The Archaeology of Medicine

Papers given at a session of the annual
conference of the Theoretical Archaeology Group
held at the University of Birmingham
on 20 December 1998

Edited by

Robert Arnott

BAR International Series 1046
2002

This title published by

Archaeopress
Publishers of British Archaeological Reports
Gordon House
276 Banbury Road
Oxford
OX2 7ED
England
www.archaeopress.com

BAR S1046

The Archaeology of Medicine: Papers given at a session of the annual conference of the Theoretical Archaeology Group held at the University of Birmingham on 20 December 1998

© the individual authors 2002

ISBN 1 84171 427 5

Printed in England by The Basingstoke Press

All BAR titles are available from:

Hadrian Books Ltd
122 Banbury Road
Oxford
OX2 7BP
England

The current BAR catalogue with details of all titles in print, prices and means of payment is available free from Hadrian Books

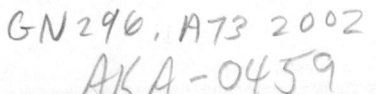

TABLE OF CONTENTS

Foreword
    Professor John Hunter (University of Birmingham)   iii

Introduction
    Robert Arnott (University of Birmingham)   v

Palaeopathology and archaeology: the current state of play   1
    Charlotte Roberts (University of Durham)

Tooth worms and pelicans: dentistry in archaeology   21
    Chrissie Freeth (University of Bradford)

Ancient bodies, but modern techniques: the utilisation of CT scanning in the study of ancient Egyptian mummies   33
    Joyce M. Filer (The British Museum)

Disease and medicine in Hittite Asia Minor   41
    Robert Arnott (University of Birmingham)

The Hippocratic patient: or an archaeology of the Greek medical mind   53
    Niall McKeown (University of Birmingham)

The Roman military *Valetudinaria*: fact or fiction?   69
    Patricia Baker (University of Kent at Canterbury)

The interpretation of medicinal plants in the archaeological context: some case-studies from Pompeii   81
    Marina Ciaraldi (University of Birmingham)

Roman surgery: the evidence of the instruments   87
    Ralph Jackson (The British Museum)

Investigating the Anglo-Saxon *Materia Medica*: archaeobotany, manuscript art, Latin and Old English   95
    Debby Banham (University of Cambridge)

Bald's *Leechbook* and archaeology: two approaches to Anglo-Saxon health and healthcare   101
    Sally Crawford (University of Birmingham) and Tony Randall (University of Oxford)

The *Mary Rose* medical chest   105
    Brendan Derham (Gloucester)

Morbid Osteology 113
Mouli Start (University of Sheffield)

Recognition and understanding of age-related bone loss and osteoporosis-related 125
fractures in the eighteenth and nineteenth centuries
Megan Brickley (University of Birmingham)

List of contributors 129

FOREWORD

John Hunter

Archaeologists have always liked finding bones. Human remains make that important link between the moribund vestiges of walls, floors, pits and objects which typically constitute the material past, and the people that built, created or used them. As a student I sat in awe listening to the late Calvin Wells relate exactly what could be achieved from a study of the human skeleton, which elements could be measured (and why), and what we might learn about trauma, and perhaps the individual's lifestyle. Even then, some thirty years ago, the study of the past was still in infancy: how people lived was somehow deemed to be archaeology because it left traces which could be measured and recorded; how people thought and interacted was considered to be more an issue of history and was thus open to debate and discussion. Much intellectual water has since flowed under the bridge, not least in arguing how aspects of the latter might be interpreted from traces of the former. This volume illustrates how the study of human remains *per se* has not only been focal to our understanding the past, but also how it has contributed to the debate and evolution as to how the past should be studied.

We might once have been more comfortable with titles such as *The History of Medicine,* or *The Archaeology of Disease,* but the title here, *The Archaeology of Medicine,* containing two seemingly irreconcilable elements, is itself an indicator of how far study of the past has developed, and indeed of the role played by *TAG* (Theoretical Archaeology Group) at whose conference the papers were delivered. The challenge of this title has been conscientiously taken up by the contributors who have admirably illustrated not only the broad range of source evidence available, but also the importance of complementarity and the need for interdisciplinary study.

This is well voiced in Charlotte Robert's opening paper which provides both context and platform for the varied contributions which follow. Like many of the other papers it combines the archaeological and the historical, as well as reflecting the interests of modern medicine. Chrissie Freeth's contribution which compares textual and archaeological evidence with respect to dentistry is a case in point. But here we are reminded how nascent some interdisciplinary elements of the subject are, 'descriptive, anecdotal, [and] case study orientated' in contrast to the great technological developments which have, for example, enabled Joyce Filer to use CT scanning for the study of Egyptian mummies.

A significant portion of the volume is taken by the analysis of historical evidence, including Robert Arnott's discussion of Hittite sources, Niall McKeown's review of Greek literary texts, and Debby Banham's investigation of Old English and Latin material. The value of Anglo-Saxon texts is further amplified by Sally Crawford and Tony Randall whose portrayal of a visit to an Anglo-Saxon surgery remains memorable to all those who attended the conference session. Related to textual matters is Marina Ciaraldi's study of medicinal plants: these not only provide the archaeological parameter, but also illustrate the importance of the palaeobotanist within the overall equation. Megan Brickley introduces some new dimensions to the relationship of osteoarchaeology and historical sources with her work on recognition and understanding of age-related loss and osteoporosis.

Archaeological discoveries are also discussed: Brendan Derham examines the medical chest from the *Mary Rose* by analysing organic residues, Ralph Jackson sets Roman surgical instruments against an historical background producing a paper which he admits raises more questions than it answers, and Patricia Baker discusses the reality or fiction of Roman military *valetudinaria* by a further balance of the archaeological and the literary. It is perhaps fitting that in the penultimate paper, Mouli Start should remind us that our study of the dead is not confined to the distant past but is equally valid in post-medieval times where once neither history nor archaeology would have dared to venture.

All the contributors, and not least Robert Arnott the editor, are to be congratulated in creating a significant milestone in the study of archaeology and medicine.

INTRODUCTION

This book arises out of a session of TAG'98 that was organised on 20 December 1998, when it was the turn of the Department of Ancient History and Archaeology and the Field Archaeology Unit of the University of Birmingham to host the conference, organised locally by a team led by Lynne Bevan. It was the first time at a TAG session, or indeed anywhere else, that archaeologists and medical historians had met in this way, and it has opened to road to future collaborations. Here at Birmingham it was one of a series of conferences that led to the establishment of the Centre for the History of Medicine within the University.

All of the papers published in this volume were presented at the session, with the exception of the paper by Niall McKeown that was written subsequently and develops some interesting views relating to our understanding and perspective of ancient Greek medicine that demand expression. I have also included my paper on Hittite Medicine. I found organising the session and presenting a paper on the same day would have proven more than stressful.

As the editor I am grateful first and foremost to the contributors, for their support and for being so efficient in returning manuscripts, even when one gave birth to twins in the meanwhile! Very special thanks must go to Rayna Andrew of the Department of Ancient History and Archaeology of the University of Birmingham who turned a series of papers produced in some varied computer programmes into what one sees here, and to Siân Williams for her heroic assistance with sub-editing. I am also grateful to Dr David Davison of Archaeopress, publishers of British Archaeological Reports, for his support and above all patience. Finally, I should like to thank our sponsors, Philip Harris Medical, a firm of leading surgical instrument, pharmaceutical and medical equipment suppliers, first established in Birmingham in 1817. Through their generosity it was possible to hold a reception at the end of the session for tired and thirsty participants and for three postgraduate students, who gave papers, to receive travelling bursaries.

John Hunter in the foreword has summed up the session supporting the argument that archaeology and medicine are no longer irreconcilable and stresses this volume is an indicator of how far our work has progressed. I hope this leads us on to more work in this field. This volume is, I am sure, the first of many.

Robert Arnott
Director
Centre for the History of Medicine
University of Birmingham Medical School December 2001

PALAEOPATHOLOGY AND ARCHAEOLOGY: THE CURRENT STATE OF PLAY

Charlotte Roberts

INTRODUCTION

'...practically all behavior patterns will affect disease incidence in some way' (Alland, 1966: 47).

To place this paper within the context of the book title, a few definitions are worth considering. This paper considers palaeopathology, whilst the rest of the book is devoted to the archaeology of medicine. In essence, this chapter sets the scene for what is to come, and introduces disease as something that humans in the past had to develop coping mechanisms to deal with. In effect, medicine (and surgery) developed to enable populations to cope with disease and injury. With this in mind the true definition of medicine is 'the science or practice of the diagnosis, treatment and prevention of disease, especially as distinct from surgical methods', whilst pathology is 'the science of bodily diseases', and disease is 'an unhealthy (i.e. state of being unwell) condition of the body or mind, illness, sickness' (Thompson, 1995).

Palaeopathology (the history of disease), classified as a subdiscipline of biological/ physical anthropology, has been studied in many parts of the world since the nineteenth century. Whilst non-human remains provided most of the focus initially, by the early twentieth century the study of human remains for evidence of disease became more popular (Aufderheide and Rodriguez-Martin, 1998). Disease is very much part of our lives today, as it potentially may result in death, and health problems affect how human and non-human populations function within their environment, whether they can adapt to changing circumstances or whether they succumb to illness and die. Everybody, past and present, has suffered, is suffering from, or will suffer from ill health. Therefore, the study of disease today, and in the past, has implications for social, political and economic systems which all may be changed as a result of the impact of disease. For example, the Black Death in Britain in the fourteenth century AD had such an impact on mortality that the reduction in population numbers meant that social/economic and political systems had to change (McNeil, 1976). Paradoxically, and taking a view from a modern context, as a result of global warming major changes in our environment and climate are occurring, and these are, in turn, affecting our health. Bhasin *et al.* (1994: 65) have eloquently reminded us that '...health is not a component but an expression of development; so that the health of a community at a given moment is the very situation of the whole social system seen from a health point of view...', and Brown *et al.* (1996: 183) indicate that '...the nature of interaction between disease and culture can be a productive way of understanding humanity'. Disease, or a deviation from normal health (whatever normal is), will also affect populations both geographically and through time, with specific patterning which will be determined by many factors intrinsic and extrinsic to the people affected. By implication, disease must be seen ultimately as a key part of the study of past human populations (and archaeology as a whole) because, without information on their health status, the rest of the archaeological evidence may be less well understood.

This chapter has a number of goals:

1. To introduce the subject of palaeopathology;
2. To highlight how health and disease is studied in the past;
3. To explore how we might recognise the care of the sick;
4. To consider how palaeopathology as a discipline has developed and contributed to our knowledge of the past;
5. To suggest recommendations for future work.

In effect, this chapter concentrates on the scientific study of unhealthy conditions of the body or mind in the past. However, bound up with disease is how people in the past perceived it, and whether any attempt was made to treat, or indeed care for, people who got sick. The focus, however, of this paper is on palaeopathology whilst most of the rest of this book concentrates on the evidence for medical treatment in the past.

Despite its importance, palaeopathology (and palaeobiological anthropology generally) has received little recognition as a major contributor to archaeological site interpretations, particularly in Britain, until recent years. Firstly, this is probably because palaeopathology has had a clinical emphasis (Bush and Zvelebil, 1991: 3) which did not allow the non-specialist reader to access the information in an understandable manner. Perhaps also, the people working in the area, especially in the 1960s and 1970s, discouraged non-medically trained personnel to work in palaeopathlogy. As Wells (1964a: 20) has stated, 'It is most unwise for anthropologists who lack clinical training to venture into the infinitely subtle field of ancient disease'. Wells was always quick to point out that anybody lacking medical training should steer well clear of studying palaeopathology, succinctly stating in the following, '...only a clinician or clinical pathologist who has spent his life studying disease as a living and ongoing process can assess the significance of the final etchings on dead bone... the great majority of physical anthropologists have enough scientific humility to recognise their limitations and incompetence in the interpretation of disease' (Chadwick Hawkes and Wells, 1983: 6–7). This is hardly encouragement for people trying to work in the field or for archaeologists to consider it worth doing! Fortunately, over the last 10 years, certainly in Britain, some undergraduate students of archaeology, anthropology and other related disciplines such as biology, genetics and anatomy, have been trained at graduate level in how to recognise, record and interpret evidence of disease in skeletal remains; this is now influencing how palaeopathological study in Britain has developed. Whilst graduates in archaeology and other subjects do not have medical backgrounds, doctors and dentists, more often than not, do not have the archaeological training to put the skeletal material into context for interpretation which also puts them at a disadvantage. However, let us emphasise that each person developing our knowledge on the history of disease has something to contribute, and each has their limitations. As Farmer (1996: 267) has said '...our approach must be dynamic, systematic and critical. In addition to historians, then, anthropologists and sociologists accountable to history and political economy have much to add, as do critical epidemiologists'.

Secondly, and associated with this barrier raised to persuade non-medically trained personnel not to become involved with studying palaeopathology, has been the lack of awareness by archaeologists to recognise the potential of the study of human skeletal remains. Again, Bush and Zvelebil (1991: 3) concisely describe this particular problem: 'Unaware of the potential of human skeletal remains, many archaeologists view them, as at best, an irrelevance, and when encountered *in situ* as objects whose excavation is time consuming and which somehow does not constitute 'real' archaeology'. Two points need to be made here. In Britain, it is likely that the reason most archaeologists do not find human skeletal remains useful is because many graduated from Universities with no awareness of the value of human remains in the final archaeological interpretation of a site, or how to excavate them properly. Put such an archaeologist on a cemetery site and there are inevitably going to be problems. In recent years, however, many University archaeology departments have seen fit to employ a (palaeo) biological anthropologist on their teaching staff, and it is gratifying to see so many students genuinely interested in courses devoted to the study and interpretation of human remains from archaeological sites. This can only be good for archaeology as a whole. However, a recent survey of the 32 universities teaching archaeology (UCAS, 1998), suggests that only ten have archaeology departments with significant teaching in biological anthropology (with some palaeopathology). By contrast, in North American universities Anthropology Departments more often than not teach biological/physical anthropology (including palaeopathology), and most graduates of anthropology have some grasp of knowledge of biological anthropology. However, in Britain at least, as many more people are being trained at Masters level in the analysis and interpretation of archaeologically derived human remains, increasing numbers of graduates are being employed to excavate cemetery sites, thus often combining an archaeological and biological anthropological background and providing a unique and broad expertise.

The second point relates to publication of data on human skeletal material. Although the situation has improved a little over the last five years, publications rarely integrate the biological information with the rest of the archaeological (cultural) evidence to ultimately say something meaningful about the population under consideration. This partly is reflected in the backgrounds of many people working in the area, partly the fault of the archaeologist responsible for the excavation of the site (and publication) not recognising the value of integrating the data, and partly the result of the formatting of publications keen to relegate 'specialist' reports to the back of the final work, thus making them isolated. Of course, cost will also affect the final format and structure of the report. Furthermore, the palaeopathological findings often tend to be placed in 'specialist' journals such as the *International Journal of Osteoarchaeology*, *Journal of Paleopathology*, *Journal of Archaeological Science*, and the *American Journal of Physical Anthropology* which many archaeologists, especially those doing fieldwork, do not have access to. However, even if archaeologists do read publications devoted to palaeopathology, they are often bombarded with medical jargon and are usually faced with isolated case studies with no archaeological context. We must make our work more accessible to all. In recent years there has been a small change and publications of human skeletal remains in archaeological journals have started to appear (e.g. Farley and Manchester, 1989; Mays, 1993; McKinley and Roberts, 1993; Roberts, 1996).

Furthermore, biocultural (linking biological and cultural evidence) population based approaches to palaeopathology are rare in Britain (e.g. Grauer and Roberts, 1996; Mays *et al.*, 1998), whilst in North America they have become the more normal approach (e.g. Jurmain, 1990; Walker, 1986). Consideration of disease in this way allows humans to be viewed as biological, social and cultural beings (McElroy, 1990). Logically, linking biology and culture, and looking at populations not individuals, is the most profitable way of approaching palaeopathology, but not everybody agrees. In 1991 Bush and Zvelebil (1991: 5) lamented that, '...in contrast to North America, the biocultural approach is yet to become established in Europe...'; unfortunately this is still the case. To support some of these findings Mays' (1997) study of publications in palaeobiological anthropology from 1991–95 illustrates the differences between UK and US work in palaeopathology. In both countries palaeopathology was the area where most publications lay but, when the numbers of 'case' versus 'population' studies were compared, more of the former were seen in the UK and more of the latter in the US (55% versus 27% in the UK and 29% versus 44% in the US). Mays clearly states (1997: 604) that, '...we need to progress towards a more population-based approach, in which osteological findings are combined with other archaeological data in order to produce a more complete picture of the human past'. Archaeologists are, after all, excavating the lives of people, '...not just their buildings, animals and pottery...' (Roberts, 1986: 111). Clearly, the UK is in a position now to address the deficiencies seen in palaeopathological work but there has to be the motivation to do it.

PALAEOPATHOLOGY: SOURCES OF EVIDENCE, METHODS OF STUDY AND LIMITATIONS

'Palaeopathological studies, in Britain at least, are uncoordinated and desperately understaffed (and therefore) there is little possibility of constructive exchange of views between archaeologists and palaeopathologists' (Cramp, 1983: 111).

Palaeopathology has a number of advantages over clinical medicine. It is a way of studying disease over long periods of prehistory and history, over many thousands of years. Through human remains it gives direct evidence of the expression of disease uninfluenced by modern drug therapy, it provides a window on how humans adapted to their environment (or did not), and what epidemiological factors were operating at the time to allow specific diseases to appear. It may even generate information on the evolution of disease-causing organisms, and diagnostic criteria not described in the clinical literature.

Sources of evidence

Many sources of evidence may be used to reconstruct the history of disease (Table 1). The primary source of evidence for palaeopathology is human remains from archaeological sites. These may be inhumed, exposed or cremated, and disposed of in a variety of funerary contexts. Some work on the palaeopathology of preserved bodies, as opposed to bones and teeth, has been done (Aufderheide and Rodriguez-Martin, 1998), although most work concentrates on the latter. However, having only the skeleton to study precludes the potential identification of diseases that only affect the soft tissues such as the plague, cholera or chickenpox. Fragmentary and poorly preserved skeletons, the lack of non-adult remains in a cemetery, and the fact that the individuals being investigated are a small sample of the original living population are some of the problems inherent in palaeopathological recording, analysis and interpretation. These, amongst other limitations, are outlined in Wood *et al.*'s (1992) important paper, and highlight that the information ultimately derived from a skeletal assemblage has many biases.

Table 1. Sources of evidence used in palaeopathology.

Primary	Skeletal remains (cremated/ inhumed/ exposed)
	Mummified remains (frozen, dessicated, deliberate, bog)
	(Clinical approach)
Secondary	Iconographic (drawings, paintings, sculpture)
	Documentary (written works)
	Archaeological (artefacts, ecofacts, structures)
	Ethnographic (traditional living populations)

Other evidence which may be utilised in the reconstruction of past human population health includes historical (written) data, and iconographic representations (paintings, drawings and sculptures). Whilst this body of evidence is classified as secondary, it has one particular advantage over human remains and that is that it records and describes disease processes affecting the soft tissues. However, it is also accepted that authors and artists, more often than not, depict the more dramatic and horrifying diseases rather than those of more minor significance, which did not necessarily look frightening. As Roberts (1971: 41) has reminded us, and many since, literary works must be studied critically '…within the traditional framework in which their facts are presented…when medical writers of Tudor times…describe rats, moles and snakes leaving their holes before plague struck, it must be remembered that in fact they are repeating Avicenna, almost verbatim'. The study of traditional living populations' health and disease (medical anthropology), where they are inhabiting parts of the world where the nature of their lifestyle and environment can be likened to past populations, has also provided some useful data with which to interpret past population health (see Sargent and Johnson, 1996; and McElroy and Townsend, 1996). Of course, there are limitations to using living population data to interpret the past, not least their distance in both space and time from archaeological groups. However, these populations are probably more similar to ancient groups than modern populations from which most of our knowledge of disease comes; their disease patterns, and coping mechanisms, are also likely to be very similar (Polunin, 1967). Nevertheless, as archaeological evidence in all its forms is fragmentary, teasing out particular factors responsible for disease occurrence and patterning in a population may be possible using medical anthropological work as a base. Archaeological evidence (artefacts, ecofacts and structures) obviously provides a wealth of information about living conditions, diet, economy, trade and contact, occupation, hygiene, climate and much more, all aspects of a society which will influence the appearance, maintenance and transmission of disease. For example, trade with other groups will allow new diseases to be introduced to a population which has never experienced them before and thus can lead to increased and rapid mortality. Furthermore, quality and quantity of diet will also affect the development and strength of the immune system and its ability to fight off disease. Without integrating archaeological evidence with palaeopathology, the final interpretation is almost useless.

Whilst there are many sources of evidence for the reconstruction of palaeopathology, human remains form the primary evidence on which the rest of this chapter is based.

Methods of study

Although there are a number of methods available for studying the palaeopathology of human remains (Roberts, 1991 and see Table 2) and, despite them providing much more detailed information normally possible with more common approaches, many are expensive, time consuming and need specific expertise. Most people worldwide use the less expensive 'macroscopic' approach for identifying and recording pathological lesions in skeletal remains; it is argued that this will always remain the case unless funding for archaeological work increases substantially in the future. It is pleasing to know that technical support and expertise exist should isotope or aDNA analysis, for example, become desirable and affordable, but most of the time people working in this discipline do not have the financial support to use these techniques.

Table 2. Methods of study for the analysis and interpretation of palaeopathology.

Macroscopic	visual examination
Radiographic	e.g. macroscopic, microscopic, computed tomography
Microscopic	low and high power, e.g. scanning electron microscopy
Biomolecular	e.g. aDNA, mycolic acids
Trace elements and isotopes	e.g. carbon, nitrogen, oxygen, lead, strontium

The Macroscopic Approach
This approach relies on the accurate identification of pathologically induced changes in the bones and teeth of the skel-

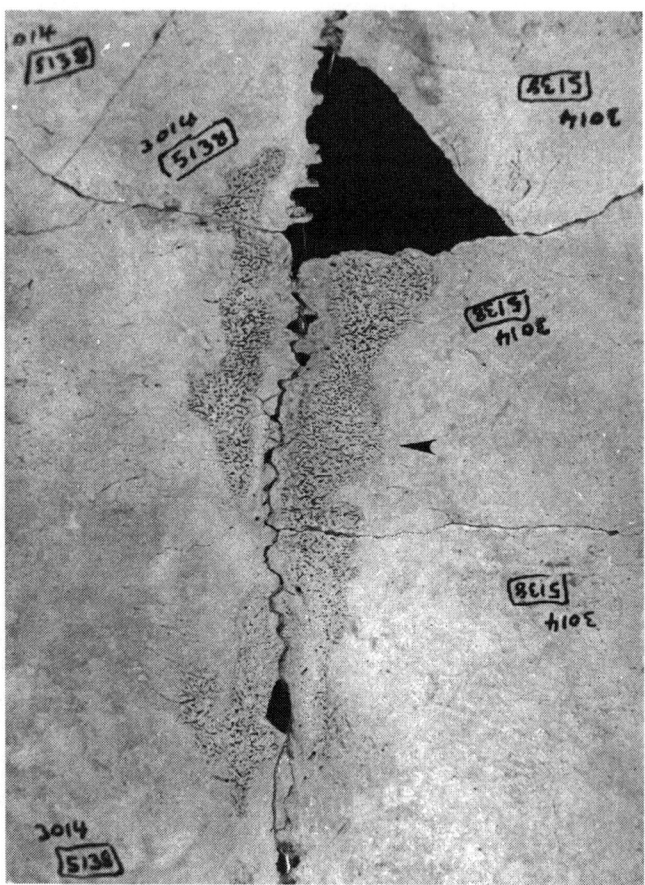

Fig. 1. New bone formation on the endocranial surface of the skull in a juvenile skeleton. Note the porous nature of the bone formed indicating that it is relatively recent in occurrence.

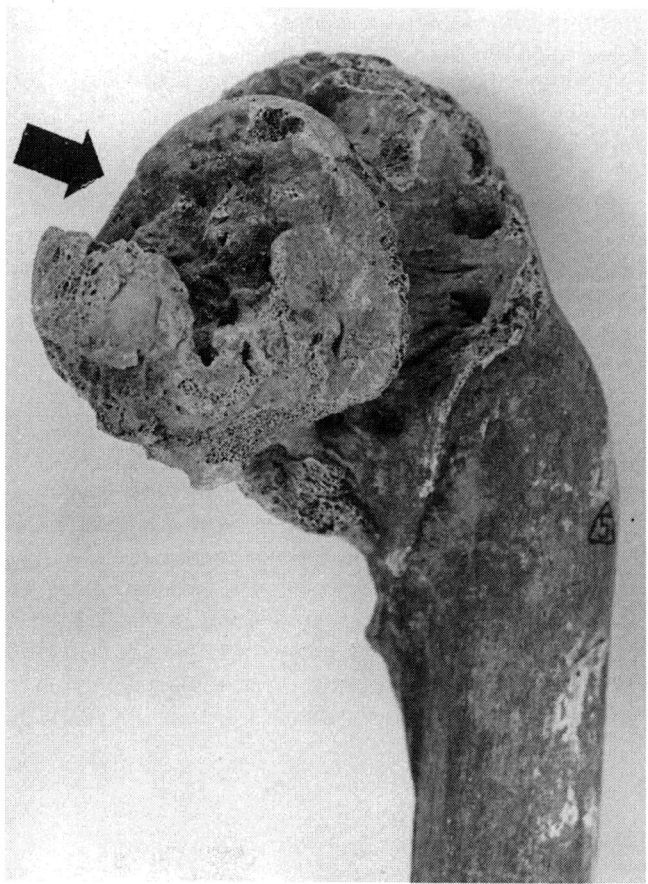

Fig. 2. Head of femur showing extensive destruction as a result of infection, possibly tuberculosis. Note that the remaining bone is remodelled or healed, suggesting that the person had the condition for a long period of time.

eton. In the bone these changes are manifest as areas of new bone formation (Fig. 1) and/or destruction (Fig. 2), with the new bone being formed being woven (porous and disorganised) or lamellar (smooth and more organised) in appearance. The former represents rapidly formed bone which illustrates that the condition was active at the time of death, whilst lamellar bone indicates a longstanding chronic (and healed) problem. In effect, any new bone formation indicates chronicity i.e. that the person has survived the acute stages of a disease to develop the chronic changes in bone; they are, in effect, the healthy ones with strong immune systems. However, it should be remembered that the absence of pathologically-induced change could indicate three scenarios: that the person was healthy, that the person died from a disease that did not leave bone damage (because they died in the acute stages or before the skeleton had chance to respond, or that it was a disease that affected only the soft tissues), or that the person's immune response was such that they had a mild form of the disease. In fact, the ultimate response of humans to a disease can result in four possible scenarios: death, acute disease and recovery, chronic illness, or the person could become a carrier of the disease with no signs or symptoms (Blumberg and Hesser, 1976: 260).

The aim of recording lesions in the skeleton is to identify abnormal areas, describe the characteristics of the bone formed or destroyed, whether the lesions are healed or not (Figs. 3 and 4), and then record their distribution pattern. Some researchers have developed sophisticated tools for recording distribution patterns (Ortner, 1991) which are extremely powerful, but most researchers at present do not have access to such hard and software. By comparing distribution pattern data with data from known clinical cases of disease affecting the skeleton, it is potentially possible to generate a number of possible differential diagnoses. Unfortunately, disease can only affect the skeleton in a limited number of ways and the changes observed may suggest a number of possible diseases. A complete skeleton is a prerequisite for successfully attempting a diagnosis, although even then it is not that easy. Research has shown that people working in palaeopathology are much more comfortable in diagnosing into a 'general' category (such as joint disease) rather than making a specific diagnosis (e.g. rheumatoid arthritis) — Miller et al. (1996). In addition, research has also shown that interobserver error and non-agreement on diagnosis are particular problems in palaeopathology (Waldron and Rogers, 1991). Clearly, diagnosis is not easy even in living people (Waldron, 1994).

To add to these problems, fragmentary skeletal material provides a major hurdle to diagnosis because the distribution pattern of lesions are not possible to record if skeletal elements are missing. For example, gout (a metabolically based joint disease) affects the joints of the big toe (usually on one side) in most cases (Resnick, 1995), and therefore if that joint is not

Fig. 3. Cranium with perimortem wound with no evidence of healing, although pitting of the bone surface around the wound indicates that the person may have lived a little time following the injury.

preserved for examination it is not possible to be sure the person did or did not have gout. However, problems in diagnosis may not only be related to those previously discussed. Palaeopathology takes its diagnostic criteria from clinical sources and these sources do not necessarily describe all changes observed in the skeleton, particularly the subtle bone formation not even seen radiographically (for example, see Roberts *et al.*, 1998a and Fig. 5). Sometimes, palaeopathology can provide additional data that might help in the diagnosis of skeletal disease. Another example is that of the work of Moller-Christensen (1961) who identified skeletal changes of leprosy in a Medieval Danish context which had not been described clinically before. Fragmentary skeletal material also has implications for recording actual prevalence rates for disease and how people working in palaeopathology record frequency data. It is essential to record the actual number of bones or teeth present for examination so that percentage prevalence rates for disease can be given. If rates are given on an individual basis, for example ten of twenty individuals had a specific infection, this assumes all bones for all skeletons were available for examination whereas it is more than likely that many bone elements and teeth will be absent, incomplete or damaged in archaeological contexts.

Furthermore, deposition, burial and excavation can damage a skeleton and mimic pathological processes (Henderson, 1987); even to the trained eye it can present problems. In addition, the representative nature of the sample needs attention. Does the sample represent the original living population (Waldron, 1994)? Was only part of the cemetery site excavated, and could there be burials still lying inhumed in the ground? Were people from that population buried elsewhere, or just particular groups, e.g. children or the diseased? Is the funerary context biasing the sample? For example, is it associated with a nunnery or a monastery, which would affect the sex profile of the population? A multitude of funerary contextual factors could affect the eventual interpretation of the site even before the burial environment, excavation and processing of skeletal material gets underway (for an example of a potentially biased sample see fig. 5 in Dawes and Magilton, 1980: 8).

The development of methods of macroscopic recording of palaeopathology has received particular attention recently, especially in North America where the need to rebury human remains has become pressing, partly as a result of the Native American Graves Protection Act passed in 1990 (Rose *et al.*, 1996). Rose *et al.* had already noted the problems of palaeopathology recording in the 1980s and was horrified at the non-comparative nature of a lot of extant data (1988). It was realised that standardisation of skeletal recording was essential if comparative population studies were to be attempted and, indeed, if useful data were to be collected. This resulted in the publication of a manual which provides methods and suggestions for the recording of human skeletal remains, including a chapter on palaeopathology (Buikstra and Ubelaker, 1994). The manual emphasises the need to use a standard terminology with no jargon (even a problem in clinical contexts), with definitions of terms used, and to describe in detail the abnormal pathologically induced changes in the skeleton before even thinking about a diagnosis. The manual also contains a coding system and photographs to illustrate abnormalities. Other recommendations were to study sex and age distribution for diseases observed and, when talking about 'severity' of lesions, to use definitions, and preferably photographs, to illustrate stages in disease manifestation. Some work on classifying the appearance of some lesions has been done, although there is generally no clear idea what the appearances actually mean (for examples see Lukacs, 1989; Sager, 1969; Stuart-Macadam, 1991). In addition, diagnostic criteria must be specified in any palaeopathological report so that readers know on what criteria diagnoses have been based. Without these basic data this information cannot be evaluated scientifically, or indeed re-evaluated in the future especially if the remains have been reburied.

The Radiographic Approach

The second most common method of analysis of human skeletal remains is through radiography, often to confirm a diagnosis or visualise the internal structure of a suspected pathological bone or tooth (Barber *et al.*, 1997; Elvery *et al.*, 1998; Fig. 6). Whilst selected bones are usually radiographed, research has shown that more pathological evidence could be identified if all bones were subject to radiography (Rothschild and Rothschild, 1995). Some disease processes just do not reveal

Fig. 4. Injury to occipital bone which has healed. Note the rounded remodelled edges.

Fig. 5. New bone formation on the visceral (lung side) of the ribs.

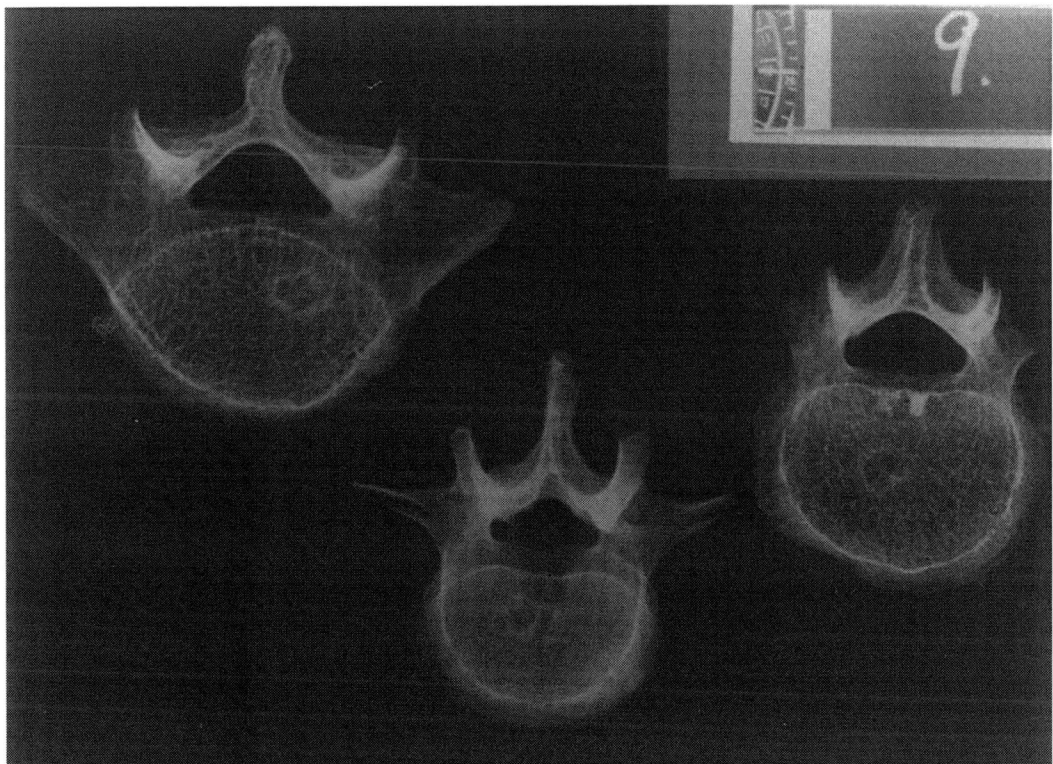

Fig. 6. Superior view of vertebrae showing circular lesions in the bodies with an opaque (sclerotic) border around them, suggesting healing has (and was) taking place at the time of death.

themselves unless radiographed and this may be because the disease is just developing (for example, in some cancers and the early stages of infections such as osteomyelitis commencing on the interior, medullary cavity, of a long bone). Plain film radiography is the most common method used, mainly because it is relatively quick and cheap, and most people working in the discipline have access to this facility. More sophisticated methods are utilised less often because of lack of availability of resources but include microradiography (Blondiaux et al., 1994) and computed tomography (Melcher et al., 1997), which are able to investigate more detailed structural changes within bone. Plain film radiography records areas of opacity and lucency which reflect bone formation and destruction, respectively; it may also provide an indication of the quality, i.e. state of healing, of bone formation. For most categories of disease it provides hidden information. For example, the overlap, apposition and angulation of fracture fragments (see Roberts, 1988 for more detail), Harris lines of arrested growth (Hughes et al.,1996; Fig. 7), the 'mosaic' patterning of Paget's disease, essential for diagnosis (Wells and Woodhouse, 1975), and the subchondral (beneath the cartilage of a joint) cysts of osteoarthritis (Rogers and Waldron, 1995; Fig. 8) are all features of health problems seen in the skeleton which would not be visible without a radiograph. There are problems with this method, however, for example the appearance of pseudopathological features which are difficult to interpret, the expense of the procedure, and getting exposure and time settings correct to bring out the best image.

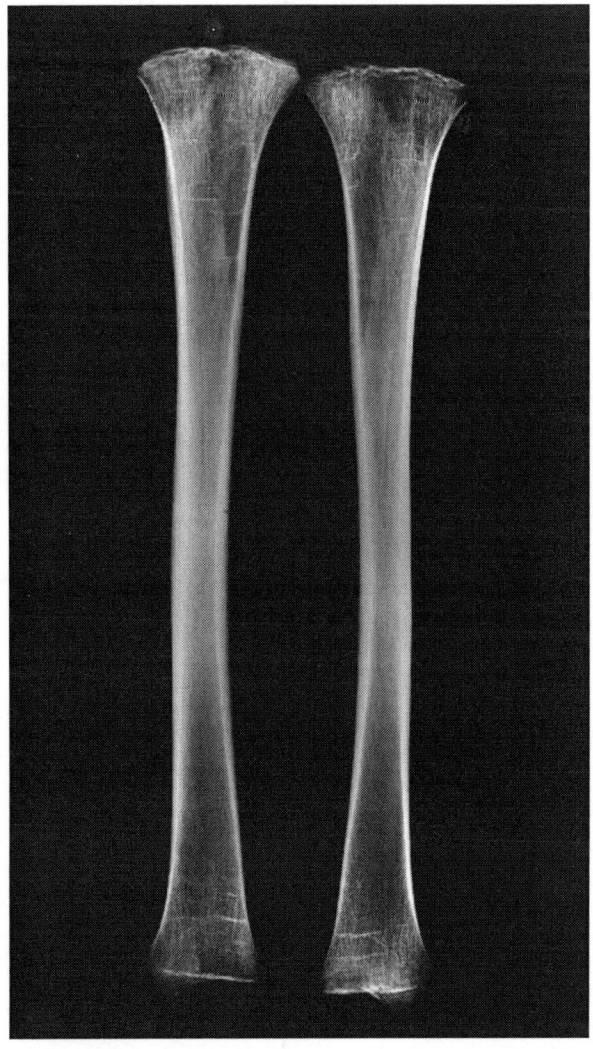

Fig. 7 (*right*). Horizontal opaque lines across the tibiae at their proximal and distal ends, suggesting stress during growth

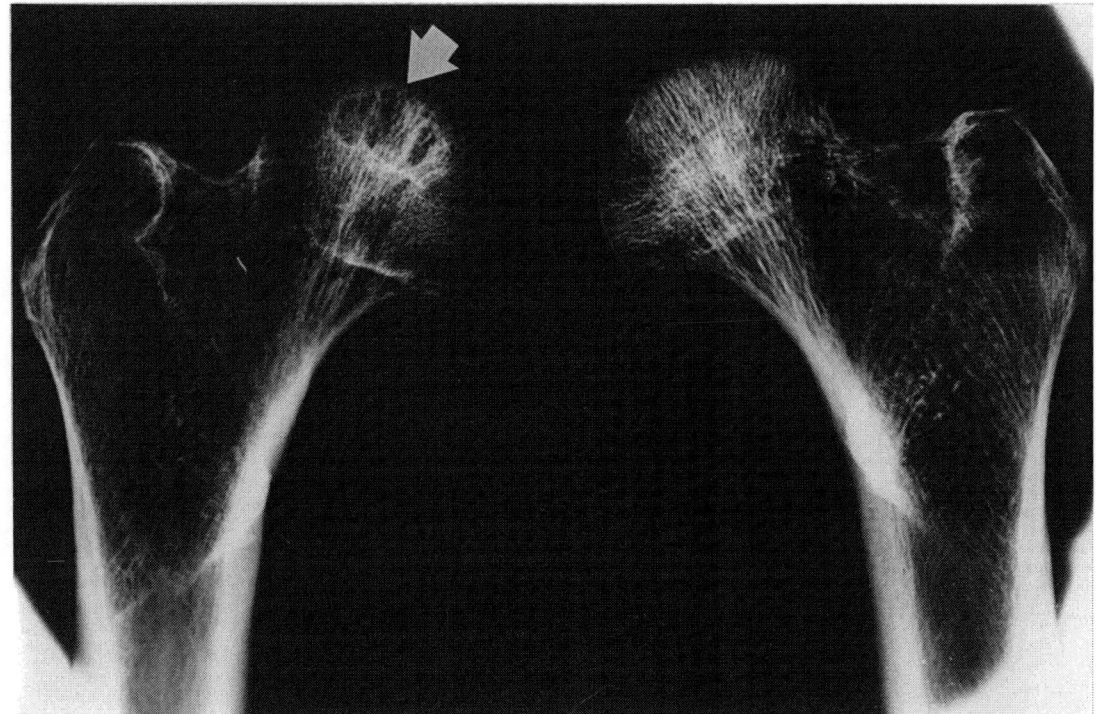

Fig. 8. Subchondral cysts in femur, a feature associated with osteoarthritis.

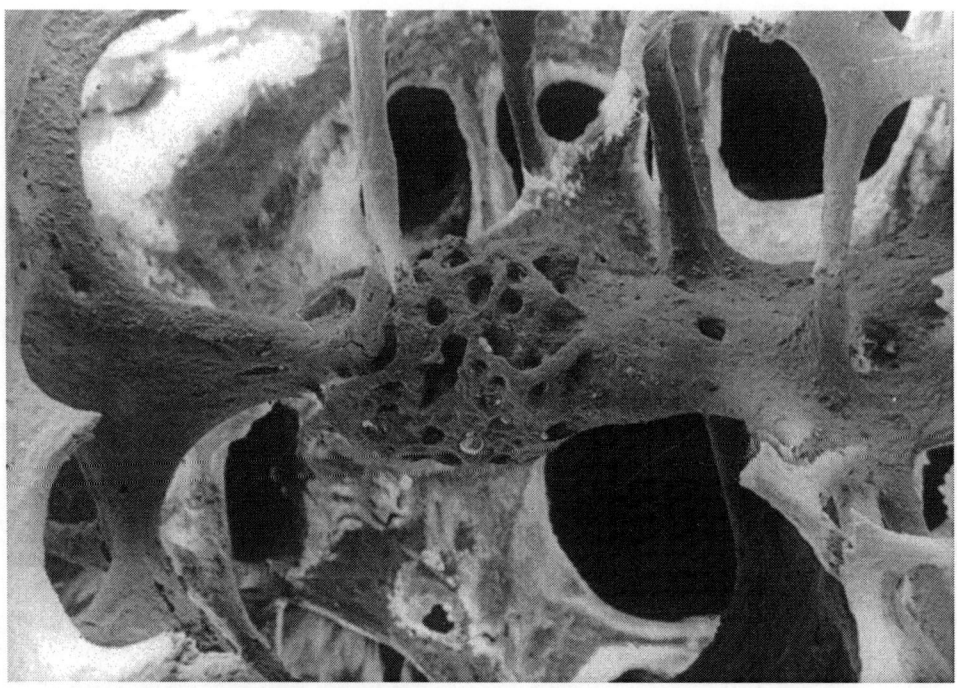

Fig. 9. A microfracture with callus (immature new bone formation) in a vertebral body (cancellous bone).

However, it remains an extremely useful tool for the interpretation of palaeopathology.

The Histological Approach

The use of histological analysis in palaeopathology, again, has seen less frequent use than macroscopic methods due the expertise, finance and time needed to pursue these methods. However, some useful research has been carried out confirming diagnoses of disease (e.g. Aaron *et al.*, 1992), looking at detailed morphological appearances using the scanning electron microscope to identify areas of bone formation and destruction at the microscopic level (Roberts and Wakely, 1992; Fig. 9), for assessing the content of calculus on the teeth (Dobney and Brothwell, 1988), and dental microwear patterns to look at quality of diet (Teaford, 1991), and also using histology to address differential diagnoses for skeletal lesions, and establishing the effect of postmortem damage on palaeopathological manifestations of bone (Bell, 1990). Whilst the histological preservation of skeletal material determines the ultimate information derived, it can be a powerful method of information generation (Pfeiffer, 2000; Bell and Piper, 2000).

The Biomolecular Approach

In recent years, biomolecular approaches to diagnosis of disease have seen increasing use particularly using aDNA (Drancourt *et al*., 1998; Fricker *et al*., 1997; Salo *et al*., 1994) and mycolic acids (Gernaey *et al*., 1999; Gernaey and Minnikin, 2000). Although most work has concentrated on tuberculosis to date, increasing emphasis is being placed on other mycobacterial diseases such as leprosy (Spigelman *et al*., 1999). The biomolecular approach has much to offer palaeopathology (Brown, 2000), particularly in identifying diseases that only affect the soft tissues, for people whose immune system resistance was so good that skeletal changes did not present themselves, or in tracing the evolution of particular organisms. Again, this method at the moment is expensive, time consuming and unpredictable, with a potential problem of contamination. Before more useful work can proceed, there is a great need to identify when these ancient biomolecules survive, i.e. in what environmental circumstances, so that time and money are not wasted trying to extract what is not there. In addition, education of those working in archaeology on the merits and problems of ancient biomolecule analysis is an overdue necessity so that assumptions of its value are not overstated. Because of the application of biomolecular methods of analysis to palaeopathology, the discipline is certainly at an exciting stage in its development where its potential has not yet been recognised.

Trace element and isotope analysis

Work in the analysis of elemental content of bones and teeth has been undertaken since the 1970s and has concentrated mainly on trying to reconstruct the palaeodiet of individuals (usually) and populations (Sandford, 1992; 1993; Sandford and Weaver, 2000). Since that time questions of whether levels of elements really do reflect life levels have made many cautious but, with care, this type of analysis has great potential. Of course, diet has a significant effect on the development of the immune system which, in turn, will affect whether a person contracts a disease or not (and how chronic that disease becomes) and therefore looking at quality of diet is highly relevant to palaeopathological studies. In addition, researchers have tried to assess the effects of pollution in the body by measuring, for example, lead (Rogers and Waldron, 1985), and measured levels of particular elements to correlate them with other (pathological) features in the skeleton (e.g. Glen-Haduch *et al*., 1997). More recent work (but also starting in the 1970s — Katzenberg, 1992) has concentrated on assessing the levels of isotopes of carbon and nitrogen to determine the quality and constituents of the diet and, even more recently, to answer questions about weaning (Katzenberg *et al*., 1996). People have also now begun to look at migration using stable lead isotopes (Carlson, 1996) and also strontium isotopes to consider changes in diet with movement of people (Sealy *et al*., 1995; Katzenberg, 2000; Mays, 2000). Clearly more work in these areas will continue and these methodologies provide potentially exciting information.

Nowithstanding the many methods available to evaluate palaeopathological evidence in skeletal and mummified remains, in order for many of those described to be used it is necessary to sample and destroy bone or teeth. Along with expense, time and necessary expertise, it is essential that people working in these methodological areas do not destroy valuable skeletal material with no particular aims, questions or problems in mind. Skeletal collections are a non-renewable resource and, in some parts of the world, a resource that is diminishing fast. To reiterate, the author believes that the macroscopic and radiographic approaches (i.e. non-destructive) will remain the predominant methods used in palaeopathology for as long as palaeopathology is studied.

HUMAN PALAEOPATHOLOGY AS A DISCIPLINE

'The progress of paleopathology, as a specific subject of research, parallels the development of many scholarly and scientific disciplines' (Ortner, 1991: 5).

There are a number of aims in palaeopathological study which workers try to address. Palaeopathology considers the occurrence of disease in human and non-human remains, its prevalence and the impact of disease load on 'population' groups. To interpret palaeopathological observations, other key parameters of the population also need to be known, which include age at death, sex and stature. How long you live will determine what organisms you will become exposed to, bearing in mind that the young and old (today and in the past) are more vulnerable to health problems, and the older you are the more severe a disease can potentially become. Biological sex will also determine diseases experienced; for example, osteoporosis (loss of bone quantity) and rheumatoid arthritis (an immune joint disease) are more common in females, while ankylosing spondylitis and Forestier's disease (both conditions affecting the spine) are more common in males. It is only in recent years that palaeopathology has begun to try to understand sex differences in disease occurrence, culminating in a recent book (Grauer and Stuart-Macadam, 1998). Thus, the palaeodemographic profile (age and sex distribution) is key to understanding palaeopathology because it indicates when and who died in that sample population. This, in turn, indicates health problems (because people are dead) which could range from cancer to infection, and even decapitation which, of course, severs important body life supporting systems.

Stature (or height) too is a very useful parameter for understanding health and disease. For example, people who are shorter than normal for their sex, age, population and period of time may have had health problems during development of the long bones which affected their normal growth. Although it would be hard to suggest exactly what caused the reduction in stature, it provides a possible indicator of health. Finally, ethnic affiliation of the individual will have an impact on what diseases the person suffers from (Polednak, 1989; Reichs, 1986). For example, the Mediterranean and south-east Asia see a high frequency of thalassaemia amongst its inhabitants, and sickle cell anaemia is more common in African countries (Aufderheide and Rodriguez-Martin, 1998).

Whilst all these parameters need attention and correlation with evidence of disease in an individual skeleton, the emphasis in recent years has been on the need to consider 'populations' of skeletons rather than 'individuals'. The original 'diagnostic/ clinical' model approach to palaeopathology (i.e. individual case studies) does still have some value because it highlights cases of certain diseases in geographic, period and funerary context (and collation of these data can contribute to a fuller picture of past health on a global scale). However, more recent years have seen a concentration on hypothesis/question driven/ problem based population studies. For example, an hypothesis to be tested might be: people living in urban Medieval environments were less healthy than those in rural environments. This indicates a 'hunch' or expectation of the data that can be tested using appropriate skeletal material. An example of a question might be: what happens to people's health when they start practising agriculture? Here, one should be thinking of investigating the living environment of the population, their diet, living conditions, hygiene, water supply etc. which may answer the question. Even more recently the physical, chemical and biological bases for pathological change in the skeleton have been a focus in palaeopathology (the integrated and process driven model — Sandford and Weaver, 1998). Why do those holes appear in the orbits in somebody suspected of having anaemia? Why do the different treponemal syndromes produce differential patterning of new bone formation on the skeleton? There is now a clear move towards questioning why rather than accepting at face value that specific pathological lesions are linked to certain diseases.

Palaeopathology, for all its problems, has always been a dynamic, progressive and changing discipline, probably because of the membership of the Paleopathology Association (founded in the US in 1973) being so varied in its expertise — archaeology, anthropology, medicine, dentistry, anatomy, genetics, history etc. To reiterate, everybody has something to offer palaeopathology and each person sees it from a different perspective. Despite this there are standards and levels to which people working in it should strive to achieve (as discussed above).

EXAMPLES OF SOME WORK IN PALAEOPATHOLOGY

'The value of the biocultural approach lies in its comprehensive view of humans as biological, social and cultural beings' (McElroy and Townsend, 1996: 244).

There has been excellent work in palaeopathology but also mediocre and very poor studies. Of course, most people have tended to concentrate on the commoner (and perhaps easier to recognise and interpret?) conditions such as infectious and joint disease, trauma and dental disease, whereas other less common conditions have seen little attention, such as neoplastic and congenital diseases. Much work, however, has consisted of individual case studies (as discussed previously). However, as numerous authors have pointed out, focusing on the individual and the disease seen in that person lets the role of the pathogen in that condition take over (Armelagos *et al.*, 1992). In a modern sense, but just as applicable to palaeopathology, a population approach enables workers to move beyond this clinical perspective and concentrate more on the complex myriad of factors in the environment which contribute to the appearance of ill health. McElroy and Townsend (1996: xxi) are quite clear in describing the limitations inherent in the clinical perspective when they say that Western medicine, '…usually considers disease as a clinical entity that can be diagnosed, and treated independently of cultural context'. In the context of treatment too, drug therapy and surgery are all well and good but a person or population's recovery depends on their environment, their diet, their hygiene and even how their psyche deals with the illness and/or operation. They go on to say (*ibid.*, 1996: 32) that '…we see neither the social context in which the disease occurs nor how the individual or family members and community perceive and experience the illness'. Wood *et al.* back in 1992, however, did note that in palaeopathology, at least, they saw a move towards the population based perspective rather than individual case studies, the latter of which they saw telling us '…little about the disease experience of ancient populations' (*ibid.*, 345). Larsen (1997) also notes that because of this it was becoming possible to create a more meaningful understanding of past human adaptation, or how people have changed and adapted to new and changing situations.

Concepts of how and why a disease enters a population, maintains itself and possibly leads to death will naturally influence how a society copes with that illness. If they think a disease is transmitted by eating a specific food then that food may be omitted from the diet, or if a pain in the head is believed to be caused by a 'demon' within then the obvious solution may be to let the demon out by creating a hole in the skull (in this case referred to as trepanation — see Backay, 1985 for more details). But what disease or illness is to one person or population may not be perceived the same in another. Work on living societies suggests that, for example, mild forms of diarrhoea may be regarded as normal, requiring no treatment (Findley, 1990). Many minor illnesses in any society today and in the past may be accepted as normal. Of course, there will be variations on this theme whereby one person may appear very ill with a minor illness, whilst another with the same illness may appear in relatively good health. Positive and negative attitudes to illness play a large part in expression of them and the ability to function and behave normally, and many factors may determine these attitudes (Roberts, 1985).

Working from a population rather than an individual perspective enables the biocultural approach to palaeopathology to be used and ultimately have an impact on the reasons behind the evolution and history of disease we understand today. Medical anthropologists have been using the biocultural approach for years to assess health problems in traditional living populations. They claim, quite rightly, that to understand the health problem you cannot isolate disease from culture because it 'manufactures' disease (Inhorn and Brown, 1990: 110). Thus, studying leprosy in populations today devoid of cultural contextual information makes the final interpretation very limited. Health reflects an individual's ability to adapt to his or her environment by biological or behavioural means and disease reflects failure to adapt (Wiley, 1992: 222). Of course, 'One can adapt to as well as adapt something to meet their (one's) own needs (*ibid.*, 229)', and 'adaptation is a useful and powerful explanatory concept and provides a model for decision making, a perspective on history and prehistory, and a way of generating and testing hypotheses about reality' (*ibid.*, 233). Whilst these ideas relate to living populations today, they are equally applicable to the past even though the evidence used is much more problematic. Perhaps because of the fragmentary nature of archaeological data this makes it even more imperative to view palaeopathology from a biocultural perspective in a very holistic way. In doing this the impact of disease on a cultural group or society living in a specific environment may be better understood, especially with respect to coping mechanisms. Whatever area of study a researcher can claim to have expertise in, he or she, '…can only claim to have one small piece of a very complex puzzle, the pieces of which are complementary, not contradictory. To discourage investigation in one domain is to deny a fundamental aspect of the human condition in health and sickness' (*ibid.*, 232). Even the Hippocratic School in fifth century BC Greece recognised the value of considering a disease in its cultural, social and geographic context when Hippocrates in '*Airs, Waters and Places*' described a successful physician as one who relates disease to environment (Furness, 1970).

In effect, the biocultural approach can be classified as an epidemiological study or, '…the study of the distribution of disease in populations and of the factors that explain disease and its distribution: the population rather than the individual is the unit of study' (McElroy and Townsend, 1996: 43). It relates disease to age, sex, ethnicity, occupation, marital status, and social class amongst other variables, and compares rates between geographic areas and time. However, it should be remembered too that some of these variables may change over the lifespan of the individual and can therefore have different effects with respect to disease, and they may vary regionally. In archaeological contexts these changes prove problematic to identify because what is examined is the state of the skeleton of an individual (and population) at their time of death. It is a static observation and usually cannot take into account the detailed life history of that person or population, especially if the evidence seen for disease is chronic and healed in nature. It also presents a major question that cannot be answered. When did this person contract the disease seen in the skeleton, and did he or she have more than one episode of the disease? One of many scenarios could be that the person was very healthy through into early adulthood and then had a period of ten years when he or she contracted a number of diseases, some not affecting the skeleton. Recovery occurred and then the person lived another 20 years. Detailed examination of the characteristics of the pathologically induced lesions may help solve some of this problem but will not give all the answers. With respect to changes in environment, diet, climate and occupation, and their effects on health through an individual's lifetime, it may be possible to see the results of these changes reflected in disease patterning in a population, and by linking the biological evidence with evidence for these variables, direct cause and effect for disease may be seen. However, a timescale for these changes would not be evident. Another example explains this concept. If a person had a malaligned healed fracture to a leg bone and the adjacent joints displayed osteoarthritis, it is often assumed (but cannot be proved) that the osteoarthritis came after the fracture (because of changed stresses through the joint) but that may not necessarily be the case. What needs emphasising is that, despite trying to take a biocultural approach to palaeopathology, it will never be possible to pick up the nuances, detailed facets and changes that a population may experience through its lifetime — but this does not mean that it should not be attempted!

There has been some extremely beneficial work in palaeopathology that has taken this biocultural approach into account when trying to understand the aetiology (cause) of le-

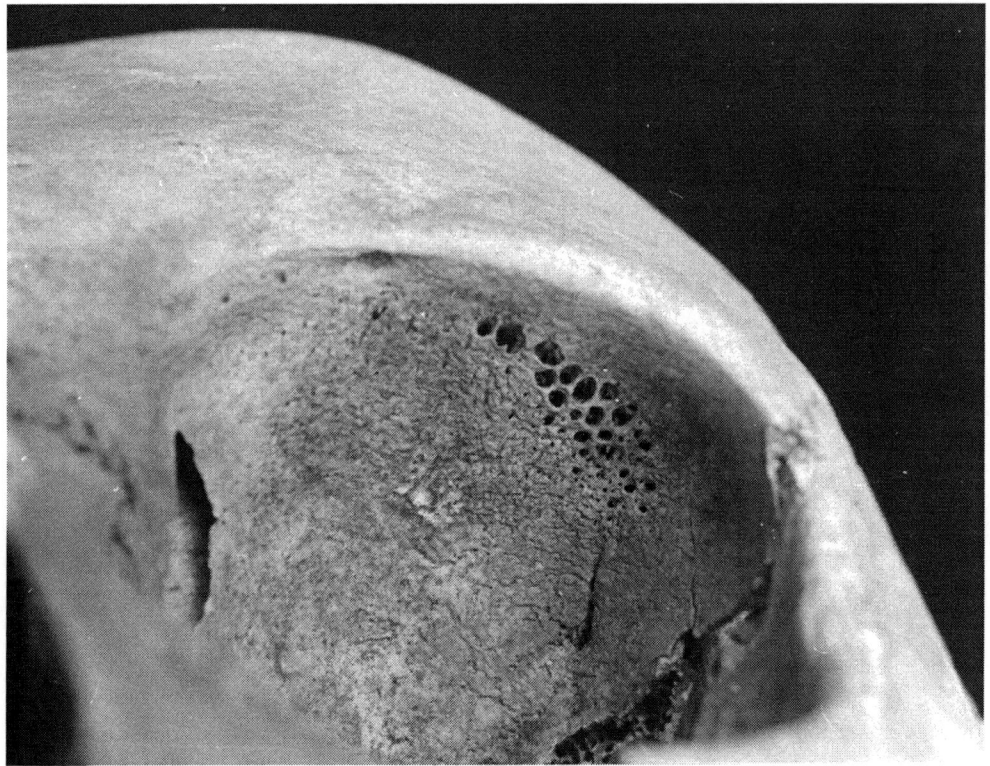

Fig. 10. Cribra orbitalia ('holes') in the left orbit of a skull.

sions in the skeleton. Three examples will illustrate the point. Firstly, a condition termed cribra orbitalia (or 'holes' in the eye sockets) has attracted much attention in palaeopathology (Fig. 10), probably because in some populations it has been seen in high frequencies, and is relatively easy to recognise and record. Stuart-Macadam (1985) has studied it both from a clinical and palaeopathological perspective, and it has been documented in agriculturally based populations in higher frequencies than for hunter-gatherers (Cohen and Armelagos, 1984). Despite much work on the condition having been done, its aetiology is not yet fully understood. A number of possible factors have been implicated for its appearance which is believed to be associated with anaemia. A diet low in iron, low birth-weight in children, a reliance on cereal in the diet, an overall high infectious disease load in the population, excessive blood loss, and intestinal problems are some of the causative factors suggested (Holland and O'Brien, 1997; Stuart-Macadam and Kent, 1992). By considering the condition from a biocultural perspective, all these factors could be considered as possible causes of the lesions. Was the population practising agriculture? Did they rely on cereals for much of their diet? Is there any evidence of infection in the population, and what factors appear to have induced it? What was the meat component of their diet? Of course, cribra orbitalia may have been caused by all these factors if these were identified in the cultural contextual data for the archaeological site, but at least this way of approaching disease causation may answer the question. If cribra orbitalia is recorded with no reference to the person's environment there is little more than can be said except that the person or population had the condition.

A second example illustrates a similar situation. New bone formation in the maxillary sinuses, the largest of the sinuses in the facial bones, has been noted in skeletal material from archaeological sites (Fig. 11). It is accepted as representing sinusitis in life (inflammation of the sinuses) — Roberts *et al.* (1998b), but there could be many potential causes. Smoking, environmental pollution, dental disease and allergies are some of the many aetiological factors involved in the appearance of the condition. Again, however, by considering later Medieval skeletal populations living in rural and urban environments it was possible to suggest causes for the sinusitis seen. Looking at cultural data indicating the quality of environment in which each group were living in, their occupations and housing, clear differences (but also similarities) were noted. Documentary and archaeological evidence in the urban centres indicated the presence of polluting industries, perhaps contributing to the rates seen there (especially for the males, who had the most severe and chronic changes in their sinuses), whilst in the less industrially (but agriculturally) polluted rural environment, other factors were identified as possibly contributing to the lower rates (for example, pollen, animal hair, etc.). Again, without the cultural contextual data the sinusitis frequencies would have remained clinical entities devoid of context.

The final example relates to lesions seen on ribs (Fig. 5) which many have suggested relate to lung infection (Kelley and Micozzi, 1984; Pfeiffer, 1992). Originally this work attempted to understand the mechanisms of the new bone formed in the ribs and its specific cause (Roberts *et al.*, 1994), suggesting that pulmonary tuberculosis was a likely candidate although it was accepted that other chronic lung diseases could have lead to the same changes. More recent work, as yet unpublished, has tried to focus on the specific environmental conditions that might lead to the rib changes. By considering populations from hunt-

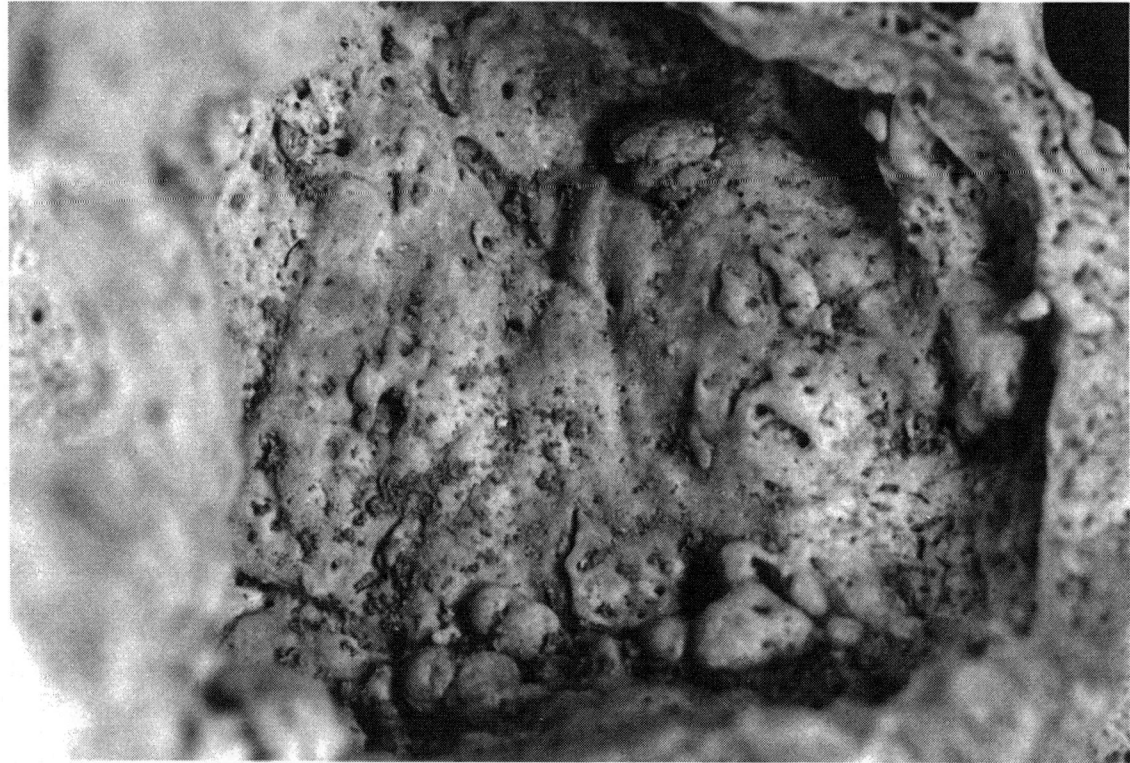

Fig. 11. Floor of maxillary sinus with extensive new bone formation, suggesting inflammation of the sinus during life.

ing and gathering and agricultural communities, desert and industrialised groups, the aim has been to try and explain more specifically what is causing the pathological lesions. If it is a respiratory disease, were the population living in close contact with each other? Did social status, sex or age have any influence on the appearance of the lesions? Are the rib changes necessarily from a lung infection or are the changes a result of irritation of the respiratory system from an external cause such as a dusty environment, or high levels of pollen in the atmosphere? Although the data is currently being worked on, the final results should make interesting reading and develop the rib lesion-lung condition theory (and probably make it even more complex!).

The inferences that are potentially possible from a bioculturally based population approach to palaeopathology are extensive and exciting and there are many questions that need approaching with respect to health in the past. For example, what were the effects of migration on health and disease in societies? Can we identify where people originated and moved to during their life? Recent work has suggested that this is possible (Carlson, 1996; Sealy *et al.*, 1995). But what are the real implications for disease when a person moves to a new area? By moving to a new place people expose themselves to new pathogens that their immune system cannot deal with, and they also take with them new diseases which the population they encounter has not experienced before which often leads to increased and rapid mortality (Swedlund and Armelagos, 1990). Trade caravans, religious pilgrimages and military manoeuvres have, in the past (and today), been responsible for mass movement of people (Wilson, 1995). In addition, acute disasters (e.g. drought), voyages of discovery and even stigma associated with a disease may lead to migration. What is important to note as was so clearly stated by Wilson (*ibid.*, 43) is that the differences in biological life in different areas and differences in receptivity and vulnerability are most important in the occurrence of disease. By linking biological evidence for disease and cultural data together to answer questions about migration, the impact of this very common human behaviour, which has had a long history, may be better understood.

Linked very much to the effect of travel on health is the immune system. The strength of the immune system or the ability of a person or population to fight off disease will be determined by exposure to pathogens during a person's lifetime, i.e. what you meet in the environment has an ongoing effect and long-lasting influence on your immune cells (comment by J. Stanford in Hamilton, 1998: 30). We assume that the improvements in living conditions, hygiene, water supply and sewage disposal are key to health but that may not necessarily be the case: '...an obsession with cleanliness and hygiene carries a hefty price tag' (*ibid.*, 26). Playing in the dirt as a child was good for us! The immune response our bodies have to a pathogen is very much determined by how many viruses, bacteria or other pathogenic organisms our immune system has had to deal with in childhood and adulthood. In a clinical sense, despite knowing much of what our immune system is about, we can only guess the strength of immune systems in the past by looking at pathological lesions: chronic healed lesions are taken to indicate that the person had a strong immune system, but was that so for all his or her life?

In transitional settings people spend a lot of time being sick (Findley, 1990), and that must have been true in the past, although few of these 'transitions' have been studied. Most of the work in palaeopathology to date has been focused on the transition to agriculture but there is room for much more work looking at, for example, migration of rural populations to urban settings (common today). Armelagos (1998) recognised three major epidemiological transitions, each sparked by human activity. The first was the transition to agriculture around the world, the second came this century when the war on the infectious diseases appeared to have been won, and the third we are experiencing now. The third is characterised by new diseases appearing over the past two decades as a result of, for example, increases in population and urbanisation of people, environmental degradation, global warming and improved transport. As he states, 'we are, quite literally, making ourselves sick' (*ibid.*: 27). However, it is possible to see other 'transitions' within these main three transitions in the past, for example the first moves to urban living, development of craft specialisation, and the development of trade and contact (Dobyns, 1993; Larsen, 1994). Each brought with it new health risks and challenges. Whilst we also generally think that we live in a healthy world in the west, there are probably more problems to face than our ancestors had to experience. Increasing length of life and development of chemotherapy has led to change in disease load seen. The degenerative diseases such as those relating to the cardiovascular system, and cancer, are prices we have to pay — '...the new survivors are not necessarily the healthy survivors' (Verbrugge, 1984). What is more, many new diseases are emerging, or old diseases re-emerging, in the world today which reflect the changes and damage we, as society, are imposing on our environments.

Start to discuss all these issues with respect to the differences between the biological sexes and, for the past, it becomes even more complex but fascinating. Differences in disease load between the sexes obviously illustrate behavioural differences which reflect social and cultural ideologies and values. Whilst people working in palaeopathology have usually provided disease data for males and females in their populations, there has been a lack of synthesis of these data with respect to why the differences are seen. A recent book (Grauer and Stuart-Macadam, 1998) has tried to redress the situation using perspectives from both medical anthropology and palaeopathology to explain sex differences in disease. Immune response, occupation and diet may be some of the more common influencing factors.

TREATMENT OF DISEASE AND INJURY

'The basic idea of medicine is to fix what goes wrong...to get back to a predetermined state of good health' (Alter, 1999: 43).

Clearly, there is much to be done despite much that has already been done in palaeopathology. Of course, accompanying disease is the treatment of disease, whether that be medically or surgically orientated. The thrust of this book is on the archaeology of medicine and it aims to show some of the evidence for treatment, and how it may be accessed and analysed. As with disease, the sources of evidence for medicine and surgery remain primary and secondary. Primary data comprises evidence on the human remains themselves, and secondary evidence may be found in documentary and art evidence (e.g. herbals, hospitals), archaeological evidence (e.g. dental and surgical instruments) and by studying traditional living societies and their concepts of disease causation and treatment. Primary evidence for treatment is limited (but more reliable) and secondary evidence is more plentiful (but less easy to interpret). Evidence for treatment of fractures (splints), head injuries (trepanations), and amputations have been found in the archaeological record (Backay, 1985; Bloom *et al.*, 1995; Elliott Smith, 1908), whilst direct application of copper plates to upper arm bones, probably to treat infection, have been noted in three different cultural contexts (Hallback, 1976–7; Janssens, 1987; Wells, 1964b; Fig. 12). Direct evidence for dental treatments are more abundant, ranging from fillings (Moller-Christensen, 1969), and drillings (Bennike, 1985) to dental restorative work (Zias, 1987).

Because dental remains tend to survive more readily in archaeological contexts, perhaps this is why there is more evidence for dental treatment than for treatment of problems in bone. Thus, while there is primary evidence for medicine and surgery, it is limited in what it can tell us about therapeutic systems, who had access to them (did specific social status, sex or age groups have priority, for example), and how effective they were. For example, poorer people may have been less likely to have access to 'first class' treatment than richer and more powerful members of a society. Indeed, today this is the case in both developed and developing countries. In fact, it has been suggested that some diseases may not be recognised as a problem (and therefore care systems not implemented) if only the poor suffer and not the rich (Farmer, 1996). Tuberculosis is one of these diseases that saw a decrease in its significance in the 1970s and 1980s in the wealthy nations of the world because of access to effective treatment. It is suggested now that tuberculosis in the poor groups of societies worldwide was still a major problem at that time which became more severe into the 1990s. Now that even the wealthier members of countries are being affected, nations are recognising the need to tackle the problem. The implication is that if a disease affects the poor then it does not matter. The alternative view of access to treatment might argue that if the poor were denied access to treatment in the past, they may have, within their own communities, developed adequate care and coping systems which worked well, i.e. don't wait for help to come, do something about it. As Withers (1961: 1) stated, '…in times of stress or of pain or of sorrow, the human being will go to any length to try and find help'.

Whilst one can guess and hypothesise about the availability of treatment for disease and injury in the past (and there is nothing as practical as a good theory — Marrow, 1969), it is mainly through secondary sources of evidence that the information comes as many of the chapters in this book will show.

THE WAY FORWARD: INTO THE TWENTY-FIRST CENTURY

'…there is growing evidence to suggest that archaeologists are incorporating skeletal studies into their research designs. This is especially the case for testing hypotheses and drawing inferences about diet and nutrition, health and disease, demography, and physical behavior and lifestyle in the past' (Larsen, 1997: 2).

So where does palaeopathology go from here and into the twenty-first century? This view is theoretical in nature which, in practice, may be difficult to achieve, especially in Britain. Notwithstanding the need to focus on linking biology with culture in palaeopathological study, a theme inherent in this chapter, recording of evidence is key to advancement. It is impor-

Fig. 12. Humerus with copper plates (originally lined with ivy leaves) indicating attempts at treatment of an infection.

tant to ensure that people working in the discipline are trained to recognise, record, and interpret pathological conditions in human remains; without this there is no point in palaeopathology. Inevitably, specialist training in this area is a prerequisite and a number of postgraduate courses exist to provide this training. Detailed recording of abnormal bone forming and destroying lesions, whether they are active or healed, and their distribution pattern on bones and teeth, and in the skeleton as a whole, form the basis of further analysis. Using a clinical base with which to interpret the distribution patterns, and providing a list of possible differential diagnoses, gives a starting point from which to think about the epidemiological aspects of the disease(s) observed. By considering age and sex, and the cultural context of the human remains, a more secure diagnosis (and specific aetiology to the disease seen) may be given. Appropriate photographs (especially for illustrating problematic or unusual cases, or to illustrate severity grading systems) and radiographs provide supporting evidence for the pathological observations seen. Methods for age and sex estimation must be given and recording methods for metrical and non-metrical data relevant to palaeopathology noted (for example, stature data, and non-metric traits which might be related to lifestyle). Details of the preservational state of the human remains (and definitions of terms used) are highly relevant to the final data collected because they will affect their quality. Not least, and of key relevance to investigating prevalence rates, is the recording of numbers of skeletal elements (including joint surfaces) and tooth types preserved so that actual prevalence rates can be determined.

HYPOTHESES, QUESTIONS, POPULATIONS VERSUS INDIVIDUALS

'In contrast to North America, the biocultural approach is yet to become established in Europe, but although population analyses are lacking... theoretical and methodological studies of measure of health are more abundant' (Bush and Zvelebil, 1991: 5).

Ideally, when recording any pathological lesion, there should be an hypothesis to test on which the work is based ('a statement of a hunch, expectation, or prediction or relationships or patterns that one seeks to test or examine' — Pelto and Pelto, 1996: 297), or a question that is being asked. This rests on considering the cultural context from which the skeletal material comes. For example, there is documentary evidence for a series of harvest failures during the period of the cemetery's use and therefore the expectation would be that the individuals from the cemetery might show signs of stress and dietary deficiency. Alternatively, a question might be: what skeletal changes (pathological and non-pathological) would be expected when a person starts to farm rather than to hunt and gather. These questions and hypotheses frame work, and should ideally be filling gaps in knowledge in a geographic area, time period or funerary context. In reality, it is not often possible to highlight these gaps because relatively little palaeopathological data has been published and still lies sitting on shelves waiting, especially in Britain. Whilst 'case studies' of interesting pathological conditions will always have their place in palaeopathology, the emphasis now should be on looking at health and disease from an aged and sexed population perspective, and preferably with large samples where analysis and interpretation will mean something. The question of sample representivity, however, should always be addressed.

To ensure good quality samples, the recommendation would be to employ trained biological anthropologists to work on cemetery site excavations whose expertise in recovering and processing skeletal material will enable due attention to be paid to the requirements of palaeopathology. For example, the recovery of all bones of the skeleton helps ultimately to diagnose disease, and the careful processing of material once excavated will ensure that delicate structures (e.g. calcified plaque, or calculus, on the teeth) do not get damaged before they reach the recording stage. Ideally, too, a bibliographic and skeletal database of previous work in palaeopathology would help in generating comparative work in the discipline. By identifying contemporary and different sites in the same and different geographic regions of the world, and assuming everybody has recorded data in the same ways, comparison of data is potentially possible and gaps in knowledge could be highlighted. Some of these databases are available but as soon as they are published they are usually incomplete and need updating. The Palaeopathology Bibliography (Tyson, 1998), and the annotated bibliography of the Paleopathology Association Newsletter, plus the numerous bibliographic database systems now available, covering most journals (obscure and not so obscure) provide an invaluable source of information for possible comparative work.

As we move into the 21st century, in many parts of the world including Britain, there exists a strong archive of skeletal material curated in museums and other institutions, supported by a strong archaeological base. This 'infrastructure' can allow very complex questions to be asked of past human behaviour in all respects. The strong archaeology base allows contextual (cultural) information to be potentially effectively integrated with biological information. However, to do this, we need the will, motivation and enthusiasm of all parties concerned. If humans are important today then surely they were so in the past. Furthermore, if they were important then if their health suffered did this not have an effect on their social, economic and political systems, and environment (and much more)? Alternatively these systems could have had an effect on their health. People are the key to understanding the past, and how better to study them but through their biological remains? However, we must reflect on what we have done already in palaeopathology, and not accept everything we read as true; never think that specific research in palaeopathology has had its final say (there is always room for improvement and extension of previous research with new data, even to the effect of demolishing of theories), and never be complacent or be frightened to admit we were wrong. We must also not study palaeopathology for its own sake; we have to justify our actions and have specific research objectives, something which is difficult to achieve with contract archaeology being dominant in many parts of the world. NAGPRA (Rose *et al.*, 1996) has shown that we must consider the study of human remains from archaeological sites as a privilege and not a right. We must ask the right questions, study the data in a scientific manner and be respectful to this valuable resource. We must also promote our studies through the media, whatever we think of that opportunity, because it is through informing the public of our work that we can show its value. With all this in mind, palaeopathology has a great future in the 21st century, a future which will contribute significantly to understanding how humans adapted to, changed and lived in their environments, and how those environments affected their health.

BIBLIOGRAPHY

Aaron, J., Rogers, J. and Kanis, J.
(1992) 'Paleohistology of Paget's disease in two Medieval skeletons', *Amer.J.Phys.Anthrop.* **89**: 325–31.

Alland, A.
(1966) 'Medical anthropology and the study of behavioural and cultural adaptation', *American Anthropologist* **68**: 40–51.

Alter, J. S.
(1999) 'Heaps of health, metaphysical fitness', *Current Anthropology* **40**: 43–66.

Armelagos, G. J.
(1998) 'The viral superhighway', *The Sciences* Jan/Feb: 24–9.

Armelagos, G. J., Leatherman, T., Ryan, M. and Sibley, L.
(1992) 'Biocultural synthesis in medical anthropology', *Medical Anthropology* **14**: 35–52.

Aufderheide, A. C. and Rodriguez-Martin, C.
(1998) *The Cambridge Encyclopedia of Human Paleopathology*, Cambridge: Cambridge University Press.

Backay, L.
(1985) *Early History of Craniotomy from Antiquity to the Napoleonic Era*, Illinois: Charles Thomas.

Barber, G., Watt, I. and Rogers, J.
(1997) 'A comparison of radiological and palaeopathological diagnostic criteria for hyperostosis frontalis interna,' *Int. J. Osteoarchaeology* **7**: 57–164.

Bell, L.
(1990) 'Palaeopathology and diagenesis: an SEM evaluation of structural change using backscattered electron imaging', *J. Archaeological Science* **17**: 85–102.

Bell, L. and Piper, K.
(2000) 'An introduction to palaeohistopathology', in M. Cox and S. Mays (eds.) *Human Osteology in Archaeology and Forensic Science*, London: Greenwich Medical Media, pp. 255–74.

Bennike, P.
(1985) *Palaeopathology of Danish skeletons. A Comparative Study of Demography, Disease and Injury*, Copenhagen: Akademisk Forlag.

Bhasin, M. K., Walter, H. and Danker-Hopfe, H.
(1994) *The People of India. An Investigation of Biological Variability in Ecological, Ethnoeconomic and Linguistic Groups*, Delhi: Kamla-Raj Enterprises.

Blondiaux, J., Duvette, J-F., Vatteon, S. and Eisenberg, L.
(1994) 'Microradiographs of leprosy from archaeological contexts', *Int. J. Osteoarchaeology* **4**: 13–20.

Bloom, A. I., Bloom, R. A., Kahila, G., Eisenberg, E. and Smith, P.
(1995) 'Amputation of the hand in the 3600 year old skeletal remains of an adult male: the first case reported from Israel', *Int. J. Osteoarchaeology* **5**: 188–91.

Blumberg, B. S. and Hesser, J. E.
(1975) 'Anthropology and infectious disease', in A. Damon (ed.) *Physiological Anthropology*, Oxford: Oxford University Press, pp. 260–94.

Brown, K.
(2000) 'Ancient DNA applications in human osteoarchaeology: achievements, problems and potential', in M. Cox and S. Mays (eds.) *Human Osteology in Archaeology and Forensic Science*, London: Greenwich Medical Media, pp. 455–73.

Brown, P. J., Inhorn, M. C. and Smith, D. J.
(1996) 'Disease, ecology, and human behavior', in C. F. Sargent and T. M. Johnson (eds.) *Medical Anthropology. Contemporary Theory and Method*, London: Praeger, pp. 183–218.

Buikstra, J. E. and Ubelaker, D. (eds.)
(1994) *Standards for Data Collection for Human Skeletal Remains*, Arkansas: Archaeological Survey Research Seminar Series 44.

Bush, H. and Zvelebil, M.
(1991) 'Pathology and health and past societies: an introduction', in H. Bush and M. Zvelebil (eds.) *Health in Past Societies. Biocultural Interpretations of Human Skeletal Remains in Archaeological Contexts*. British Archaeological Reports, International Series 567, Oxford: Tempus Reparatum, pp. 3–9.

Carlson, A. K.
(1996) 'Lead isotope analysis of human bone for addressing cultural affinity: a case study from Rocky Mountain House, Alberta', *J.Archaeological Science* **23**: 557–67.

Chadwick Hawkes, S. C. and Wells, C.
(1983) 'The inhumed skeletal material from an early Anglo-Saxon cemetery in Worthy Park, Kingsworthy, Hampshire, Southern England, *Paleobios* **1**, (1–2): 3–46.

Cohen, M. and Armelagos, G. J. (eds.)
(1984) *Paleopathology at the origins of agriculture*, London: Academic Press.

Cramp, R.
(1983) 'The archaeologist's view — general', in G. D. Hart (ed.) *Disease in Ancient Man*, Toronto: Clarke Irwin, pp. 11–20.

Dawes, J. D. and Magilton, J. R.
(1980) *The Cemetery of St Helen-on-the-Walls, Aldwark*. The archaeology of York. The Medieval cemeteries 12/1, London: Council for British Archaeology.

Dobney, K. and Brothwell, D.
(1988) 'A scanning electron microscope study of archaeological dental calculus', in S. Olsen (ed.) *Scanning Electron Microscopy in Archaeology*. British Archaeological Reports, International Series 452, Oxford, pp. 372–85.

Dobyns, H. F.
(1993) 'Disease transfer at contact', *Annual Rev. of Anthropology* **22**: 273–91.

Drancourt, M., Aboudharam, G., Signoli, M., Dutour, O. and Raoult, D.
(1998) 'Detection of 400-year-old Yersinia perstis DNA in human dental pulp: an approach to the diagnosis of ancient septicemia', *Proc. National Academy of Science* **95**: 12637–40.

Elliott Smith, G.
(1908) 'The most ancient splints', *British Medical J.* **1**: 732.

Elvery, M. W., Savage, N. W. and Wood, W. B.
(1998) 'Radiographic study of the Broadbeach Aboriginal dentition', *Amer.J.Phys.Anthrop.* **107**: 211–19.

Farley, M. and Manchester, K.
(1989) 'The cemetery of the leper hospital of St Margaret, High Wycombe, Buckinghamshire', *Medieval Archaeology* **33**: 82–9.

Farmer, P.
(1996) 'Social inequalities and emerging infectious disease', *Emerging Infectious Diseases* **2**, (4): 259–69.

Findley, S. E.
(1990) 'Social reflections of changing morbidity during health transitions', in J. Caldwell, S. Findley, P. Caldwell, G. Santow, W. Cosford, J. Braid, and D. Broers-Freeman (eds.) *What We Know About Health Transitions. The Cultural, Social and Behavioural Determinants of Health.* Proceedings of an International Workshop, Canberra, May 1989, Canberra: Australian National University, Health Transition Centre, pp. 311–29.

Fricker, E. J., Spigelman, M. and Fricker, C. R.
(1997) 'The detection of *E. coli* DNA in the ancient remains of Lindow man using the polymerase chain reaction', *Letters in Applied Microbiology* **24**: 531–4.

Furness, S. B.
(1970) 'Changes in non-infectious diseases associated with the processes of civilisation', in S. V. Boyden (ed.) *The Impact of Civilisation on the Biology of Man*, Canberra: Australian National University Press, pp. 75–108.

Gernaey, A. and Minnikin, D.
(2000) 'Chemical methods in palaeopathology', in M. Cox and S. Mays (eds.) *Human Osteology in Archaeology and Forensic Science*, London: Greenwich Medical Media, 239–53.

Gernaey, A., Minnikin, D. E., Copley, M. S., Ahmed, A. M. S., Robertson, D. J., Nolan, J., and Chamberlain, A. T.
(1999) 'Correlation of the occurrence of mycolic acids with tuberculosis in an archaeological population', in G. Palfi, O. Dutour, J. Deak and I. Hutas (eds.) *Tuberculosis. Past and Present.* Golden Book Publisher Ltd., and Tuberculosis Foundation, pp. 275–82.

Glen-Haduch, E., Szostek, K. and Glab, H.
(1997) 'Cribra orbitalia and trace element content in human teeth from Neolithic and Early Bronze Age graves in Southern Poland', *Amer.J.Phys.Anthrop.* **103**: 201–07.

Grauer, A. L. and Roberts, C. A.
(1996) 'Paleoepidemiology, healing and possible treatment of trauma in the Medieval cemetery of St. Helen-on-the-Walls, York, England', *Amer.J.Phys.Anthrop.* **100**, (4): 531–44.

Grauer, A. L. and Stuart-Macadam, P. (eds.)
(1998) *Sex and Gender in Paleopathological Perspective*, Cambridge: Cambridge University Press.

Hallback, H.
(1976–77) 'A Medieval bone with a copper plate support indicating open surgical treatment', *Ossa* **3/4**: 63–82.

Hamilton, G.
(1998) 'Let them eat dirt', *New Scientist* eighteenth July: 26–31.

Henderson, J.
(1987) 'Factors determining the state of preservation of human remains', in A. Boddington, A. N. Garland and R. C. Janaway (eds.) *Death, Decay and Reconstruction. Approaches to Archaeology and Forensic Science*, Manchester: Manchester University Press, pp. 43–54.

Holland, T. D. and O'Brien, M. J.
(1997) 'Parasites, porotic hyperostosis and the implications of changing perspectives', *American Antiquity* **62**(2): 183–93.

Hughes, C., Heylings, D. J. A. and Power, C.
(1996) 'Transverse (Harris) lines in Irish archaeological remains', *Amer.J.Phys.Anthrop.* **101**: 115–31.

Inhorn, M. C. and Brown, P. J.
(1990) 'The anthropology of infectious disease', *Annual Review of Anthropology* **19**: 89–117.

Janssens, P.
(1987) 'A copper plate on the upper arm in a burial at the church of Vrasene, Belgium', *J.Paleopathology* **1** (1): 15–18.

Jurmain, R.
(1990) 'Paleoepidemiology of a Central Californian prehistoric population from CA-ALA-329. III Degenerative joint disease', *Amer.J.Phys.Anthrop.* **83**: 83–94.

Katzenberg, M. A.
(1992) 'Advances in stable isotope analysis of prehistoric bones', in S. R. Saunders and M. A. Katzenberg (eds.) *Skeletal Biology of Past Peoples. Research Methods*, New York: Wiley Liss, pp. 105–19.

(2000) 'Stable isotope analysis: a tool for studying past diet, demography, and life history', in M. A. Katzenberg and S. R. Saunders (eds.) *Biological Anthropology of the Human Skeleton*, New York, Wiley-Liss, 305–27.

Katzenberg, M. A., Herring, D. A. and Saunders, S. R.
(1996) 'Weaning and infant mortality: evaluating the skeletal evidence', *Amer.J.Phys.Anthrop.* **39**: 177–99.

Kelley, M. and Micozzi, M.
(1984) 'Rib lesions in pulmonary tuberculosis', *Amer. J. Phys. Anthrop.* **65**: 381–6.

Larsen, C. S.
(1994) 'In the wake of contact: native population biology in the Postcontact Americas', *Yearbook of Phys.Anthrop.* **37**: 109–54.

(1997) *Bioarchaeology. Interpreting Behavior from the Human Skeleton*, Cambridge: Cambridge University Press.

Lukacs, J. R.
(1989) 'Dental palaeopathology: methods for reconstructing dietary patterns', in M. Y. Iscan and K. A. R. Kennedy (eds.) *Reconstruction of Life from the Skeleton*, New York: Alan R. Liss, pp. 261–86.

Marrow, A.
(1969) *The Practical Theorist. The Life and Work of Kurt Lewin*, New York: Basic Books.

Mays, S.
(1993) 'Infanticide in Roman Britain', *Antiquity* **67**: 883–8.
(1997) 'A perspective on human osteoarchaeology in Britain', *International J. Osteoarchaeology* **7**: 600–04.

(2000) 'New directions in the analysis of stable isotopes in excavated bones and teeth', in M. Cox and S. Mays (eds.) *Human Osteology in Archaeology and Forensic Science*, London: Greenwich Medical Media, pp. 425–38.

Mays, S., Lees, B., and Stevenson, J. C.
(1998) 'Age-dependent bone loss in a Medieval population', *Int. J. Osteoarchaeology* **8**, (2): 97–106

McElroy, A.
(1990) 'Biocultural models in studies of human health and adaptation', *Medical Anthropology* **4**: 243–65.

McElroy, A. and Townsend, P. K.
(1996) *Medical Anthropology in Ecological Perspective*, Oxford: Westview Press.

McKinley, J. and Roberts, C. A.
(1993) *Excavation and Post-excavation Treatment of Cremated and Inhumed Remains*, Birmingham: Institute of Field Archaeologists Technical Paper 13.

McNeill, W.
(1976) *Plagues and People*, Oxford: Blackwell.

Melcher, A. H., Holowka, S., Pharaoh, M. and Lewin, P. K.
(1997) 'Non-invasive computed tomography and three-dimensional reconstruction of the dentition of a 2800 year old Egyptian mummy exhibiting extensive dental disease', *Amer. J. Phys.Anthrop.* **103**: 329–40.

Miller, E., Ragsdale, B. D. and Ortner, D. J.
(1996) 'Accuracy in dry bone diagnosis: a comment on palaeopathological methods', *International J. Osteoarchaeology* **6**: 21–229.

Moller-Christensen, V.
(1961) *Bone Changes in Leprosy*, Copenhagen: Munksgaard.
(1969) *A Rosary Bead Used as a Tooth Filling Material in a Human Mandibular Canine Tooth. A Unique Case from the Danish Middle Ages*, 21st International Congress of the History of Medicine, Siena, Italy, 1968.

Ortner, D.
(1991) 'Theoretical and methodological issues in paleopathology', in D. J. Ortner and A. C. Aufderheide (eds.) *Human Paleopathology. Current Syntheses and Future Options*, Washington DC: Smithsonian Institution Press, pp. 5–11.

Pelto, P. J. and Pelto, G. H.
(1996) 'Research designs in medical anthropology', in C. F. Sargent and T. M. Johnson (eds.) *Medical Anthropology. Contemporary Theory and Method*, London: Praeger, pp. 293–324.

Pfeiffer, S.
(1991) 'Rib lesions and New World tuberculosis', *Int. J. Osteoarchaeology* **1**: 191–8.
(2000) 'Palaeohistology: health and disease', in M. A. Katzenberg and S. R. Saunders (eds.) *Biological Anthropology of the Human Skeleton*, New York, Wiley-Liss, pp. 287–302.

Polednak, A.
(1989) *Racial and Ethnic Differences in Disease*, Oxford: Oxford University Press.

Polunin, V.
(1967) 'Health and disease in contemporary primitive societies', in D. Brothwell and A. T. Sandison (eds.) *Diseases in Antiquity*, Illinois: Charles Thomas, pp. 69–97.

Reichs, K.
(1986) 'Forensic implications of skeletal pathology: ancestry', in K. Reichs (ed.) *Forensic Osteology. Advances in the Identification of Human Remains*, Illinois: Charles Thomas, pp. 196–217.

Resnick, D.
(1995) *Diagnosis of Bone and Joint Disorders*, Edinburgh: W. B. Saunders Company.

Roberts, C. A.
(1986) 'Palaeopathology: cottage industry or interacting discipline', in J. Bintliff and C. Gaffney (eds.) *Archaeology at the Interface. Studies of Archaeology's Relationships with History, Geography, Biology and Physical Sciences*, British Archaeological Reports, International Series 300, Oxford, pp. 110–28.
(1988) 'Trauma and treatment in British antiquity: a radiographic study', in E. Slater and J. Tate (eds.) *Science and Archaeology. Glasgow 1987*, British Archaeological Reports, British Series 96(ii), Oxford, 339–59.
(1991) 'Scientific methods in palaeopathology: past, present and future', in P. Budd, B. Chapman, C. Jackson, R. Janaway and B. Ottaway (eds.) *Archaeological Sciences 1989. Proceedings of a Conference on the Application of Scientific Techniques to Archaeology, Bradford, September 1989*, Oxford: Oxbow Books, pp. 373–85.
(1996) 'The biological evidence or what the people say', in 'Archaeological study of church cemeteries: past, present and future' by E. O'Brien and C. A. Roberts, in J. Blair and C. Pyrah (eds.) *Church Archaeology. Research Directions for the Future*, Council for British Archaeology Research Report 104, York: Council for British Archaeology, pp. 166–81.

Roberts, C. A. and Wakely, J.
(1992) 'Microscopical findings associated with a diagnosis of osteoporosis in palaeopathology', *International J. Osteoarchaeology* **2**: 23–30.

Roberts, C. A., Lucy, D. and Manchester, K.
(1994) 'Inflammatory lesions of ribs: an analysis of the Terry Collection', *Amer.J.Phys.Anthrop.* **95**(2): 169–82.

Roberts, C. A., Boylston, A., Buckley, L., Chamberlain, A. T. and Murphy, E. M.
(1998a) 'Rib lesions and tuberculosis: the palaeopathological evidence', *Tubercle and Lung Disease* **79**, (1): 55–60.

Roberts, C. A., Lewis, M. E. and Boocock, P.
(1998b) 'Infectious disease, sex and gender: the complexity of it all', in A. L. Grauer and P. Stuart-Macadam (eds.) *Exploring the Difference: sex and gender in paleopathological perspective*, Cambridge: Cambridge University Press, pp. 93–113.

Roberts, N. M.
(1985) *Psychological aspects of rehabilitation in three orthopaedic populations. Health attitudes and moods correlating with disability and pain in arthritic patients, back surgery patients and general orthopaedic surgery patients*, Unpublished PhD thesis, University of Bradford.

Roberts, R. S.
(1971) 'The use of literary and documentary evidence in the

history of medicine', in E. Clarke (ed.) *Modern Methods in the History of Medicine*, Canada: Athlone Press, pp. 36–57.

Rogers, J. and Waldron, T.
(1985) 'Lead concentrations in bones from a Neolithic long barrow', *J. Archaeological Science* **12**: 93–6.
(1995) *A Field Guide to Joint Disease in Archaeology*, Chichester: Wiley.

Rose, J. C., Anton, S. C., Aufderheide, A. C., Eisenberg, L., Gregg, J. B., Neiburger, E. J. and Rothschild, B. M.
(1988) *Skeletal Database Committee Recommendations*, Detroit, Ilinois: Paleopathology Association.

Rose, J. C., Green, T. J. and Green, V. D.
(1996) 'NAGPRA IS FOREVER. Osteology and the repatriation of skeletons', *Annual Review of Anthropology* **25**: 81–103.

Rothschild, B. and Rothschild, C.
(1995) 'Comparison of radiologic and gross examination for detection of cancer in defleshed skeletons', *Amer.J.Phys.Anthrop.* **96**: 357–63.

Sager, P.
(1969) *Spondylosis Cervicalis*, Copenhagen: Munksgaard.

Salo, W. L., Aufderheide, A. C., Buikstra, J. E. and Holcomb, T. A.
(1994) 'Identification of *Mycobacterium tuberculosis* DNA in a pre-Columbian Peruvian mummy', *Proc. National Academy of Sciences* **91**: 2091–4.

Sandford, M. K.
(1992) 'A reconsideration of trace element analysis in prehistoric bone', in S. R. Saunders and A. Katzenberg (eds.) *Skeletal Biology of Past Peoples: Research Methods*, New York: John Wiley and Sons, pp. 79–103.
(1993) 'Understanding the biogenic-diagenetic continuum: interpreting elemental concentrations of archaeological bone', in M. K. Sandford (ed.) *Investigations of Ancient Human Tissues. Chemical Analyses in Anthropology*, Pennsylvania: Gordon and Breach, pp. 3–57.

Sandford, M. K. and Weaver, D. S.
(1998) *Paleopathology: Future Directions and Challenge*, Paper presented at the American Anthropological Association 97th Annual Meeting, Philadelphia, December 1998.
(2000) 'Trace element research in anthropology: new perspectives and challenges', in M. A. Katzenberg and S. R. Saunders (eds.) *Biological Anthropology of the Human Skeleton*, New York, Wiley-Liss, 329–50.

Sargent, C. F. and Johnson, T. M. (eds.)
(1996) *Medical Anthropology. Contemporary Theory and Method*, London: Praeger.

Sealy, J., Armstrong, R. and Schrire, C.
(1995) 'Beyond lifetime averages: tracing life histories through isotopic analysis of different calcified tissues from archaeological human skeletons', *Antiquity* **69**: 290–300.

Spigelman, M., Donaghue, H. D. and Hershkovitz, I.
(in press) *The Study of Ancient DNA Answers, a Palaeopathological Question*, Proc. of the Third International Congress on the Evolution and Palaeoepidemiology of Infectious Diseases: the Past and Present of Leprosy, Oxford: Archaeopress.

Stuart-Macadam, P.
(1985) 'Porotic hyperostosis: representative of a childhood condition,' *Amer.J.Phys.Anthrop.* **66**: 391–8.
(1991) 'Anaemia in Roman Britain: Poundbury Camp', in H. Bush and M. Zvelebil (eds.) *Health in Past Societies. Biocultural Interpretations of Human Skeletal Remains in Archaeological Contexts*, British Archaeological Reports, International Series 567, Oxford: Tempus Reparatum, pp. 101–13.

Stuart-Macadam, P. and Kent, S. (eds.)
(1992) *Diet, Demography and Disease. Changing Perspectives on Anemia*, New York: Aldine de Gruyter.

Swedlund, A. C. and Armelagos, G. J.
(1990) *Disease in Transition. Anthropological and Epidemiological Perspectives*, New York: Bergin and Garvey.

Teaford, M. F.
(1991) 'Dental microwear: What can it tell us about diet and dental function?' in M. Kelley and C. S. Larsen (eds.) *Advances in Dental Anthropology*, New York: Wiley Liss Inc., pp. 341–6.

Thompson, D. (ed.)
(1995) *The Concise Oxford Dictionary of Current English*, Oxford: Clarendon Press.

Tyson, R. (ed.)
(1998) *Human Paleopathology and Related Subjects. An International Bibliography*, San Diego: Museum of Man.

U.C.A.S.
(1998) *Universities and college admission services entry 1999*, U.C.A.S.

Verbrugge, L.
(1984) 'Longer life but worsening health? Trends in health and mortality of middle aged and older persons', *Milbank Memorial Fund Quarterly/Health and Society* **62**: 475–519.

Waldron, T.
(1994) *Counting the Dead. The Epidemiology of Skeletal Populations,* Chichester: Wiley.

Waldron, T. and Rogers, J.
(1991) 'Interobserver variation in coding osteoarthritis in human skeletal remains', *International J. Osteoarchaeology* **1(1)**: 49–56.

Walker, P.
(1986) 'Porotic hyperostosis in a marine-dependent Californian Indian population', *Amer. J. Phys. Anthrop.* **69**: 345–54.

Wells, C.
(1964a) *Bones, Bodies and Disease*, London: Thames and Hudson.
(1964b) 'The study of ancient disease', *Surgo* **32**: 3–7.

Wells, C. and Woodhouse, N.
(1975) 'Paget's disease in an Anglo-Saxon', *Medical History* **19**, (4): 396–400.

Wiley, A. S.
(1992) 'Adaptation and the biocultural paradigm in medical anthropology: a critical review', *Medical Anthropology* **6**, (3): 216–36.

Wilson
(1995) 'Travel and the emergence of infectious diseases', *Emerging Infectious Diseases* **1**, (2): 39–46

Withers, R. T.
(1961) 'On bone setting', *Ulster Medical J.* **29** (1): 1–13.

Wood, J. W., Milner, G. R., Harpending, H. C. and Weiss, K. M.
(1992) 'The osteological paradox. Problems of inferring health from the skeleton', *Current Anthropology* **33**: 343–70.

Zias, J.
(1987) 'Operative dentistry in the 2nd century BC', *J. Amer. Dental Assoc.* **114**: 665–6.

TOOTH WORMS AND PELICANS: DENTISTRY IN ARCHAEOLOGY

Chrissie Freeth

INTRODUCTION

The study of the archaeological evidence for dentistry seems to be at the stage where the study of palaeopathology was a few decades ago: descriptive, anecdotal, case study orientated, and executed by those with a medical/dental background rather than an archaeological one. This is unfortunate as this untapped source of information has, as discussed later, a great potential of information to contribute to the field of archaeology.

Palaeopathology must, as an integral part to the study of disease in the past, examine evidence (documentary and artefactual) on ways of treating disease. How it was treated and what people's perceptions of it were may reflect its presence in the archaeological record and therefore its subsequent interpretation. This is especially so with the dental diseases. The main reasons for this are twofold: survivability and accessibility.

The teeth are the hardest part of the body and more likely to survive burial than bone. Any marks made on the teeth, accidentally or intentionally, will also be preserved as a permanent record as such evidence cannot be remodelled away. The use of inorganic material in prosthetic devices should also promote preservation of the evidence of intentional intervention. Organic structures or fillings may decay but tell-tale signs, as discussed below, may remain. There are some problems regarding preservation as discussed later in this chapter, but on the whole, the potential for the evidence of dental treatment to survive is encouraging.

Dental disease affects most people in one form or another and can be a depressing and preoccupying discomfort. Unlike the other tissues palaeopathologists examine, the dental tissues were also visible to their owners and others in life. This accessibility, and therefore potential to manipulate, add to and remove the dental tissues means that it is naive to assume that people in the past would not try to treat the discomfort. It is also naive to assume that people of the past did not have successful and trusted methods of treatment since lost to us. However, this is an easy trap to fall into as only the more bizarre and unusual remedies tend to be discussed in many texts on the subject of dentistry in the past.

Although many of these remedies and treatments used by people in the past may not leave evidence on the teeth, for example application of herbs, a number of treatments may leave their mark on the teeth. These include evidence of oral hygiene, filling, filing, drilling, extraction, cosmetic modification and the use of prosthetic devices. This chapter will review the reported evidence of such treatments and summarise ways in which they may be seen on skeletal remains. This chapter will then identify the limitations in this study and their cause. The potential benefits of the study of dentistry in the past will be discussed and ways forward for this fascinating and understudied area of archaeology will be proposed.

THE NON-DENTAL EVIDENCE

Most evidence regarding the *archaeology* of dentistry has been anecdotally tagged onto the *history* of dentistry. This is no great surprise considering it is *historians* (or dentists) rather than *archaeologists* who have been studying dentistry in the past. The historical record provides a rich source of information. For example, texts written by dentists may describe what treatments were practised and the types of instruments used. Literary references and iconographic evidence may also provide some of this information, but it may also provide an insight into who was being treated and what the contemporary perceptions of dentistry and dental health were. Summaries of such evidence can be found in standard texts on the history of dentistry such as Ring (1992), Hillam (1990), Axthelm (1981) and Wynbrandt (1998).

Other non-dental evidence for dentistry in the past includes evidence for the tools used in the treatment of dental disease. Bennion's (1986) review of the instruments and equipment associated with various dental treatments provides a useful guide to their development, function and identification. However, not surprisingly, the bulk of the evidence reviewed is historic rather than archaeological. This discrepancy may be due to archaeologically recovered instruments not being recognised as such or their lack of survival in the archaeological record. Nevertheless, a set of ten Roman silver instruments has been identified as a dental set (Longfield-Jones, 1984).

By examining parallels between the ethnographic and archaeological record, information regarding oral hygiene and dental practises where the documentary evidence is sparse or non-existent may be of use. For example, what were the treatments, who were the practitioners, who were the patients, what equipment is associated with them, what evidence is left on the dental tissues?

THE DENTAL EVIDENCE

Oral Hygiene

There are four types of evidence that may remain on dental remains from antiquity that indicate oral hygiene practise: appliance abrasion, dentifrice abrasion, scaling and interproximal grooves.

Appliance Abrasion
Appliance abrasion caused by a cleaning appliance may be due to the use of a toothbrush or, as in the case of Isabella d'Aragona

(1470–1524), the use of a pumice stone or cuttlefish (d'Errico et al., 1986–87). The enamel surfaces of this individual's teeth had been so severely abraded the enamel and some dentine had been completely removed on the buccal surfaces with only a thin blackened margin of enamel remaining. The abrasion was the most severe in the upper and lower incisors. Microscopically, horizontal long and thin parallel striations were visible and were more oblique posteriorly; vertical striae were also present. It was concluded, because of the lack of occlusal wear, that these were not mastication striae but caused by particles freed from the instrument. Wide grooves on the mesial and distal borders were also present and interpreted as being caused by a metal toothpick. The black staining visible on the unabraded surfaces of the teeth, which had a high content of mercury, was probably a side effect of chronic mercury intoxication as a result of its use to treat syphilis.

Toothbrush abrasion is said to be common today (Soames and Southam, 1993) and is seen most often on the exposed root surfaces of the maxillary anterior teeth. The abrasion is recognised as wedge-shaped grooves with polished dentine surfaces. There may be an asymmetric distribution depending on whether the individual was left or right-handed. It seems reasonable to assume that because of increased root exposure in antiquity (due to periodontal disease and continuing eruption), more examples of this type of abrasion would be known in the archaeological record. However, toothbrushes are a relatively modern phenomenon. For example, even into the beginning of this century it was not uncommon for poorer families, boarding houses and college dormitories to share a common toothbrush (Mandel, 1990).

There are conflicting references as to the date of the introduction of toothbrushes. Mandel (1990) refers to the first toothbrush being of hog bristles set in oxbone and dating to 1490, and of brushes made of ivory handles with horse-mane bristles from China in 1000. However, Bennion (1986) argues that the 'accepted view' is that they were introduced to France from Spain c. 1590 and consisted of horse hair or animal bristles mounted in tubular handles and thus resembling a paintbrush. However, by the eighteenth century toothbrushes were more common for the select few and became part of the vanity case or travelling kit with decorative handles with interchangeable heads. With the introduction of nylon bristles in the 1930s and wooden or plastic handles, access by the masses to toothbrushes was made possible. As well as these artificial toothbrushes, natural ones were available. The use of a siwak or misswak, a twig of the *Salvadora persica* tree which had been soaked in water to separate the fibres which were then exposed and used to brush the teeth, was recommended by Muhammad, the sixth century prophet (Ring, 1992).

As well as the availability of toothbrushes, the material used to make the bristles may also have an effect on the prevalence of toothbrush abrasion. However, it would appear that toothbrushes of different harshness were available as indicated by the comments of Jean Baptisie Gariot, who in 1843 stated (cited by Bennion, 1986: 134): 'Delicate females, who take a great care of their mouths, and whose teeth are easily cleaned, should use a soft brush. Men, who clean their teeth but seldom require a hard one.'

Dentrifice Abrasion

Prior to the availability of a toothbrush, a cloth, sponge or digit would have been used to apply a dentrifice. However, if the appliance itself did not result in abrasion the dentrifice might. An abrasive compound has been attributed as the cause of macroscopic loss of enamel and multiple, fine, mostly transverse scratches seen microscopically on the labial surfaces of the maxillary anterior teeth and premolars of King Christian III of Denmark and Norway (1503–1559) (Pedersen, 1979).

The presence of abrasion is not surprising considering the contents of some of these compounds. These contents would have been devised and kept secret by their makers, but Bennion (1986) lists several examples: ground pebbles, honey, verdigris, incense and pulverised fruit (Ebers Papyrus 1500 BC); burnt shells, coral, talc, salt and honey (Ancient Greek); three mice, the head of a hare and white stone (Hippocrates); ground oyster and egg shells, cattle hooves and horns, myrrh and an aromatic (Roman); dried bread (nibbled by mouse), cuttlefish, rock-salt, pumice, nitre, alum, burnt staghorn and oris-root (Middle Ages); meerschaum, salt and the burnt shells of snails and oysters, sal ammoniac, burnt gypsum and verdigris with honey (Avicenna, 980–1037); honey and burnt shells tied inside a piece of loosely woven cloth (Giovanni d'Arcoli); magistery of pearls, powder of coral, dragon's blood and red rose water (Charles Allen, 1687). Fauchard argued against the use of cuttlefish, powdered alabaster, brick dust, pumice or vitriol which suggests these were in use during his time (Bennion, 1986). Added to these lists can be china, earthenware and soot, which Hillam (1990: 7) suggests were in use until 'recently'. Such compounds would have been made at home or by the apothecary; in the early nineteenth century dentrifice compounds were sold in stoneware pots but before this may have been held in compartmentalised powder boxes which were part of the toothbrush and toilet set (Bennion, 1986). By the late nineteenth century pastes in collapsible metal tubes were introduced (Hillam, 1990).

The published examples of appliance and dentrifice abrasion mentioned above (d'Errico et al., 1986–87; Pedersen, 1979) are examples of the extreme end of the manifestation of such practises. The use of abrasive dentrifice in moderation is likely to be only visible as microscopic scratches rather than extensive loss of enamel. However, because teeth are usually only routinely examined macroscopically, it is possible that this phenomenon is not being identified. The parallel scratches reported by d'Errico et al. (1986–87) are used to indicate a rigid appliance as the cause. However, if unparallel microscopic abrasion is identified it may be problematic to distinguish abrasion caused by a dentrifice and abrasion caused by a coarse diet. The examination of populations with a less abrasive diet, i.e., as indicated by less occlusal wear, may provide an opportunity to examine dentrifice abrasion. However, such populations are rare during the British Medieval and earlier periods. This is unfortunate as it would be interesting to know who had access to such compounds. The two reported cases are of a King and the daughter of a King, and it would be of interest to know if these cases indicate that only high status individuals had access to this treatment. However, it is also important that the abrasion of the teeth of Isabella d'Aragona was not caused by daily hygiene but an effort to remove staining.

Scaling

One other instrument may produce abrasion that, although used by dentists, did eventually make its way into the toilet set of the 'well to do' during the eighteenth and beginning of the nineteenth centuries (Bennion, 1986). Although Woodforde (1968) credits the Arabian Albucasis (1050–1122) as being the first to describe and illustrate dental scrapers (also known as scalers and gravers) in *De Chiurgia* (he designed a set of fourteen scalers and wrote a chapter on scraping the teeth), Bennion (1986) cites Avicenna (980–1037) as having described fourteen scalers, and Cremona (1114–1187) of illustrating eight scalers. Woodforde (1968) describes the use of these instruments by a barber-surgeon to scrape teeth, after which the teeth would be rubbed with a stick dipped in aqua fortis (a solution of nitric acid) which also may cause damage to the enamel. Fauchard recommended that only steel should be used to make scalers as gold and silver were not hard enough (Bennion, 1986). It is possible that the use of these instruments to remove stubborn calculus deposits may result in some abrasion to the enamel and may be identifiable in dental remains.

Interproximal Grooves

Interproximal grooves, which have been associated with the use of an inflexible object to pick one's teeth, are widely reported in the literature. The earliest known example is associated with the remains of a *Homo habilis* from Ethiopia dating to 1.8 million years ago (Puech and Cianfarani, 1988). The use of a 'toothpick' has also been observed in non-human primates, namely chimpanzees (McGrew and Tutin, 1973). For an extensive review, Milner and Larsen (1991) cite many examples but a review of some of these (Ubelaker *et al.*, 1969; Berryman *et al.*, 1979; Frayer, 1991; Frayer and Russel, 1987; Formicola, 1988; Puech and Cianfarani, 1988; Turner, 1988) serves to illustrate the diagnostic features of this phenomenon. Grooves associated with toothpick use are most commonly seen on the maxillary, posterior dentition. They are located on the interproximal surface around the CEJ. They are usually narrow, trough-like grooves which rarely extend across the whole interproximal surface, and they are usually deeper and wider buccally. In some cases the orientation of the grooves is more oblique posteriorly. Some examples are associated with polishing and the formation of secondary cementum. Microscopically, these grooves are floored by parallel bucco-lingual scratches.

Although some authors argue that these grooves are caused by the repeated back and forth movement of an inflexible object, other authors have proposed different explanations. Grooves may be formed by passing fibres between the teeth interproximally and occlusally in order to process them (Schultz, 1977; Brown and Molnar, 1990). However, these grooves would be more common on the anterior teeth rather than the posterior and would be more likely to form grooves that extend across the whole of the interproximal surface (Frayer, 1991). Grit-laden saliva is an alternative suggested by Wallace (1974), but although it may be a factor in the instigation of the use of a toothpick, if it were the cause, the grooves would be present on the anterior teeth and would not cause parallel striations (Schultz, 1977). Eckhardt and Piermarini (1988) cite Wells (1967) as proposing taphonomic erosion due to rootlets as a possible cause, but this would not account for the evidence of secondary cementum formation. Root caries, proposed by Brothwell (1963) as an alternative to toothpick use, would not affect the enamel. A toothpick may have been employed to dislodge irritants caused by a coarse diet i.e. grit or impacted food. A high correlation was found by Ubelaker *et al.* (1969) between these grooves and the presence of periodontal disease and caries, suggesting a palliative aim. However, other studies have found no such correlation and have led to the hypothesis that the use of a toothpick was not just for therapeutic and palliative purposes (Formicola, 1988) and therefore a 'non-functional pastime that was cultural rather than practical' (Bahn, 1989: 693). Berryman *et al.* (1979) also suggested a cultural factor in their use, as the interproximal grooves they observed in a Protohistoric Arikara skeletal series were predominantly seen in the males rather than females. However, this may have been due to differential access to irritation-inducing foods.

The hypothesis that toothpicks and their use had a cultural significance is not as unusual as it may appear. In the sixteenth to eighteenth centuries the use of toothpicks became fashionable and a status symbol, indicating the need for them due to a plentiful meal. Both d'Errico *et al.* (1986–87) and Pedersen (1979) report evidence of interproximal grooves associated with a probably metal toothpick in their respective Renaissance aristocrats already mentioned above. Once a status symbol, the decoration of toothpicks and their cases resulted in prized material being used for toothpicks unlike earlier centuries (Bennion, 1986). Many naturally available materials were also used as toothpicks, as Bennion (1986) records: cypress, pine, rosemary, juniper (Giovanni d'Arcoli, 1412–1484); root of marshmallow or lucerne or a quill as opposed to metal toothpicks, pins or the point of a knife (Fauchard); silver (Nero); porcupine quill (Pliny); splinter of wood/reed (Talmud); mastic tree, quills, feathers, straws (Ancient Greeks). Mandel (1990) cites the use of gold or silver (sixteenth to seventeenth centuries) and the use of willow or poplar trees to manufacture modern toothpicks. Metallic toothpicks have also been found as part of a common form of toilet set consisting of a toothpick, ear scoop and tweezers attached to a common ring from Sumeria and Mesopotamia (Garfield, 1972; Mandel, 1990).

Fillings

It was believed, even into the mid-eighteenth century, that toothache was caused by the tooth worm. The first reference to the tooth worm is in a Babylonian clay tablet which describes the creation; the worm on being told to live in figs and apricots decided he would rather live in people's teeth (Bennion, 1986). An eighteenth century French ivory carving of a tooth conceals inside a carving of a demon-like worm, which amply illustrates the contemporary perception of the tooth worm having demonic associations. There are a number of reasons that may explain the origins of the belief that a worm caused toothache. Garfield (1972) suggests that worms found in the mouth were in fact caused by worms and maggots in fruit. He also suggests that the pulp of an extracted tooth may look like a worm. Bennion (1986) suggests that because putrefaction of the body was associated with worms, it was only logical that the decay of teeth was also associated with worms. The use of concealed maggots or pods of henbane seeds proclaimed to be tooth worms extracted by charlatans (Hillam, 1990) probably did little to contradict this common view.

Bennion (1986) suggests that the belief that worms caused toothache may account for the number of remedies that contained worms or maggots. The extraction of a tooth was frowned upon and seen as a last resort. This is attested to by the plethora of the most bizarre remedies recommended for curing toothache and for making a tooth fall out of its own accord. Many are unlikely to survive and be recoverable archaeologically. For example, Pliny recommended touching the tooth with the frontal bone of a lizard taken during the full moon (Garfield, 1972). Another remedy was the use of a new nail to make the gum bleed and then driving it into an oak (Hillam, 1990). However, the use of fillings, either in an attempt to cure the toothache or in an attempt to prevent a crown breaking on extraction may be recognisable. The use of fillings as a remedy is unlikely to be successful, as the decayed areas of the tooth often were not removed beforehand. However, fillings may have been of use to prevent pain caused by the exposed pulp (Garfield, 1972). Bennion describes early Medieval fillings such as wax from the paschal candle, gum and resin, raven's dung (rural Germany), stale bread, mastic and lead. However, the Persian Rhazes (850–923) recommended filling cavities with alum and mastic, but this was prone to dissolution by saliva (Moller-Christensen, 1969).

In 1969, Moller-Christensen published the case of a male excavated from Aebelholt Abbey, in the Northern part of Sjaelland near Copenhagen. A small perforated bone rosary bead was found embedded in the mandibular right canine. It has been suggested that this bead was used to allow the worm to crawl out through the perforation, as well as the religious connection. There was evidence that the cavity had been prepared, i.e. enlarged so that the bead would fit into the cavity. The bead would have been fixed into the cavity with wax.

The first reference to the use of gold leaf as a filling, which was gradually pressed into the cavity, is attributed to Giovanni d'Arcoli (1412–1484) (Garfield, 1972). Such procedures would have been time-consuming to perform, expensive and prone to failure. The use of non-precious metals included amalgams such as fuseable metal which were composed of bismuth, lead, tin and mercury. This amalgam had a low melting point (212°F) which enabled it to be melted in boiling water and poured through funnels into the carious cavity and then allowed to solidify. A later development of an amalgam with an even lower melting point allowed the insertion of the metal directly into the cavity and which was subsequently melted in situ with hot instruments (Garfield, 1972). Another example of an amalgam was introduced in 1826 by Taveau, known as Silver Paste; this consisted of mercury and silver from coins. These early amalgams were problematic as they would often shrink or expand and cause the tooth to break. If the amalgam expanded but did not split the tooth it may have raised above the crown causing incorrect bite and subsequent pain (Garfield, 1972). These problems and the poor reputation of the Royal Mineral Succedaneum amalgam that was used by the Crawcour brothers did little to improve its reputation. In the 1840s the 'Amalgam War' resulted in members of the American Society of Dental Surgeons having to pledge not to use it (Garfield, 1972). However, individuals worked in secret, improving the amalgams that would eventually lead to the silver amalgams in use today. A further development was the introduction of the first electric drill in 1874 that allowed easier and more effective cavity preparation, and therefore allowed successful insertion of filling material and removal of decayed matter.

Examples of metallic fillings have been reported from at least two post-Medieval sites. At Spitalfields, London, metallic fillings were reported in three individuals (Whittaker, 1993; Whittaker and Hargreaves, 1991). An amalgam of mercury and silver was located in an upper right canine in an unnamed individual. Eliza Favenc who died in 1809 had six gold fillings and showed evidence of recurrent caries on treated teeth. Another unnamed individual had compressed gold foil in carious lesions in their upper left second premolar and first molar. Remains excavated from St Brides Church, also in London, contained five individuals with examples of fillings (Harvey, 1968). Gold plugs were found in individuals who had died between 1820 and 1834. Two of these individuals were male and two female, both males aged 59 and the females 18 and 23. In a male interment who had died in 1824 when 24 years old, a metal filling was found in his maxillary first premolar. The filling had caused staining on nearby teeth. The amalgam was found to contain silver (46%), mercury (53%), iron (0.07%), and copper (0.02%).

As well as the presence of a foreign object in situ, other features may indicate an attempt to fill a cavity. Koritzer (1968) reported the example of the second molar from an individual excavated from Illinois, where the margins of a carious lesion appear to have been modified through the removal of the carious lesion. However White et al., (1997) question this as evidence of preparation associated with the treatment of caries. Gibson (1971) and St Hoyme and Koritzer (1971) report on another example from Illinois that dates to c. 600. The lesions that are argued to have been treated were present on the roots of the lower right first molar, first premolar and canine, although no evidence of a filling was found in the molar tooth. The authors argue that the cavities were intentionally prepared and that shell or bone may have been used as a filling in the carious cavities.

Drilling

The application of a cautery may have been used to treat post-extraction haemorrhage, root canal treatment, abscesses, toothache and pyorrhoea. Direct application of a cautery could be applied by making a hole in the tooth as recommended by Giovanni d'Arcolli (1412–1484) (Bennion, 1986). As well as cautery application, drilling was also used as a method to drain an infected pulp as recommended by Archigenese (81–117), a Syrian who lived in Rome (Garfield, 1972). Later, drilling was practised to enable crowns, bridges and dentures to be attached to roots in situ. As will be seen later, teeth were also drilled to allow the insertion of decorative inlays.

Several examples of drilled teeth identified in the archaeological record have been published. Most recently White et al. (1997) published a case of an individual excavated from a household site from the Formative period in Fremont, Colorado, in south-west America and dating to c. 1025. The remains were disturbed and disarticulated so that only the mandible of this individual is described as being present. The perforation was located on the occlusal surface of a heavily-worn lower right canine. The perforation is conical with its rootward tip 3 mm below the occlusal surface. Microscopic analysis reveals dense and mostly parallel, though irregular in depth, circumferential striae. The hypothesis that these striae were due to a mechanical cause was tested by the authors on another tooth on which they used an obsidian flake attached to a rod which was twisted rapidly in a drilling motion with the palms together on the shaft. The perforation on the tooth on which this was performed also resulted in irregular circumferential striations. Microfractures were present on this example, but this was attributed to the brittle dentine in the non-living tooth. The motive behind such a procedure may be hinted at by the presence of a periapical abscess, but this may have been a post-operative feature especially as a lower lateral incisor, which also had a periapical abscess, showed no evidence of attempts to treat it. White *et al.* (1997) also argue that the motive would not have been cosmetic as the perforation would not have been visible. They also argue that a possible motive may have been an occlusal carious lesion that was subsequently drilled out by the procedure. The perforation was argued to be an antemortem feature as the striae had been truncated obliquely by tooth wear.

Schwartz *et al.* (1995) reported another North American example but from Point Hope, Alaska which dates to 1300–1700. A complete and partial perforation was present on the lower left incisor. The perforation is present on the labial surface of the root and is orientated obliquely down. As well as the presence of the perforations, this individual also had evidence of caries and tori and, for the population, this too was unusual. The authors argued that the perforation was not performed postmortem, a congenital defect, due to the extraction of samples for analysis or having been conducted for cosmetic means. They argue that it may have been associated with an abscess being present, but again, this may be a post-operative feature.

A drilled perforation was observed in the tooth of a male adult from a passage grave at Langeland, Denmark (2000–3000 BC) (Bennike, 1985; Bennike and Fredebo, 1986). The perforation is located between the buccal roots of the upper right second molar. Partial perforations were also located on this tooth and the first molar. The complete perforation was circular and conical and had a maximum diameter of 4 mm and a depth of 6 mm. Again, an abscess is associated with this perforation as is a carious lesion on this tooth and the first molar. Despite the obvious difficulty regarding access to the buccal surface of the second molar by a drill, the presence of calculus within the perforation has been used as evidence of the procedure being performed antemortem. It is interesting to note that also within this group of fifty-three individuals excavated from the grave, as well as this drilled tooth, one individual had evidence of a healed trepanation, indicating some medical skill and knowledge was present in this population. A flint drill was reconstructed by Bennike (1985) and used to drill through a second molar; it was found to take five and a half minutes to perforate the tooth. Similarities in shape and circumferential striations were found between the original and contemporary tooth.

Hanson (1988) reports occlusal perforation on opposing left canines of an adult male from Rota, Mariana Islands. Both perforations were conical and 1.5 mm in diameter, and both were initiated in the enamel and range from 0.5–1.5 mm in depth. No caries or other indication of motive for the procedure was evident. An unpublished example (Cook *et al.*, n.d.) cited by Milner and Larsen (1991) describes a maxillary left canine with a circular perforation labial to the CEJ from Illinois.

A number of difficulties are present in studying evidence of drilling in antiquity. Drilled perforations may be dismissed as caries, wear-induced pulp exposure or postmortem damage, or assumed to have been due to samples taken by another researcher. Furthermore, periapical lesions present in the bone may be mistaken for drilled perforations (Leek, 1967). Another limitation is that the anterior teeth are more accessible and therefore more likely to be subjected to this procedure. However the anterior teeth are less likely, compared to the posterior teeth, to require this treatment if periapical abscess due to caries are the cause; posterior teeth are more likely to be affected by caries than the anterior dentition. Also, as the anterior teeth are more likely to be lost postmortem the evidence may also be lost. Furthermore, the use of the drill and subsequent pulp exposure and abscess may lead to antemortem tooth loss, again resulting in loss of evidence.

Cosmetic Modification

The practise of filing, filling and drilling in order to modify the dentition for appearance rather than therapeutic ends is demonstrated in populations from the Americas, Africa and Asia. Examples of these modifications are widely reported in the literature and have been reviewed by Milner and Larsen (1991). Romero (1970) has classified the various patterns and combinations of these modifications. The modifications include filing and notching of the occlusal and labial surface, the drilling of the labial surfaces of the upper anterior teeth and the insertion of fillings such as jade and turquoise with the aid of a cement. Decorative inlays would have been produced over a number of sittings to prevent pulp exposure by allowing secondary dentine to form; a higher association with abscess is seen in filed modifications (Langsjoen, 1998). The motive behind these procedures may have been purely cosmetic, or they may have had some ritual significance, such as marking a rite of passage, or they may be associated with tribal identification or social status (Langsjoen, 1998).

Filing

In the Old World, filing was conducted to level uneven teeth, as recommended by Albucasis, and to round off rough edges caused by caries as recommended by Celsus (Bennion, 1986). Fauchard recommended filing between carious and healthy teeth in order to separate them. Fauchard also recommended the use of a file to trim the roots of teeth that were to be transplanted to enable a better fit; he also suggested filing to even off a root that was to be drilled in order to allow a crown to be attached (Bennion, 1986). Theoretically, the use of a file in these cases would be recognisable as abrasion on a carious lesion or fracture margins; or on a root, occlusal or interproximal surface.

Tooth Extraction

The early writers did not approve of tooth extraction and this disfavour persisted into the Middle Ages. The reasons for such disapproval are clear considering the possible sequelae following extraction; fracture and dislocation of the jaw, fracture of teeth, damage to neighbouring healthy teeth, exposure of the pulp, infection and, potentially, even death. The use of extraction as a last resort was, according to Cicero, first advised by Aesculapius (1300 BC) (Weinberger, 1934). It was recommended that loose teeth should be extracted digitally, but the forceps could be used if necessary; Greek and Roman examples of these instruments have been recovered. Forceps and an extracted tooth are commonly seen in the depiction of St Appollonia who was martyred in 246 after having all of her teeth removed, her jaw fractured and being burnt alive. She is the patron saint of toothache sufferers and of dentists. If forceps were to be used, it was recommended that the tooth was loosened digitally by rocking the tooth beforehand. Filling to prevent the crown from breaking has already been mentioned. Another preliminary task was to detach the gum from the tooth (Bennion, 1986).

The pelican was first mentioned by Guy de Chauliac (1300–1368), although the first illustration was provided in 1460 by Giovanni d'Arcolis (1412–1484) (Bennion, 1986). The pelican consisted of a bolster that was placed against the buccal or labial surface of the gum or roots and a claw that extended to the lingual surface of the tooth. When pressure was applied to the handle the bolster (cushioned with linen or leather) acted as a fulcrum and enabled the claw to prise out the tooth sideways. The pelican varies in the number and size of the claws, shape of the bolster and material used to make the instrument. It was based on a cooper's tool that was used to force the last hoop onto the barrel and gets its name from the resemblance of the bolster and claw to the beak of a pelican. A number of problems were associated with the use of the pelican; because of the pressure applied, gum damage was possible, as was the extraction of the wrong tooth, damage to the adjacent teeth and breakage of the tooth.

The use of the pelican was eventually superseded by the key, which was probably in use by c. 1730 although it is only first mentioned in 1742 by Alexander Morro (Bennion, 1986). The bolster was placed against the gum or root and a hinged claw was placed over the crown. The key was then turned as if in a lock, causing the tooth to be dislocated. The key was much quicker than the pelican, which may explain its popularity; it was still in use into the twentieth century in some areas. However, as with the pelican, the risk of fracturing the crown leaving the root in place, accidental extraction or damage to neighbouring teeth was still possible.

If the result was the fracture of the crown and the roots were left *in situ*, the elevator may have been used. This instrument was also used to extract anterior teeth. The blade of the elevator was placed between the tooth to be removed and the adjacent healthy tooth. Using the healthy tooth as a fulcrum the blade was turned, prising out the root to be removed. But, of course, damage to the tooth acting as the fulcrum was possible. Albucasis was the first to illustrate the elevator, but there were various types available.

Although the use of instruments such as the pelican and key may seem painful, this may not have been the case. The furnicate of the roots was likely to be exposed above the gum line either through periodontal disease or continuing eruption allowing the claw of the pelican and the key to fit into it. Furthermore, because of periodontal disease or continuing eruption the tooth would have been loose. Kerr (1998) argues that the decline in tooth wear and therefore continuing eruption meant that these procedures did become more painful as access to the furnicate involved cutting the gum. This, he argues, was one of the factors that pushed dentistry from a trade to a profession as better, less painful methods were demanded.

As already discussed, the absence of teeth is not an uncommon finding in archaeological dentitions. The antemortem loss of a tooth may be due to periodontal disease, continuing eruption, trauma or pulp exposure caused by wear or caries. Teeth may have been intentionally removed for ritual or cosmetic reasons as seen in Australian and African people (Langsjoen, 1998 citing Thoma, 1944) or to ease over-crowding as recommended in the mid-eighteenth century by Etienne Bourdet (Bennion, 1986). However, the identification of a tooth expelled digitally or aided by the use of one of the procedures mentioned above is more difficult. The identification of fractured crowns of teeth adjacent to a tooth lost antemortem, fractured crowns of a tooth that disintegrated on an attempted extraction, evidence of a fractured or dislocated jaw or the presence of cut marks on the bone caused during the separation of the gum from the tooth may help to identify the method of extraction used or attempted.

Many of these clues were found in remains reported by Hendersen *et al.* (1996). A number of skeletons which showed evidence of having been autopsied, and those discarded as clinical waste, were excavated from Lady Yesters Kirkyard. The remains were associated with the nearby Royal Infirmary at Edinburgh and dated to the later half of the eighteenth century. Of the eight complete or partial dentitions all had no incisors or canines present; in five cases the premolar was also removed. In all cases the buccal alveolar bone had been damaged and cut marks on one individual was also discovered, as were teeth with the crown snapped off. Hendersen *et al.* (1996) argued that the postmortem extraction of these teeth may have been conducted by a worker in the hospital prior to burial and the teeth sold on to denture manufacturers (see below).

Prosthetics

The loss of teeth has a number of personal and sociological consequences. Digestive problems, deafness and speech problems are examples of the former. Loss of teeth symbolises old age and loss of vitality and, therefore, the ability to contribute to a society. It cannot be surprising that attempts have been made in the past, as well as today, to compensate for tooth loss by the use of prosthetics such as transplants, implants, dentures, bridges and crowns. Despite the fact that 37% of the modern English and Welsh population over the age of sixteen had, in the 1960s, no natural teeth remaining (Silverstone *et al.*, 1981, citing Gray *et al.*, 1970), the use of false teeth today is met with acute embarrassment. Such embarrassment is a relatively modern phenomenon and may be due to the use of false teeth being associated with poor oral hygiene and therefore low social class (Bennion, 1986). However, the reverse is true prior to the middle of the last century. Only the very rich could have afforded false teeth and any attempts to disguise their use would have been futile, especially at the dinner table where they would had to have been removed before eating.

The earliest dental prosthesis identified in the archaeological record was discovered in 1862 in a Phoenician grave at Sidon, Italy, and dates to the sixth to fourth centuries BC. This prosthesis consists of gold wires to which were attached carved ivory teeth. The most proficient manufacturers of prosthetic appliances in the archaeological record are the Etruscans, to whom approximately nineteen of these prostheses are attributed. Typically they are constructed with gold rings to which are riveted the false tooth (usually made from human or animal teeth or gold). The most lateral rings of the device would have anchored around the teeth present either side of the gap of lost teeth in order to hold it in place.

Becker (1994b: 69) states that: 'a significant recent discovery is that these Etruscan bridges were worn only by females, suggesting that cosmetics and vanity was the principal 'dental' concern of these people'. However, in at least one case reported by Becker (1994a) the individual was sexed based on the size of the teeth. If it is the case that other reported prostheses have been recovered without the human remains to which they belonged, the size of the teeth may well be the only criteria available to sex the individuals. However, sex determination using the teeth is not always accurate (Roberts, 1996) and therefore the declaration that these prostheses were only worn by females cannot be taken as a fact. Furthermore, just because they were associated with females, it does not mean they were associated with vanity. If vanity was the cause behind their development wouldn't these prostheses have been designed to be less visible when worn? If then, as now, loss of teeth is associated with a loss of vitality, strength and worth, surely the males would have been more keen to have access to these prosthetics. Furthermore, some of these prostheses may not have been an attempt to replace lost teeth but worn in an attempt to stabilise loose teeth due to periodontal disease or continuing eruption. If this is the case one would expect it to be a genderless motive. If this was the original intent, the craftsmanship of the jewellers who probably made these devices as stabilisers could have easily added teeth to fill gaps; this may have altered their original function from stabilisers to false teeth.

One of the earliest Etruscan examples identified is of a gold band with a gold tooth attached. As this is the only example with a gold tooth known, Becker (1994a) argues that soon after this device was created a more natural appearance was preferred and human or carved teeth were used instead of gold. But, as this is based on the belief that no other gold examples exist, the old archaeological adage that 'absence of evidence is not evidence of absence' should be borne in mind. This is especially so as prosthetics with gold teeth as well as bands may have been more attractive to grave looters and therefore may explain to some extent their absence in the archaeological record. What cannot be disputed is that following the assimilation by the Romans, the output of such prostheses diminished. A number of reasons can be proposed to explain this; their removal before burial, looting, poor documentation on recovery, or loss of the skill needed as the Etruscan culture faded (Becker, 1994b).

Bennion (1986) cites numerous references in the documentary evidence to prosthetics and stabilisers. For example, Albucasis (936–1013) advised wiring loose teeth together with fine gold wire and using oxbone to fill gaps. However, this suggests that the primary function behind such prostheses was stabilising loose teeth rather than supply new ones. Other texts referring to prosthetics include Gerard of Cremora (1114–1187), Guy de Chauliac (1300–1368), and Francisco Mautinez (1518–1588), who produced in 1557 a book with a chapter devoted to prosthetics. Jacques Guillemeau (1550–1613) is credited with being the first to suggest the use of inorganic material to make false teeth, namely white coral and pearls.

However, despite such references it appears that it is not until the eighteenth century that prosthetics are seen again in the archaeological record in any significant number. This may have been spurred on by the necessity of Parisian fashions to look young (Hillam, 1990), and the very beginnings of a dental profession, which began to some limited extent to share innovations. Only a hundred to a hundred and fifty years later the dentistry profession was established, regulated and trained. With the introduction of anaesthetics and therefore a greater number of extractions, affordable, naturalistic and comfortable dentures available to the masses were needed and eventually provided with the introduction of vulcanite and eventually acrylic resins. However, until such developments the edentulous middle and upper classes of the eighteenth and nineteenth centuries had the option to endure the sequelae of tooth loss or endure the discomfort that prosthetic devices available during this period caused.

If any original upper teeth survived, dentures and bridges could be fixed with the use of ligatures. However, as these were difficult to tie, they often remained in place for some time causing discomfort. Woodforde (1968: 27) cites Thomas Berdmore who in 1768 recommended the use of silk rather than wire ligature as this was less likely to 'cut deep into sound teeth'. Although full lower dentures could be weighed down with lead (Woodforde, 1968), if teeth were present, lower dentures could be secured using (usually wooden) posts placed into any remaining roots and onto which a prosthesis could be attached. The wood swelled on becoming wet and kept the device in place, and the same principle was used for metallic posts covered in linen. However, there was a risk that the wooden posts could swell too much and split the root (Woodforde, 1968). As well as using such posts to attach dentures, single carved crowns could also be attached over wooden or gold posts inserted into prepared roots. Later dentures with gold bases provided wire that would clasp around any remaining teeth which would have aided anchoring the prosthetic device in place (Hillam, 1990).

Because of the method of their manufacture, upper sets were horseshoe shaped (see below). This resulted in a lack of suction available to hold the prosthetic in place and therefore alternatives were sought. Fauchard mentions 'floating teeth'; if there were no upper teeth to which a bridge could be anchored, the gums could be pierced to allow the hook of a row of front teeth to be suspended like an earring (Woodforde, 1968). He was against such practise due to the obvious damage it caused; he introduced the use of whale bone, and then eventually flat steel, 'springs' attached to the back of the upper and lower dentures. However, there were a number of problems as there was a constant pressure of the prosthetic on the gums, which would be especially painful if the fit were poor. It also resulted in the need for considerable pressure to close the mouth and often, the prosthetic tended to jut forward and could easily slip sideways (Woodforde, 1968). An alternative was a frame, attached to the upper set, which was placed over the arch of the lower teeth *in situ*, or dentures, and thus supported the upper sets, however this type of prosthetic was still prone to slipping sideways; prompting their removal prior to eating. By the mid eighteenth century flat springs dropped out of favour for coil springs which were placed near the first molars and which evened out the pressure on the gum (Woodforde, 1968).

The very early dentures would have been constructed using measurements from a compass and card outlines, with the final carving completed at the chair-side of the client (Hillam, 1990). The patient's gums would be painted and the ivory dentures placed over them, and the areas on the dentures that had picked up the paint would be scraped away (Woodforde, 1968). This was a time-consuming and expensive process and rarely provided a good fit. Purman (1648–1711) recommended the use of wax models and Pfaff (1716–1790) produced models in Plaster of Paris (Garfield, 1972). As model making improved, zinc was used to make swaging blocks over which gold could be shaped to make the base (Hillam, 1990).

The most common material used was ivory from which was carved both the gum and the teeth; ivory was still being sold to manufacture dentures in 1875 (Woodforde, 1968). Alternatively, ivory may have been used to make the base and posterior teeth but other material used to make the anterior teeth, which were then riveted onto the ivory base. Examples include animal teeth or bone, silver, mother of pearl, porcelain, and what is now known as 'Waterloo teeth'. These were human teeth extracted from hanged convicts, plundered vaults, crypts or graveyards, from the destitute willing to sell them, dissecting rooms and mortuaries (see above), and from the battlefield dead where of course they get their name. Apparently, they were shipped over in abundance during the American Civil War (Woodforde, 1968). The roots of these teeth were filed off and the crown posted or riveted onto the denture base.

The use of ivory was problematic and more than adequately summarised by the comments of a dentist of the time, who, when talking of ivory bases with human teeth attached, said: 'to say nothing of this contaminating putrid accumulation being carried to the stomach of the unfortunate wearers, the unavoidable thickness, the liability to discoloration, decay and the expense of renewing, are insurmountable objections to the use of human set on a base of bone' (Hillam, 1990: 16). George Washington's response to these problems was to soak his ivory dentures in port to try to get rid of the taste and smell but of course they did discolour somewhat (Bennion, 1986). Not surprisingly, alternatives were sought and included tin, lead, tortoise shell and gold but these were expensive, corroded and did not look at all natural.

In the eighteenth century, complete sets of porcelain dentures were introduced by a Parisian dentist (Nicholas Dubois de Chemant), but were in fact developed by Alexis Duchateau, an apothecary who had sought de Chemant's advice and who eventually took the credit (Woodforde, 1968). Although porcelain dentures didn't decay, they were expensive and subject to shrinkage during firing making them difficult to fit; they also easily broke and tended to make a strange noise. Not surprisingly porcelain dentures did not prove popular, but the use of porcelain to make individual teeth was more successful. Guiseppangelo Fonzi, an Italian working in Paris, introduced individual porcelain teeth known as Fonzi or bean teeth in 1808. A small metal hook imbedded in the porcelain was used to attach the tooth to the denture base. However, the teeth looked artificial and were still prone to breakage (Woodforde, 1968). The bean teeth were eventually improved in the 1830s with Claudius Ash's introduction of tube teeth which contained a sleeve of gold into which a post on a denture base or prepared roots could be inserted (Hillam, 1990).

The identification of the use of prosthetics and stabilisers can be seen though the presence of the prosthetic *in situ*, and through drilled and filed roots into which a prosthetic was attached to the dentition. As some bridges were held in place by ligatures the marks left by the use of ligatures may be identifiable; these potential clues which may indicate the use of a prosthetic, if that prosthetic is no longer *in situ*. Most of these clues have been found in the post-Medieval prosthetic devices excavated from the British sites of Spitalfields and at St Brides; nine examples in the former (Whittaker, 1993; Whittaker and Hargreaves, 1991) and four from the latter (Harvey, 1968).

Another prosthetic device that may be identified *in situ* in the oral cavity is the use of obturators. These were artificial palates used in such cases as syphilis or congenital cleft palate. Although simple obturators would have included the use of linen or a sponge, Fauchard designed more complex devices made from ivory, but by the 1850s vulcanite was in use (Hillam, 1990). Earlier examples may be recognisable by observing the device *in situ* or through the presence of ligatures or ligature marks used to hold the device in place.

Transplants and Implants

Another method employed to replace lost teeth is the use of transplants (other people's teeth) or implants (non-human material shaped liked a tooth). The first reference to transplanted teeth is by Guy de Chauliac (1300–1368), but its peak of popularity was during the eighteenth century, largely due to its promotion by John Hunter (1728–1793). Its popularity began to decrease following the improvement of dentures in the nineteenth century (Woodforde, 1968). The difficulty of finding teeth to fit another person's socket resulted in the need for building up a stock of possible teeth to be transplanted, either through 'live donors' or Waterloo teeth (see above). The filing of the root to enable easier fitting was recommended by Fauchard as already mentioned.

One case of a transplant and several of implants are reported in the literature. The example of the transplant was first reported by Saville (1913) and was found in Esmeraldas in North Ecuador. Instead of the right upper middle incisor, a right upper lateral incisor was implanted. The upper incisors had gold decorative inlays on the labial surface. Weinberger (1934) supports the view that this was an antemortem phenomenon and argues that about quarter of an inch had been removed from the root, presumably to enable fit. However, it has been argued by Fastlicht (1962) that the 'implants' may have been placed post-mortem by an Indian vendor trying to sell them.

Ring (1992) describes the example discovered in 1931 in the Ulua Valley in Honduras dated to 600. Only a fragment of the mandible remains, but it reveals three crudely fashioned shell implants replacing the two lower left incisors and the right central incisor. At the base of two of the implants compact bone is present, suggesting they were antemortem implants. It is interesting to note that from the photograph of this specimen it appears that hypoplastic lines present on the remaining teeth have been recreated on the implants. Another example from the Americas was found in Copan, Honduras and was published by Andrews (1893). The implant that replaced the left lateral incisor was said to be made of a fine dark stone and shaped like an incisor. No ligatures were present to hold it into place, but the presence of calculus was used to suggest the implant was inserted antemortem.

Another stone implant is reported by Atilla (1993). This example, excavated from a looted sarcophagus in the Kalabak Necropolis in Anatolia, is dated to 550 BC. The 'tooth-like structure' was found, presumably not *in situ*, along with 'some bones' and a gold hair-spiral. On the basis of the hair-spiral the individual was judged to be female and, based on dental development, aged 14–16 years of age at death. The implant is argued to be shaped like an upper right canine, and eroded lines at the neck, in which gold particles were found, are used as evidence of gold wires used to hold the implant in place. Erosion and abrasion on the 'incisal edge' is also used as evidence of the structure being an implant. Because of the sex and age of the individual the implant was argued to be aesthetic; but the estimation of sex of this individual based on a grave good such as a hair-spiral leaves room for doubt as to the sex of the individual. If, as it seems, the alveolar bone is absent (although this is not clearly stated), the identification of the use of this structure as an implant leaves much room for doubt.

A more secure case is put forward by Crubezy *et al.* (1998). This male individual was excavated from the Gallo-Roman necropolis at Chantambre (Essonne, France) and dates to the first to second centuries AD. The implant is located in the socket of the upper right second premolar and is made of wrought iron. It is argued that the good fit is due to the use of the original tooth as a model for the implant. It is argued that this implant may have been inserted to keep the right side of the jaw functional due to an early loss of molars on the left side of the jaw.

Zias and Numeroff (1987) describe a 2.5mm bronze wire inserted into the root canal of a heavily worn upper right lateral incisor. The individual was excavated from Northern Negrev, Israel, and dates to 200 BC. The root canal was artificially widened to a depth of 2.5mm in preparation for the implant. A number of reasons were suggested to account for the presence of this implant. It is argued that the implant was inserted to prevent the tooth worm burrowing into the tooth; and that the operation may have been an attempt to drain a large periapical abscess that was present, or that it was a post used to hold an artificial crown since lost. The tooth was green which prompted the x-ray, which revealed the presence of the wire. The authors suggested that bronze was fraudulently substituted for gold as the bronze wire would have been toxic and corrosive to the wearer.

The use of implants may be identified through the identification of a tooth-like object *in situ* i.e., in the socket, but of course they have single roots and are liable to fall out postmortem so they may not be *in situ* at all. Identification of transplanted teeth is also difficult as it is very easy to dismiss a tooth that fails to fit as a post-excavation 'mix up'. Other clues may be the presence of filed roots to aid fitting and the identification of ligatures and ligature marks which were used to hold the implant or transplant in place.

PROBLEMS AND BENEFITS OF STUDY

The review of the literature above illustrates that there are a number of therapeutic, cosmetic and ritual modifications to the dentition that can be described as evidence of dentistry and can be preserved in the archaeological record and be interpreted as such by modern researchers. However, it seems a logical assumption that there should be much more dental evidence than there seems to have been reported. This, as already discussed, is in part due to the survivability of the dental tissues, and to their ease of access which enabled the application of treatment. Further factors in the favour of the expectation of more evidence is the range of potential evidence described and the amount of documentary evidence testifying to the fact that dental treatments were practised. If this assumption is correct, one is forced to ask — where is the evidence?

There are a number of answers to this question. It may be that the evidence was simply not buried, especially in the case of prosthetics and those made from valued materials. The evidence may not survive burial. This may be due to plundering of graves, or the degradation of, for example, organic fillings or silk ligatures. As the anterior teeth are more accessible and have a single root they may have been more likely to have been transplanted or drilled. However, because they are single rooted they are more likely to have been lost before or after death. Another possible answer to the question is that the evidence is not being excavated, i.e., only a particular strata of a society may have had access to such treatment. However, of all the possible answers to the question, another explanation may be the most likely and fortunately the most rectifiable; the evidence is not being recognised both during excavation and examination of the osteological evidence. Examples of this problem include the potential for interproximal grooves to be misdiagnosed as caries, cavity preparation not noticed, drilled holes mistaken for caries or postmortem damage, ligature marks missed, as well as transplanted teeth being dismissed as 'mix-ups'. This lack of recognition is of course compounded by its absence in the literature. The evidence that is published in the literature is scattered and infrequently described. If it is published, it is published in medical, dental, historical, ethnographic and archaeological journals, or in published and unpublished bone reports. Furthermore, much of the published cases are in many different languages and some examples, especially of prosthetics, were found in the nineteenth century resulting in questionable and conflicted information regarding their archaeological context.

Despite these limitations in the evidence for dentistry, by far the most unfortunate limitation is the study of the archaeological evidence of dentistry from an historical or case study approach, rather than its study as an integral part of the battery of archaeological evidence that informs about the lifeways and health of past populations. The study of the archaeology of dentistry can provide information on the technological development of a past population, for example, by looking at the manufacture of prosthetics and implants. Also, it may provide an insight into their medical understanding — did treatments have a therapeutic basis or were they purely cosmetic? By studying evidence of dentistry it can help us understand and interpret evidence of dental disease; for example, evidence of oral hygiene practice may help to explain the prevalence of particular diseases. If only particular strata of a society has access to treatment, the evidence of it may tell us about the status of the individual or population. Evidence of modifications associated with ritual behaviour, for example the filling and filing seen in Mayans, may help to identify such practises in the population under study. And, of course, the dental evidence can also help in the understanding and interpretation of the documentary evidence.

CONCLUSIONS

The study of the archaeology of dentistry offers the opportunity to integrate archaeological, iconographic, historical, literary and ethnographic data, and these data may be of relevance to the studies of archaeologists, anthropologists, ethnographers and medical and dental historians. To archaeologists, such data has the potential to contribute to the study of technology, economy, dental disease, medical understanding and ritual practises. However, such studies are dependent on the recognition of dental intervention in the archaeological record. A comprehensive synthesis of the archaeological evidence is needed in order to maximise the recognition of dental intervention in the archaeological record. This synthesis should provide clear diagnostic criteria, establish the temporal and geographic distribution of dental treatments as well as to place the evidence of dental treatment within a biocultural context.

BIBLIOGRAPHY

Andrews, R. R.
(1893) 'Evidences of Prehistoric Dentistry In Central America', *Transactions of The Pan-American Medical Congress* 2, 1872–3.
Atilla, G.
(1993) 'A rare find in Anatolia—a tooth implant (mid-sixth century BC)', *Journal of Oral Implantology* XIX: 54–7.
Axthelm, W. H.
(1981) *History of Dentistry,* Germany: Quintessenz Verlags.
Bahn, P. G.
(1989) 'Early teething troubles', *Nature* 337: 693.
Becker, M. J.
(1994a) 'Etruscan gold dental appliances, origins and functions as indicated by an example from Orvieto, Italy in the Danish National Museum', *Dental Anthropology Newsletter* 8: 2–8.
(1994b) 'Etruscan gold dental appliances, origins and functions as indicated by an example from Valsiarosa, Italy', *Journal of Palaeopathology* 6: 69–92.
Bennike, P.
(1985) *Palaeopathology of Danish Skeletons,* Copenhagen: Akademisk Forlag.
Bennike P, and Fredebo, L.
(1986) 'Dental treatment in the Stone Age', *Bulletin of the History of Dentistry* 34: 81–7.
Bennion, E.
(1986) *Antique Dental Instruments,* London: Sotheby's.
Berryman, H., Owsley, D. and Henderson, A.
(1979) 'Non-carious interproximal grooves in Arikara Indian dentitions', *Amer.J.Phys.Anthrop.* 50: 209–12.
Brothwell, D.
(1963) 'The macroscopic dental pathology of some earlier human populations', in D. Brothwell (ed.), *Dental Anthropology,* New York: Pergamon Press, pp. 271–88.
Brown, T. and Molnar, S.
(1990) 'Interproximal grooving and task activity in Australia', *Amer.J.Phys.Anthrop.* 81: 545–53.
Cook, D., Pickering, R. and Furia, E.
(n.d.) 'Therapeutic dental drilling in a prehistoric Midwestern Indian', *Ms In Possession of Milner and Larsen.*
Crubezy, E., Murail, P., Girard, L., and Bernadou, J.
(1998) 'False teeth of the Roman world', *Nature* 391: 29.
D'Erricio, F., Villa, G. and Fornaciari, G.
(1986–1987) 'Dental esthetics of an Italian Renaissance noblewoman, Isabella d'Aragona. A case of chronic mercury intoxication', *OSSA* 13: 207–28.
Eckhardt, R. and Piermarini, A.
(1988) 'Interproximal grooving of teeth: additional evidence and interpretation', *Current Anthropology* 29: 668–70.
Fastlicht, S.
(1962) 'Dental inlays and fillings among the Ancient Mayas', *Journal of The History of Medicine* 17: 393–401.
Formicola, V.
(1988) 'Interproximal grooving of teeth: additional evidence and interpretation', *Current Anthropology* 29: 663–71.
Frayer, D. W. and Russell, M. D.
(1987) 'Artificial grooves on the Krapina Neanderthal teeth', *Amer.J.Phys.Anthrop.* 74: 393–405.
Frayer, D. W.
(1991) 'On the etiology of interproximal grooves', *Amer.J.Phys.Anthrop.* 85: 299–304.
Garfield, S.
(1972) *Teeth Teeth Teeth: A Treatise On Teeth and Related Parts of Man Land and Water Animals From Earth's Beginning To The Future of Time,* London: Arlington Books.
Gibson, H.
(1971) 'Multi-spectrum investigation of prehistoric teeth', *Dental Radiography and Photography* 44: 57–64.
Gray, P. G., Todd, T. E., Slack, G. L. and Bulman, J. S.
(1970) *Adult Dental Health in England and Wales 1968,* London, HMSO.

Hanson, D.
(1988) 'Prehistoric mortuary practices and human biology', in B. Butler (ed.), *Archaeological Investigations On The North Coast of Rota, Mariana Islands*, Cent. Archaeol. Invest. South Ill. Univ. Occ. Pap. 8.

Harvey, W.
(1968) 'Some dental and social conditions of 1969–1852 connected with St Brides Church, Fleet Street, London', *Medical History* XII: 62–75.

Henderson, D., Collard, M., and Johnston, D. A.
(1996) 'Archaeological evidence for 18th-century medical practice in the Old Town of Edinburgh: excavations at 13 Infirmary Street and Surgeons' Square', *Proceedings of the Society of Antiquaries of Scotland* 126: 929–41.

Hillam, C. (ed.)
(1990) *Roots of Dentistry*, London: British Dental Journal.

Kerr, N. W.
(1998) 'Dental pain and suffering prior to the advent of modern dentistry', *British Dental Journal* 184: 397–9.

Koritzer, R.
(1968) 'Apparent tooth preparation in a Middle Mississippi Indian culture', *Journal of Dental Research* 47: 839.

Langsjoen, O.
(1998) 'Disease of the dentition', in A. C. Aufderheide and C. Rodriguez, *The Cambridge Encyclopaedia of Human Paleopathology*, Cambridge: Cambridge University Press, pp. 393–424.

Leek, F.
(1967) 'Reputed Early Egyptian dental operation, an appraisal', in D. Brothwell and S. Sandison (eds.), *Diseases In Antiquity*, Springfield: Charles C. Thomas, pp. 702–5.

Longfield-Jones, G. M.
(1984) 'A set of silver dental instruments from the new Milton Collection', *Medical History* 28: 42–8.

Mandel, I. D.
(1990) 'Why pick on teeth?', *Journal of the American Dental Association* 121: 129–32.

McGrew, W. and Tutin, C.
(1973) 'Chimpanzee tool use in dental grooming', *Nature* 241: 477–8.

Milner, G. and Larsen, C.
(1991) 'Teeth as artifacts of human behaviour: intentional mutilation and accidental modification', in M. Kelley and C. Larsen (eds.), *Advances In Dental Anthropology*, New York: Wiley-Liss, pp. 357–78.

Moller-Christensen, V.
(1969) 'A rosary bead used as tooth filling material in a human mandibular canine tooth. A unique case from the Danish Middle Ages', *Paginas Storia Medicas* 13: 46–58.

Pedersen, P. O.
(1979) 'The dentition of King Christian The Third, dental disease and oral hygiene habits of a sixteenth century king of Denmark and Norway', *OSSA* 6: 229–41.

Puech, P. and Cianfarani, F.
(1988) 'Interproximal grooving of teeth: additional evidence and interpretation', *Current Anthropology* 29: 665–8.

Ring, M. E.
(1992) *Dentistry: An Illustrated History*, Abrams.

Roberts, C.
(1996) 'Forensic anthropology 1: the contribution of biological anthropology to forensic contexts', in J. Hunter, C. Roberts and A. Martin (eds.) *Studies in Crime: An Introduction to Forensic Archaeology*, London: BT Batsford, pp. 101–21.

Romero, J.
(1970) 'Dental mutilation, trephination and cranial deformation', in T. Stewart (ed.), *Handbook of Middle American Indians*, Austin: University of Texas Press.

Saville, M. H.
(1913) 'Pre-Columbian decoration of the teeth in Ecuador with some account of the occurrence of the custom in other parts of North and South America', *American Anthropologist* 15: 377–94.

Schulz, P. D.
(1977) 'Task activity and anterior tooth grooving in prehistoric Californian Indians', *Amer.J.Phys.Anthrop.* 46: 87–92.

Schwartz, J. H., Brauer, J., and Gordon-Larsen, P.
(1995) 'Brief communication: Tigaran (Point Hope, Alaska) tooth drilling', *Amer.J.Phys.Anthrop.* 97: 77–82.

Silverstone, L., Johnston, N., Hardie, J. and Williams, R,
(1981) *Dental Caries. Aetiology, Pathology and Prevention,* London: Macmillan.

Soames, J. and Southam, J.
(1993) *Oral Pathology,* Oxford: Oxford University Press.

St-Hoyme, L. and Koritzer, R.
(1971) 'Commentary on prehistoric dentistry', *Dental Radiology and Photography* 44: 65.

Thoma, K. H.
(1944) *Oral Pathology*, St Louis-Baltimore: C. V. Mosby Co.

Turner, C.
(1988) 'Interproximal grooving of teeth: additional evidence and interpretation', *Current Anthropology* 29: 664–5.

Ubelaker, D., Phenice, T., and Bass, W.
(1969) 'Artificial interproximal grooving of the teeth of American Indians', *Amer.J.Phys.Anthrop.* 30: 145–50.

Wallace, J. A.
(1974) 'Approximal grooving of teeth', *Amer.J.Phys.Anthrop.* 40: 385–90.

Weinberger, B. W.
(1934) 'Ancient dentistry in the Old and New World', *Annals of Medical History*, pp. 264–79.

Wells, C.
(1967) 'Pseudopathology' in D. Brothwell and T. Sandison (eds.), *Diseases In Antiquity,* Springfield: Charles C Thomas, pp. 5–19.

White, T. D., Degusta, D., Richards, G. D. and Baker, S. G.
(1997) 'Brief communication: prehistoric dentistry in the American Southwest: a drilled canine from Sky Aerie, Colorado', *Amer.J.Phys.Anthrop.* 103: 409–14.

Whittaker, D.
(1993) 'Oral health', in T. Molleson and M. Cox (eds.), *The Spitalfields Project. Volume 2: The Anthropology: The Middling Sort*, York: Council For British Archaeology Research Report 86.

Whittaker, D. K. and Hargreaves, A. S.
(1991) 'Dental restorations and artificial teeth in a Georgian population', *British Dental Journal* **171**: 371–6.

Woodforde, J.
(1968) *The Strange Story of False Teeth,* London: Routledge & Kegan Paul.

Wynbrandt, J.
(1998) *Excruciating History of Dentistry*, St Martins PUS.

Zias, J. and Numeroff, K.
(1987) 'Operative dentistry in the second century BCE', *Journal of the American Dental Association* **114**: 665–6.

ANCIENT BODIES, BUT MODERN TECHNIQUES: THE UTILISATION OF CT SCANNING IN THE STUDY OF ANCIENT EGYPTIAN MUMMIES

Joyce M. Filer

During the eighteenth, nineteenth and early twentieth centuries, increasing numbers of ancient Egyptian mummies were brought into Europe, and, before the advent of radiography, the only way of ascertaining their contents was by unwrapping them. In many cases, the corpses within were dissected — a destructive and irreversible process. A nineteenth century painting by Phillipoteaux (Filer, 1995: pl. IV) shows the autopsy of a mummy in progress, and the presence of a group of fashionably dressed women in the scene underlines the fact that many of these public dissections were viewed as social entertainment. In the majority of cases neither the remains of the mummies nor notes on findings during the examinations were retained, with the consequent loss of both ancient artefacts and scientific knowledge. In one particular case, however, portions of the autopsied mummy were kept (now held in the British Museum) and the observations during the examination published. In the early 1800s, Augustus Granville, a physician to the Duke of Clarence, unwrapped and dissected the mummy of an adult female named Irtyersenu who, judging from the style of coffin lid which accompanies the body, lived during the Twenty-sixth Dynasty or later (c. 727–332 BC). Granville, in his own words, decided to 'sacrifice a most complete specimen of the Egyptian art of embalming, in hopes of eliciting some new facts illustrative of so curious and interesting a subject' (Granville, 1825: 281). Granville judged the lady to have been between fifty and fifty-five years of age at death and that she had borne children. Two issues were of palaeopathological interest: Irtyersenu had suffered from porrigo decalvans, a cutaneous affliction of the head which destroys the hair and prevents its growth, and, during his examination, Granville noted that the lady's uterus had been diseased for some time prior to death. In Granville's opinion it was this latter condition — which he termed ovarian dropsy — which was the cause of death. That Irtyersenu had some ovarian disease was in fact correct, but a subsequent re-examination of the extant uterus has revealed she had a benign cyst (Tapp, forthcoming) which, whilst not being the life-threatening condition suggested by Granville, is certainly one of the earliest recorded neoplasms.

Many decades after the discovery and development of X-ray technology, an advanced form — computed tomography (henceforth CT) scanning — has proved extremely useful in the non-invasive examination of mummies. In this technique a scanner takes a series of X-ray projections through a subject. The term tomography derives from the Greek *tomos*, meaning 'slice' or 'section', the principle upon which this scanning technique is founded, thus, the X-ray projections are often called 'slices'. The tissues of the mummy, whether soft tissues or skeletal, attenuate the X-ray beam according to their particular composition and thickness and so the structures within a mummy package can be easily demonstrated. In CT scanning, as the name implies, a computer is used to record and store the data in digital form for display as required: in a form similar to conventional X-rays or in the form of a 3D reconstruction.

As alluded to above, the foremost advantage of utilising CT scanning in Egyptological studies is its non-invasive and non-destructive nature. Other information which can be obtained include: the gender and age at death of the individual within the mummy package, evidence of pathology and details of the mummification process together with any amulets and jewellery used in the preparation of the body for burial. In recent years the Department of Egyptian Antiquities, British Museum, has been engaged in a project CT scanning some of the mummies in its collection. The results of some of these examinations are outlined below. The letters EA denote Egyptian Antiquities, followed by the departmental accession number for that particular mummy.

Whilst some studies of ancient Egyptian human remains indicate that the majority of people did not live beyond forty years of age, it is clear from the evidence from CT scanning examinations that some individuals did live longer. A mummy (EA 6679) of Ptolemaic date (332–30 BC) is contained in a skilfully decorated cartonnage case bearing the name 'Hornedjitef', an illustration of which can be seen in Dawson and Gray (1968: pl. XIIIb). The CT scans have revealed that the body within is in good anatomical order with the arms crossed over the chest and is that of a mature male well advanced into his fifth decade. The scans reveal interesting information about the mummification techniques employed in the preparation of this mummy. The thorax and abdomen contain four cylindrical packages that are, in all likelihood, the internal organs wrapped in linen and returned to the body following treatment with natron salt. A large, densely opaque oval object can be seen near the left scapula. This may be a heart scarab that has slipped from its original position. Following the removal of the brain via the nose, a liquid resin-like substance was poured into the cranial cavity. The scans show a clear and even resin line on a level parallel with the mastoid processes indicating that the corpse lay unmoved in a supine position until the resin had hardened (Fig. 1). This forms an interesting contrast, for example, with the skull of Tutankhamun where two levels of resin can be seen (Filer, 1995: frontispiece) indicating that the young king's body had been moved around during the preparation of his body. With regard to jewellery included with Hornedjitef's body, the scans reveal a square-bezelled ring on the left hand and a wide band, probably of gold, on the left first toe. Amulets conferring magical protection are scattered around the chest area. From a pathological point of view the CT scans reveal that Hornedjitef's left lower third molar is impacted and that parts of the vertebral column show degenerative changes. There also appears to be a loss of bone density suggesting osteoporosis, which seems in keeping with Hornedjief's mature age.

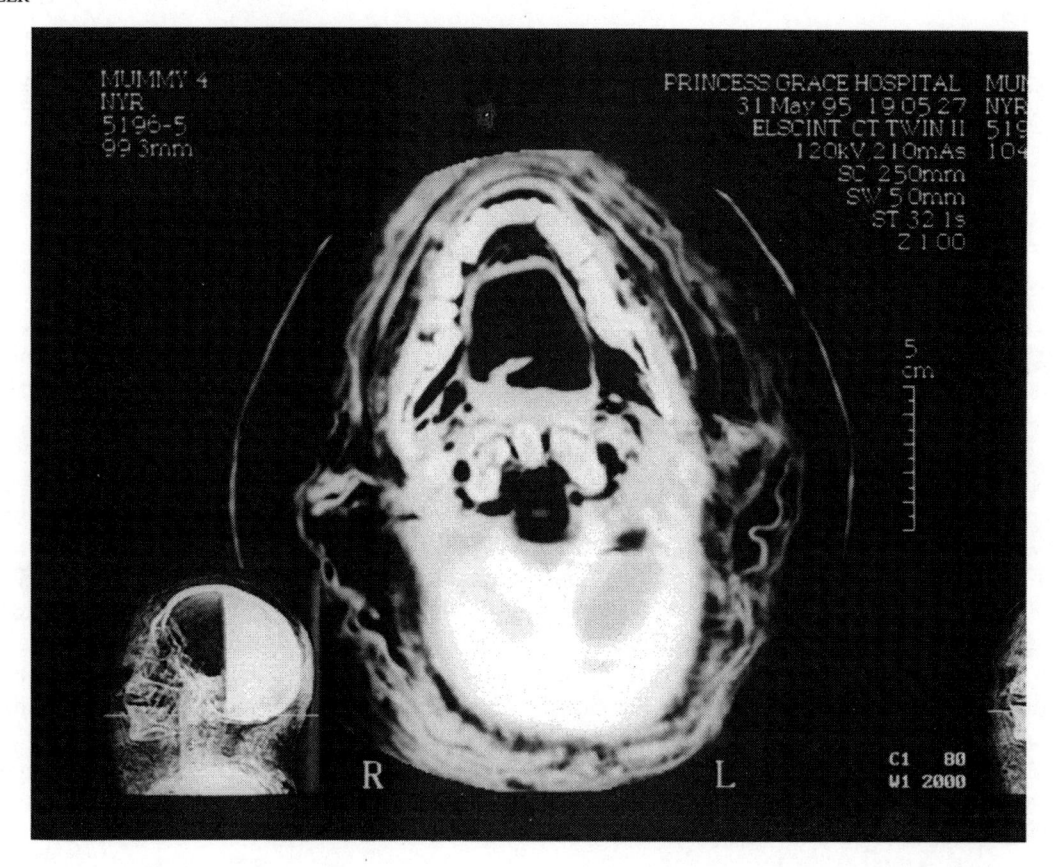

Fig. 1. View through the skull of Hornedjitef showing the resin level (courtesy British Museum).

Another mummy showing all the signs that the individual concerned died at an advanced age is that of a woman named Katebet (EA 6665), of possible New Kingdom or later date. Although the mummy of Katebet has only recently been scanned, it is possible to give some preliminary observations. The mummy lies fully extended with the hands over the pubic area. This is at odds with the wooden mask over the head and torso, which presents the arms as crossed over the chest. Views through the skull (Fig. 2) show the remains of Katebet's brain or possibly some textile packing material. The thorax and abdomen appear to be empty of organs or packages and a few of her ribs are dislocated. A large amount of seemingly mud-like material has been packed around the outer aspect of the abdominal and the upper thigh area. Views of her skull reveal that Katebet was almost endentulous at death, with only two teeth remaining (Fig. 3). Arthritic changes in the spine are apparent.

Several of the mummies CT scanned proved to be those of individuals in the late adolescent to young adult age range at death. One mummy that has been of great interest is EA 6707 (Fig. 4), purporting to be the mummy of a female child. Named 'Cleopatra, daughter of Candace' the mummy is from the Roman period, and being a member of the well-known Soter family, can be more firmly dated to the second century AD. The mummy is approximately 1.6 m in length and is covered with a painted linen shroud. Both the length of the mummy and the image of the deceased depicted on the shroud would suggest an individual older than a child at death, yet a hieroglyphic inscription on the accompanying wooden coffin (EA 6706) giving Cleopatra's age at death has been traditionally translated as 11 years, 1 month and 25 days. The scan reveals that the body has been

Fig. 2. The mummy of Katebet (EA 6665) (courtesy British Museum).

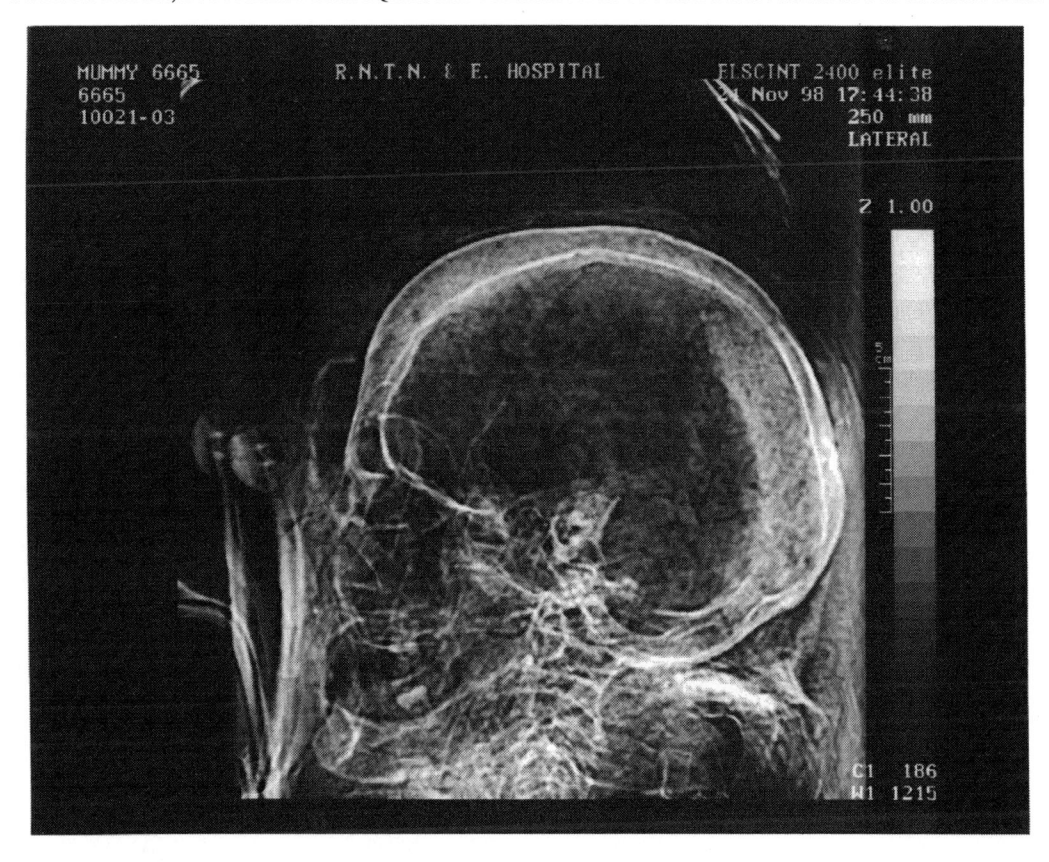

Fig. 3. View through the skull of Katebet showing an almost endentulous mouth (courtesy British Museum).

Fig. 4. The mummy of Cleopatra (EA 6707) (courtesy British Museum).

wrapped in many layers of linen and this, together with mud packing, accounts for the rather substantial weight (at *c.* 75 kg) of the mummy. Cleopatra's skeleton is in good condition and anatomical order and there are several 'packages' within the bodily cavities which, again, are likely to be the internal organs returned to the body (Fig. 5). One elongated object, approximately 9 cm in length in the abdominal area, may be a roll of linen or papyrus, or a figurine. There are no obvious pathological changes. An examination of Cleopatra's skeleton was essential in resolving the apparent discrepancy between the image on the shroud and the age at death inscribed on the coffin. As various parts of the skeleton are known to fuse at particular times it is possible to determine an individual's age at death, and for Cleopatra it is quite clear from the scans that she was in her late teens, between 16 and 18, when she died. The traditional translation of the first digits of the hieroglyphic inscription has been questioned by Renate Germer (pers. comm., 1995), who suggested that the inscription may have been poorly written in antiquity and that '11 years' should be read as '17 years'. The new CT examination of Cleopatra's body would indeed seem to support Germer's revision that 'Cleopatra, daughter of Candace, died aged 17 years, 1 month and 25 days'.

EA 6704 is a mummy of Roman date (after 30 BC) but presents a very interesting combination of styles in its preparation. The external presentation shows the limbs wrapped individually but without an all-enveloping shroud. The facial features — eyes, eyebrows and mouth — are depicted in black paint, an archaising style of decorating mummies that harks back to the Old Kingdom period (*c.* 2613–2160 BC); whilst the lower arms are wrapped in an intricate geometric pattern utilising dark and light coloured linens, which is very much a feature of the Ptolemaic period. The mummy can be seen in Dawson and Gray (1968: pl. XVIIb). As with the mummy of Katebet described above, EA 6704 has also only recently been scanned; thus, the following remarks are brief, preliminary observations. As the breasts

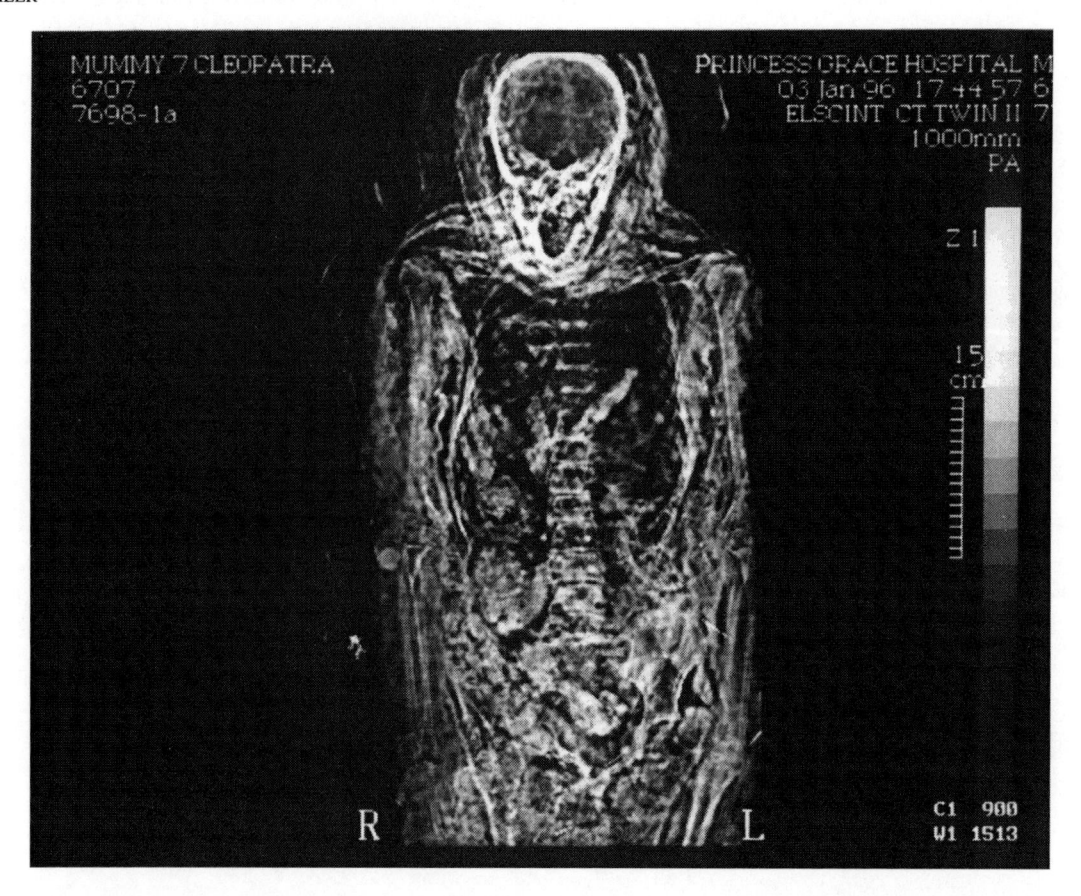

Fig. 5. View of Cleopatra's body showing internal packages (courtesy British Museum).

and upper thighs are well-padded it has often been thought that this is the mummy of a female; the scans, however, show quite clearly that this is a male. The skeletal and dental development would indicate a young man between eighteen and twenty-one years of age at death.

Mummy EA 21810, dating to AD 100–20, is contained within a red-painted stucco case that is finely decorated with traditional ancient Egyptian funerary scenes in gold leaf (Fig. 6). A portrait of the deceased, in encaustic on limewood, is incorporated within the case and it shows a young man, perhaps in his early twenties. The young man has dark hair and eyes, a long nose and large lips; his skin appears sunburned. Beneath the portrait is a conventional Greek inscription, 'Farewell Artemidorus' and this is set within a Roman format *tabula ansata* flanked by serpents. Thus, interestingly, the mummy of Artemidorus provides an excellent example of the merging of different cultural influences: a Greek personal name and a Romanised portrait combined with traditional Egyptian funerary practices. Within the case the body is fully extended with the hands over the pelvic area. Unusually, the feet are placed with the walking surfaces together. Scans of the skeleton can be seen in Filer (1998: fig. 3). The skeleton is complete but there is some displacement of the thoracic vertebrae and ribs. This may be due to the application of overly tight wrappings during the mummification process. Based upon developmental features of the skeleton, including the incomplete fusion of the innominate bones, it is suggested that Artemidorus was no older than his early twenties when he died, which is in keeping with the age suggested by the accompanying portrait. Rarely in archaeological studies do we have any indications as to an individual's cause

Fig. 6. The mummy of Artemidorus (EA 21810) (courtesy British Museum).

of death but from an examination of the body of Artemidorus we come close to 'witnessing' a peri-mortem event. The CT scans show evidence of damage to the head. The bridge of the nose appears crushed and there are long fractures radiating from the occipital bone into the left and right parietal bones. A three-dimensional reconstruction of the injuries has shown that there are no signs of healing and it is possible that this may indicate death from a violent assault or from accidental injury (Fig. 7). However, that the damage to the skull occurred as a consequence of rough handling by the ancient embalmers during the mummification process cannot be ruled out.

The mummy inscribed 'Hermione grammatike' was loaned to the British Museum as part of the *Ancient Faces* exhibition. With the kind permission of the owners, Girton College, Cambridge, the mummy of Hermione underwent a CT scanning examination. The mummy is carefully wrapped in many layers of linen arranged in a rhomboid pattern but without decorative gilt studs. A head and shoulders portrait, thought to be of the deceased, is executed in the encaustic technique on a shroud within the wrappings. An excellent illustration of Hermione can be seen in Doxiadis (1995: pl. 33). In the portrait the young woman has an oval-shaped face with deep-set eyes, a longish nose, a rather pursed mouth and well-defined ears. The hair is parted centrally and drawn up, in a severe style, away from the

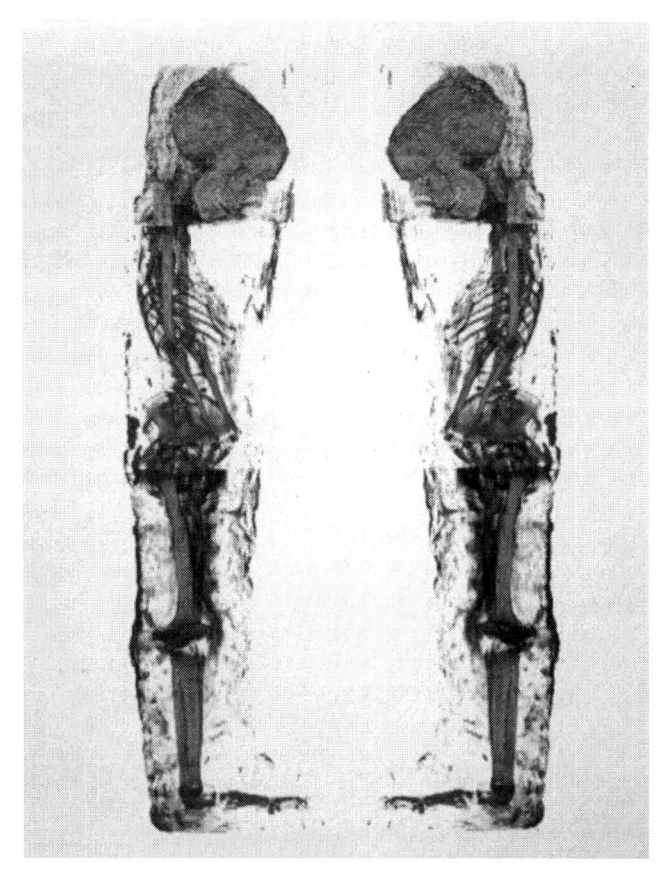

Fig. 8. View of Hermione's skeleton and hair (courtesy British Museum).

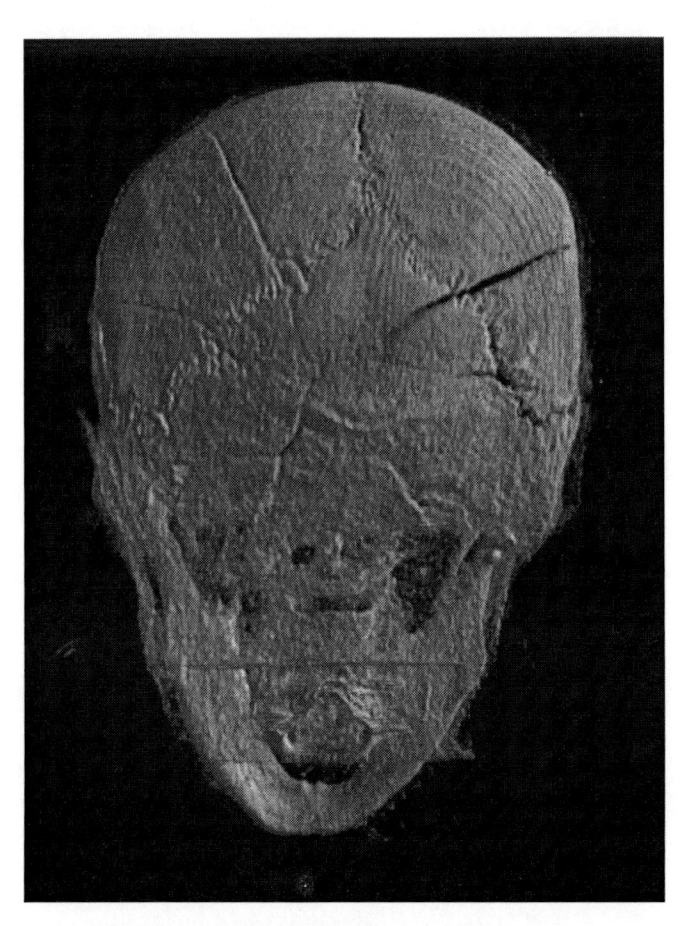

Fig. 7. Three-dimensional reconstruction of the skull of Artemidorus showing unhealed fractures (courtesy British Museum).

face. A Greek inscription above the subject's right shoulder gives her name: *Hermione*. The exact meaning of the following word, *grammatike*, has been the subject of much discussion and revision. Perhaps the most useful translation is that by Montserrat (1996: 177; 1997: 225–6), who suggests *grammatike* to be an epithet praising the deceased woman for her learning. Despite the overall slimness of the mummy, the scans show that a considerable amount of linen was used to wrap the body. The scans also show Hermione's skeleton to be complete (Fig. 8), but that it has sustained some damage to some of the ribs and, again, this may have occurred as a result of overly-tight wrappings during the preparation of the mummy. A previous X-ray study of this mummy suggested Hermione's age at death to have been about twenty-four years (Bourriau and Bashford, 1980: 169); however, from this re-examination of the anatomical development it seems more likely that Hermione was younger when she died, perhaps no more than twenty-one years of age. The scans reveal damage to the ethmoid bones, which suggests that the brain was evacuated via the nose, and a three-dimensional reconstruction of her skull and remaining facial soft tissues show that the left nostril, being very distended, was the area of entry into the skull. The cranial cavity was left empty yet packing material, probably linen, was used to fill the nasal and oral cavities. Interestingly, the scanner detected the remains of Hermione's hair, which provides a useful opportunity to compare her actual coiffure with that depicted on her portrait. The outline of her hair can be seen along the top of her skull finishing piled up in a loose bun on top of her head (see also Fig. 8), which compares favourably with the style shown in the portrait. Further details of Hermione's hair can be seen in Filer (1999: 81–2).

JOYCE M. FILER

There are many extant mummies which testify to the fact that ancient Egypt, like many other ancient societies, endured a high infant mortality. Several of the child mummies in the British Museum were included in this scanning project. EA 13595, is a beautifully wrapped mummy featuring a portrait of an adolescent boy (Fig. 9). Found at Hawara in the Fayum and dated to AD 100–20, the mummy is contained within linen wrappings executed in a rhomboid pattern finished off with gilt stucco studs. The portrait, in encaustic on wood, is inserted within the wrappings and depicts the head and shoulders of a youth, perhaps about thirteen years of age. Whilst both the portrait and the wrappings demonstrate care and attention to detail, the scans reveal that the same cannot be said of the body within. The skeleton is very disarticulated and it would appear that the body was already in some state of decompostition when it was wrapped (Fig. 10). Much granulous material, probably sand or mud, has been used to pad out the mummy and this certainly obscures some of the detail. However, from the long bones that can be examined it is clear that this is an immature individual, which agrees with the age indicated by the portrait.

A second child mummy, EA 6715, is wrapped in a decorated linen shroud depicting a full-length view of a young boy wearing a white tunic. The mummy can be seen in Dawson and Gray (1968: pl. XVIIId). The mummy, dating to AD 230–50, is in a shallow painted wooden coffin set on two battens. The CT scans show a fully extended body in excellent condition. The development of the skeleton indicates a child between eight and ten years of age which concurs with the depiction of the child's head as shaven except for four tufts of hair above the brow — a traditional ancient Egyptian way of indicating a juvenile.

Fig. 9. The mummy of EA 13595 (courtesy British Museum).

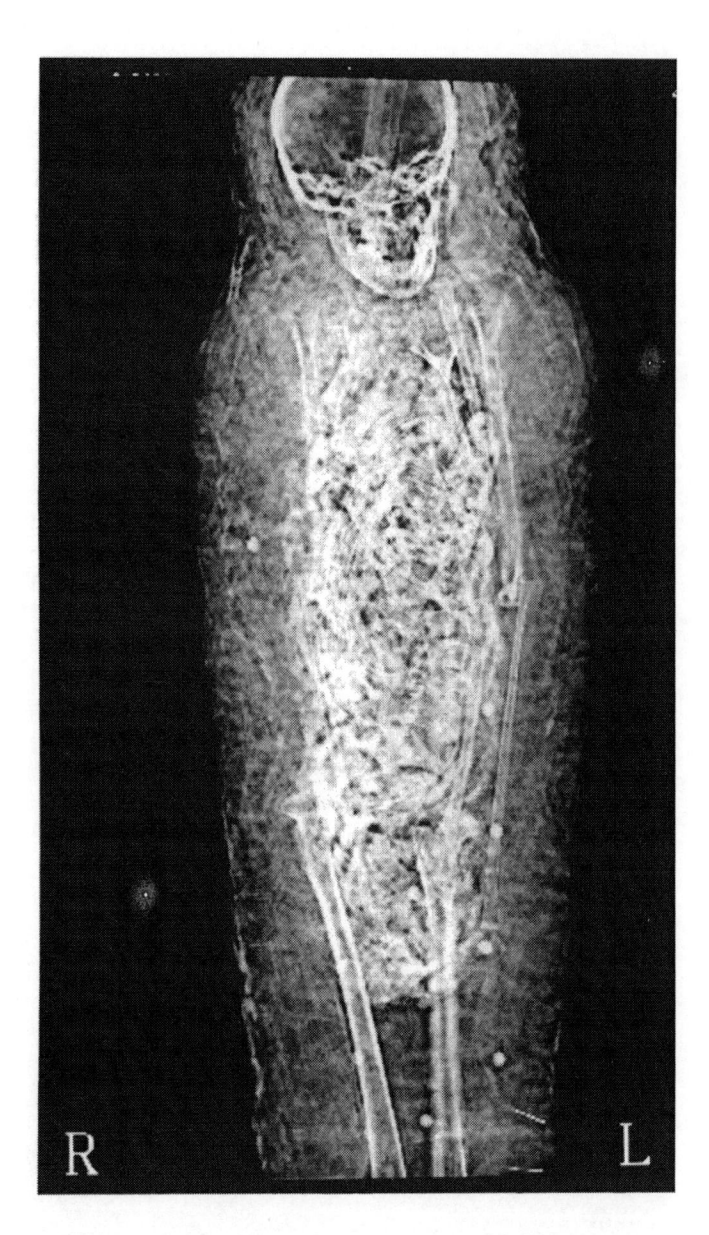

Fig. 10. View of the skeleton of EA 13595, showing its disorder and granulous material (courtesy British Museum).

The two final mummies in this discussion form an interesting contrast with regards to style of preparation, and yet both were found together and it is thought that they are roughly contemporaneous. EA 22108 and EA 21809 were found with an adult female mummy and another child mummy at Hawara. EA 22108, dating to AD 40–60, has been provided with a gilded headpiece that, although in keeping with traditional Egyptian funerary practices, does not give the impression of individuality implied by those mummies with a painted portrait (Fig. 11). The lack of jewellery represented on the headpiece and the style of the draping of the shroud suggests that this is a male child (Walker and Bierbrier, 1997: 80), but it has not been possible to confirm this through the CT scans. Beneath this headpiece is a linen shroud painted with fairly typical funerary scenes. The skeleton within is in good order and is that of an infant. Interestingly, on the headpiece the child's hands are depicted folded across the chest whereas in reality they are over the pubic area (Fig. 12). Mummy EA 21809, as noted above, was found in association with EA 22108. The mummy is enclosed in a linen shroud painted with mythological scenes and this includes a portrait of

38

a young boy. The mummy can be seen in Dawson and Gray (1968: XVIb). Both the portrait and the linen shroud show signs of wear and tear and the scans reveal that the mummy has sustained dislocations to the thoracic spine, the ribs and the pelvis. The dislocations to the pelvis have resulted in the femora shifting to the right. The immature age of the individual, as suggested by the portrait, is confirmed by the development of the skeleton within the wrappings.

From this brief discussion, it can be seen that a wide range of information can be obtained from ancient Egyptian mummies without resorting to destructive methods. Encouragingly, as radiographic techniques improve and are refined, the possibilities of gaining an even greater depth of information are becoming a reality.

ACKNOWLEDGMENTS

I would like to thank the following London hospitals for providing the CT scans: Princess Grace, The Royal Free Hospitals, The Royal National Throat, Nose and Ear Hospital. Grateful thanks are due to The Institute of Laryngology and Otology, University College London for the three-dimensional reconstructions of the Artemidorus head injuries, in particular G. Alusi, A. C. Tan, J. Campos and A. Alusi.

Fig. 11. The mummy of EA 22108 (courtesy British Museum).

BIBLIOGRAPHY

Bourriau, J. and Bashford, J.
(1980) 'Radiological examination of two mummies of the Roman era', *Museums Applied Science Center For Archaeology*, Vol. **1 (6)** Mummification Supplement: 168–71.

Dawson, W. R. and Gray, P. H. K.
(1968) *Catalogue Of Egyptian Antiquities In The British Museum I: Mummies and Human Remains*, London: British Museum Press.

Doxiadis, E.
(1995) *The Mysterious Fayum Portraits*, London: British Museum Press.

Filer, J. M.
(1995) *Disease*, London: British Museum Press.
(1997) 'Revealing Hermione's secrets', *Egyptian Archaeology* **11**: 32–4.
(1998) 'Revealing the face of Artemidorus', *Minerva* **9, 4**: 21–4.
(1999) 'Ein Blick auf die Menschen hinter den Portrats: eine Untersuchung agyptischer Mumien mit Hilfe von Computertomographie und Gesichtsrekonstruktion' in K. Parlasca and H. Seemann (eds.), *Au Genblicke. Mumienportrats und agyptische Grabkunst aus romischer Zeit*, Frankfurt: Schirn Kunsthalle, pp. 79–86.

Granville, A.
(1825) 'An essay on Egyptian mummies: with observations on the art of embalming among the ancient Egyptians', *Philosophical Transactions*, Read April 14, 1825: 269–316.

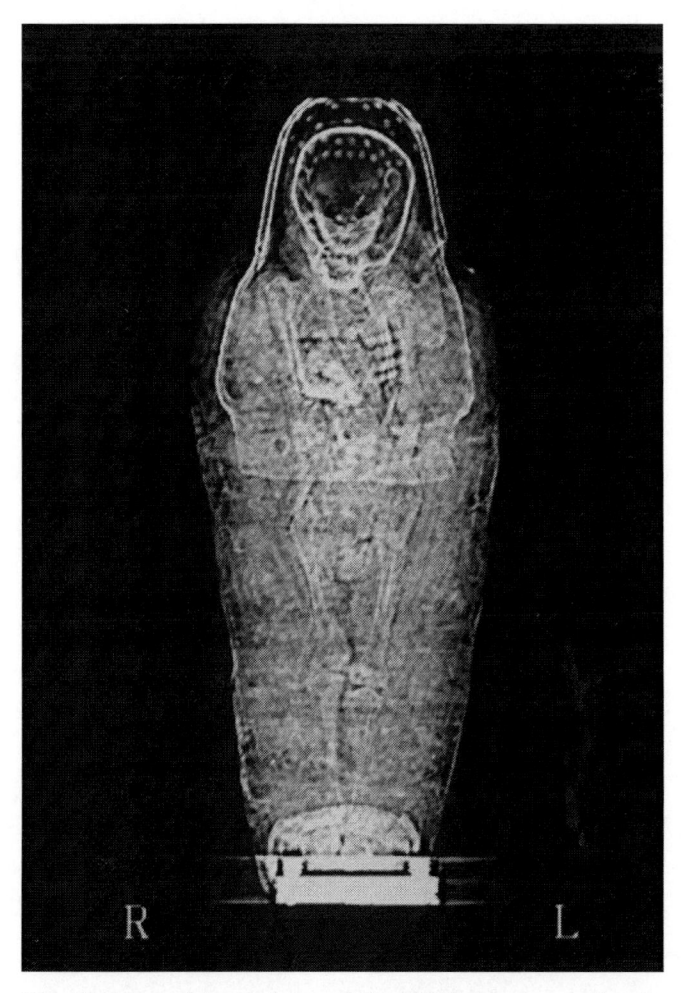

Fig. 12. View of the skeleton of EA 22108 showing the hands over the pubic area (courtesy British Museum).

Montserrat, D.
(1996) 'Your name will reach the Hall of the Western Mountains: some aspects of mummy portrait inscriptions' in D. Bailey (ed.), *Archaeological Research in Roman Egypt,* Michigan: Ann Arbor, pp. 177–85.
(1997) 'Heron Bearer of Philosophia and Hermione Grammatike', *Journal of Egyptian Archaeology* **83**: 223–6.

Walker, S. and Bierbrier, M.
(1997) *Ancient Faces: Mummy Portraits From Roman Egypt,* London: British Museum Press.

DISEASE AND MEDICINE IN HITTITE ASIA MINOR

Robert Arnott

INTRODUCTON

The late Hans G. Güterbock, speaking at the thirty-fourth annual meeting of the American Association for the History of Medicine in Chicago in May 1961, began with the emphatic statement that: 'There is no Hittite medicine!' (Güterbock, 1962: 109). Based upon the state of knowledge at the time, his instincts may well have been right, but in the forty years since his remarks, a great deal of new work on the subject, principally on the texts, has been undertaken. Utilising the results of this published work, I am able to present a brief review of the evidence, both textual and archaeological, that we have for the existence of disease and medical practice amongst the Hittites.

Like all ancient societies, the Hittites suffered both illness and physical trauma, and within their society there emerged individuals whose role it was to dispense the remedies and provide the skills necessary for healing. As Beckman has emphasised, '…the Hittite texts reveal many instances in which therapeutic intervention was deemed appropriate for responding to physical problems or restoring soundness of body' (Beckman, 1990: 629).

THE HITTITE EMPIRE

The Hittite Empire was one of the great Bronze Age powers of the Ancient Near East for a relatively short time between c. 1380 and 1200 BC (Gurney, 1980; Macqueen, 1986). It was based on the central Anatolian plateau, where the Hittites had established themselves in approximately 1650 BC, and was centred on their capital Hattuša, present-day Boğazköy (Bittel, 1970). At the peak of its power, the Hittite Empire included subordinate states as far west as the Aegean, and as far south as Syria. Under the Old Kingdom (c. 1700–1400 BC), two kings, Hattušili I (1650–1620 BC) and his adopted son and successor Muršili I (1620–1590 BC), anxious to secure supplies of raw materials from the mines and forests of eastern and western Anatolia, established military and diplomatic alliances that were to last. The Hittite kings also sought to stabilise centres of power within a state that lacked secure natural frontiers, which were often threatened on all sides. By the establishment of vassal kings, they ensured effective control over the important trade routes south-eastward through Syria to Mesopotamia; in a military campaign in c. 1595 BC, King Muršili I succeeded in sacking Babylon and ending the dynasty of Hammurabi.

Throughout the period of the New Kingdom (c. 1400–1200 BC), the Hittites vied with the Egyptians for control of the Euphrates trade route, and in c. 1370 BC, during the reign of King Šuppiluliuma I (1380–1340 BC), they incorporated the northern parts of Syria and Mesopotamia into their empire after consolidating their power in Anatolia. This hegemony in North Syria came under threat from the Egyptians during the time of King Muwatalli II (1306–1282 BC), which culminated in his army meeting that of Pharaoh Rameses II on the River Orontes at the Battle of Kadeš in 1300 BC, a decisive victory for neither side. The Hittite Empire lasted until shortly after 1200 BC, when it collapsed as the result of complex internal and external forces that involved, amongst others, the great migrations of the 'Sea Peoples', although its legacy lived on in the Neo-Hittite states of northern Syria, centred around Carchemish.

The Hittites were originally one of a small number of Indo-European tribes, that migrated into Anatolia from the north, probably towards the end of the third millennium BC. Hittite society was complex, multi-lingual and multi-ethnic, with a ruling class whose wealth depended partly on slavery, and whose semi-feudal nature evolved slowly and did not attain the form best known to us from the archives of the Hittite kings until the period of the New Kingdom. It incorporated administrative structures originally developed by the Neolithic and Early Bronze Age village communities of central Anatolia, and which underpinned the whole of the Hittite economic and social system. The king, who represented on the earth the supreme weather or storm god, also had special status of chief priest, and owned all the land, which he then distributed. He also presided over all-important religious festivals, with its many cults representing the diverse cultural heritage of the Hittite state. This state had a mainly agricultural economy, which was largely organised in a condition of perpetual readiness for war, both for conquest and defence against attack from the north (Gurney, 1980).

Unlike other Late Bronze Age societies of Western Asia, the Hittites, like their far neighbours the Mycenaeans, were of Indo-European stock, although they wrote their language in cuneiform, adopted from Mesopotamia, leaving behind in the ruins of Hattuša thousands of inscribed baked tablets. They referred to the people of their own kingdom as 'men of the Hatti land', and they described their language as Nešili or Neš(umn)ili, meaning 'of (the men of) Neša' or Kaneš, the site of the Old Assyrian trading post of the early second millennium BC, now modern Kültepe (Kültepe-Karum). Their language had a close affinity with another Indo-European language, Luwian, spoken by those who settled in western Anatolia, and later, in the southeast. This gave rise to a Hurro-Luwian culture after the Luwian and the Hurrian cultures merged in Kizzuwatna, which now approximates to ancient Cilicia. Beckman has emphasised that Luwian and Luwian-speaking scribes had an increasingly strong influence on Hittite language texts during the New Kingdom, particularly as much of the Mesopotamian acculturation which penetrated to the Hittites by the time of the New Kingdom came through Hurrian intermediaries, who had assimilated and often remoulded the ancient myths and religious traditions of Sumer and Akkad (Beckman, 1983a: 102), although there would also

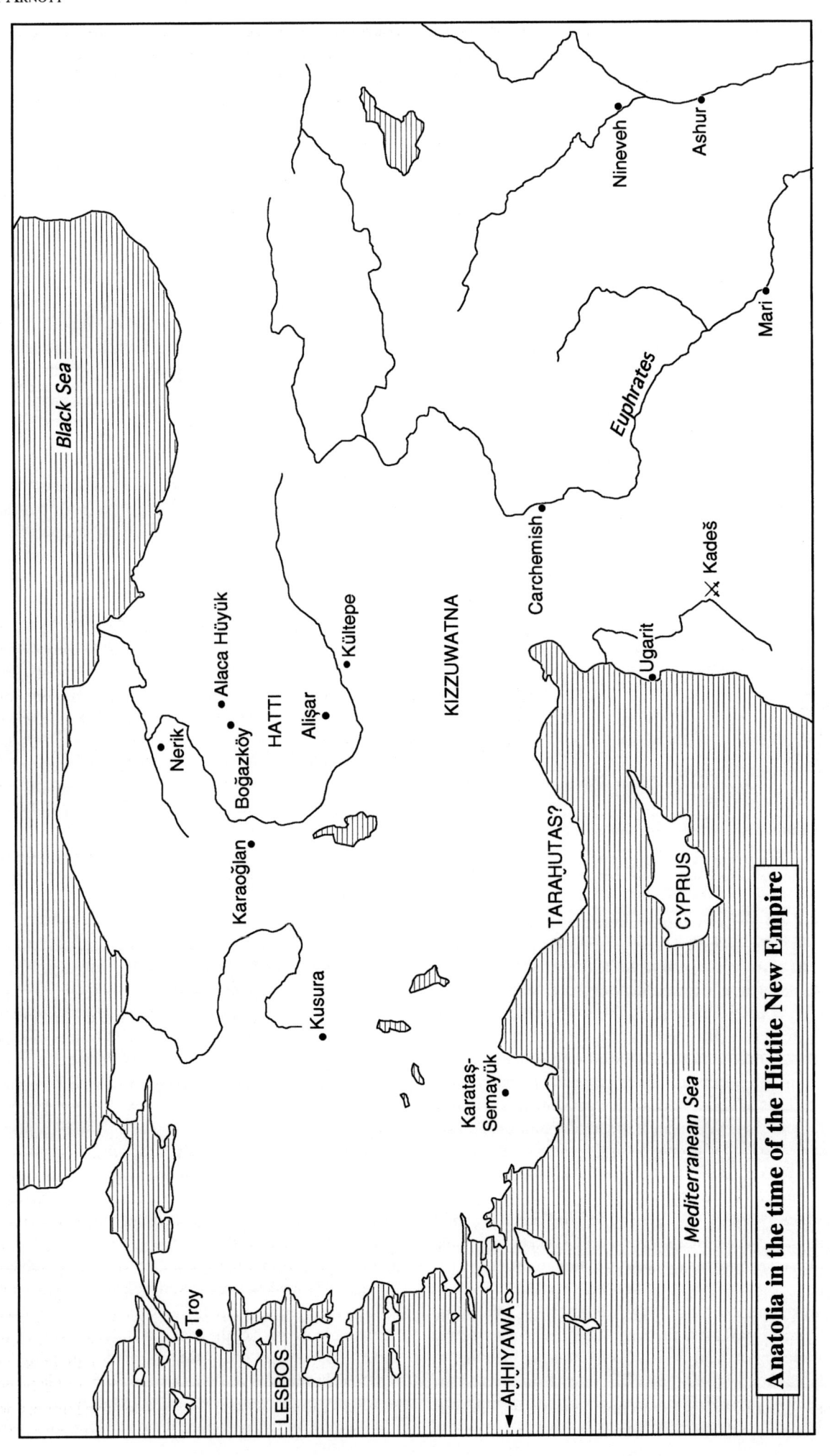

Fig. 1. Anatolia in the time of the Hittite New Empire.

have been some direct cultural importation from Mesopotamia. Like other contemporary societies of the Late Bronze Age, literacy was restricted to serve the social elite, and was conducted by a highly trained class of professional scribes. The training of these scribes included the learning of Akkadian, or Old Babylonian, not only because it was the instrument of much diplomatic correspondence and was the *lingua franca* throughout the whole of the Ancient Near East at this time, but because the system of writing itself, a combination of syllables and word-signs that could only have been learned within the framework of the language or language group for which it had originally been developed. Therefore, a scribe's training included not only Akkadian texts, but also some of the texts from Old Sumerian, for which cuneiform writing had been invented. The languages from which Akkadian borrowed its script therefore directly influenced Hittite, and ready-made Akkadian word signs now expressed some Hittite words. It must be, as Beckman believes, that the adoption of cuneiform implied the borrowing of an entire cultural tradition, and that scribal education was the means by which that tradition was transmitted (Beckman, 1983a: 98). As Labat has pointed out, the Hittites borrowed from, rather than contributed to, that knowledge (Labat, 1965: 67). Many of the extant medical texts in the Hittite language are just translations of Mesopotamian medical writings and little more. They did not contribute anything to the broad corpus of medical knowledge in the ancient world.

THE EVIDENCE OF THE TEXTS: DIAGNOSES AND THERAPEUTICS

Hittite medicine was not much advanced beyond the stage of magic and simple remedies, and the textual evidence for medical practice and purification found mostly in the Boğazköy-Hattuša archives provides few systematic descriptions of rational medical practice, prescriptions or techniques. Like many early societies, magic was used to drive out disease and to restore impaired bodily function through different devices employed in the rituals, all of which were largely based on analogy. They were combined with prayers and offerings to the gods (Güterbock, 1962: 110; Wilhelm, 1994). Unlike some contemporary early societies, they did little that can be considered to contribute to the progress of medical practice.

Of the religious texts concerning healing, Güterbock established that these texts generally fall into two main types: (i) diagnostic texts, which are collections of simple statements in the form of predictions, for example, 'If a man has…(here is mentioned a symptom) then he will die or recover' — whatever the case may be; and (ii) prescription texts: collections of somewhat longer items, each of which also begins with a description of a symptom or symptoms and ends with the statement '…then he will recover,' but mainly describes the ritual procedures to be applied (Güterbock, 1962: 111–12). This is particularly evident in the series of tablets of Babylonian diagnostic medical texts found at Boğazköy, attributed to a Babylonian scholar active around 1067–1046 BC, although the texts are originally earlier (Wilhelm, 1994).

The few exclusively Hittite New Kingdom medical texts that include aspects of practice are incantation texts, with several among the compositions imported from Mesopotamia (Beckman, 1983a: 98; Beckman, 1993: 26–7). One of the latter (KUB XXXVII 1) is an Akkadian-language text about the making and application of poultices (Köcher, 1952–3). Its poor quality, as well as the presence of Hittite and Luwian glosses, shows that it is the product of a Hittite student scribe who probably had an Assyrian master (Beckman, 1993: 26). In contrast to this, two of the texts included within CTH 809 (KUB XXXVII 2; KUB XXXVII 12), a series concerning diseases of the eye and their treatment, seems according to Beckman to be copies imported from the south, whilst a third (KUB IV 55) may be a local copy. The diagnostic texts CTH 537, most of which are Akkadian, include one text (KUB XXXVII 190) which has a Hittite gloss, and two (KBo XIII 32; KBo XIII 33) are translations into the Hittite language (Beckman, 1993: 26). However, the small number of pure Hittite-language medical texts and fragments, edited by Burde, seem to be of local origin (Burde, 1974). Their poor state of conservation combined with our ignorance of the implication of many of the technical terms makes understanding very difficult, but it is quite apparent that many of the therapeutics described are medical; the central theme is the internal and topical administration of practical remedies. Wounds (KUB XLIV 63; KUB XIII 38), diseases and disorders of the eyes (KUB XLIV 63; KUB VIII 38), intestinal complaints (KUB XLIV 61), possibly flatulence (KUB XLIV 64) and problems of the neck and throat (KBo XXI 74; KBo XXI 21), were among the conditions treated. There is a text (CTH 406) which outlines a ritual against impotence (Hoffner, 1987). One text (KUB VIII 36), the largest, details prescriptions for the treatment of problems of the eyes, throat and mouth (Beckman, 1993: 26–7). These medical texts were not simply exercises for the more advanced students in the scribal schools; they were possibly manuals of medical practice (Beckman, 1993: 26–7). Some further texts contain prescriptions against fevers (CTH 811) (Meier, 1939: 200–13), and for assisting childbirth (CTH 810) (Meier, 1939: 198). Beckman believes that a number of medical texts have been lost (Beckman, 1990: 630), although, if found, they are unlikely to change our view on the quality of medical practice within the Hittite Empire.

Many medico-religious texts are ascribed to particular authors, although there are only three (KUB IX 31; KUB XXXV 9; KUB XXXV 10) which have the title of *asû* or physician. These concern three separate rituals to be used at times of an epidemic or pestilence. In these originally Luwian ritual texts of Zarpiya, physician of Kizzuwatna, he prescribes simple magic, inserting Luwian charms into his ritual without any rational basis, and in which he himself, plays a leading role (Schwartz 1938; Starke, 1985: 46–55). Another religious text (KBo XVII 61), again purely magical, prescribes the following procedure to be applied by a 'wise-woman' or ^SAL^*hašauwa-*, whereby nine parts of a male goat are fitted to 'nine body parts' of a new-born baby, and, as a consequence, each goat part is supposed to remove the illness from the corresponding part of the body of the child. The list comprises more than nine items, so 'the nine body parts' must be a fixed figure of speech, or have some religious significance (Beckman, 1983b: 45, 56), although it may just be schematic. If the repetitions of the list of parts of the body are disregarded, it would appear that it would have been as follows: eyes, eyebrows, ears, mouth, liver, gall bladder, pelvis, anus, testicles, knees and feet. This list by no means covers all the names of body parts known in Hittite, nor is it the only way of listing them; it is what one particular author considers essential parts of the body. In another common number attested with body parts in Hittite ritual is twelve (Güterbock, 1962: 111–12). There are references in other texts to other parts of the human body: head, throat, arms, hands, fingers, finger nails, ribs or side, toes, toe nails, bones, ligaments and veins (although it is uncertain which of the two is meant) and the blood (Güterbock, 1962: 111–12). In the same text, there also contains what might be seen as an element of rational therapeutics. The ^{SAL}*hašauwa*- administers to a child a remedy:

> 'And I come (and) further, a copper-box (and) medicine I give to him. I take cr(ocus), (?), lettuce (and) one + vessel(s) of cheap beer for drinking' (Beckman, 1983b: 43).

Pringle also refers to the giving of a remedy to a child whose 'inner parts are eaten' — an expression possibly referring to paediatric gastro-enteritis. On the first day, she will make offerings and pronounce prayers to the 'sun-god of illness.' On the second day, she takes a number of garden plants (some twenty plant names are listed, but none yet identified), which are then crushed and mixed with a liquid consisting of active yeast dissolved in beer, with a sprinkling of water upon the top. The child's mouth is washed out with the mixture, and then a little is administered orally; the rest is then poured over the child's head and body and served as an enema, to the accompaniment of incantations and sacrifices, with a final treatment of the body parts by a salve containing more plants and sheep's fat. Ritual bathing then follows. What then occurs is purely magical (Pringle, 1983: 137). Even if we were able to identify the plants used, and even if they had known medicinal properties — purgative, soothing or whatever, the indiscriminate external and internal application of this remedy would not have had a particular therapeutic effect. Of course, a combination of simple home remedies with magic, whereby these remedies form an integral part of a basic magic procedure, or a 'placebo effect' is a common characteristic of most primitive medicine. Other ritual texts refer to other forms of healing. For example, the ritual of Ammitatua (Kbo V 2) describes the treatment of food poisoning by magic (Lebrun, 1979).

Of the extensive textual evidence that exists for plants in Anatolia at the time of the Hittites and which we know had medical use elsewhere in contemporary Late Bronze Age societies of the Eastern Mediterranean, we can identify the spring-flowering crocus (*Crocus albiflorus* L.), probably the *an.tah.šum*^{SAR} (Hoffner, 1974: 16–18, 109), cumin (*Cuminum cymiumn* L.) *ú.tin.tir* (KUB XV 39) (Hoffner, 1974: 103–4), coriander (*Coriandrum sativum* L.) *še-lú*^{SAR} (Hoffner, 1974, 105–6), the broad bean (*Vicia faba* L.), *gú.gal.gal* (KBo V 5) (Hoffner, 1974: 98–9) used as a purgative (Arnott, 1996: 268) and the onion or garlic (*Alium Sepa* L.) *šuppiwašhar*$^{(SAR)}$ (KUB XXIX 7) (Hoffner, 1974: 108). The bitter vetch (*Vicia ervilia* Wild) *gú.šeš* is attested only at Boğazköy, although *ú.gú.šeš* is mentioned in Mesopotamian medical texts and has been so identified. It occurs in four texts and one of them (KBo XIII 101) shows bitter vetch being used as a component of a ritual drink which is applied to the head of a patient, accompanied by an incantation, to drive away evil from the eyes, likely to be an eye disease (Hoffner, 1974: 99–104). Wine would also have been used for both internal and external applications as it is antiseptic (although not known to them as such) and could have been used, for example, for cleaning wounds and ulcers.

MEDICAL PRACTITIONERS: PALACE AND COMMUNITY

The Hittite texts tell us that like many of their contemporary societies in Mesopotamia, Syro-Palestine and the Aegean, medicine would have developed along the lines of having both magico-religious and practical elements, and therefore amongst the early Hittites, there developed two contemporaneous sets of medical practitioners, the magical-expert and the practical healer, who would have been at the same time, supplementary, competitive and interactive.

For the word for 'physician' or practical healer, the Hittites adopted the Sumerian word ^{LÚ}A.ZU or the Akkadian *asû*, 'one who practices a physician's skill' (Ritter, 1965) which I shall henceforth refer to as a physician, although he would have probably primarily served royal households and other elite families. The corresponding word in Hittite is seemingly lost. He would have undertaken the practice of medicine, dispensing herbal remedies, focusing on obvious symptoms and likely performing very minor surgical operations. According to Beckman, the physician is attested in a number of texts (Beckman, 1990: 630), some dating back to the Old Kingdom. It is also possible that a hieroglyph that appears on a number of seals denotes a physician (Rainer and Güterbock, 1987: 66 no. 188; Beckman, 1990: 630).

Although most references to physicians are general, eight are known by name (Beckman, 1993: 28): Akiya, Hutubi, Lurma, Zarpiya, the Egyptian Pariamahu, the Akkadian Rabâ-sa-Marduk (Burde, 1974: 5 n. 13), and the Luwian Tuwatta-ziti and Piha-Tarhunta (Burde, 1974: 3–5). To this list can also be added Mittanamuwa, who cared for the young King Hattušili III, although the title given to him (KBo IV 12) is GAL DUB.SAR, or 'chief of the scribes' (Beckman, 1990: 630). There are also references to the 'overseer of the physicians' or UGULA ^{LÚ}A.ZU (KUB V 12), 'chief of physicians' or GAL $^{LÚ.MEŠ}$A.ZU (IBoT II 44), as well as 'head physician' or LÚA.ZU TAG (KBo XXI 42) and 'apprentice or junior physician' ^{LÚ}A.ZU TUR KAB.ZU.ZU (KBo XI 1), from which Beckman deduces that the profession was hierarchically structured (Beckman, 1990: 631). Nothing is known of their education or training. The vast majority were men, but as in ancient Egypt, a few may have been women; and there are two attestations of female physicians in KUB XXX 42 and KUB XXXIX 31, although Otten and Rüster believe that these references from the Hittite texts refer not to female physicians (*âsu*) working in the Hittite Empire, but in the mixed cultural area of north Syria and Upper Mesopotamia in the middle of the second millennium BC. They refer to the mention in one of the Mari letters to two female physicians listed by name and occupation (Otten and Rüster, 1993). It seems, therefore, that in the heart of the Hittite Empire as well as in Mesopotamia, the medical profession was essentially the preserve of men (Beckman, 1993: 28 n. 25). However, in texts emphasising the magical approach, women are very prominent (Beckman, 1993: 28, 36–7).

Hittite laws are known from the early Old Kingdom, and in them, the physician is recognised. In the laws on assault and compensation (KBo VI 2, KBo VI 3, KBo VI 5, KBo XXIX 13) (Goetze, 1969a: 189; Hoffner, 1997: 23–4, 176–7) it is recorded that:

> 'If anyone injures a (free) person and temporarily incapacitates him, he shall provide medical care for him. In his place he shall provide a person to work on his estate until he recovers. When he recovers, (his assailant) shall pay him 6 shekels of silver and shall pay the physician's fee as well (Hoffner, 1997: 23–4, Law §10).

An earlier Late Kingdom later parallel version of this law (KBo VI 4) (Hrozný, 1922: 74–99; Friedrich, 1959: 48–61; Hoffner, 1997: 24) reads:

> 'If anyone injures a free man's head, he shall provide medical care for him. And in his place he shall provide a person to work on his estate until he recovers. When he recovers, (his assailant) shall pay him 10 shekels of silver and shall pay the 3 shekel physician's fee as well. If it is a slave, he shall pay 2 shekels of silver (Hoffner, 1997: 24).

This is significant in that it establishes the physician within the law, although it does not specify whether such an individual practised within the community or served the ruling elite. In some cases fines are graded according to the social status or sex of the offender (Roth, 1995: 215–16) and no doubt the status of the physician varied the size of his fee accordingly. Hoffner points out that the later edition extends the coverage of the law to slaves. The ratio of 10:2 (or 5:1) for compensation for free to slave is not the usual one, which is 2:1 (Hoffner, 1997: 177). It should be noted that in the New Kingdom the law does not specify a physician's fee in the case of a slave.

As Beckman points out, the actual contexts in which Hittite physicians practised their medicine marks the inadequacy of their culture to make a distinction between the magical and the medical in the healing process (Beckman, 1993: 27). For example, the measures taken by the physician Zarpiya against plague (CTH 757) are entirely magical, consisting of a ritual meal and incantations (Beckman, 1990: 631). There are also records of physicians participating in cult activities with no connection with healing as in a festival at Nerik where a physician chants in the Hattic (or Hittite) language (KUB XXVIII 80), or a ritual for Telipinu in which a physician sings whilst accompanying himself on a musical instrument (KUB LIII 15) (Beckman, 1990: 631).

There was also the magical-healer, the Akkadian *āšipu*, or 'incantation priest', which would seem to describe their activities more accurately (Beckman, 1990: 631). Unlike the *asû* they were probably literate and dealt with diagnostics, incantations and perhaps also physiognomy. Their aim would have been healing in a holistic sense and they were also distinct from the *asû* or physician who were focused on immediate medical problems and treated them. However, they both worked at the royal court at Hattuša (Beckman, 1983a: 108), although much of the activity of the *āšipu* would have been in the temple. There was an incantation priest at the court of King Muršili II (KBo 16 99) and an incantation priest and a physician at the court of King Muwatali (KBo 1 10), and an incantation priest at the court of King Hattušili III (KUB III 7). The primary role of the *āšipu* was both the diagnosis of ailments and the provision of magical cures, although they probably would have referred patients to the *asû*, a practitioner of more rational skills, working with herbal remedies and bandages. Generally, the Hittites would not have differentiated between therapies based upon physiological techniques such as the administration of drugs, the treatment of injured limbs and occasionally surgery, with those of a purely magical character; they likely applied both types of intervention in a unified regimen of treatment. Spirits or deities would largely have been considered responsible for a disease, condition or dysfunction, and as a consequence, invocations made to a healing god, possibly Kamrusepa, god of magic and healing, to cure them (Beckman, 1993: 30–6).

The royal courts of Hatti did not confine themselves to the talents of native physicians, but sought additional expertise from abroad (Beckman, 1993: 631). The importation from the royal courts of Egypt and Mesopotamia of physicians is well documented in the diplomatic correspondence found at Hattuša and elsewhere. Foreign physicians and incantation priests were viewed as 'prestige goods' and the transfer of a physician from one court to another was part of the dynamics and formal apparatus of the practice of gift-exchange (Zaccagnini, 1983: 250). For example, there is a letter, dated to *c.* 1300 BC, sent from Pharaoh Rameses II to King Hattušili III (1275–1250 BC), and another to Queen Puduhepa, concerning two royal physicians obviously in great demand, present and practising at the court of King Kurunta of Tarhuntassa, the nephew of King Hattušili III, and a Hittite vassal (Bryce, 1998: 296). One of these tablets (KUB III 67) asks the king to pass an Egyptian physician named Pariamakhû on to another Hittite vassal king, and on the other (KUB III 66) to permit two other Egyptian physicians at the court of Tarhuntassa to return home. Perhaps they had failed to cure the king. One of the texts (KUB III 67) also includes references to the preparation of herbal remedies by the physician. It reads:

> '…now I have clamoured for a learned physician (and) they have allowed Pariamakhû to come so as to prepare herbs from Kurunta, the king of Tarhuntassa; and he requested (a selection) from all the herbs in accordance with what you had written me…' (Goetze, 1947: 248).

Medical assistance from Egypt to the Hittites is well documented (Edel, 1976), and there is also another letter (CTH 155) from Pharaoh Rameses II to King Hattušili III, which attests to the dispatch of medicines to treat the king's eye problems.

> 'And I had all good drugs brought for the eyes of my Brother, and I had a Chariot Officer go with Pirihnawa and the Officer went to Bentesina Prince of Amurri with my Ambassador; and gave him all the drugs, and Bentesina had a sargu-officer go to my Brother with the drugs…and I wrote a letter to the Prince of Amurri…I had a medicine brought to my Brother for his eyes' (Beckman, 1990: 631).

A physician is not sent, but a known Egyptian emissary, Pirihnawa, is asked to deliver the necessary drugs. As to whether a specific medication was asked for on the basis of a diagnosis made by the Egyptian physician in the Hittite court is not known, but what we do know from this letter is that there was a delay in delivering the drugs, which the Pharaoh had to confirm, but denies any responsibility (Beckman, 1990: 631).

The oddest request is Hattušili's letter to the Pharaoh, now in the form of three complimentary fragments (Edel, 1976: 68–75; Beckman, 1983b: 253–4; Beckman, 1990: 631), requesting that he send a gynaecologist to Hattuša to aid his sister, Princess Matanazi, in conceiving (Royal Letter 652/f+28/n+127n). It reads:

'[That which my brother] wrote [to me concerning] Mata[n]az[i], his [sis]ter: 'Let my brother send a man, so that medicines might be prepared for her, so that she might be caused to give birth!' '(Edel, 1976: 68–75).

The reply of the Pharaoh was forthright, according to this translation by Edel; although acting diplomatically he did agree to send a physician and incantation priest, supplied with the necessary drugs, in the vain hope that a miracle might occur:

'So (spoke) Wasmuarea Satepnare (Rameses II) The Great King, the King of the Land of Egypt, Son of the Sun, Ramesešsa. Mai-Am ana (Beloved of Amun), the Great King, the King of the Land of Egypt to Hattušili, the Great King, the King of the Land of Hatti, my brother: See, I find myself well, I, King of the Land of Egypt, your Brother. So to my Brother: What my Brother wrote to me on account of Matanazi, my sister. My brother would like me to send a man to prepare for her a drug to let her be with child. So has my brother written. So do I say to my Brother. See, Matanazi, the sister of my brother, the King your brother knows her, Is she fifty years old? Nonsense! She is sixty. And see, a woman fifty years old, No! one who is sixty, One cannot prepare for her a drug, to let her be with child. Indeed, the Sun god and the Weather god may — to please her — Issue an order and the dispositions thereof will be lastingly dispensed to her and I, the King, your Brother, Will send you an able exorciser priest and an able physician. And they will prepare to her intent drugs so that she be with child. Now I am sending you a greetings present' (Edel, 1976: 69).

The sheer naiveté of Hattušili's first letter tells us a great deal about the limitations of Hittite medical knowledge, and the difference between a developed and underdeveloped medical culture. Beckman is of the view that if there were those in the Hittite royal court who knew something about the treatment of gynaecological problems, then the king might have been advised of the absurdity of his request (Beckman, 1983b: 254).

There are other instances of Hittite kings requesting Egyptian royal physicians (Zaccagnini, 1983: 247–8, 250–3; Beckman, 1983: 106–7; Cline, 1995: 276–7). The most significant are King Hattušili III's letters (CTH 172) written in Akkadian to King Kadašman-Enlil II of Babylon in c. 1280 BC, concerning two Babylonian physicians and two incantation priests sent to Hattuša (Oppenheim, 1967: 145; Zaccagnini, 1983: 251). One letter concerns an incident in around 1270 BC, when the King of Babylon sent a physician to the Hittite court, where he unfortunately died. The Hittite king's letter to him is full of excuses and regrets for the incident, and why an incantation priest, similarly sent, decided to remain at Hattuša. The text reads:

'Say t[o my brother] concerning the physician whom my brother dispatched here: 'When they received the physician, he accomplished many [go]od thin[gs]. When disease seized him, I exerted myself constantly on his behalf. I performed many extispicies for him, but when his (appointed) day […] arrived, he died…I would in no way have detained the physician.' Sa[y (further) to my brother:] 'When they received an incantation priest (*āšipu*) and a physician (*asû*) during the reign of my brother Muwatalli and detained him [in Hat]ti, I argued with him, saying Why are you detaining them? Detaining [them] is not correct! And should I now have detained the physician? [Of the for]mer [experts] whom they received here, perhaps the incantation priest died, [but the physician] is alive — the woman whom he married is a relative of mine — and proprietor of a fine household. [If he should say] that 'I will go (back) to my native land! let him arise and go […] Would I have detained a great physician of the Marduk?' (Beckman, 1983a: 106–7 n. 49)

These texts are particularly significant in that they indicate that physicians and the incantation priests imported from foreign powers were of significant importance in the royal court to warrant the personal attention of the king and his diplomatic correspondence.

The Hittite kings called in not only foreign physicians but also foreign healing deities, such as the healing god of Ahhiyawâ. A divination text of great length (KUB V 6) found at Hattuša and dated to *c.* 1330 BC, during the reign of King Muršili II (*c.* 1350–1320 BC) (Sommer, 1932: 283; Huxley, 1960: 5, text no. 10; Košak, 1980: 42; Mellink, 1983: 140; Güterbock, 1983: 134; Bryce, 1989a: 8 n. 36; Cline, 1994: 122. C8) concerns the king's illness, a speech affliction, possibly brought on by a mild stroke, if the symptom as described by the king himself 'my mouth went sideways' (CTH 486) is to be properly understood (Bryce, 1998: 238–40). It records both questions and answers put to an oracle by divination priests to find out the cause of the divine anger against him. The text, in part (KUB V 6 II 57–60) reads:

'The deity from Ahhiyawâ and the deity from Lazpa…afflicted persons, and also my Sun (myself)…' and 'Likewise, also for the deity from Ahhiyawâ and the deity from Lazpa three days…' (Sommer, 1932: 283).

The god of Ahhiyawâ, as well as the god of Lazpa, most likely in the form of a localised cult statuette, and his own personal god had been summoned to succour him, but was unaware of the correct ritual, suggesting that the representations of the Aegean deities were not accompanied by attendants. There is no indication in the tablet of where Ahhiyawâ or Lazpa are located, but assuming, as many scholars have suggested, Ahhiyawâ is the Mycenaean heartland (Huxley, 1960; Cline, 1994: 69–70; *contra* Košak, 1980), or at least a Mycenaean state on the Eastern Aegean coast, and Lazpa is Lesbos (Huxley, 1960: 12–13), the Hittite officials would have known enough of the reputation and sacral contents of Mycenaean healing cult to send for one of their deities to benefit the ailing king (Mellink, 1983: 140). This suggests the Mycenaeans worshipped a god of healing whose fame and potency spread as far as the Hittite Empire of central Anatolia (Arnott, 1996: 267). As for the healing deity from Lazpa, Huxley is of the view that it can be identified with the Lesbian pre-Greek oracular deity, Smintheus, later identified with Apollo (Huxley, 1960: 13).

Other than what we know from some New Kingdom religious medical texts that include some therapies, where both the texts and archaeology are generally silent is any explanation about the day-to-day practice of Hittite medicine. No medical or surgical instruments have been found, and it is only possible to conjecture that instruments similar to those found in a Mycenaean chamber tomb at Nauplion and dated to *c*. 1425 BC (Arnott, 1997: 271–5) or mentioned in a text (UT 2050) found at Ugarit (Ras Shamra) (Steiglitz, 1981: 52–5) of similar date, were used by Hittite healers.

Of surgical practice of the period, there is, at present, little evidence. However, the cut-off part of the occipital region of a cranium, found in Level II at Kültepe-Karum (*c*. 2000–1850 BC), ancient Kaneš, and examined by Senyürek, shows evidence of proficient trepanation on an approximately 50 year old male, with evidence of healing and osseous regeneration around the operation site, showing signs that it was successful and that the patient lived for some time after undergoing the operation (Senyürek, 1958: 51–2). An Early Chalcolithic (*c*. 4000 BC) trepanation has recently been identified at Kuraçay-Höyök, in which a drill may have been used (Güleç, 1995: 6). Until this discovery, the oldest recorded trepanation in the region has come from Elmali-Karatas (522 Ka.), dated to approximately 2300 BC, where a female was unsuccessfully trepanned after a massive left temporal head injury (Angel, 1966: 255). This suggests that trepanation was known in central and southern Anatolia much earlier than the beginning of the second millennium BC, although not referred to in the texts.

OBSTETRICS AND GYNAECOLOGY

Some of the texts also refer to gynaecological problems, although, as we have seen, the correspondence between King Hattušili III and the Pharaoh Rameses II concerning the infertility of Hattušili's sister, leads one to conclude that Hittite physicians had no real knowledge of understanding of gynaecology.

As regards obstetrics, although we know from the textual records a great deal about Hittite birth ritual (Beckman, 1983b; Pringle, 1983), and placing the religious elements aside for one moment, it is possible to detect from the texts some details of basic rational obstetric practice. For example, there is the use of specific furniture and equipment. Births occurred in the mother's own home, where the midwife would put out two stools or ^{GIŠ}*kuppiššar* (Symington, 1996: 118–19) and three cushions (KUB XXX 29), or two footstools (KBo XVII 62+63) (Beckman, 1983b: 250), with the mother sat on one and the midwife facing her on the other, with a cushion or blanket also placed in between to catch the baby immediately upon delivery (Beckman, 1983b: 102–4, 151; Pringle, 1983: 132; Beckman, 1993: 36–8). The concept of a woman giving birth in the seated position was already well known in the Neolithic period. A clay figurine from Çatal Hüyük is of a seated woman in the act of parturition, supported by two felines (Mellaart, 1967: 156).

The only mention of possible surgical aids in the midwife's equipment is of a midwife preparing some objects, most for cleaning the newly-born baby, and a bronze knife (KBo XVII 61) that may have been used to cut the umbilical cord. Four bronze pegs are also mentioned (KUB IX 22) (Beckman, 1983b: 99), but they have ritual use, with the best explanation whereby objects were hung on them to ward off evil during the birth, although this is uncertain (Pringle, 1983: 133). The principal practitioners or midwives were women — the ^{SAL}*haš(ša)nupalla-* or Sumerian ^{MÍ}ŠÀ.ZU — literally the 'woman who knows the internal organs' (von Soden, 1957–8: 119–21), whose practice included incantations during the birth itself and again after the birth to ward off evil sprits, and the ^{SAL}*hašauwa-*, meaning the 'one of birth giving', or specialist midwife, identified with the 'wise woman' of the family or community, whose specialisations may have included midwife, nurse or wet-nurse and magico-ritual attendant. She may be the same as the Sumerian ^{MÍ}ŠU.GI or 'Old Woman' of the Hittite Old Kingdom, who performed a wide variety of simple purificatory and healing rituals (Beckman, 1983b: 233–5; Pringle, 1983: 132–4; Beckman, 1993: 36–8).

The mass of the native population of Hatti were peasants, apparently free to move within the country but subject to labour obligations called *luzzi* and presumably to a form of taxation in kind. A number were, however, slaves (Goetze, 1957: 103). Their ailments, diseases and trauma would have been treated in the community by various forms of practitioner, perhaps dominated by the 'wise-woman' or ^{SAL}*hašauwa-*, or other forms, which combined both practical and magical elements. Some would have worked with herbal medicine, performing unsophisticated surgery, such as the removal of bladder stones, or simple ear, nose and throat procedures. For example, midwives with a much wider healing competence are well known from other early societies. Some were possible barbers or smiths with particular skills, perhaps dentistry, put to everyday use. Some may even have been peripatetic. However, the Hittite texts are records of royal courts and their vassals, and it is unlikely that what went on amongst the poor will ever be known.

DISEASE AND TRAUMA

There are records of Kings Šuppiluliuma I dying in 1340 BC and Arnuwanda II dying in 1339 BC, probably as the result of an epidemic of unknown nature and aetiology, which started in 1346 BC, when a Hittite army under the command of Arnuwanda, son of King Šuppiluliuma I (1380–1340 BC), crossed the Egyptian frontiers in southern Syria and launched an attack on towns and cities in the region. Many thousands of

Egyptian prisoners-of-war were taken and transported back to the Hittite homeland. The prisoners brought back with them an epidemic disease, which for the next twenty years spread throughout the kingdom and decimated its population (Gurney, 1980: 33; Bryce, 1998: 198–9). Large armies billeted under poor sanitary conditions would have been exposed to any number of cyclical epidemics. This epidemic, which lasted from approximately 1346–1320 BC, and which decimated the population, is the principal subject of the 'plague prayers' of King Muršili II (1339–1306 BC) (KUB XIV 8 and duplicates KUB XIV 10+KUB XXVI 86, KUB XIV 11 and KUB XXIV 1–4), which also appears in oracle questions (KUB V 4; KUB XV 1; KUB XV 15) and in administrative correspondence (KBo XVIII 10) (Beckman, 1990: 629–30). They look to be a desperate appeal to the gods to understand the epidemic and for it to end. In one prayer, which outlines the effect of the epidemic on the economy, King Muršili pleads:

> 'What is this, o gods, that you have done? A plague you have let into the land. The land of Hatti, all of it, is dying; so no one prepares sacrificial loaves and libations for you. The ploughmen who used to work the fields of the god are dead…Man has lost his wits, and there is nothing that we do aright. Oh gods, whatever sin you behold, either let a prophet rise and declare it, or let the sibyls or the priests learn about it by incubation, or let man see it in a dream! Oh gods, take pity again on the land of Hatti! On the one hand it is afflicted with a plague, on the other hand, it is afflicted with hostility. The protectorates beyond the frontier (namely) the land of Mitanni and the land of Arzawa, each one has rebelled…Moreover those countries which belong of Hatti, (namely) the land of Kaska, also the land of Arawawna, the land of Kalasma, the land of Lukka, the land of Pitassa — these lands have also renounced the Sun goddess of Arinna… Now all the surrounding countries have begun to attack the land of Hatti. Let it again become a matter of concern to the Sun goddess Arinna! On god, bring not your name into disrepute!' (Translation after Goetze, 1969b: 396). Plague Prayers of Muršili II to the Sun Goddess Arinna, KUB XXIV 3(+) (CTH 376).

The precise nature and aetiology of this epidemic that afflicted the Hittites remains unknown. Smallpox is a strong possibility; but it would appear they could do nothing to combat large scale mortality other than to seek divine intervention and remove their most important officials to a place of safety (Beckman, 1990: 630). How the epidemic ended is also unknown, but what is known is that it could well have had a significant effect on the economy and possibly the social structure. This may well be the same epidemic (the 'Canaanite' or 'Asiatic' sickness) that some think seriously affected Egypt during the Amarna period of the New Kingdom which was similarly brought back by the Egyptian army from Syria (Goedicke, 1984). What we do know is that in order to prevent further spread of the disease, all contacts between the Hittites and the Egyptians remained frozen for over thirty years (Goedicke, 1984: 92).

The few recorded medical conditions in which a physician was consulted for which we have evidence include diseases of the eyes (KUB XXII 61), of the throat (KUB XLVIII 123), fever (KUB XXXIV 45 + KBo XVI 63), 'plague' (KBo XVI 99) and reproductive problems (KBo VIII 130; KBo XXVIII 30). Symptoms recorded in both the diagnostic and prescriptions texts are not precise enough to allow for the recognition of any specific or non-specific disease, as are the unspecified illnesses that affected prominent persons such as an important early Late Kingdom official, perhaps a member of the royal family, named Kantuzzili (CTH 373, esp. KUB XXX 10), King Hattušili III's first wife Queen Gaššuliawiya (CTH 380) and the king himself, who was a sickly child (KBo IV 12) and was often ill as an adult, a condition reflected in the vow made by his second wife, Queen Puduhepa, to the goddess Lelwani seeking improvements in his health (CTH 585) (Beckman, 1990: 630).

In the two millennia before the Old Kingdom, innovations associated with agriculture would have heightened exposure to infectious diseases. While agriculture increased the availability of food for humans, it also had negative repercussions in terms of human health and nutrition, which if expressed in terms of deficiencies, may have made humans more susceptible to disease. Various diseases were associated with animal husbandry and the expansion of agriculture to new environments, and the domestication of animals brought the potential of contracting animal-borne diseases or zoonoses, such as tuberculosis and brucellosis. Spectacular growth in population, with its concentration in urban centres, presented the greatest risk to health as it increased densities above the limits imposed by various parasitic and infectious diseases. Even ploughing the soil probably increased the risk of acquiring fungal diseases and tetanus. Human nucleation into larger communities that followed the development of agriculture brought increased population sizes and densities and a greater likelihood of exposure to droplet-borne infectious agents, and facilitated the spread of many of them, which also brought with it health problems associated with sanitation and the contamination of food and water supplies by human detritus and the wastes of domesticated animals, with its inherent risk of causing disease. Urbanisation brought with it standing water reservoirs, breeding grounds of the vectors of parasitic diseases such as malaria.

Extended trade also enhanced the possibility of the spread of infectious agents between different parts of the Ancient Near East and the Eastern Mediterranean, such as the epidemic which struck the Hittite Empire between the reigns of Kings Šuppiluliuma I and Muršili II, and the wholesale movement of populations in the prehistory of Anatolia may well have led to the introduction and spread of new infectious diseases (Cockburn, 1963: 87). The development of remedies was likely stimulated by need, and practical medicine as we know it today will have arisen parallel to the increase of diseases of civilisation (Wells, 1978: 5–13; Johns, 1990: 263).

For those who owned the land and controlled trade, good living and a nutritious diet would have been a reality; but not for the ordinary people — the vast majority who worked the land, or as labourers or craftsmen in the towns. Although the everyday life of the ordinary citizens was mostly concerned with agriculture, and therefore the principal unit of society was the small village community, many would have been crowded together into a few densely-populated urban centres, and been subject to the many diseases that were endemic in the Near East and Eastern Mediterranean at this time. In these towns, like Hattuša, overcrowding, poor sanitation, and possible contamination of drinking water, when combined with a meagre, unbalanced and often seasonal diet, would have taken its toll on the population, weakening resistance to diseases such as dysentery, hookworm and tetanus, and in children, rickets. Immunity to infection would have begun to disappear so even childhood diseases such as infant diarrhoea, diphtheria, whooping cough and scarlet fever would often have been fatal. Another significant parasitical disease, largely seasonal, would have been malaria, especially *Falciparum* malaria, which would have been found in both coastal and highland regions.

Like most contemporary societies, the average life expectancy of the Hittites was low. Research by Senyürek fixed the average age of deceased adults in Early Bronze Age Anatolia at 35 for men and 28 for women (Senyürek, 1951a: 447–68; 1957: 95–110). This is explained by the increase in the number of various infectious diseases and the overall effect of a process of urbanisation on a considerable number of the population. Senyürek's work on the Hittite period graves from Alaca Höyük, Aliçar Höyük, Karaoglan and Kasura (Senyürek, 1947: 55–66) and Krogman's work also at Aliçar Höyük (Krogman, 1937: 213–84) have, however, not provided precise enough information in order to confirm this hypothesis.

The population of Hattuša has been estimated by Macqueen to have been approximately forty thousand (Macqueen, 1986: 77), and was certainly large enough to sustain certain communicable density dependent diseases such as poliomyelitis, tuberculosis, cholera, typhoid and smallpox. At the same time, both urban and rural social conditions must have created the conditions for the existence of avitaminosis, rickets and scurvy, together with a whole range of degenerative diseases associated with heavy manual labour, such as osteoarthritis, osteoporosis and periostisis, not to mention examples of bone fractures, the most common being forearm and spinal injuries. (Angel, 1974: 9–18) With the Hittites being so often at war, battle injuries both for the warrior elites and the common foot soldier would have been common. However, much more palaeopathological evidence is required in order to substantiate these claims. However, the insufficiency of studied human skeletal remains only allows for these preliminary conclusions.

PUBLIC HEALTH

Sufficiently large areas of Hittite towns have been excavated to give a reasonable picture of the layout and domestic architecture. Attention was paid to town planning and to problems of drainage and sanitation. Some streets had large drainage channels, painstakingly built and roofed with stone slabs, running down the middle and connected to lesser channels or clay pipes which carried dirty water into them from the houses of the elites on either side. Similar channels drained public buildings and crossed open spaces. The urban houses of the non-elites, which had no such drainage systems, varied in shapes and sizes dependent upon the space available, and were usually built together in self-contained blocks enclosed by roads and lanes (Macqueen, 1986: 61). A review of Hittite drainage, water supply and public health has been published by Ünal (1993). He offers a similar picture of limited infrastructure and what there is largely restricted to the elite. However, the larger Hittite cities such as Hattusa-Boğazköy were built upon steep hillsides and slopes, which would allow an element of natural drainage. As Ünal notes from Kbo X 37: 'As the rain water cleanses the streets from urine and filth.' This suggests that because of the lack of sanitation outside the elite areas, those streets were being used as toilets (Ünal, 1993: 120). Not only unpleasant, it would have led to increased incidence of ova, worms and other parasites as carriers of infectious diseases and the pollutants of the storage and supply of drinking water. This seems to contradict what we know of the so-called concept of cleanliness, but as Ünal points out (1993: 121), this relates to ritual purity and not domestic cleanliness; trying to ward off the consequences of impurity in some way as they dealt with maladies as they relate to magic.

The very existence of 'washing houses' or bathtubs in some houses, and certain cleanliness rituals, imply that the Hittites were concerned with physical purity. Not so, as Ünal points out; physical and spiritual purity were valuable commodities in religious life only, and they lacked hygienic rules in everyday life (Ünal, 1993: 123). As in many other ancient societies, the neglect of hygiene and public health was a contributory factor to the spread of disease. There are some texts which related to the sanitary practices of the King and Queen, but again, they relate more to the place of the royal family in the religious structure of society and have little significance in our understanding of overall sanitary practices of the time (Ünal, 1993: 128–36).

Water supply and waste water disposal in Hittite urban centres has been summarised by Ünal, who emphasises the problems of collecting and storing rainwater, a threat to public health itself, together with drainage that seems to have served only public buildings and elite dwellings (Ünal, 1993: 124–6, 137–9).

EPILOGUE

Based upon the little textual and palaeopathological evidence that exists, it has been no easy matter to discover what we now know of disease and the practice of Hittite medicine. Whilst Hittite medicine was no doubt greatly influenced by imported medical texts and practices from Mesopotamia, physicians from Egypt and Mesopotamia, or a healing deity from the Mycenaeans, Beckman has established that a native Hittite medical practice is reflected in the medical texts written in the Hittite language and in areas such as pregnancy and childbirth (Beckman, 1990: 631). But in all aspects of Hittite medicine, magic and the priests would have dominated.

Some however, including Ünal, believe that there were no truly rational medical practices in the Hittite world (Ünal, 1993: 123–4). He believes that the *āšipu* were the more realistic and proficient in treating ailments because some of their practices were 'empirical and therefore pseudo-medical' (Ünal, 1993: 124; Burde, 1974: 3), and that the *asû* were really only like community practitioners who presumably used folk remedies already widely known, and copied Mesopotamian and Egyptian medical practices (Ünal, 1993: 124). This is, of course, too simplistic a solution to account for what was likely to be a complex interplay of many types of practice that would have existed, including various forms of healers working amongst the peasants and slaves, and others, both *asû*, *āšipu* and the ᔆᴬᴸ*hašauwa-*.

Other than the study of the physical anthropology of crania (Angel, 1951; Senyürek, 1951b: 43–61; 1956: 205–9; 1959: 57–84), which has produced largely insignificant and often irrelevant results, and the work of Angel on osteoarthritis (Angel, 1978: 38–43), little palaeopathological work has so far been undertaken in order to evaluate what the non-cremated skeletal remains from Hittite cemeteries can tell us about what palaeopathology can reveal in terms of disease, trauma, and to some extent, medical practice (Roberts and Manchester, 1995: 2–14).

For the future, those working on deciphering the texts from Boğazköy and elsewhere, will, no doubt, bring a great deal more to our attention in the next few years. However, much of the future belongs to the palaeopathologists, and what they can tell us about the nature of disease, medical practice, and the social and economic history of the period. It may be that we should now make the study of the skeletal material in their graves as the *starting* point for the correct interpretation of the remaining finds.

ACKNOWLEDGEMENTS

This paper was first read on 4 January 1999 to a meeting of the British Association for Near Eastern Archaeology, held at the University of Birmingham, and I am grateful to all those who stimulated me with comments at the time. I also acknowledge with thanks the help or valued criticism of Professor Gary M. Beckman, Dr. Irving L. Finkel, Professor Mark Geller, Professor Harry A. Hoffner, Jr., Dr. Alasdair Livingstone, Professor Wilfred Lambert FBA, Dr. Frances Reynolds, Professor Marten Stol, and Dr. Siân Williams, although any errors or solecisms are mine alone. This work would not have been possible without the financial support of The Wellcome Trust, to whom I am, as always, deeply indebted.

ABBREVIATIONS IN THE TEXT

CTH	*Catalogue des textes hittite.* After E. Laroche, *Catalogue des textes hittites*, 1971, Paris: Éditions Klincksieck (*Études et commentaires* 75).
IBoT	*Istanbul Arkeoloji Müzelerinde bulunan Boğazköy Tabletleri (unden Seçme Metinler)*, vols. I–III, Istanbul, 1944, 1947, 1954.
KBo	*Keilschrifttexte aus Boghazköi*, vols. I–VI, Leipzig, 1916–23, vols. VII– (in progress), Berlin, 1923–.
KUB	*Keilschrifturkunden aus Boghazköi*, vols. I– (in progress), Berlin, 1921–.

BIBLIOGRAPHY

Angel, J. L.
(1951) *Troy: The Human Remains*, Supplementary Monograph I, *Troy: excavations conducted by the University of Cincinnati, 1932–1938*, Princeton: Princeton University Press.
(1966) 'Appendix: Human skeletal remains at Karatas', in Machteld J. Mellink, 'Excavations at Karatas-Semayük in Lycia, 1965', *American Journal of Archaeology* 70: 255–7.
(1974) 'Patterns of fractures from Neolithic to modern times', *Anthrop. Közlemenyek* 18: 9–18.
(1978) 'Osteoarthritis in prehistoric Turkey and medieval Byzantium', *Henry Ford Hospital Medical Journal* 27: 38–43.

Arnott, Robert
(1996) 'Healing and medicine in the Aegean Bronze Age', *Journal of the Royal Society of Medicine* 89: 265–70.
(1997) 'Surgical practice in the Prehistoric Aegean', *Medizinhistorisches Journal* 32: 249–78.

Beckman, Gary M.
(1983a) *Hittite Birth Rituals*, 2nd ed., Wiesbaden: Otto Harrassowitz (*Studien zu den Boğazköy-Texten* 29).
(1983b) 'Mesopotamians and Mesopotamian learning at Hattusa', *Journal of Cuneiform Studies* 35: 7–114.
(1990) 'Medizin. B. Bei den Hethitern', in *Reallexikon der Assyriologie und Vorderasiatischen Archäologie*, Band 7, Lieferung 7/8, Berlin: Walter de Gruyter, pp. 629–31.
(1993) 'From cradle to grave: women's role in Hittite medicine and magic', *Journal of Ancient Civilizations* 8: 25–39.

Bittel, K.
(1970) *Hattusha, the Capital of the Hittites*, New York: Oxford University Press.

Bryce, T. R.
(1989) 'The nature of Mycenaean involvement in Western Anatolia', *Historia* 38: 1–21.
(1998) *The Kingdom of the Hittites*, Oxford: Oxford University Press.

Burde, Cornelia
(1974) *Hethitische medizinische Texte*, Wiesbaden: Otto Harrassowitz (*Studien zu den Boğazköy-Texten* 19).

Cline, Eric H.
(1994) *Sailing the Wine-Dark Sea: International Trade and the Late Bronze Age Aegean*, vol. S 591, British Archaeological Reports, International Series, Oxford: Tempus Reparatum.
(1995) 'Tinker, tailor, soldier, sailor: Minoans and Mycenaeans abroad', in Robert Laffineur and Wolf-Dietrich Niemeier (eds.), *Politeia: Society and State in the Aegean Bronze Age, Proceedings of the 5th International Aegean Conference, University of Heidelberg Archäologisches Institut, 10–13 April 1994*, Liège, Histoire de l'art et archéologie de la Grèce antique, University of Liège (*Aegaeum* 12), pp. 265–83.

Cockburn, Aiden
(1963) *The Evolution and Eradication of Infectious Diseases*, Baltimore: Johns Hopkins University Press.

Edel, Elmar
(1976) *Ägyptische Ärzte und ägyptische Medizin am hethitischen Königshof: Neue Funde von Keilschriftbriefen Rameses II aus Boğazköy*, Düsseldorf, Rheinisch-Westfälische Akademie der Wissenschaften, Vorträge, G205.

Friedrich, Johannes
(1959) *Die hethitischen Gesetze*, Leiden: E. J. Brill (Documenta et Monumenta Orientis Antiqui 7).

Goedicke, Hans
(1984) 'The Canaanite Illness', *Studien zur Altägyptischen Kultur* **11**: 91–105 (Festschrift für Wolfgang Helck zu seinen 70. Geburtstag).

Goetze, Albrecht
(1947) 'A new letter from Rameses to Hattusilis', *Journal of Cuneiform Studies* **1**: 241–51.
(1957) *Kulturgeschichte Kleinasiens*, 2nd ed., Munich (*Handbuch der Altertumswissenschaft* III/1 iii).
(1969a) 'The Hittite laws', in J. B. Pritchard (ed.), *Ancient Near Eastern Texts related to the Old Testament*, 3rd ed., Princeton: Princeton University Press, pp. 199–7.
(1969b) 'Hittite prayers', in J. B. Pritchard (ed.), *Ancient Near Eastern Texts related to the Old Testament*, 3rd ed., Princeton: Princeton University Press, pp. 393–401.

Grapow, H.
(1956) *Kranker, Krankheiten und Arzt*, vol. III, *Grundriss der Medizin der Alten Ägypter*, Berlin: Akademie-Verlag.

Güleç, Erskin
(1995) 'Trepanation in ancient Anatolia: six new case studies' (abstract), *Papers on Paleopathology Presented to the Twenty Second Meeting of the Paleopathology Association, Oakland, 28–29 March 1995*, Paleopathology Association, p. 6.

Gurney, O. R.
(1980) *The Hittites*, 2nd ed., Harmondsworth: Penguin Books.

Güterbock, Hans G.
(1962) 'Hittite Medicine', *Bulletin of the History of Medicine* **36**: 109–13.

Güterbock, Hans G. and M. J. Mellink
(1983) 'The Hittites and the Aegean World: 1. The Ahhiyawa problem reconsidered', *American Journal of Archaeology* **87**: 133–8.

Hoffner, Harry A. Jr.
(1974) *Alimenta Hethaeorum: Food Production in Hittite Asia Minor*, New Haven: American Oriental Society (*American Oriental Series* Vol. 55).
(1987) 'Paskuwatti's ritual against impotence (CTH 406)', *Aula Orientalis* **5**: 271–87.
(1997) *The Laws of the Hittites: A Critical Edition*, Leiden: E. J. Brill (*Documenta et Monumenta Orientis Antiqui* 23).

Hrozný, Frédéric
(1922) *Code Hittite provenant de l'Asie Mineure (vers 1350 av. J.-C.)* Part 1, *Transcriptions, traductions française*, Paris: Librairie orientaliste Paul Geunther (*Hethitica*, Volume 1, Part 1).

Huxley, G. L.
(1960) *Achaeans and Hittites*, Oxford: Vincent-Baxter Press.

Johns, Timothy
(1990) *With Bitter Herbs They Shall Eat It: Chemical Ecology and the Origins of Human Diet and Medicine*, Tucson: University of Arizona Press (*Arizona Studies in Human Ecology*).

Köcher, Frank
(1952–3) 'Ein akkadischer medizinischer Schülertext aus Boğazköy', *Archiv für Orientforschung* **16**: 47–56

Košak, S.
(1980) 'The Hittites and the Greeks', *Linguistica* **20**: 35–47.

Krogman, W. M.
(1937) 'Cranial types from Alishar Hüyük and their relation to other racial types, ancient and modern, of Europe and Western Asia', in H. H. von der Osten, *The Alishar Hüyük, seasons of 1930–1932*, Part III, Chicago: Oriental Institute, pp. 213–84.

Labat, René
(1965) 'Mesopotamia', in René Taton (ed.), *Ancient and Medieval Science from Prehistory to AD 1450, vol. I, A General History of the Sciences*, London: Thames and Hudson, pp. 65–121.

Laroche, Emmanuel
(1971) *Catalogue des textes hittites*, Paris: Éditions Klincksieck (*Études et commentaires* 75).

Lebrun, R.
(1979) 'Les rituels d'Ammihatna Tulbi et Mati contre une impurete', *Hethitica* **3**: 139–64.

Macqueen, J. G.
(1986) *The Hittites and their Contemporaries in Asia Minor*, London: Thames and Hudson.

McNeill, William H.
(1977) *Plagues and Peoples*, Oxford: Basil Blackwell.

Meier, Gerard
(1939) 'Ein akkadisches Heilungsritual aus Bogasköy', *Zeitschrift für Assyriologie* **45**: 195–215.

Mellaart, James
(1967) *Çatal Hüyük: a Neolithic Town in Anatolia*, London: Thames and Hudson.

Mellink, M. J.
(1983) 'The Hittites and the Aegean World: 2. Archaeological comments on Ahhiyawa-Achaians in Western Anatolia', *American Journal of Archaeology* **87**: 139–41.

Oppenheim, A. L.
(1967) *Letters from Mesopotamia*, Chicago: Oriental Institute.

Otten, Heinrich and Christel Rüster
(1993) 'Ärztin im hethitischen Schrifttum' in Machteld Mellink, et al., *Aspects of Art and Iconography: Anatolia and its Neighbours: Studies in Honor of Nimet Özgüc*, Ankara, pp. 539–41.

Pringle, Jackie
(1983) 'Hittite birth rituals', in Averil Cameron and Amelie Kuhrt (eds.), *Images of Women in Antiquity*, London: Croom Helm, pp. 128–41.

Rainer, M. B. and Hans G. Güterbock
(1987) *Glyptik aus dem Stadtgebiet von Boğazköy*, vol. XIV: II, *Boğazköy-Hattuša: Ergebnisse der Ausgrabungen*, Berlin: Walter de Gruyter.

Ritter, Edith K.
(1965) 'Magical-Expert (=Ašipu) and Physician (=Asû): notes on two complementary professions in Babylonian medicine', in Hans G. Güterbock and Thorkild Jacobsen (eds.), *Studies in Honor of Benno Landsberger on his Seventy-fifth Birthday, April 21, 1965*, Chicago: University of Chicago Press (*Oriental Institute of the University of Chicago Assyriological Studies* 16), pp. 299–321.

Roberts, Charlotte A. and Keith Manchester
(1995) *The Archaeology of Disease*, 2nd ed., Stroud: Alan Sutton.

Roth, Maria T.
(1995) *Law Collections from Mesopotamia and Asia Minor*, Atlanta, Georgia: Scholars Press (Writings from the Ancient World, Society for Biblical Literature, volume 6).

Schwartz, Benjamin
(1938) 'The Hittite and Luwian ritual of Zarpiya of Kizzuwatna', *Journal of the American Oriental Society* **58**: 344–53.

Starke, F.
(1985) *Die keilschrift-luwischen Texte in Umschrift*, Wiesbaden: Otto Harrassowitz (*Studien zu den Boğazköy Texten* 30).

Senyürek, M. S.
(1947) 'A note on the duration of life of the ancient inhabitants of Anatolia', *Amer.J.Phys.Anthrop.* **5**: 55–86.
(1951a) 'The longevity of the Chalcolithic and Copper Age inhabitants of Anatolia', *Türk Tarih Kurumu Basimevi Belleten* **15(60)**: 447–68.
(1951b) 'A note on the human skeletons in the Alaca Höyök Museum', *Ankara Universitesi Dil ve Tarih-Cografya Fakültesi Dergisi* **9(1–2)**: 43–61.
(1956) 'A short review of the anthropology of the ancient inhabitants of Anatolia, from the Chalcolithic age to the end of the Hittite empire', Appendix I in Seton Lloyd, *Early Anatolia*, Harmondsworth: Pelican Books, pp. 205–9.
(1957) 'The duration of life in the Chalcolithic and Copper Age population of Anatolia', *Anatolia* **2**: 95–110.
(1958) 'A case of trepanation among the inhabitants of the Assyrian trading colony of Kültepe', *Anatolia* **3**: 51–2.
(1959) 'A note on three skulls from Alaca Höyük', *Türk Tarih Kurumu Basimevi Belleten* **14(53)**: 57–84.

Sommer, F.
(1932) *Die Ahhijawa-Urkunden*, Munich: Verlag Bayerischen Akademie der Wissenschaften (C. H. Beck'schen).

Stieglitz, Robert S.
(1981) 'A physician's equipment list from Ugarit', *Journal of Cuneiform Studies* **33**: 52–5.

Symington, Dorit
(1996) 'Hittite and Neo-Hittite furniture', in Georgina Herrmann (ed.), *The Furniture of Western Asia: Ancient and Traditional*, Mainz: Philipp von Zabern, pp. 111–38.

Ünal, Ahmet
(1993) 'Ritual purity versus physical impurity in Hittite Anatolia: public health and structures for sanitation according to cuneiform texts and archaeological remains', in HIH Prince Takahito Mikasa (ed.), *Essays on Anatolian Archaeology*, Wiesbaden: Otto Harrassowitz (*Bulletin of the Middle East Center of Japan*, no. 7), pp. 119–39.

von Soden, W.
(1957–8) 'Die Hebamme in Babylonien und Assyrien', *Archiv für Orientforschung* **18**: 119–21.

Wells, Calvin
(1978) 'Disease and evolution', *Biology and Human Affairs* **43**: 5–13.

Wilhelm, Gernot
(1994) *Medizinische Omina aus Hattusa in akkadischer Sprache*, Wiesbaden: Otto Harrassowitz (*Studien zu den Boğazköy-Texten* 36).

Zaccagnini, C.
(1983) 'Patterns of mobility among ancient Near Eastern craftsmen', *Journal of Near Eastern Studies* **42**: 245–64.

THE HIPPOCRATIC PATIENT: OR AN ARCHAEOLOGY OF THE GREEK MEDICAL MIND

Niall McKeown

PROLOGUE: THE PROBLEM AND A LITTLE ASTRONOMY

Archaeologists have long been aware of the difficulties of interpreting material culture. The purpose of this paper is to sound some cautionary notes about the reading of some of the literary evidence often used to give some context to the archaeology of the classical Greek medicine: the Hippocratic medical texts. Tools tell us little unless we can place them in the context of a belief system (on the tools, see Milne, 1907; Krug, 1993: 70–103; or Bliquez, 1984 for a popular introduction). I want to examine the basic nature of those texts and the types of medicine enshrined in them. I will suggest that the success of the Hippocratic corpus is perhaps much more of a paradox than it is sometimes believed, and that to understand it fully we have to examine it more in the context of ancient *Greek* ideas and less in the context of our own.

I would like to begin, strangely enough, not with medicine, but with some astronomy. Anaxagoras was a fifth century Greek philosopher/scientist whose ideas have survived only in fragments. In one of those surviving fragments, he lays bare his ideas on the cosmos (Kirk, Ravenscroft and Schofield, 1983: 381). The earth was flat. The moisture of the earth came from evaporation from the sea. The sun, the moon and the stars were fiery hot stones. The sun was, he believed, bigger than all of southern Greece and the stars were so far away and in such a cold part of the cosmos that we could not feel their heat. The moon was lit only by the light of the sun. Finally the moon was made of earth, with plains and chasms. A striking number of correct ideas, one might feel. A pity that he believed that the earth was flat and, almost certainly, he also would have believed that the earth was at the centre of the universe and didn't move. He is, however, well on the way to a 'modern' understanding of the universe, is he not? But wait. Appearances may be deceptive. We cannot tell *how* he had come to these conclusions. Paradoxically, the areas where he could call upon the evidence of his senses would suggest that the world was flat and was the unmoving centre of the universe. After all one certainly cannot feel any sensation of the movement of the earth (which moves at some hundreds of miles per hour just on its axis, never mind its movement around the sun or the sun's movement around the centre of our galaxy, and so on) and everything falls in only one direction, which one could assume was the centre of the universe. Further, when the sun sets over the sea or a plain, what shape is described by it as it dips beneath the horizon? Not a curve, as proponents of a spherical earth might argue, but a straight line, suggesting a flat earth. Now, we cannot tell whether Anaxagoras deployed such arguments (though later Greeks did employ some of them: see Aristotle, *On the Heavens* 2.13, 294a and 2.14, 296b–7a). Nor do I have any desire to delve into the deeper mysteries of Greek astronomy.

I merely wish to make a fundamental point: we cannot assume that ancient writers think like us simply because some of their conclusions look superficially like ours, or different because their conclusions look different. Anaxagoras may be 'correct' about the surface of the moon, but how could he have known? The 'incorrect' conclusions (about the unmoving flat earth) can actually sometimes be more easily defended in terms of *our* rationality.

II. HIPPOCRATES AND IMPACT OF HIPPOCRATIC MEDICINE IN CLASSICAL GREECE

The fifth century Greek doctor Hippocrates is one of the greatest figures in the history of science, but he presents us with a series of paradoxes. The first is that, despite his fame, we know very little about the man himself (though see Jouanna, 1999: chapters 1–2 for a very optimistic attempt at reconstructing his life). The second is that many of the medical works ascribed to him are in fact the work of others, produced over a period of several centuries or more (though with the bulk belonging to the late fifth, fourth and third centuries BC). The third is much more important. This paper will suggest that the modern debate about the 'Hippocratic corpus', focusing largely on how similar or dissimilar it is from modern (western/scientific) medicine may often make it more rather than less difficult to understand the workings of the medical system(s) found within the texts. It typically removes one of the most important elements from the equation: the ancient patient. This leads on to a final paradox. The most important question about 'Hippocratic' medicine may not be the gauging of the level of its success, but rather explaining its popularity in the face of other competing systems of medical care. Greek doctors may have been less, rather than more effective (in modern terms) the more 'Hippocratic' they were. Why did the *patient* want this system of care?

'Hippocratic medicine' is enshrined in over sixty medical treatises. The texts can differ radically from one another in literary style and in underlying medical theory, and as already noted, they are certainly not the product of any one individual. Few give consistently detailed reports on therapeutics (for the exceptions, see especially *Diseases* 2; *Fractures*; and *Diseases of Women*). Some focus largely on prognosis (for example, *Epidemics* 1 and 3). Other texts deal with ethics (*Oath*), or with the self-presentation of the doctor to his customers (*Precepts*; *Decorum*; *The Physician*; *The Art*; *In the Surgery*). Others read like philosophical or rhetorical set-pieces (see, for example, *Generation*; *The Sacred Disease*; *Airs, Waters, Places*; *Breaths*). Often it seems that the only common thread is diversity. It is probable, however, that we only have a biased sample of even the Hippocratic tradition. In general, only a tiny percentage of ancient texts have survived, and the Hippocratic texts in particular passed through a number of 'editorial' filters even in Antiquity (see especially Smith, 1989).

Even if it *were* safe to assume that the 'Hippocratic' texts that have survived represented a cross-section of the written medical texts of their time, nonetheless it would be foolish to regard them as a summary of the health care of their day. Theory and practice can often differ. While the kind of medicine represented in these texts was very famous in Classical and later Greece, they form part of only one strand of Greek medicine, that which was literary and philosophically-inclined. Religious medicine, such as the cult of Asclepius, was also important (Edelstein, 1945; Krug, 1993: 120–87). Finally, the story of non-literate medicine (on the level of root-cutters and wise women) is, by definition, lost to us almost entirely, except in so far as part of it was incorporated into Hippocratic medicine (Gordon, 1995, with references to earlier debate, and see also section VII, below).

This leads on to a further problem: what degree of access would there have been to the kind of care discussed in the Hippocratic texts? There are some statements apparently encouraging practitioners against charging a patient more than they could bear (e.g. *Precepts* 4–6; *Decorum* 2). How far doctors heeded such advice, and what precisely they did charge, is unknown. There were some doctors who received payment from the state, but it is unclear whether such payments covered actual treatment or whether they were a form of 'retainer' to ensure that the physician stayed in town (see Cohn-Haft, 1956: chs. IV–V). Having a famous doctor in residence could also enhance a town's prestige, in just the same way as having a famous poet. We cannot simply assume that the poor received cheaper treatment from such practitioners. Our surviving texts generally had little reason to include information about the social status of patients, though there are the important exceptions of *Epidemics* 4, 5 and 7 (for a handful of indicators beyond these texts, see *Humours* 20; *Diseases of Women* 2.138 and 2.153; *Epidemics* 1.21; *Nature of the Child* 13). While many of the clientele would seem to have been wealthy (Deichgraeber, 1982), artisans (such as fullers and carpenters) and indeed slaves are also present (see particularly *Epidemics* 4, for example 4.2, 9, 13, 20d, 20e, 20f, 23, 25 etc.), though the fact that, unlike some other patients, they remain unnamed, may be indicative of some authorial condescension. Mention of slaves should not necessarily surprise us, however. Treatment would have probably been paid for by their master: one should remember that they constituted a valuable property that needed to be protected, quite apart from any humanitarian feelings. Their access to health care was probably dependent on the relative wealth of their master. There has been some discussion as to whether slaves were given a different kind of medical treatment to free people, though this suggestion is based, in the main, on one rather dubious piece of evidence (Plato, *Laws* 720a–e, on which, see Kudlien, 1968). Overall, the evidence seems consistent with another rather rhetorical passage from Plato (*Republic* 405a–6e): while some forms of treatment (especially those involving dietetics and exercise) may have been difficult for the poor to follow (see *Regimen* 3.68–69), many poorer members of society do seem to have had access to the kind of health care represented in our surviving 'Hippocratic' texts.

III. DIFFERENT APPROACHES TO THE TEXTS

The Hippocratics therefore represent only one of a number of medical traditions within ancient Greece, albeit one that was socially important and intellectually prestigious and relatively widely available. There are also major debates among modern historians about the Hippocratic corpus itself. Some of the most heated arguments in the past have revolved around the existence or otherwise of two ancient 'schools' of thought, the 'Coan' or the 'Cnidian'. The 'Coan' school was generally seen as the more theoretical and sophisticated, focusing on the patient. The Cnidian was seen as more concerned with actual therapy, focusing on the disease and containing less sophisticated material (see e.g. Langholf, 1990: ch. 1; Smith, 1973; Lonie, 1978; cf. Jouanna, 1998: chs. 3–4). Not all modern scholars would accept the exisitence of a 'Coan' or 'Cnidian' strand of thought. Today, indeed, there seems to be almost as many different ways of reading the Hippocratic texts as there are historians. One can take a philological approach, examining the way language is used within them and comparing such use with non-Hippocratic texts. Or one can adopt a more philosophical approach, putting the corpus in the context of presocratic and fourth century thought. *Historians* have tended to adopt one of two other approaches (see the elegant statement of Kearns, 1987: 331–2). The first one might call the medico-historical. It tends to stress the progress represented by Hippocratic medicine when compared with the kind of religious-based ideas that had proceeded it, and thus fits well with some of the more philosophical approaches (Phillips, 1987; Longrigg, 1993; Jouanna, 1998 and 1999). Similarities of thought between ancient and modern are often highlighted. The second approach is the anthropological, asking a different question: how does ancient medicine reflect the social and intellectual world of its day? For an early manifestation of such ideas, see Joly, 1966, and, more generally, the extremely influential work of G. Lloyd (e.g. 1979; 1983; 1987; 1991; 1996: ch. 6; but see 1992 for a fine summary). This approach fits well with some recent feminist and post-modernist influenced theories which stress the role of medicine in reinforcing male power over women and in reinforcing social hierarchies rather than its therapeutical role (see, e.g., Manuli, 1983; Demand, 1994; Barton, 1994). These writers are *not* primarily interested in how effective ancient medicine may have been. They tend to look for the differences between ancient medicine and our own. One does need, however, to avoid exaggeration. The two 'historical' approaches listed are not entirely mutually exclusive. They form two poles in a spectrum of possible viewpoints. John Longrigg, for example, might entitle his book *Greek Rational Medicine*, but he was well aware of the problem of defining a term such as 'rational' (Longrigg, 1993: 4). An 'anthropologically' inclined author such as Geoffrey Lloyd might investigate the 'unscientific' elements of Greek medicine but was, nonetheless, still happy to recognise the difference between Hippocratic cures and the incantations over the wounded that one can find in the texts of Homer of the eighth century BC (Lloyd, 1987: 335–6; cf. criticism of Lloyd in Barton, 1994: 188 fn. 44). Nonetheless it would be legitimate to talk of two *tendencies*, one looking at ancient medicine primarily within the context of later medicine, the other looking at it more within in the context of the society and ideologies of the ancient world. It must be stressed that *both* approaches have their validity (as do the philological and philosophical). There is a danger, however, that these differences in approach can too easily descend into a rather sterile debate about whether there was 'progress' in classical Greek medicine compared to earlier medicine, a debate which too often fails to specify whether the discussion is dealing with theory or with practice (note Joly's pained 1980 response to the criticisms of his 1966 book). What I would like to do is to approach the debate from a slightly different direction — that of the Hippocratic patient, rather than the Hippocratic doctor.

IV. THE ETHICAL DEBATE — FULL OF SOUND AND FURY, SIGNIFYING ... NOT VERY MUCH?

Few Hippocratic texts are as famous as the *Oath*, which pledges the doctor to respect and act in the interests of his patient. However important this document may be to the modern world, it provides a very fine example of how difficult it is to interpret the realities of *ancient* medicine. The ideals of the *Oath*, and the injunctions found in many other texts concerning professional presentation and deportment (*The Physician* especially 1, 4; *Decorum* especially 5, 7ff; *Precepts* 1, 8, 10) do seem quite impressive, but it is difficult to tell how far such ideals were kept to. The *Oath* may represent an attempt to regulate medical behaviour but its popularity and significance in Antiquity are subjects of considerable doubt (for two very different views, see Edelstein, 1967: 1–63; and Harig and Kollesch, 1978). More importantly, there were important structural problems which the *Oath* hints at but could not of itself solve. It is obvious from reading it that the worst penalty available for medical incompetence was loss of face (see also *Laws* 1). It is also obvious that guild controls were very weak (see, e.g. Nutton, 1995; though cf. Nutton, 1992). Ancient Greece was a world in which anyone who wished to could claim to be a doctor, even if a variety of texts stress that true medical knowledge could not be acquired quickly (see, for example, *Aphorisms* 1; *Places of Man* 41; *Precepts* 13; *Laws* 4 and especially 2, with Kudlien, 1970). Obviously this lack of control could lead to disaster. Hippocratic texts themselves attack ill-qualified and poor practitioners (for example, *Regimen in Acute Diseases* 6, 8, 40ff; *Laws* 1; *Regimen* 1.1; *Fractures* 1–2, 7; *Joints* 11; *The Physician* 4 and 6; *Diseases of Women* 1.62). Later Roman sources such as the elder Pliny (*Natural History* 29.1ff) were particularly keen to repeat (and elaborate upon) these kinds of accusations of incompetence and wrong-doing, and it would be easy to produce a grimly entertaining picture of professional incompetence (see Nutton, 1985; Gourevitch, 1984: 323–414; André, 1987, esp. chs. 9–10; Ferngren, 1985).

All this is quite depressing, whatever the strictures of the *Oath*. One might cling to one hope, however. Might not the very situation (the unregulated 'medical marketplace') which helped to create these problems have helped also to solve them? Could the free market in medicine, rather than create a breeding ground for incompetence, have actually helped (in the long run) to keep the number of charlatans down, with good medicine driving out bad (see *Ancient Medicine* 9, cf. Nutton, 1990)? Who would choose a bad doctor when there was a wide choice available? This is, unfortunately, a little optimistic. It may have been quite difficult to spot the difference between bad luck and incompetence (and indeed good luck and competence). All medical systems have methods to explain away failure, and Hippocratic medicine was no exception. One could cite the strength of the disease (*The Art* 8; cf. *Diseases of Women* 1.62). One might blame the patient for not carrying out the treament properly (*The Art* 7 and 14; cf. *Prorrhetic* 2.3–4) or for doing (or eating) something unsuitable (for example, *Epidemics* 3.17, 5.29; *Fractures* 9; *Diseases of Women* 3.230: some of the cures in this last text almost seem designed to elicit such an excuse). One could blind the patient (or their family) with science (*Precepts* 13; compare *Regimen in Acute Diseases* 58 for what looks like an example of a post-eventum justification — a cure is effective *except* in such cases as the patient is already mortally ill, where it can make things worse). Unfortunately these excuses could be used by all, whether their failures were justified or not.

Yet, if the texts might lead us to exaggerate some of the advances made by Hippocratic medicine, they may equally lead us to exaggerate some of the problems. Historical evidence is always the product of human minds, and we cannot just assume that the agendas of those minds are the same as our own. Firstly, the Roman sources often quoted to attack Greek medicine had their own particular racial (anti-Greek) and class (anti-craft) biases and should not be taken at face value (Wallace-Hadrill, 1988; Nutton, 1986). Secondly, doctors of all periods have made mistakes and been criticized for them. Unsuccessful treatment has always lent itself to charges of incompetence, and all medical systems have had their fair share of failure. *Joints* 13 notes that even good doctors can get it badly wrong, and several texts recommend that one avoid incurable cases for fear of what they would do to one's reputation (*The Art* 3; cf. *Fractures* 36; contra *Precepts* 7). One should have some sympathy with the author of *The Art* 4 who writes that some attack the doctor whenever a patient dies but also claim that any success is due to luck (cf. *Diseases* 1.8): heavy criticism is to be expected. Thirdly, all medical systems (indeed, all professions) have their share of incompetents and charlatans (as *Ancient Medicine* 1 was keen to point out), and it is doubtful what would be gained by simply focusing exclusively on them. Fourthly, and lastly, we should note that most of the surviving charges of incompetence are found within the Hippocratic texts themselves. One should remember why these texts exist. It would be pleasant to believe that ancient doctors formed a community of disinterested seekers after the truth who simply wanted to share their knowledge. In reality the Hippocratics needed to compete for business to make a living, and the medical texts are often part of that struggle. We should not necessarily believe everything negative that they say about their competitors. On the other hand, we should not necessarily believe what they say about their own high standards (however important such statements may have been in inspiring posterity).

V. THE LIMITS OF INTERVENTION

The Hippocratic texts can, therefore, both praise and damn the ethics and professional standards of classical Greek doctors. It is perhaps more profitable then to turn from ethics to therapeutics, and the methods by which Hippocratics actually attempted to treat ill-health. We shall find that treatments that appear more 'modern' from our perspective were not necessarily more beneficial than those that don't.

The Hippocratics had very distinctive ideas of what caused disease. Instead of disease as, for example, a function of parasitic

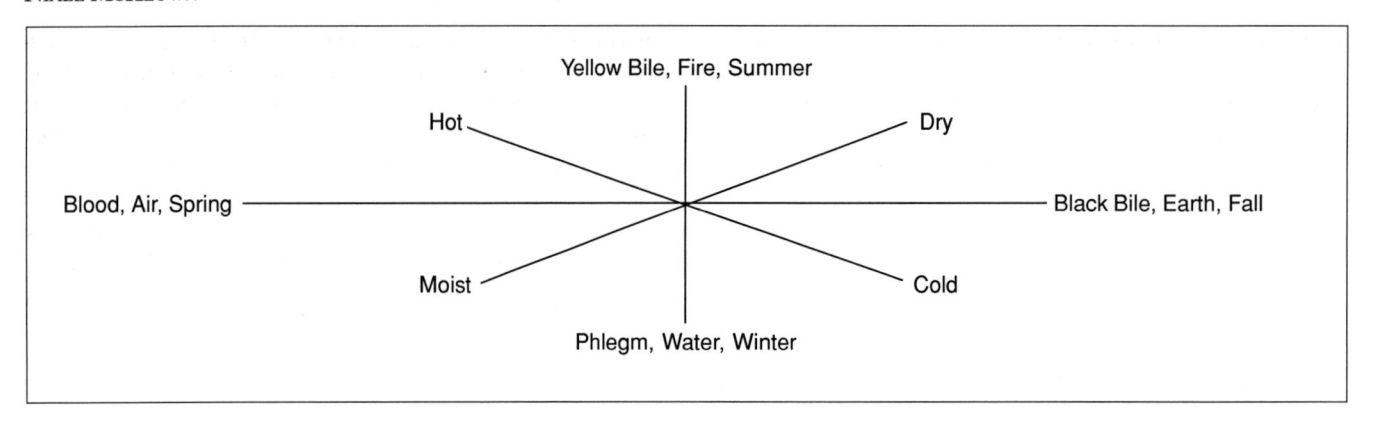

```
                    Yellow Bile, Fire, Summer
                Hot  \         |         / Dry
                      \        |        /
                       \       |       /
Blood, Air, Spring ─────────────────────── Black Bile, Earth, Fall
                       /       |       \
                      /        |        \
               Moist /         |         \ Cold
                    Phlegm, Water, Winter
```

Fig. 1 (after Sigerist, 1961: 323).

attack or external contagion (though see Nutton, 1983; and Parker, 1983) the Hippocratics *usually* worked on the assumption that disease occurred when the balance of various substances (humors) in the body had been disturbed. Henry Sigerist (1961: 323) famously produced a diagram to explain how their mental map of disease might have looked (Fig. 1).

Some warnings are appropriate at this point. Hippocratic writers could also employ more mechanical models to explain disruptions to the body, and we should note the possibility that the prevalence of humoral theory in the extant literary texts has been exaggerated by later editorial filters, particularly Galen (see e.g. Smith, 1979 esp. ch. 2; Temkin, 1991 esp. ch. 5). The full implications of humoral theory could vary in practice. While ancient Greeks did often structure their understanding of the world by means of pairs of opposites (see Lloyd, 1966), Sigerist's diagram should only be seen as illustrating some *possibilities*. It is quite appropriate in a number of texts: *Nature of Man* 4 and 7 (on which it was based) and *perhaps Epidemics* 6 (e.g. 6.5.8 — (yellow) bile is indicated by a greeny-yellow tongue). Other four-humor systems were possible however (for example *Generation* 3 introduces blood, phlegm, bile and water). Some authors felt that some of the elements were more important than others (for example, *Affections* 1 and *Haemorrhoids* 1 suggest that bile and phlegm cause all diseases, cf. Nutton, 1999: 33). Other sets of opposites were possible (see, e.g. *Nature of Woman* 1). One text (*Ancient Medicine* 13ff) rejected the use of opposites altogether.

Nonetheless, countering disease was generally seen as a question of restoring balance. A cure might be attempted by means of elements which caused or reflected the imbalance (homeopathy) as well as (more commonly) opposite elements (allopathy). Once again, diversity is the watchword. There were a number of ways of intervening on the body to achieve a new balance that are outlined in the Hippocratic texts: surgery; burning (cautery); bleeding; diet and exercise (including bathing and sex); drugs (including pessaries, fumigations and clysters). For examples of varied and detailed therapies, see (e.g.) *Places in Man*; *Diseases of Women* and *Diseases* II. *Joints* 50 (dealing with contusion of flesh around the ribs) recommends and lessening diet, keeping still, avoiding sexual intercourse, cutting a vein in the elbow, silence, padding the bruised parts, something to sooth the innards, and, in extremis, cauterisation (cf. *Diseases* 2.47, which involves diet, drugs, bathing, and surgical intervention to drain pus). Combinations of treatments are typical.

The chief difference between ancient and modern doctors was perhaps the attitude towards invasive surgery (for a rather jaundiced view, see Majno 1975). It was much less common in Antiquity. The Hippocratic text *Haemorrhoids* graphically illustrates some of the reasons for this. It recommends that the doctor allow the patient to shout during the cutting out of the haemorrhoids (2). It also suggests that one should distract the patient's attention with conversation during one procedure, so as to take him unawares (4). Anesthesia and pain killers may not have been entirely unknown to the Hippocratics, but there is little evidence that they are used to dull pain in the course of operations (Scarborough, 1995: 5 for references to opium, but see King, 1988; Byl, 1992). The more serious problem (as it was long to remain) was the absence of effective post-operative antiseptic (or indeed real knowledge of the mechanisms of infection). This meant that whatever guesses Hippocratic doctors made on the internal workings of the body (itself problematical in a society in which the dissection of bodies would appear to have been something of a taboo) were likely to be of only theoretical interest (e.g. the theories on the anatomy of the eye and brain in *Places in Man* 2). Frustration at this state of affairs could occasionally break through in the texts. *Joints* 46 notes the impossibility of carrying out any effective treatment in one case without killing the patient. Hippocratics themselves seem to have realised that any serious medical invasion of the body was likely to lead to death. A few procedures could be safely attempted, but they were limited in scope. Draining of pus was one of the few procedures involving cutting that they apparently were willing to try (see, e.g. *Internal Affections* 9; *Diseases* 1.9, 2.47, 2.60). Amputation would seem to have been reasonably commonplace, judging from the discussion of gangrene in *Joints* 69ff. *Instruments of Reduction* 34 also suggests some degree of success with the operation. Trephination of the skull might seem colourful but it is a relatively safe and simple surgical procedure and it seems to have been used, as it is today, in cases of fractures of the skull (*Wounds to the Head* 9 and 12), and the potential pitfalls were known (*Wounds to the Head* 32). The Hippocratics were also prepared to cut or rip out growths in the nose (*Diseases* 2.33, 35), use the knife as part of the treatment of growths in the throat (*Diseases* 2.29; *Affections* 34) and excise haemorrhoids (*Haemorrhoids*; cf.

Regimen in Acute Diseases 62). The gynecological treatises describe the surgical removal of a dead fetus (e.g. *Superfetation* 5, 7–8; *Excision of the Foetus* 1; *Diseases of Women* 1.70, 3.249 etc.), and *Nature of Woman* 65 mentions a procedure of cutting out warts from the womb. Generally mechanical intervention in women's diseases with anything more than finger probe or pessary was not encouraged (*Superfetation* 15 mentions that doctors sometimes had to intervene with labour, but that such children have little hope of survival, itself partly a prejudice linked to their belief in the active role the child was supposed to take in the birthing process: see Demand, 1994: ch. 1; Hanson, 1991: 87ff). Succussion could be used as an alternate to internal intervention in gynecological cases (*Excision of the Foetus* 4). Giving something that will cause the patient to sneeze, then holding her nose and mouth is recommended also for expelling a dead fetus (*Diseases of Women* 68). All in all, this is a very limited range of intervention, but, as I have suggested, this should be seen as a Hippocratic virtue rather than a Hippocratic failing. They were aware of the need for skill if they ever did need to intervene with the knife (e.g. *The Physician* 5) and, more importantly, of the dangers of this form of intervention (see, e.g. *Aphorisms* 6.27).

There was one branch of surgery, however, in which the Hippocratics did show rather greater confidence in their abilities: their work on dislocations and on the settings of bones, summarised in particular in *Fractures*; *Joints*; *Instruments of Reduction* and *Wounds to the Head* (see, e.g., Roselli, 1975). Bone setting has been practised successfully by humans since Neolithic times, but there is no doubt that these texts are amongst the most systematic in the corpus. They also deal with a number of areas, such as bandaging (on which see also *On the Surgery* 7ff), or the use of the Hippocratic 'ladder' (see *Fractures* 13, but especially *Joints* 43–4, and also 70, 72), which seem to have been important ways in which a practitioner could impress potential customers.

Aside from bone-setting, however, manual intervention was seen as potentially quite dangerous. The same was also true of the second method of intervention: cautery (*Places in Man* 40; cf. *Aphorisms* 6.27). It was used for a wide variety of disorders (see especially *Diseases* 2, e.g. 2.53, 55, 60, 62). Sometimes the ancient applications mirror more recent uses (e.g. *Epidemics* 7.111 to deal with an eating sore or cancer; *Diseases* 2.34 and a nasal polyp). On other occasions, however, its use was more probably connected to the idea that burning can counteract cold or wet disorders (*Places in Man* 20, dealing with dropsy; cf. *Internal Affections* 51). This might also explain its relative uncommoness in the gynecological texts, given that women were wet and not supposed to be dried out (though see an interesting exception of diarrhea in *Diseases of Women* 2.134). At least one case has managed to elicit sarcasm from a modern commentator when it was used to 'cure' a dislocation of the shoulder (Majno, 1975: 191 on *Joints* 11).

Bleeding, a third mechanism of intervention, was recommended for everything from a sore throat to diseases of the spleen and flatulence (e.g. *Affections* 20, *Internal Affections* 37, *Places in Man* 22, *Diseases* 1.38, 2.26, *Epidemics* 2.5.5, 2.6.12). As with cautery, and possibly for the same reason (if not quite to the same extent), bleeding seems to be less common in the gynecological texts than elsewhere. There were two ways of bleeding the patient — cupping (*Places in Man* 12, *The Physician* 7–8), or incision (*Places in Man* 13, *The Physician* 6), though they could be used together (*Epidemics* 5.8). Hippocratic authors once again recognised potential dangers (e.g. *Ulcers* 2.6, but cf. *Regimen in Acute Diseases* 31). One should note that the prevalence of bleeding cups in the artistic representations of doctors (Krug, 1993: 29) need only mean that it was an easily recognisable distinctive symbol, *not* (judging from our literary texts) that it was the doctor's main means of intervention.

The types of treatments we have been examining thus far represent, however, the minority of medical interventions outlined in the Hippocratic texts. The bulk of therapies involved exercise, diet and pharmacology. Exercise and diet were often grouped together as 'dietetics' (Craik, 1995; Woehrli, 1990). Exercise presents some facets which, to the modern eye, might seem a little odd. The first is that it is more usually seen as part of a cure (see *Regimen* 3.68 for a classic statement on the use of exercise (walking), cf. e.g. *Epidemics* 5.70, 6.3.1, *Diseases* 2.52, 2.55, 2.66), than as a mechanism to maintain good health (though see *Regimen in Acute Diseases* 9 and *Epidemics* 6.4.23). They are also seen as only part of treatment involving a whole range of other therapeutic devices. Secondly, Hippocratic doctors could as easily warn against certain kinds of exercise as recommend them (e.g. *Diseases* 2.53, 2.62, 2.73). Thirdly, bathing and sex were included within curing 'regimes'. This is perhaps less surprising when we keep in mind the 'balancing' model of hot/cold, dry/wet. For some applications and general statements on washing, see *Regimen in Acute Diseases* 65–8 (including potential dangers) and *Diseases* 2.12–14 etc. Bathing is, in fact, an extremely common form of treatment in the therapeutic texts. Vapour baths and fomentations are also found (e.g. *Diseases* 2.26, 2.51; *Epidemics* 5.58; *Diseases* 1.38) and were commonly prescribed as mechanisms of pain relief (Byl, 1992; King, 1988). Bathing (or particular kinds of bathing) could, however, also be seen as dangerous in some circumstances (e.g. *Diseases* 2.19, 2.68; *Epidemics* 7.71). Sex could help cure a variety of disorders, including diseases caused by phlegm (e.g. *Epidemics* 6.5.15) and even dysentery (*Epidemics* 7.122; cf. *Regimen* 3.80 and 3.85). *Regimen* 2.58 refers to its moistening and warming character. It was also used commonly as both cure and evidence of cure in the gynecological texts (discussed below, section VII). As with bathing, there were potential negatives as well as pluses (e.g. *Internal Affections* 28; *Regimen in Acute diseases (appendix)* 55).

By a process of elimination we are moving towards the most important weapons in the arsenal of a Greek doctor: diet and pharmacology. *Regimen* 2.39ff is the most famous statement of the curative powers of everyday foodstuffs, categorising them as heating or cooling, wetting or drying (see also *Regimen in Acute Diseases* 39ff and 50ff, but cf. some rather different categories in *Ancient Medicine* 13–15). References to food in therapy are so numerous as to defy listing, but they are particularly prominent throughout *Regimen* and *Regimen in Acute Diseases*, and are also very evident in *Epidemics* 7 and *Diseases* 2 (e.g., *Epidemics* 7.97, 7.101; *Diseases* 2.47, 50, 70–1). Diet therapy was used in the treatment of just about every conceivable form of illness, including recovery from broken bones (*Fractures* 7–8). Abstinence could also be important (e.g. *Epidemics* 6.4.4 recommends the avoidance of garlic, piglet, mutton, beef, shouting and anger). Soups and gruels were quite popular (e.g. *Epidemics* 2.6.3, 5.10, 7.108; *Regimen in Acute Diseases* 10). While fresh food and fruit are described as healthy (*Regimen* 2.55–56), fresh uncooked vegetables could be dangerous in winter (*Regimen in Health* 1; *Regimen* 3.68) and a number of foods bad for the eyes were listed (e.g. *Epidemics* 5.58 with lentils, fruit, sweet things and greens cf. 5.54). One should stress again that there was no single, prescriptive, theory of foods within the texts. Modern writers have sometimes been unconvinced as to the usefulness of a dietetic system that favoured starving the patient with gruel quite as much as the Hippocratics seem to have done (Majno, 1975: 189, 418; Lloyd, 1987: 20; cf. Joly, 1966: ch. 3). Once again, however, at least some of the Hippocratic authors were aware of potential problems (e.g. *Regimen in Acute Diseases* 16, 26–7; *Precepts* 14).

We move finally to treatment by drugs (see, e.g. Stannard, 1961; Harig, 1980; Scarborough, 1981; Riddle, 1985 and 1992: ch. 8). One should state immediately, however, that it can be quite difficult to distinguish drug from food in the Hippocratic corpus (note, for example, the wide definition of *pharmakon* in *Places in Man* 45). The materials applied and ingested are usually not mineral but organic. Hydromel and oxymel are popular pharmacological substances, and they are nothing more than mixtures of honey and water and vinegar and honey (see e.g. *Regimen in Acute Diseases* 50, 53–62. Compare the use of corn meal and cabbage as evacuants in *Diseases* 2.19). Materials usually eaten could also, of course, be used in new ways. Onions were placed up the patient's nose to cure loss of voice after drunkenness (a potentially fatal disease: *Diseases* 2.22). It was treatments with these substances, and others like them, that provide the most common mechanism of intervention for Hippocratic doctors. They did not have to be ingested but could be used in poultices, pessaries, suppositories, clysters and fumigations as well. We shall investigate perhaps the finest Hippocratic pharmacological text — the *Diseases of Women* — in more detail later, but every Hippocratic text dealing with therapy mentions drug intervention at some point. *Epidemics* 2, 5, and 7; *Diseases* 2 and *Ulcers* 11ff are among the richest of the non-gynecological works (though one should not expect consistency of use between, or even within, texts). For some typical examples, see, e.g., *Diseases* 1.17 (a poultice), 2.14 (mentioning laxatives and a mixture to be applied to the ears), 2.27 (a gargle mix), 2.37 (a detailed treatment to bring forth pus from a suppurating lung); *Epidemics* 2.5.22 (a detailed treatment for the eyes), 2.6.29 (a mixture of food and diet, designed to ensure conception). The *Epidemics* have a general fondness for emetics or purgatives (e.g. 5.31–5), with melicrat, linozostis and particularly hellebore often used (writers were well aware how dangerous the latter could be: e.g. *Regimen in Acute Diseases* 40).

There have been some attempts to assess the effectiveness of Hippocratic pharmacology (see Nutton, 1986: 43 and 55–6 fn. 67; and Corvisier, 1985: ch. IV; Riddle, 1992), but any such attempts face serious difficulties for a number of reasons (see Riddle, 1985: 40ff; and Stannard, 1961). Hippocratic authors typically use a combination of substances at any one time ('polypharmacy'), often without specifying amounts (perhaps deliberately: why give away one's secrets to others?). Even if we can be confident of equating an ancient Greek term with a modern substance we need to bear in mind that plants, for example, can and do evolve and change their properties over time (see Sallares, 1990). We must also assume a certain degree of adulteration in the practical use of these substances (Nutton, 1986). There even remains the tricky problem of defining precisely what disease they were meant to cure. Greeks were capable of combining diseases that we might keep separate (Grmek, 1989: esp. ch. 12) and could create diseases that we no longer believe exist (e.g. see below on the wandering womb). This is not to say that one cannot *attempt* to judge the efficacy of cures but there will always be a worrying possible margin for error between a result on paper and what was actually happening in classical Greece. Finally, one should also be careful before assuming that a substance which is found to be useful in modern medicine was used by the ancients *because they found it to be useful in the same way* (Stannard, 1961: 507). John Scarborough has investigated one Hippocratic poultice for a wound and found that it did indeed contain efficacious ingredients: as an antidepressant for menopausal women (Scarborough, 1983: 319). The Hippocratics sometimes had rather a blunderbuss approach to the use of pharmacological substances and it is inevitable that things may have been rather hit and miss.

But if Hippocratic pharmacology and dietary lore did not represent the most exciting aspect of the Hippocratic corpus, if they failed to anticipate the future of medicine in the way that some of the ethical and philosophical texts and surgical enquiries did, if they offered no 'breakthroughs', they were still, nonetheless, vitally important. Firstly because this was the type of medicine that the Hippocratic *patient* was most likely to encounter, not least because the practitioners themselves recognised the dangers of the more drastic forms of intervention which are sometimes more prominent in the *historiographical* tradition. Secondly, because such treatments allow us a somewhat different perspective on classical medicine than the more theoretical Hippocratic texts. Prior to the Hippocratics (and indeed alongside them) existed a tradition of (one assumes) largely non-literate drug lore from groups such as root cutters and herbalists, what we might today see as folklore (Gordon, 1995; Lloyd, 1983: 119ff; Calame, 1983; Scarborough, 1991: 162–3). These herbalists and dietary advisors would have operated with a mixture of knowledge gained from experience and culturally received ideas (with one, of course, affecting the other). When comparing them to the Hippocratics we need, however, to be careful not to equate 'folkloric' with 'primitive'. The Hippocratic 'advance' may not have been quite what it seems. To the experience and preconceptions of the existing tradition they added their own experience, and their own preconceptions. The theories they developed about the body, disease and various forms of balance served to add an extra layer to existing drug and food lore, a layer which was unlikely often to be of particularly benefit to the patient. Hippocratic theories about the internal workings and anatomy of the body would have to wait many generations before they would bear fruit. They were of little practical use to contemporaries, whatever their philosophical significance. Indeed, it could be argued that the closer Hippocratic medicine was to the existing herbalist tradition, the more, not less, it was likely to be 'effective' in a modern therapeutic sense.

VI. A SOUNDER METHOD?

One might argue that laying stress on the technology of curing is to miss the essential point about Hippocratic medicine. All pre-industrial medical systems must have had more failures than successes. Surely the major advance of the Hippocratics was not in therapeutics, but in *method*? It has been suggested that even a perverse rational theory that can be challenged is an advance on a religious conception of a disease which cannot (e.g. Longrigg, 1993: 5). The Hippocratics were also at times willing to admit their limits and mistakes (e.g. *Joints* 47 and *Epidemics* 5.27). Their most important advances would, however, seem to have been in promoting a secular rather than religious view of disease, in providing theories as to the cause and cure of diseases that could be tested, and their emphasis on the close observation of disease. We shall see once again, however, that this may have been another area of Hippocratic medicine that meant more for the subsequent development of health care than it did for the patient of the time.

It is certainly true that the Hippocratics do seem to have removed incantations, gods and religious explanation and treatment from (their form of) medicine and therefore could be said to represent a step away from the kind of medicine sometimes found earlier, even if they themselves were not *necessarily* responsible for taking that step. The *Sacred Disease* begins with an attack on religious and magical theories on epilepsy (1–4: though one should perhaps be a little cautious before one necessarily believes the strength of the opposition that its author claimed he faced in his crusade on behalf of rationality and reason). Sufferers of the disease would, no doubt, have been glad to be relieved of the stigma of being 'cursed'. Geoffrey Lloyd has, however, pointed out some of the ideas put forward by the author of the *Sacred Disease* to explain the incidence of epilepsy (involving the impact of hot and cold winds on phlegm in the head) were scarcely more testable than those he sought to replace (Lloyd, 1979: 15–29). Once again one might doubt how much help this was to the patient of the time. Ancient doctors themselves seem to have been aware of this. Much of the division between dogmatic and empiricist medicine in the Hellenistic period (discussed below) largely revolved around the issue of whether theory was of any practical use at all.

Hippocratic observation is also a little less impressive than it might seem at first sight. The *Epidemics* provide perhaps the most famous examples of close observation in classical Greek medicine (for lists of things to be observed, see *Epidemics* 1.23, 2.1.6, 4.43). Successful prognosis was vital to ensure a continuing supply of customers (*Prognosis* 1, but cf. *Prorrhetics* 2.2). There are, however, some peculiarities about Hippocratic observation. The most striking concerns the issue of 'critical days', that is the idea that certain days were more dangerous or more propitious for cures (or the appearance of symptoms) than others. One reads, for example, that dislocations were to be cured on the first, second and tenth day, but never on the fourth (*Instruments of Reduction* 31, cf. 41–2). There are numerous other examples of what would appear to be the influence of number theory: e.g., *Fleshes* 19; *Epidemics* 2.6.10–11, 6.8.6; *Internal Affections* 40L; *Aphorisms* 2.13–14; *Nature of Woman* 5; *Seven Month's Child* 9; *Eight Month's Child* 13; *Diseases* 4.46–8. One might attempt to explain such ideas by the prevalence of malaria within the classical Greek world, a disease which has very distinctive cyclical rhythms. The commonness of malaria may have led doctors to read all fevers, and indeed, many other diseases, in a cyclical manner too (Jones, 1909). There is, however, a second possible explanation for the prevalence of the 'critical day' theory, which is just as plausible, if not more so. The concept that certain days were more 'special' or luckier than others was also an important part of Greek religion and mysticism from the time of the peasant-poet Hesiod onwards (see, e.g. *Works and Days* 765ff), and it gained a particular impetus from the work of Pythagoras and those who later claimed to follow his teachings (Guthrie, 1962). The importance of numbers such as three and seven to the Hippocratics may have had nothing to do with observation in our sense.

Volker Langholf has gone further in showing how Hippocratic theory could get in the way of observation even in texts as acclaimed as the *Epidemics* (Langholf, 1990). The key issue of dating could be manipulated by the authors of the *Epidemics* (Langholf, 1990: 93ff, esp. 108ff). For example, *Epidemics* 3.1 case 1 has some difficulty actually dating the beginning of a disease. This seems to have allowed the author to set a beginning date which fitted with his ideas on when the final crisis should occur — here the fortieth day after an initial crisis, itself ten days into the course of the disease. In addition, some Hippocratic definitions for the key phenomena they were observing could be rather vague (Langholf, 1990: 126ff). 'Apostasis', for example, described the manner in which harmful materials which had caused disease might leave the body and so lead to a cure. This could occur in any part of the body and in a very wide variety of ways. For example, in *Epidemics* 4.47 an observer states that, in the absence of the cough he had been expecting, red blotches on the skin must have served the purpose of the *apostasis* (Langholf, 1990: 210). For an example, where the *apostasis* occurs in the expected form, but does not have the expected result, note the case of Timenes' niece, where the *apostasis* occurs in a finger, but this site did not prove *large* enough to get rid of the problem and she died (*Epidemics* 2.1.7; Langholf, 1990: 212). Finally, *Epidemics* 1.14 notes that patients suffering from *kausos* never die when they have bled through the nose, so long as they have bled *abundantly*. One can imagine how researchers might manipulate these ideas (in the same way as we have seen that unsuccesful doctors would have had rhetorical techniques to deal with their failures). There is, however, a vital point one needs to make about these descriptions. They were not the product of intellectual bad faith. All scientific systems have ways of 'saving the phenomenon', of insulating themselves against uncomfortable facts, even when researchers consider themselves to be of a critical cast of mind. The authors of the *Epidemics* were willing to attack traditional ideas that critical days could only fall on odd days rather than even days (*Epidemics* 1.26, with Langholf, 1990: 102ff, esp. 123). What they were not prepared to do, however, was abandon the idea of critical days altogether.

So, Hippocratic observation had its cultural limits, no matter how careful it claimed to be. The Hippocratics were prepared to consider 'experiment', but by this they generally meant a thought experiment usually designed to offer the reader a convincing analogy (often mechanical) for a process being discussed, rather than a 'proof' determined by testing (see e.g.,

Sacred Disease 7ff, 16, 20, though cf. *Airs, Waters, Places* 8–9; *Fleshes* 8–9, and see section VII for references to the gynecological texts). Occasionally they would make use of analogy from the plant or animal world (e.g., *Sacred Disease* 14), but it is difficult to see how such 'experimentation' would change existing ideas. An example from the Hellenistic period illustrates what could happen. Hellenistic Greek doctors debated what was carried by arteries: blood or air? They had an advantage over their Hippocratic predecessors in that they were able to dissect cadavers (and possibly even engage in human vivisection — though see Lloyd, 1991: ch. 8 with references to the debate on this issue). When arteries were opened, blood was found. This failed to convince those who believed that they normally carried air. It was argued that the blood only entered the arteries when they were cut and injured (see Longrigg, 1993: 209). I should conclude, however, with a Hippocratic example. *Diseases of Women* 214 recommends that a woman is given a pessary containing the oil of bitter almonds. If she is able to conceive, her breath should smell of it the next day. This theory rests on the assumption of an open tube running the whole length of the body (cf. also *Fleshes* 3). If the text has any relationship with therapeutical practice, one can only assume that some doctors at least must have found themselves satisfied that they could cure their patient and that they could therefore smell the almonds via this route. We may (quite legitimately) look back to Hippocratic rationalism and Hippocratic observation as cornerstones of our own medical system, but we always need to remember that they were moulded by the society that produced them. Once again one can legitimately doubt how far they actually helped to cure patients better than more traditional methods of trial and error and herbal lore.

VII. GREEK DOCTORS AND THE SOCIAL IDEAS OF THEIR TIME

My aim is not to damn Hippocratic medicine simply because it failed to meet some notional standard of modern medicine. Modern medicine itself no doubt has many peculiarities that will be only too easy to spot with hindsight. What is important, however, is the recognition that Hippocratic medicine operated within a specific cultural matrix. It *is* vital, as the 'anthropologically' inclined historians have argued, to investigate the ways in which Greek society left its imprint on medical ideas and research. We must understand Greek medicine in its own terms. Let us take two examples, the treatment of slaves and of women, and examine (the slightly different) stories that they tell us.

The treatment of slaves offers one occasion when Hippocratic doctors do seem to have been able to escape some of the preconceptions of their age (though cf. Demand, 1998). Aristotle, perhaps the greatest of all Greek philosophers, suggested that slaves, usually foreigners, were in essence different types of creatures from Greek free-born citizens (*Politics* 1.5–6; Demand, 1998: 83). This was a view that would seem to have had considerable resonance at the time (see Hall, 1991 on the whole issue of the definition of 'outsiders'). While one Hippocratic would seem to offer Aristotle support (*Airs, Waters, Places* 12ff), it is striking that the rest of the corpus makes no such suggestion. Potential differences between climates and countries was recognised (*Regimen* 2.37), but there is little overt racism (or rather, hellenocentrism), or indeed reference to foreigners and 'barbarians' at all (as one might have expected given the number of slaves who appear in the texts). If *Ancient Medicine* 5 suggests that some 'barbarians' had no idea of regimen, it says the same of some Greeks too. Only once is the non-Greek origin of a patient mentioned: *Epidemics* 5.35 refers to a slave woman who was a 'barbarian', though nothing in the text allows us to see this as anything more than a description (the term need not, for an ancient Greek, have quite the same negative connotations it has in English today).

There has, however, been one area of Greek medicine where it has been suggested that not only were Hippocratic doctors imprisoned within traditional ideas, but that those ideas may actually have led to harm for a large number of their patients: the treatment of women (see e.g Manuli, 1983; Demand, 1994; Dean-Jones, 1994; King, 1998; with shorter introductions by Hanson, 1990; King, 1994 and 1995; Dean-Jones, 1994a; Demand, 1998). Indeed, it has been one of the battlegrounds between proponents of the 'medico-historical' or 'philosophical' approaches to the Hippocratics on the one hand (who tend to down-play gynecology, e.g. Jouanna, 1999 deals with it in five pages: 141–6, with just one paragraph in his 1998 survey: 57–8) and proponents of the anthropological approach on the other (who tend to focus on it — e.g. Lloyd, 1983: parts II–III, and Joly, 1966: chs. 1–2).

There are short statements on gynecology in texts such as *Aphorisms* 5.28ff; *Places in Man* 47; *Prorrhetics* 2.24–28; *Regimen* 1.27ff (a rather philosophically inclined piece). Our main source of evidence comes, however, from the dedicated gynecological works, most notably *Diseases of Women* and *Nature of Woman* and a number of other texts such as *Generation*. There are three areas where they might surprise a modern reader.

1. The nature of physiological differences claimed between men and women (notably that women were 'wetter' than men);
2. The nature of some of the diseases they claimed to identify (in particular, the disease of the wandering womb, prominent in ancient medicine but not recognised today);
3. The nature of some of the cures (including the use of dung and beetles).

At one level, one can defend the rationality of even some of the oddest of Hippocratic gynecological ideas. Women are generally seen in the texts as softer, weaker, and particularly wetter than men (*Diseases of Women* 1; *Illnesses of Young Girls* 1; *Regimen* 1.27 and 1.33–4; *Glands* 16; *Nature of the Child* 15; though cf. *Diseases of Women* 1.62). Menstruation is given a striking prominence, not just in the discussion of medical problems, but even in some cures (e.g., *Epidemics* 2.28 for girl cured of paralysis at the time her menses break out, 7.100 for arthritic pain caused by failure of menses). The idea that women are somehow 'wetter' than men may seem ludicrous to us, but not when one should bear in mind the importance of bleeding within the narrow range of Hippocratic therapeutics discussed above. This may make the importance attached to menstruation a little more explicable. One should note that bleeding through the nose and haemorrhoidal bleeding (of men and women) were also of great interest to the writers of the Hippocratic corpus (see *Epidemics* 1.14, 2.1.7, 6.4.2, etc., on nosebleeds. See *Epidemics*

6.5.15, and *Humors* 20 on haemorrhoids, and Dean-Jones, 1994a: 142).

Hysteria is perhaps the most famous example of an invented gynecological disease. It was believed to be caused when the womb 'wandered' around the body producing a series of baleful psychological and physical symptoms (e.g. *Diseases of Women* 1.7, 2.123ff; *Nature of Woman* e.g. 26, 48–9, 54, 75 etc.; and *Places in Man* 47; cf. King, 1998: ch. 11; Lefkowitz, 1981: ch. 2). One should not be too quick, however, in condemning Greek doctors for possessing an over-active imagination. The Greeks had only a rudimentary knowledge of the internal organs. The womb can suffer prolapse, and this *may* have convinced some writers that it was capable of movement. Dean-Jones (1991: 126) and Hanson (1991: 82) raise a second possibility — that Hippocratic doctors, reading female anatomy from male, could see no natural 'home' for the organ (there was obviously none in the male body), and so allowed it to wander. This is a possibility, but there is no direct ancient evidence to suggest this (and cf. Dean-Jones, 1991: 129–30). To defend the Hippocratics further, even if the womb was immobile, the *symptoms* associated with its supposed movement may have manifested themselves and have required treatment. The Hippocratics could have been misdiagnosing what was in fact a range of problems. There was therefore some point to their attempted cures, and it is even possible that some of them may have been effective, however ignorant doctors of the time may have been of the *cause* of whatever they were treating. Perhaps we shouldn't laugh at hysteria after all. Or at least, not too much.

We should also perhaps not recoil quite so much from some of the (detailed) cures that we can find in *Diseases of Women* and the *Nature of Woman*. There are indeed many sections of the gynecological texts which appear very strange to modern eyes. For example, *Diseases of Women* 2.185 gives a recipe (for bad breath!) which includes mice and the head of a hare. *Diseases of Women* 2.192 has potions which involve crabs drowned in wine and also asses' dung, and compare 2.203 (a cornucopia of interesting substances), or *Nature of Woman* 2, 34, 109 etc. The use of beetles and especially feces is perhaps most repellent to some modern sensitivities. One must, however, be very careful. There is always a danger of naivety in our response to some of the materials used in ancient medicine. As *medical* substances go, using beetles (for example) needn't be any 'odder' than other substances (and see *Internal Affections* 36 for one non-gynecological use of beetles). The use of feces is, of course, a rather more interesting problem, since there is little doubt that the Greeks found it as repellent a substance as Western Europeans generally do today (see especially, Von Staden, 1992: 9). There is still, however, a danger that we may be exaggerating its significance to Hippocratic gynecology. Firstly, it may not be entirely safe to conclude that feces were only used in the treatment of women rather than men given that the *Diseases of Women* text presents us with by far the most detailed pharmacology in all of the extent Hippocratic texts. It is *probable* that men were not treated with such substances, but one would feel much more certain if one had in one's possession a similarly detailed and extensive general pharmacological text. This leads to a second point. Whilst some sections of the gynecological texts do emphasise treatment with feces, it still represents a very small selection in a very large text (Hanson, 1990: 311 argues that feces and urine are more common in the *Epidemics*,

but does not differentiate prognostic from therapeutic use). Thirdly, one needs to bear in mind precisely how some of these substances may have been used. Dung, for example, appears *mainly* in fumigations (though there are some exceptions — e.g. *Diseases of Women* 2.192 (dung in a drink, cf. *Nature of Woman* 90; Von Staden, 1992: 10); *Nature of Woman* 82 (dung in a pessary). The association may not be dung/female but rather dung/fumigation. One could imagine how it might be believed that stronger-smelling substances might be more effective in fumigations and why dung would be chosen.

One *could* attempt to defend the 'modernity' of the Hippocratics in this way, but one might then be falling into the trap of seeing the Greeks as more like us than they actually were. The defence breaks down at a number of key points.

1. Whatever the cause for the belief in the wetness of the female body, it should be remembered that other later authors (such as Soranus) developed very different views even though they were operating effectively within the same technological level. Seeing women as soft, whilst plausible given the existence of many Greek women of the time, made a physiological absolute out of a cultural norm. Other problems also remain, which are difficult to explain in any other terms but cultural prejudice. The female fetus allegedly developed slower than males (*Diseases of Women* 1.71; *Nature of the Child* 18, 21), though quicker development after birth could also be explained paradoxically by their weakness compared to boys (*Seven Month's Child* 9). Women were also associated with the 'left', ill-omened side of the body (see *Epidemics* 2.6.15, and note the implication of *Superfetation* 31).

2. There were key areas in which observation once again broke down. Perhaps the two most famous examples concern menstruation and birth and its aftermath. The Hippocratics calculated average menstrual flow at an astonishing eight times what we believe today (*Diseases of Women* 1.6, with Dean-Jones, 1994: 86ff, cf. 1989, explaining the belief in terms of the mechanical conceptions Hippocratics had of the womb). With regards to birth, it was believed that the lochial flow continued longer after female births than male, since the male fetus, being stronger than the female fetus, used up more of the liquids in the womb (*Diseases of Women* 1.72 and Dean-Jones, 1994: 213), something fairly obviously connected with the idea of male strong/female weak which affected ideas of the development of the fetus. For further examples of what would appear to us as theory-driven observations, one could also examine the Hippocratic discussion of the age of menarchy (e.g. King, 1995: 210), and the survival or otherwise of the 'eighth month child' (see Hanson, 1987).

3. Some of the cures in the gynecological texts should indeed cause us to pause for thought. Not because they are 'disgusting', but because they have strong cultural associations that have little to do with modern concepts of medicine, but are rather religious and indeed magical. Von Staden's work on (for example) the uses and connotations of asphalt, sulphur and squill is perhaps the most striking examination of this phenomenon (Von

Staden, 1992; 17–18). Here the problem comes not so much from ingredients such as the 'genitals of a stag' (*Diseases of Women* 2.224) but rather sections such as *Diseases of Women* 199 which in short order mentions wine, ivy and deer horn, all materials which can be found in close relationship with the god Dionysos (Burkert, 1985: 166). The prominent use of substances such as Cnidian grain and cumin (for example, *Diseases of Women* 34, 78, 80) becomes much more interesting when one traces the etymology of '*kokkos*' and the *ku-* root of the word cumin, which have strong sexual connections (in the case of cumin obviously connected to the shape of the seeds). The sounds of words may be significant: for example, the accumulation of *kappa* and *chi* sounds in passages such as *Nature of Woman* 1.32. It is true that neither Cnidian grains nor alliteration are confined to solely gynecological texts (see *Diseases* 2.48 for an example of both in a non-gynecological context) and the latter may simply be a stylistic conceit, but this should nonetheless alert us to the possibility of deeper layers in these texts. There are also times when the colour-associations of substances seem to come to the forefront. Black substances can be prominent in the gynecological texts (for example, *Diseases of Women* 26, 43, 126 (with 96) and 231; *Nature of Woman* 52), but white, red or other colours can be important too (*Diseases of Women* 232; *Nature of Woman* 94). Finally, if one attempts to defend the rationality of the use of feces in terms of its appropriateness in fumigations, one still has to explain why fumigations are quite so popular in gynecological cures. It is difficult not to explain this at least partly in terms of a preexisting idea of the womb as an animal with its own sense of smell, even if the Hippocratics would have explicitly denied such a belief (e.g. Hanson, 1991: 83, cf. Sissa, 1990: 149).

4. If the wandering womb might receive some plausibility from the fact of prolapse, one must still wonder how doctors continued to believe this idea after dissecting female animals (where they found that the womb couldn't simply move at random) when they were prepared to use such dissections as evidence for other aspects of the functioning of the womb (*Nature of the Child* 31 on pockets in the womb). And whatever its cause, it did effectively underpin a model of the female body prone to disequilibrium in a different way from that suffered in illnesses of men, with very different effects and very different cures; cures which reinforced the existing sexual hierarchy (e.g. Manuli, 1983: 159). Women were, on a number of levels, seen as inherently unstable (prone not just to the effects of the wandering womb but to the general problems of maintaining a balance between dryness and wetness). This is true whatever position one takes on hysteria: whether it was a disease reported by women, or created by men, or a function of the experiences of both (see Demand, 1994: 55ff for a summary of the debate).

5. Most importantly of all, Hipppocratic doctors do seem to have seen women as baby-making machines, connecting the majority of their problems with the functioning of their wombs (Dean-Jones, 1994). Sex (and pregnancy) are usually seen either as something that will protect the health of a woman and aid cures, or as proof that she is well. This is commonplace in the gynecological works, beginning with general statements and then manifesting itself in large numbers of individual cases (e.g. *Diseases of Women* 1.1, 1.2, 1.4, 2.115, 2.118 etc., *Illnesses of Young Girls* 1; *Nature of Woman* 2, 3, cf. 35, 43 etc.). This is not just because many of the texts that have survived for us are *directly* connected with problems of reproduction (so one could hardly be surprised that successful pregnancy is seen as the end point of the exercise). These ideas also appear in non-gynecological texts too, for example the *Epidemics* (e.g. 2.2.18 and 5.12). In *Epidemics* 5.25 we even find a woman cured by what could be described as a mock pregnancy (a stone shaped like a spindle weight is produced from the mouth of the womb) and in 6.1.1 headaches follow miscarriage until the time when the child *ought* to have been born. Given the belief that sex both lubricated and relaxed the mechanical operation of the female body (see e.g., *Diseases of Women* 1.2 for a womb drying out without sex, cf. *Generation* 4), there was an implicit bias towards early marriage and frequent sex. There were some occasions when the Hippocratics recognised sex as problematic, usually when it occurred too soon after pregnancy, causing a prolapse of the womb (e.g., *Diseases of Women* 1.5, 2.143–4, 3.247; *Nature of Woman* 4) but the stress on intercourse, given the problems with childbearing and the comparative lack of contraceptive or abortifacient advice in the texts (though see, for example, *Nature of Woman* 98) would not necessarily have been to the benefit of the female patient.

So there is a strangeness to these texts, at least to the modern eye, a strangeness we should not try to rationalise away. There is also, however, a further point that should be raised. There is a case to be made that the gynecological texts, whatever their oddities, look in other ways closer to modern medicine than many other Hippocratic writings.

Firstly, there are many attempts to explain what causes diseases which spills over into a greater willingness to use thought-experiment and experiment by analogy. The ideas of disease in *Diseases of Women* are obviously underpinned by a quite detailed model of the female body based on hydraulics (e.g., 1.2, 1.32, 1.61, 3.213, 3.217, cf. *Superfetation* 29 and *Illnesses of Young Girls* 1). *Diseases of Women* even begins (1.1) with an attempt to reason *why* women are 'wetter' than men, starting from the premise that they are softer, and then arguing from analogy that wool, a soft substance, soaks up more liquid from its surroundings than a denser cloth (though see Hanson, 1992: 37 on the cultural connection between wool-working and women). It has been suggested that such 'mechanical' or 'hydraulic' models are themselves a representation of a sexist view of the body, with women seen as mechanical and so 'base' in some sense (Hanson, 1991: 87). They are not, however, the *only* texts supplying such a mechanical model of the body: one can find it also in the *Sacred Disease* and *Generation* where it is applied to the bodies of men too. Such criticism also *presupposes* that the 'humoral' model of explaining disease, which is more prevalent in the non-gynecological texts represents a 'higher' form of explanation to the ancients than the hydraulic, mechanical model, a view easier to assert than prove. Whilst hydraulic explanations did have more far-reaching consequences for women (since their fluid 'balance' seems to have been much more under threat than that of men), they still represent a striking attempt to explain the aetiology of particular disorders. Apart from such conceptions there are also some more specific 'thought experiments'. *Generation/Nature of the Child* is perhaps the most striking example in the entire Hippocratic corpus of proof by thought-experiment and the use of analogy from the natural and animal world. It compares the development of human embryoes and those of birds (29), and draws parallels between the wombs of dogs, pigs and humans (31). It also offers a fine sustained argument to explain why *both* men and women must supply seed for the development of a child (6ff). This would appear, incidentally, to offer another example of the Hippocratics *escaping* some of the more major social prejudices of their time. There are even a few practical experiments in the gynecological texts: *Nature of Woman* 99 supplies a test to see if a woman was pregnant and there are a number of examples of tests designed to check whether a particular discharge is phlegmatic or cholic (cf. *Diseases of Women* 1.11, 1.22, etc., cf. *Nature of Woman* e.g. 22 and 106).

Secondly, these texts compare well with the best in the corpus (e.g. *Epidemics* 1 and 3; *Diseases* 1–3; *Internal Affections*; *Fractures* and *Joints*) for prognosis and diagnosis and therapy. For diagnosis and prognosis, see e.g. *Illnesses of Women* 4, 8–9, 26, 29, 41, 61 etc., and the first half of *Nature of Woman*. For detailed therapy see, e.g. *Diseases of Women* 13 (on a pessary). 23, 46, 53 (on a poultice), 75, 78, 133 (on another pessary, and a fumigation) and 230 (fumigation again); cf. *Nature of Woman* e.g. 29, 32, 62, and especially 109).

There have been many attempts in the past to separate the gynecological texts from the rest of the corpus. Some have tried to argue that they are 'Cnidian' (as opposed to the more philosophical and truly Hippocratical Coan) or 'primitive' (for the debate, see, e.g. Hanson, 1991: 75ff). Others have debated how far the texts represent the folk-loric knowledge of women and women healers (for a summary, see King, 1995: 206ff). This latter position is often dictated by a laudable desire to rescue the silent voice of ancient women, though there seems little possibility of establishing clear evidence for it (or for the increasing orthodoxy that texts such as *Diseases of Women* represent female knowledge overlaid with male theoretical elaboration). Yet, whatever way one categorizes these texts, there can be little doubt that they represent currents of thought present *throughout* the corpus. In any case, one can hardly simply put to one side texts which form to up to a quarter of all the extant Hippocratic writings and dealing with how doctors sought to heal between a quarter and a half of their patients. That many have sought to do just that says much for the way that modern ideas have led to us to wilfully misread the way Hippocratic medicine actually worked for its patients.

Feminist (and indeed post-modernist) thought provides us today with perhaps the most striking reading of the significance of the gynecological texts. Nancy Demand is at the forefront of those arguing that Hippocratic gynecology *in toto* represents an attempt by men to gain control over female reproduction and over an area of knowledge previously controlled by (wise) women (Demand, 1994: esp. 68–70, 146–7). One could, and should, expand on this argument. As she herself pointed out, the Hippocratic corpus *could* be read as an attempt generally to gain extra control and authority over *all* bodies, male as well as female (Demand, 1994: 206 fn 101, but not developed). Similarly, while she has argued that Hippocratic gynecology may actually have made things *worse* for female patients (by introducing inappropriate treatments based on erroneous theories: Demand, 1994: 86, 152), it should be obvious from what I have said above that I do believe that such a position need not be gender specific. Much of the theoretical side of Hippocratic medicine may have operated against male as well as female patients (though I would never deny a basic gender bias in the way ancient society or ancient medicine operated). It is time to take this point further and to come to a conclusion.

VIII. CONCLUSION

I would like to finish, as I began, by citing a non-Hippocratic author, indeed a non-Greek. Celsus was a Roman who wrote centuries after the acme of Hippocratic medicine. In his introduction to his handbook on medicine he sketched a debate that took place in the Hellenistic period, a hundred years or more after the death of Hippocrates. A number of groups had taken over the mantle of the Hippocratics in the production of literary medicine. Celsus described two such groups — the empiricists and the dogmatists. Again, the rights and wrongs of this particular debate (and indeed the accuracy of Celsus' report) are not my primary concern, but rather what the nature of the debate may tell us about our reading of ancient medicine. Dogmatists, apparently, wanted to look for the hidden as well as the more obvious, surface causes of disease, wishing to develop theories about the workings of the body and even investigate its internal workings directly (Celsus, *Prooemium* 13ff. I would prefer to leave aside the vexed question of human vivisection here, on which see Longrigg, 1993: 188ff). Their teachings were then compared by Celsus with those of the empiricists (*Prooemium* 27ff). The empiricists attacked the whole idea of opening bodies (living or dead) in order to investigate disease (41–2). They also refused (27–8) to go beyond evident causes or engage in theoretical debates. Rather unfairly they pointed to the very existence of the debates themselves and the failure to produce a single theory of disease as proof of the uselessness of such theory. Experience, they argued, taught what treatment should be used (32): trial and error (particularly with dietary cures), not abstract theorising, was what was important.

Now, which appears the more scientific, the more modern position? I would suggest that most readers would choose the dogmatists. But let us change the question. Which type of doctor might we prefer *treatment* from? Here the answer might be rather different. However impressive dogmatists might be in abstract terms I would suggest that, in the terms of the debate put to us by Celsus (and in view of the realities of ancient medicine sketched earlier in this text), the empiricists would have been a much safer choice, given the difficulties with any type of invasive medical technique (however well justified such techniques might be in modern terms). Empiricist medicine might seem much closer to folk medicine, but would it have been less likely or more likely to have been effective for that reason?

This does leave us, however, with what might appear a final paradox. Dogmatists were popular. More importantly for us, so was the approach enshrined in the Hippocratic theorists. They were famed at the time and that fame helps explain why they have survived for us to read. We have, however, little reason to believe that they were more likely to be effective in modern therapeutic terms than traditional forms of healing. Their methodological advances have been exaggerated and their ideas were often only likely to have added an extra layer of unsubstantiated theory to existing folk medicine. The more dramatic their intervention, indeed, the greater the danger that they might make things considerably worse. Why, then, the popularity? I stated that this *appears* a paradox, because it is a product of our peculiar attitude to Hippocratic medicine, which is often treated differently from other similar phenomena in the ancient world. Oracles and soothsaying were also very popular in antiquity, but few modern scholars seem interested in deciding how far the Delphic oracle (to give just one example) actually could tell the future. Instead they examine some of the functions that the oracle might have fulfilled. An oracular response might render difficult decisions easier to make. It might provide reassurance. Hippocratic medicine should also be examined within its social context. Curiously, more work has been done on this aspect of medicine for the Roman world rather than the Greek (though such an approach is implied in Langholf, 1990: 234–54. For the Roman period, see Gourevitch, 1984: 414–58, and, controversially, Barton, 1994: ch. 3). In the modern world, so in the ancient: doctors could fulfill a range of roles, and have an 'effectiveness' well beyond the narrow confines of the material technology of therapy. The doctor could help patients understand and accept illness, help society isolate it and control it in a psychological sense, provide companionship, hope, entertainment, even something or someone to blame. It was part of a greater philosophical tradition (beginning with the Presocratics and continuing with the Sophists) that claimed that man was the measure of his world and had control over his own destiny (for an introduction to Greek thought at the time, see Guthrie, 1965 and 1969).

A final twist: we may be too quick to condemn types of ancient health care which fit ill with our modern preconceptions, be they the charlatans and the witchdoctors of the opening sections of the *Sacred Disease* or the authors of some of the more exotic cures we saw in the gynecological texts. One should never forget that odd and unusual ingredients or colourful treatments (particularly if used at the end of long and complicated curative regimes) may well have had a profound psychological effect. This is not to claim that Hippocratic doctors indulged very much in psychotherapy (Lain-Etralgo, 1970: ch. 4; though cf. *Epidemics* 6.5.7). We should, nonetheless, not underestimate the placebo effect of such treatment. Indeed, in many cases it is difficult to see how cures could have been affected *other* than by the placebo effect. This leads us back to our charlatans and witchdoctors. There is a sense in which the charlatan may well have been as successful as the Hippocratic writers who complained about them. Indeed, given that a significant amount of the Hippocratic corpus may have been produced to encourage the confidence of the prospective patient, there may have been less difference between the two types of practitioners than the texts themselves would like to make us think.

Hippocratic medicine has to be seen as a social, not a scientific, phenomenon. Reading it as a 'science' inevitably imports modern concerns which distort the manner in which it operated and would have been perceived in antiquity. If it succeeded, it may well have succeeded in spite of, rather than because of, precisely those things for which it is most lauded today. In terms of modern therapeutic efficiency it was probably at its safest — and best — when it looks *least* modern to us. We should not exaggerate the technical side of ancient medicine. The tools of the trade will only ever give us a partial picture, in every sense of the term.

BIBLIOGRAPHY

All ancient works are cited from the Loeb Classical Library editions, excepting *Diseases of Women*; *Nature of Woman*; *Seven Months' Child*; *Eight Months' Child*; *Excision of the Foetus*; *Superfetation*; *Generation*; *Nature of the Child* and *Diseases IV*, which are from the edition of E. Littré, *Oeuvres complètes d'Hippocrates Vols. VII and VIII*, Amsterdam (1962): A. M. Hakert. For the Loeb editions, see W. H. S. Jones, W. D. Smith and P. Potter (tr.), *Hippocrates,* Vols. I–VIII, London and Cambridge Mass. (1923–95): Harvard University Press.

André, J.
(1987) *Être médecin à Rome*, Paris: Les Belles Lettres.
Barton, T.
(1994) *Power and Knowledge: Astrology, Physiognomics, and Medicine under the Roman Empire*, Ann Arbor: The University of Michigan Press.
Bliquez, J. L.
(1984) 'Greek and Roman medicine', *Archaeology* **34**:11–17.
Byl, S.
(1991) 'Le traitement de la doleur dans le Corpus hippocratique', in J. A. López Férez (ed.), *Tratados Hipocráticos (Estudios acerca de su contenido, forma e influencia): Actas del VIIe Colloque International Hippocratique (Madrid, 24–29 septiembre de 1990)*, Madrid, Universidad Nacional de Educacion a Distancia, pp. 203–13.
Calame, C.
(1983) 'Les avatars hippocratiques de quelques procédés de médecine traditionelle', in *Formes De Pensée dans la collection Hippocratique: Actes du IVe Colloque International Hippocratique (Lausanne, 21–26 Septembre 1981)*, Édition préparée par François Lassere et Philippe Mudry, Geneva, Libraire Droz S.A., pp. 129–36.
Corvisier, J. N.
(1985) *Santé et Société en Grèce Ancienne*, Paris: Économica.
Craik, E.
(1995) 'Diet, Diaitia and dietetics', in A. Powell (ed.), *The Greek World*, London: Routledge, pp. 387–402.
Cohn-Haft, L.
(1956) *The Public Physicians of Ancient Greece* (Smith College Studies in History, 42) Northampton, Mass, Department of History of Smith College.

Dean-Jones, L.
(1989) 'Menstrual bleeding according to the Hippocratics and Aristotle', *Transactions of the American Philological Association* **119**: 177–92.
(1991) 'The cultural construct of the female body in classical Greek science', in S. B. Pomeroy (ed.), *Women's History and Ancient History*, Chapel Hill and London: The University of North Carolina Press, pp. 111–37.
(1994a) *Women's Bodies in Classical Greek Science*, Oxford: Oxford University Press.
(1994b) 'Medicine: The "proof" of anatomy' in E. Fantham, H. P. Foley, N. B. Kampen, S. B. Pomeroy and H. A. Shapiro (eds.), *Women in the Classical World*, Oxford: Oxford University Press.

Deichgräber, K.
(1982) *Die Patienten des Hippokrates: historisch-prosopographische Beiträge zu den Epidemien des Corpus Hippocraticum*, Mainz: Akademie der Wissenschaft und der Literatur.

Demand, N.
(1994) *Birth, Death, and Motherhood in Classical Greece*, Baltimore and London: The Johns Hopkins University Press.
(1998) 'Women and slaves as Hippocratic patients', in S. R. Joshel and S. Murnaghan (eds.), *Women and Slaves in Greco-Roman culture: Differential Equations*, London: Routledge, pp. 69–84.

Edelstein, L and Edelstein, E.
(1945) *Asclepius: a collection and interpretation of the testimonies*, 2 vols, Baltimore: Johns Hopkins University Press.

Edelstein, L.
(1967) *Ancient Medicine: Selected papers of Ludwig Edelstein* (O. Temkin and C. Temkin eds.), Baltimore: Johns Hopkins University Press.

Ferngren, G. B.
(1985) 'Lay attitudes towards medical experimentation', *Bulletin of the History of Medicine* **59.4**: 495–505.

Gordon, R.
(1995) 'The healing event in Graeco-Roman folk-medicine', in Ph. J. van der Eijk, H. F. G. Horstmanshoff, P. H. Schrijvers (eds.), *Ancient Medicine in its socio-cultural context*, Vol 2, Amsterdam: Rodopi, pp. 363–76

Gourevitch, D.
(1984) *Le triangle hippocratique dans le monde Gréco-Roman: la malade, sa maladie et son médecin*, Paris: École Française de Rome.

Grmek, M.
(1989) *Diseases in the Ancient Greek World*, Baltimore: Johns Hopkins University Press.

Guthrie, W. K. C.
(1962) *A History of Greek Philosophy Vol. 1: The Earlier Presocratics and the Pythagoreans*, Cambridge: Cambridge University Press.
(1965) *A History of Greek Philosophy Vol. 2: The Presocratic Tradition from Parmenides to Democritus*, Cambridge: Cambridge University Press.
(1969) *A History of Greek Philosophy Vol. 3: The Fifth Century Enlightenment*, Cambridge: Cambridge University Press.

Hall, E.
(1991) *Inventing the Barbarian*, Oxford: Clarendon Press.

Hanson, A. E.
(1987) 'The eighth month child: obsit omen', *Bulletin of the History of Medicine* **61**: 589–602.
(1990) 'The medical writer's woman', in D. Halperin (ed.), *Before Sexuality*, Cambridge Mass.: Princeton University Press, pp. 309–37.
(1991) 'Continuity and change: three case studies in Hippocratic gynecological therapy and theory', in S. B. Pomeroy (ed.), *Women's History and Ancient History*, Chapel Hill and London: The University of North Carolina Press, pp. 73–110.

Harig, G.
(1980) 'Anfänge der theoretischen Pharmakologie im Corpus Hippocraticum', in M. Grmek (ed.), *Hippocratica: Actes du Colloque hippocratique de Paris (4–9 septembre 1978)*, Paris: CNRS 1980, pp. 223–46.

Harig, G. and Kollesch, J.
(1978) 'Der Hippokratische Eid: Zur Entstehung der antiken medizinischen Deontologie', *Philologus* **122**: 157–76.

Joly, R.
(1966) *Le niveau de la science hippocratique. Contribution à la psychologie de l'histoire des sciences*, Paris: Les Belles Lettres.
(1980) 'Un peu d'épistémologie historique pour hippocratisants', in M. Grmek (ed.) *Hippocratica: Actes du Colloque hippocratique de Paris (4–9 septembre 1978)*, Paris: CNRS 1980, pp. 285–98.

Jones, W. H. S.
(1909) *Malaria and Greek History*, Oxford: Oxford University Press.

Jouanna, J
(1998) 'The birth of Western medical art', in M. Grmek (ed.) *Western Medical Thought from Antiquity to the Middle Ages*, Cambridge, Mass: Harvard University Press, pp. 22–71.
(1999) *Hippocrates*, Baltimore and London: Johns Hopkins University Press.

Kearns, E.
(1987) 'Review of A. Krug *Heilkunst und Heilkult*', *Classical Review* **37**: 331–2.

King, H.
(1988) 'The early anodynes: pain in the ancient world', in R. D. Mann (ed.), *The History of the Management of Pain: From Early Principles to Present Practices*, Park Ridge N.J.: Parthenon Publishing Group, pp. 51–62.
(1994) 'Producing women: Hippocratic gynecology', in L. Archer, S. Fischler and M. Wyke (eds.), *Women in Ancient Societies: An Illusion of the Night*, London: Routledge, pp. 102–14.
(1995) 'Medical texts as a source for women's history', in A. Powell (ed.), *The Greek World*, London, pp. 199–218.
(1998) *Hippocrates' Woman: Reading the Female Body in Ancient Greece*, London: Routledge.

Kirk, G. S, Raven, J. E. and Schofield, M.
(1983) *The Presocratic Philosophers*, 2nd edition, Cambridge: Cambridge University Press.

Krug, A.
(1993) *Heilkunst und Heilkult: Medizin in der Antike*, 2nd edition, Munich: C. H. Beck.

Kudlien, F.
(1968) *Die Sklaven in der griechischen Medizin der klassischen und hellenistischen Zeit,* Wiesbaden: Steiner.
(1970) 'Medical education in classical antiquity', in C. D. O'Malley (ed.), *The History of Medical Education,* Berkeley: University of California Press, pp. 3–37.

Lain-Entralgo, P.
(1970) *The Therapy of the Word in Classical Antiquity*, New Haven and London: Yale University Press.

Langholf, V.
(1990) *Medical Theories in Hippocrates — Early Texts and the 'Epidemics'*, Berlin, New York: W. de Gruyter.

Lloyd, G. E. R.
(1966) *Polarity and Analogy: Two Types of Argumentation in Early Greek Thought*, Cambridge: Cambridge University Press.
(1979) *Magic, Reason, and Experience: Studies in the Origin and Development of Greek Science*, Cambridge: Cambridge University Press.
(1983) *Science, Folklore and Ideology,* Cambridge: Cambridge University Press.
(1987) *The Revolutions of Wisdom: Studies in the Claims and Practice of Ancient Greek Science*, Berkeley and London: University of California Press.
(1991) *Methods and Problems in Greek Science,* Cambridge: Cambridge University Press.
(1992) 'The transformation of ancient medicine', *Bulletin of the History of Medicine* **66.1**: 114–32.
(1996) *Adversaries and Authorities: Investigations into Ancient Greek and Chinese Science,* Cambridge: Cambridge University Press.

Lonie, I. M.
(1978) 'Cos versus Cnidus and the historians', *History of Science* **16**: 42–75, 77–92.

Longrigg, J.
(1993) *Greek Rational Medicine: Philosophy and Medicine from Alcmaeon to the Alexandrians*, London: Routledge.

Majno, G.
(1975) *The Healing Hand: Man and Wound in the Ancient World*, Cambridge, Mass.: Harvard University Press.

Manuli, P.
(1983) 'Donne masculine, femmine sterile, vergini perpetue: la ginecologia greca tra ippocrate e sorano' in S. Campese, P. Manuli and G. Sissa (eds.), *Madre Materia: Sociologia e biologia della donna greca,* Turin: Boringhieri, pp. 149–85.

Milne, J. S.
(1907) *Surgical Instruments in Greek and Roman Times,* Oxford: Clarendon Press.

Nutton, V.
(1983) 'The seeds of disease — an explanation of contagion and infection from the Greeks to the Renaissance', *Medical History* **27.1**: 1–34.
(1986) 'The perils of patriotism: Pliny and Roman medicine', in P. Green and F. Greenaway (eds.), *Science in the Early Roman Empire: Pliny the Elder and his Sources*, London: Croom Helm, pp. 30–58.
(1990) 'The patient's choice, a new treatise by Galen', *Classical Quarterly* **40.1**: 236–57.
(1992) 'Healers in the medical market place: towards a social history of Graeco-Roman medicine', in A. Wear (ed.) *Medicine in Society: Historical Essays,* Cambridge: Cambridge University Press, pp. 15–59.
(1995) 'The medical meeting place', in Ph. J. van der Eijk, H. F. G. Horstmanshoff, P. H. Schrijvers (eds.), *Ancient Medicine in its Socio-cultural Context: Vol 1*, Amsterdam: Rodopi, pp. 3–26.
(1999) 'Healers and the healing act in Classical Greece', *European Review* **7.1**: 27–35.

Parker, R.
(1983) *Miasma: Pollution and Purification in Early Greek Religion,* Oxford: Clarendon Press.

Phillips, E. D
(1987) *Aspects of Greek Medicine*, London: Croom Helm.

Riddle, J. M.
(1985) *Diocorides on Pharmacy and Medicine,* Austin: University of Texas Press.
(1992) *Contraception and Abortion from the Ancient World to the Renaissance,* Cambridge, Mass: Harvard University Press.

Roselli, A.
(1975) *La chirurgia ippocratica*, Florence: La Nuova Italia Editrice.

Sallares, R.
(1990) *The Ecology of the Ancient Greek World*, London: Duckworth.

Scarborough, J.
(1983) 'Theoretical assumptions in Hippocratic pharmacology', in *Formes De Pensée dans la collection Hippocratique: Actes du IVe Colloque International Hippocratique* (Lausanne, 21–26 Septembre 1981), Édition préparée par François Lassere et Philippe Mudry, pp. 307–26.
(1991) 'The pharmacology of sacred plants, herbs and roots', in C. A. Faraone and D. Obbink (eds.), *Magika Hiera: Ancient Greek Magic and Religion,* Oxford: Oxford University Press, pp. 138–74.
(1995) 'The opium poppy in Hellenistic and Roman medicine', in R. Porter and M. Teich (eds.), *Drugs and Narcotics in History,* Cambridge: Cambridge University Press, pp. 4–23.

Sigerist, H.
(1961) *A History of Medicine. — Vol. 2: Early Greek, Hindu, and Persian medicine*, New York: Oxford University Press.

Sissa, G.
(1990) *Greek Virginity,* Cambridge, Mass.: Harvard University Press.

Smith, W. D.
(1973) 'Galen on Coan vs Cnidian', *Bulletin of the History of Medicine* **47**: 569–85.
(1979) *The Hippocratic Tradition,* Ithaca and London: Cornell University Press.

Stannard, J.
(1961) 'Hippocratic pharmacology', *Bulletin of the History of Medicine* **35**: 497–518.

Temkin, O.
(1991) *Hippocrates in a World of Pagans and Christians*, Baltimore: Johns Hopkins University Press.

Von Staden, H.
(1992) 'Women, dirt and exotica in the Hippocratic corpus', *Helios* **19**: 7–30.

Wallace-Hadrill, A.
(1988) 'Greek knowledge and Roman power', *Classical Philology* **83**: 224–33.

Wörhle, G.
(1990) *Studien zur Theorie der Antiken Gesundheitslehre* Stuttgart: Franz Steiner Verlag.

THE ROMAN MILITARY *VALETUDINARIA*: FACT OR FICTION?

Patricia Baker

INTRODUCTION

The first Roman military *valetudinarium* or hospital to be identified was that at the legionary fortress of Novaesium, located in Neuss on the lower Rhine. Previously, military hospitals in fortifications were known only from Hyginus in his *Liber de Munitionibus Castrorum*, a late first century text on the arrangement of marching fortifications. Hyginus stated that a hospital was to be found in every fortress, but he did not provide a description of its layout — only its location (*gromat.* 4). Thus, without any discussion of the building's plan, none had been distinguished until Koenen identified a previously undetermined structure at Neuss as a *valetudinarium*. He identified the building as a hospital because the layout suited his idea of what a hospital should be: a building with a number of small rooms, or wards, divided by small hallways that would aid in keeping the rooms quiet. Furthermore, one room in the structure at Neuss had a number of instruments that can be categorised as having both the qualities of surgical and toilet implements, which further convinced Koenen of the function of the building (1904: 180–2). Following his discovery, other buildings with a similar design were accepted as *valetudinaria* without question, as they still tend to be by archaeologists and ancient historians. As Bidwell says, 'Courtyard buildings in or behind the central range have long been identified as hospitals; conclusive evidence of their function has never been forthcoming from auxiliary forts, but much larger courtyard buildings in fortresses have been satisfactorily identified as hospitals' (1997: 71). Yet Bidwell does not explain what the evidence is for this satisfactory identification. Press also shows a willingness to accept Koenen's discovery as she says, 'the discovery of the building at Neuss brought an answer to the question concerning the layout of the legionary hospital's design and plan'. Press goes on to say, 'some archaeologists had doubts as to the correctness of the identification of the building, but the discovery of other buildings with a similar plan confirmed Koenen's opinion' (1988: 69). Yet how could a building with a similar plan confirm the identification when it merely demonstrates that other buildings of this design were constructed in other fortresses? It should not be taken for granted that they were intended to be hospitals. Since these buildings are accepted to be hospitals, other writers have used the evidence for their arguments about medical care without much question of the structure. Wilmanns, for example, uses the identification of legionary hospitals to support her argument that there was a need for doctors in legionary fortresses (1995: 103–16). Therefore, this inclination to accept the identification of a building on the basis of one room with (sometimes non-surgical) instruments, along with an anachronistic preconception of how a hospital should be arranged, demonstrates that there is a need to re-examine the evidence.

LITERARY EVIDENCE

The epigraphic and literary evidence informs us that hospitals did exist in both legionary and auxiliary fortifications. An inscription from an auxiliary fort at Stojnik in Serbia, occupied by the second cohort of equites (*CIL* III 14537=*ILS* 9147), has the word *valetudinarium* inscribed on it, as does one from Aleppo in Syria (*AE* 1987: 952). Sadly the provenances of the inscriptions are not noted. Had each inscription been associated with a particular building than perhaps the structure might have provided a precise idea about how the plan or layout of the hospital appeared. Inscriptions that mention the *optio valetudinarii*, a person in charge of the hospital, provide supporting evidence. For example there are two *optio valetudinarii* recorded at Lambaesis in Africa (*CIL* VIII 2553 and *CIL* VIII 2563), one from Bonn (*CIL* XIII 8099) and one from Italy (*CIL* VI 175). The first three are from legionary fortresses, whilst the latter is not specified, but again these inscriptions never seem to have been associated with a particular building.

To further support the existence of hospitals, a damaged list from Vindolanda mentions 343 men who were associated with the workshop. One line has the word *valetudinarium* inscribed on it (Bowman and Thomas, 1994: 155). However, since the fragment is damaged there is nothing surviving that indicates the significance of the word. It can probably be assumed that the word was referring to those who built the hospital, as part of the tablet mentions the tasks that people who belonged to the *fabrica* were expected to perform. Perhaps it was referring to people who worked in, or made supplies for, the hospital. It could possibly have been an indication that those who worked in the hospital, such as doctors or *medici*, were associated with the *fabrica* because the body was repaired in the hospital just as objects were in the workshops. The word might also be an implication that the hospital was actually part of the workshops, rather than being a separate building itself. It is not impossible that the *valetudinaria* were rooms in sections of other buildings, rather than being a complete building itself; although this is something that we would not consider today due to sanitary reasons. The Romans were aware of cleanliness being a part of good health, as they were obviously concerned with personal hygiene, evident from the number of baths and toilet instruments found in the archaeological record. Despite this, they were still unaware of the bacteria that caused disease, so a place that appeared clean was not necessarily sterile, and it is possible that the Romans used areas of other buildings for hospitals if they appeared clean.

Finally a papyrus fragment found in Egypt also indicates the existence of hospitals. The fragment is an order form from a military hospital in Cappodocia requesting a white blanket to be sent to the fortification hospital. The order requested that the blanket should be plain and white. It was also asked in the order that the blanket be of good, soft, pure white wool without any stain and that is to be well woven, firm, with finished hems, satisfactory without damage (*BGU* 1564=Sp 395, papyrus Egypt 138; Campbell, 1994: 239). Despite the fact that there is no evidence for how the hospital might have appeared, there is some indication that they might have been clean structures as the fragment requests that the blanket be so.

As mentioned above, there is only one source that provides any information about the hospitals as structures and that was Hyginus (*gromat.* 4), who also provides us with a better understanding of the location of the building. According to Hyginus the hospital was to be constructed above or beyond the *praetorium*, or commanding officer's house. He suggests that this is a quiet area of the fortification. It is often assumed by archaeologists that his suggestion for the location of the building was always followed by the people who constructed the site (e.g. von Petrikovitz, 1975: 98), but when comparing fortifications of both legionary and auxiliary units, it immediately becomes apparent that not all of the so-called hospitals were placed in the same position in every fortification.

Another interesting point about Hyginus' suggestion for the location of the hospitals is that they were to be located near the *fabrica* and the *veterinarium,* as all three buildings were used for the repair of something. The aforementioned Vindolanda tablet supports this, as the word *valetudinarium* was mentioned along with other aspects of the workshops. Thus, there is the possibility that the hospital was actually considered to be part of the system of workshops, or it may have been built in the workshop, rather then having been a separate building.

Other primary literary sources have been used to further support the idea that there were hospitals (e.g. Conrad *et al,* 1995: 49–51; Davies, 1989: 221–2; Nutton, 1969: 261–3; Scarborough, 1976: 78–9). However, when the Latin or Greek is examined carefully, it becomes clear that some statements have been over-interpreted. One such example, interpreted by Davies, is from Hadrian's biography, in which a statement is made about how he would visit the sick in their quarters, which is a demonstration of his being a concerned emperor whilst on campaign, *Aegros milites in hospitiis suis videret* (*SHA* 10. 3). It is important to point out from this passage that Hadrian visited the sick in the *hospitium*, rather than in a *valetudinarium*. *Hospitium* is similar in meaning to the Greek word xenodoceion, and can be translated to mean a place for foreigners to stay, literally a place to receive hospitality. In a more specific military context it can be translated to mean quarters or barracks rather than a hospital, showing that Davies' interpretation can be challenged. Thus the Latin indicates that the sick and wounded would not necessarily be placed in a hospital building for treatment or recuperation.

The biography of Severus Alexander describes him visiting the sick in their tents *aegrotantes ipse visitavit per tentoria milites* (*SHA* Severus Alexander 47.2), implying that this was probably a common practice, or at least expected of good emperors and generals. Since the writer uses the word for tent rather than hospital, it may suggest that the soldiers were placed in the tents along with others, healthy or wounded, from their ranks. Moreover, since the plural for tents is used, there is greater evidence that the emperor was not visiting a single tent used for a hospital. There is a further suggestion from Tacitus that the soldiers were placed in their regular tents, which states that in the same tents some nursed the wounds of brothers, others of relatives: *Isdem tentoriis alii fratrum, alii propinquorum volnera fovebant* (*Histories* 2. 45). From these three statements it is difficult to decide whether hospitals were instituted during campaigns and if so, if every camp had one and if they were placed in the same areas of the fortification.

According to Majno (1975: 382), a quotation by Livy (10. 35. 7) provides the reason why hospitals were created in marching camps and then became part of permanent structures. Livy states that during the Samnite Wars in 294 BC soldiers sharing quarters with the casualties were dispirited because they were kept awake by the groans of the wounded and the dying, ...*sed militum iacere animos; tota nocte inter volnera et gemitus morientium vigilatum esse*. Yet, even two hundred years later, during the time of Julius Caesar, the soldiers were still with the sick on campaign (*BG* 1. 26. 5), as they most likely were during the reign of Hadrian (*SHA Hadrian* 10. 3). Majno's statement does not seem to show that the hospitals were created because of such reasons, but it does display the fact that soldiers were possibly living with the wounded.

For soldiers not on campaign there is the possibility that perhaps only patients suffering from certain diseases or wounds were expected to be placed in the hospital for recuperation. A daily report from Vindolanda lists the number of soldiers who were available for their duties and the numbers and whereabouts of those who were absent (Bowman and Thomas, 1991: 62–73). Ten percent of the soldiers who were absent were missing on account of illness. Those who were ill were divided into three categories: those suffering from eye problems, injury and illness. It is possible that the three groups were divided because they had different places to convalesce. For example, those who were absent because of illness might have been left to recuperate in their barracks, and this is supported by a papyrus fragment of a soldier's letter to his parents from Egypt (P. Mich. 478). The soldier was ill because of food poisoning due to rancid fish. In his letter he mentions being fed by members of his troop. This might mean that fellow soldiers attended him — had he been in a *valetudinarium* he would probably have mentioned a doctor or someone else associated with the medical field feeding him. However, it might also be an indication that soldiers sometimes helped their ill comrades, yet it still seems that he might have mentioned the word *valetudinarium*. This could indicate that the soldiers, when ill, may have stayed in their barracks, depending upon the nature of the disease. Again, more questions are raised about the nature of the hospital from this statement rather than answers. It might have implied that a specific doctor was provided for certain treatments, but then one must ask where the treatments were being offered, demonstrating the possibility that there might have been different ideas about what a hospital should be in Roman thought. As for the wounded and those suffering from eye diseases, they too might have been placed elsewhere, but again no specific information is provided.

ARCHITECTURAL EVIDENCE

Although the literary evidence proves that hospitals did exist, there is no specific description about how the buildings may have appeared. Thus, an examination of the architecture is necessary to the question whether there is enough evidence in the archaeological record to support the identification of structures as hospitals. The legionary fortresses that are thought to have contained hospitals are Haltern, Vetera I and II, Neuss, Bonn, Vindonissa, Carnuntum, Novae, Inchtuthil and Caerleon. Hospitals have also been argued for the legionary fortresses at Regensburg, Chester, Lauriacum and Vindobona, but there is even less structural evidence to support the argument. One has even been claimed for Aquincum, but there is hardly any evidence on which to base the identification (Póczy, 1976: 27). A number of auxiliary forts — Valkenburg, Wiesbaden, Oberstimm, Künzing, Housesteads, Benwell, Hodd Hill, Wallsend, Fendoch and Pen Llysten — have structures that have, at some point, also been argued to be hospitals. Nevertheless, in some instances the structures appear similar to the layout of *fabrica*, such as with the building at Valkenburg (Schönberger, 1979).

According to Pitts and St. Joseph, all legionary fortress *valetudinaria* were constructed on a similar plan (1985: 91). Nonetheless, the size and shape of the 'hospitals' vary, illustrating the difficulties in defining the structures as such on appearances only. In shape, legionary fortress hospitals generally consist of two rectangular halls of rooms arranged around a central courtyard. The rooms, or wards, tend to be organised so that two rooms were placed next to each other forming a single set that was divided from another set of rooms by a small hallway, such as at Vetera I (Fig. 1). Auxiliary fort hospitals tend to be of two general types: smaller versions of the legionary hospital, but with a single rectangle of rooms surrounding a courtyard such as at Housesteads (Fig. 2), Benwell and Wallsend; or a long rectangular building with a central hall such as at Künzing (Fig. 3), Oberstimm, Fendoch, Valkenburg and Wiesbaden. Although there were some buildings in fortifications that were constructed on a set of similar plans, such as the barracks, headquarters buildings, granaries and baths, even these are not entirely alike from fort to fort. Moreover, there are other buildings such as *fabrica* and storage facilities that have greater variations in their plan and sometimes have very little resemblance to structures in other Roman fortifications, and the artefacts are too few to provide a precise identification of what the building was intended to be.

The size of the structures ranges from 73.0 × 58.4 metres at Vetera I to 123.0 × 68.0 metres at Lotschitz. The central hall style buildings identified as hospitals located in auxiliary forts range from 18.0 × 13.0 metres at Oberstimm, to 35.0 × 12.0 metres at Valkenburg; and the courtyard-style structures in auxiliary forts range from 30.0 × 22.0 metres at Housesteads to 24.7 × 22.5 metres at Benwell. The noticeable difference in the sizes of the structures demonstrates that if the buildings are hospitals then they were not constructed on a standard plan, as is expected.

Fig. 1. The legionary 'hospital' plan from Vetera I (after Johnson, 1983).

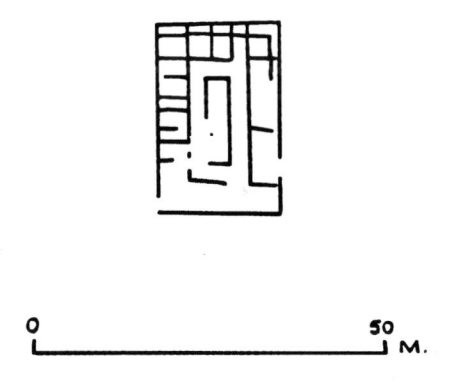

Fig. 2. The auxiliary 'hospital' plan from Housesteads (after Johnson, 1983).

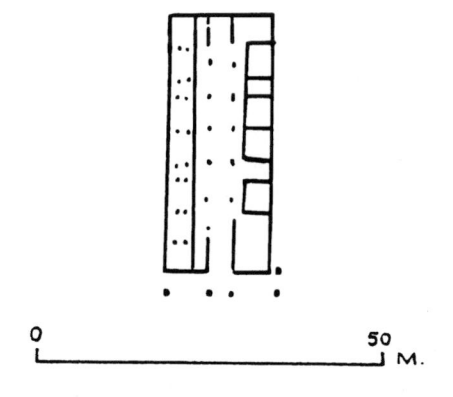

Fig. 3. The auxiliary 'hospital' plan from Künzing (after Johnson, 1983).

The interior of each structure contains different arrangements and sizes of rooms, again making their identification even more questionable. In the legionary fortresses, those buildings that have been excavated thoroughly all have a courtyard plan with two rows of wards; yet, the wards are of different sizes. Although these do not vary as much in comparison with entire hospital sizes as a whole, even a minor difference implies that the buildings might not have been intended for the same purpose. If they were, then they had been adjusted according to the needs of those occupying the fortification.

There are specific rooms that are thought by a number of writers to have been part of every hospital: baths, operating theatres and latrines (e.g. von Petrikovitz, 1975; Press, 1988). The so-called hospital in Vetera I had a bath, and some rooms in Neuss and Carnuntum had a hypocaust system, often associated with bathing. However, hypocausts were also used to heat other rooms in the fortifications. Warm rooms would have been sensible for the sick and wounded soldiers, in addition to the provision of their own baths, preventing the need for them to leave the comfort and warmth of the *valetudinarium*. Nonetheless, there is not enough structural evidence to support the idea that every hospital had a bath. Bathing was a means of treatment in Roman times and some soldiers were even sent to specially designated baths for recovery, such as at Baden Baden in Germania Superior, Baden in Switzerland and Aquae Sulis (Bath) in Britannia (Doppler, 1970/71: 26). However, perhaps some hospitals did not have private baths for the sick, but the soldiers were either sponge-bathed, or sent to the camp bath.

Latrines are also assumed to be present in all so-called fortification hospitals. Yet again, there is little evidence for them. There was a possible latrine found at Housesteads and one at Wallsend. Other fortifications such as at Neuss and Vindonissa have drains assumed to have been for latrines, but their intended purpose is not clearly seen.

Operating theatres are integral to any modern hospital, so most Roman *valetudinaria* are expected to have had one as well. In spite of this claim there is no description of their existence in Roman literary sources. The only idea provided to us about where the doctors performed their surgery is from Celsus, who recommends a well-lit area to perform a cataract operation, *Post haec in advorso collocandus est, luco lucido, lumine adverso* (7. 7. 14C). Archaeologists believe that the physical remains of rooms that protrude into the courtyard such as at Neuss and Vetera I were operating theatres, because it is believed they would have had brighter light and fresher air (von Petrikovitz, 1975: 101). Larger rooms in other structures such as at Housesteads, Wallsend, Künzing and Oberstimm have been defined as operating theatres because the space would allow room for more equipment and for doctor's movement. Nevertheless, when reading any description of how Roman surgical procedures were to be performed it seems as if the doctor often had to be in a position close to the patient. Quite often it is suggested that the patient sat rather than lay down (e.g. Celsus 7. 7. 14C). In comparison, modern operating theatres need the space for an operating table, electronic equipment, a team of surgeons and nurses, large lamps and tanks for anaesthetic gases. No Roman operating theatre, if they existed, would have needed room to accommodate the same number of instruments and people that are required in modern operating theatres. Again it is demonstrated that anachronistic preconceptions are imposed on conceptions of Roman hospitals.

The final two rooms that are mentioned repeatedly in archaeological descriptions of hospitals are the possible kitchen and cult room. Some of the structures have hearths within them that were originally suggested as being used by doctors to sterilise their instruments (Schultze, 1934: 55). However, as it became clear that this was not a Roman practise, the hearths were then said to be a component in kitchens. Kitchens in Roman fortifications, however, are not widely known of because it seems that most soldiers were expected to cook their own meals, and hearths are often found throughout many buildings and could have had a variety of functions, such as cooking and heating. Without artefactual evidence of food remains or cooking implements, one cannot indicate with certainty if kitchens were part of the *valetudinaria*. This is a reasonable suggestion, though the 'hospital' at Housesteads has hearths with evidence of high temperature burning (Crow, 1995: 50–1), probably an indication of metal-working.

The cult rooms claimed to have been part of all the hospitals are also lacking in evidence. The structure at Vindobona had two altars found within one room. However, one of the altars had been reused as *spolia* in part of the wall of the building, whilst the other was found *in situ*. The altar found *in situ* was dedicated to Aesculapius along with Jupiter, whilst the other was dedicated to Apollo (Neumann, 1965: 103). A building that has two altars dedicated to gods of health does not necessarily make the structure a hospital. Some forts had buildings used for places for socialising and these were often based around religious activity, making it plausible that the room at Vindobona might have been used for a social or religious function.

When looking at the placement of the so-called hospitals in their fortifications, evidently the advice of Hyginus might not have been followed because the 'hospitals' were not all constructed in the same area of each fortification. The legionary fortresses of Haltern, Vetera I, Bonn, Vindonissa, Vindobona, Lotschitz, Lauriacum, Caerleon and Novae had buildings claimed to be hospitals in the *praetentora*, whilst others were constructed in the *latera praetorii*: Neuss, Carnuntum, Inchtuthil and Chester. In the auxiliary forts the so-called hospitals located in the *praetentora* were at Valkenburg, Wiesbaden, Künzing, Benwell and Hodd Hill. Those in the *latera praetorii* were found at Oberstimm, Housesteads, Wallsend and Fendoch. Since the buildings identified as hospitals appear in a couple of areas of the fortifications it either suggests that Hyginus' advice was not always followed, or if all the structures were located behind the Commanding Officer's house then they do not follow a similar plan. Had there been a standard system then all of the structures would probably have been built with an identical layout in the same location.

Although Hyginus suggests that hospitals be in a quiet place, the locations of many so-called hospitals do not appear to be in quiet areas. Vetera I was located next to a gate with possible shops placed at its entrance, whilst Künzing's argued hospital was built next to a granary without any surrounding buildings. This brings us to questioning what the Romans thought of as quiet, as one would not expect shops and the granary during deliveries and distributions would have been peaceful places.

Many of the structures did not have buildings constructed around them, showing that they may have varied in their construction, or that perhaps they were part of other structures, or were located in various areas of the fort depending on where was considered to have the least amount of noise.

The finer details of the *valetudinarium* arrangements are also described as if the buildings were modern hospitals. The sleeping arrangements are discussed by Majno (1975: 387) and von Petrikovitz (1975: 101), who state that there was probably space for four or five people, each having their own bed (Fig. 4). To the modern reader, this seems perfectly reasonable; nonetheless we know very little about the sleeping arrangements of the Romans. When looking at other cultures it becomes clear that the one person or couple per bed is not always the norm. The Pennsylvania Dutch or Amish practice bundling, whereby they use their beds as couches in the winter months. Since the Amish do not have heating in their houses they find that it is more comfortable and practical to invite a guest to sit under the covers of their beds for warmth. In order to avoid possible 'temptation', a length of wood known as a bundling board is placed down the centre of the bed separating the two occupants. Mention can also be made of the 16th century 'great bed of Ware' (held in the Victoria and Albert Museum) that could have slept about fifteen people. In the inns of colonial America an overnight visitor paid for a space rather than a room and might have had to sleep in the same bed with a stranger, or even on the floor. It is possible, therefore, that soldiers might have had different sleeping arrangements while they were sick or even when healthy in their barracks. These cross-cultural examples further demonstrate the problems with applying modern western habits onto those of the Romans.

Overall, when looking at the arrangement of these buildings, they appear to offer a beneficial design for a hospital with small wards, possible operating theatres, kitchens, baths and latrines. However, this is the modern perception of how a hospital should be arranged. According to Thomas we write the past in the present, and archaeologists tend to use their experiences as a means of explaining how things functioned in the past (1990: 18–23). Clearly this has been done with the identification of the 'hospitals'. Evans points out that such institutionalised buildings designed for a specific purpose, as we think of them, tend to be a feature of the 18th century and later (1990: 648). It is clear that there were some similar buildings in the military that might be classed as institutional, such as the barracks and the headquarters building and other internal buildings. However, even these differ from fortification to fortification (Johnson, 1983: 105–56). Therefore, it is possible that the hospital was not an institutionalised building in the sense of conforming to a prescribed style or plan. The comparisons shown above indicate that the expectation that all hospitals were built with the same integral features is merely an assumption, and the structural evidence shows very little of what is often expected to have been typical.

An examination of civilian Roman hospitals might shed some light onto how the military hospitals were arranged, though there is even less evidence for these than the military hospitals. In the literary sources Celsus mentions hospitals, commenting that the larger the building the less treatment available to the people by the person in charge of running the structure: *et qui ampla valetudinaria nutriunt, quia singulis summa cura consulere non sustinent, ad communia ista confugiunt* (*Proemium* 65). This statement in itself implies that such structures did exist. Jackson refers to *Taberna Medicae* or places where civilians could go to receive treatment, much like a modern doctor's office (1988: 65). It is also known from Galen that doctors would visit their patients at their homes (Horstmanshoff, 1995: 84–5). Yet, Horstmanshoff concludes that Galen preferred to treat wealthier patients (1995: 91), so it is possible that poorer patients might not have received visiting doctors, but had to go to the doctor themselves, providing many doctors held the same attitudes as Galen about whom they preferred to treat. These literary statements are further proof of the number of different places civilians could receive treatment and this may have been the case for the military as well.

Since there are many questions about the identification of the Roman hospital's structure, a comparison of the Medieval English hospital might provide more evidence about the arrangement of the *valetudinarium*. If we follow the logic that the Roman hospitals were expected to have been similar to the early 20th century hospitals, than one would expect the Medieval hospital to be based on a similar plan. The Medieval hospitals were designed in an open basilica, similar to a church, possibly because many were run by the church. Most large Medieval buildings follow one of two plans. The first is the church plan or basilica, and the second is the large open hall used in the construction of high status structures. The limited range of both institutionalised and domestic structures can be seen in Medieval towns, such as Cambridge (*RCHME* 1959). In Medieval basilica hospitals there was usually a chapel or a group of chapels at the end of the nave so patients could witness the daily celebrations. St. Mary's in Newark, Leicestershire, had room for thirty inmates with a single bed each. Some were able to see the service given from balconies. There was separate accommodation for hospital staff, usually in an unattached building located off the side of the infirmary. Travellers often lodged with the sick, in the same rooms, and there does not seem to have been a division of genders (Carlin, 1989: 28). Renaissance Italian hospitals were also based on the basilica plan. In some cases the hospitals were constructed in a cruciform design where eve-

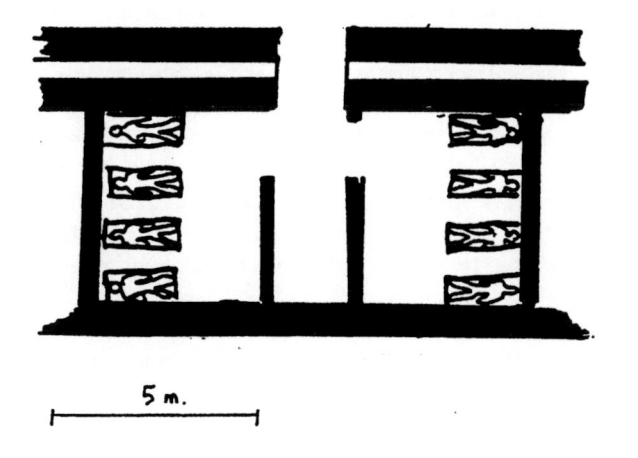

Fig. 4. Conjectured sleeping arrangement in 'hospitals' (after Majno, 1975).

ryone could observe the daily religious services taking place in the centre of the building (Henderson, 1989: 76). The plan of the hospital seems to be determined by the dictates of religious services – religion defines the organisation of treatment. Thus, the Medieval hospital, for which there is more evidence, looks nothing like a Roman hospital is thought to be. Perhaps the Medieval doctors rejected the idea of the Roman hospital, or perhaps the design does follow the Roman one, and the Roman hospital plan has been mis-identified. The Byzantine hospital also does not seem to have developed from a Roman military design. Miller argues that they developed as houses for the sick and poor (1985: 5). He also points out that it is rather difficult to determine whether there were buildings or an organisation that was specifically meant for the sick in the Byzantine era (1985: 24–5). So it seems that there was not a military plan that was followed for further development of hospitals.

When looking at the structural evidence it becomes clear that there is very little on which to base the identification of the hospital. The layout is based on a modern (or at least a late nineteenth or early twentieth century) ideal, but since there is little surviving in the literary evidence stating how the Roman hospitals functioned and appeared makes this identification on structural evidence questionable. Moreover, the argument is made even weaker because some of the structures, especially those in auxiliary forts, look like buildings that have been identified as *fabrica* or storehouses.

ARTEFACTUAL EVIDENCE

The final aspect that should be investigated relates to where remains of surgical or surgical/toilet instruments were found in the fortifications, because this might provide a better indication of where the *valetudinarium* was located. Since many of the fortifications were excavated at the turn of the century, the provenance of the instruments was not always recorded with much care.

None of the instruments from the auxiliary forts in Germania Inferior were recorded with much detail. Yet the provenance of the instruments from the legionary fortress of Neuss is well recorded. The distribution of instruments from Neuss is of interest because a number of surgical/toilet instruments were found in the so-called hospital; however this structure was not the only building to have instruments within the fortification (Fig. 5). Four scalpels and ten surgical/toilet instruments were found in the building. The majority of these were found in a single room, room 51, tending to suggest some form of storage rather than a surgical area, especially since they were not all strictly surgical. Furthermore, instruments were found in the baths, which tends to be common, as one would expect surgical/toilet instruments to have been used given their association with personal hygiene. The *principia* has seven of these dual purpose instruments, pointing to the possibility that people were either grooming themselves in public, or that the instruments might have had another function. Instruments were found in the barracks and other buildings in the fortress. Thus the majority of the instruments do not come from the so-called hospital building, and furthermore it shows that their uses were probably not strictly medical or hygienic.

In Germania Superior the majority of recorded instruments come from auxiliary fortifications. The forts at Ladenburg, Okarben and Hofheim have surgical instruments from the baths associated with the military structures, showing a possibility that not all treatment was made available to the soldiers through a hospital. At Holzhausen two dual-purpose instruments were found in the west corner of the fort. Since one of the probes was found broken it may be an indication that this area was used as a dumping ground for trash. Another explanation is that the instruments were being used by soldiers in areas of the fort in which one might not expect people to clean themselves, suggesting that there were no social stipulations about grooming oneself in public, or if there were they were not always followed. Perhaps in certain places there was no *valetudinarium* so the fort doctor was provided with a room or set of rooms to work from wherever there was available space in the fortification. Alternatively, the location of the instrument in a tower or corner of a structure might suggest an area where trash was discarded, as there is some evidence of this at Caerleon in Wales (P. Macdonald, pers. comm.).

The legionary fortress at Vindonissa has a comparatively high number of instruments that have survived in good condition. The central area of the fort, Breite, also had a large number of instruments. Since not all the instruments were broken, some form of treatment might have been made available in this area of the fort. The so-called hospital was identified in the area known as Königsfelden. Yet only one scalpel was found in that area, along with four broken spoon probes, and they were not found within the structure. The remaining instruments to have find spots recorded were found throughout the fortress. Many of the tools were broken spatulae and spoon probes. With such a high number of instruments recorded in this fortress, it becomes apparent that it is rather difficult to tell exactly where medical treatment was being offered.

Compared to other provinces, Britain has more instruments with adequate contextual information — a product of the number of excavations that have taken place, and the recording techniques used. In the fortress at Caerleon (Fig. 6), a scalpel was found in a rubbish pit along Isca Grange, located outside the fortification, and a needle handle was found in a possible workshop. The remainder of the surgical/toilet instruments were found in the baths, barracks, drains and amphitheatre. The finds from the amphitheatre illustrate that instruments can be found in many different places. The distribution of instruments throughout the site suggests that treatment could have been offered anywhere in the fortification. Furthermore, since none were found in the so-called hospital there is greater support to the argument that the structure might have been incorrectly identified.

The fortress at Chester has a small number of finds, all of them surgical/toilet instruments that were found throughout the fortress (Fig. 7). The amphitheatre, like that at Caerleon, had a pair of surgical tweezers, again perhaps indicating that there were no social mores against people cleaning themselves in public. Outside the fortress were three ear probes and one set of surgical tweezers. The instruments do not define a particular area that could have been used as a hospital.

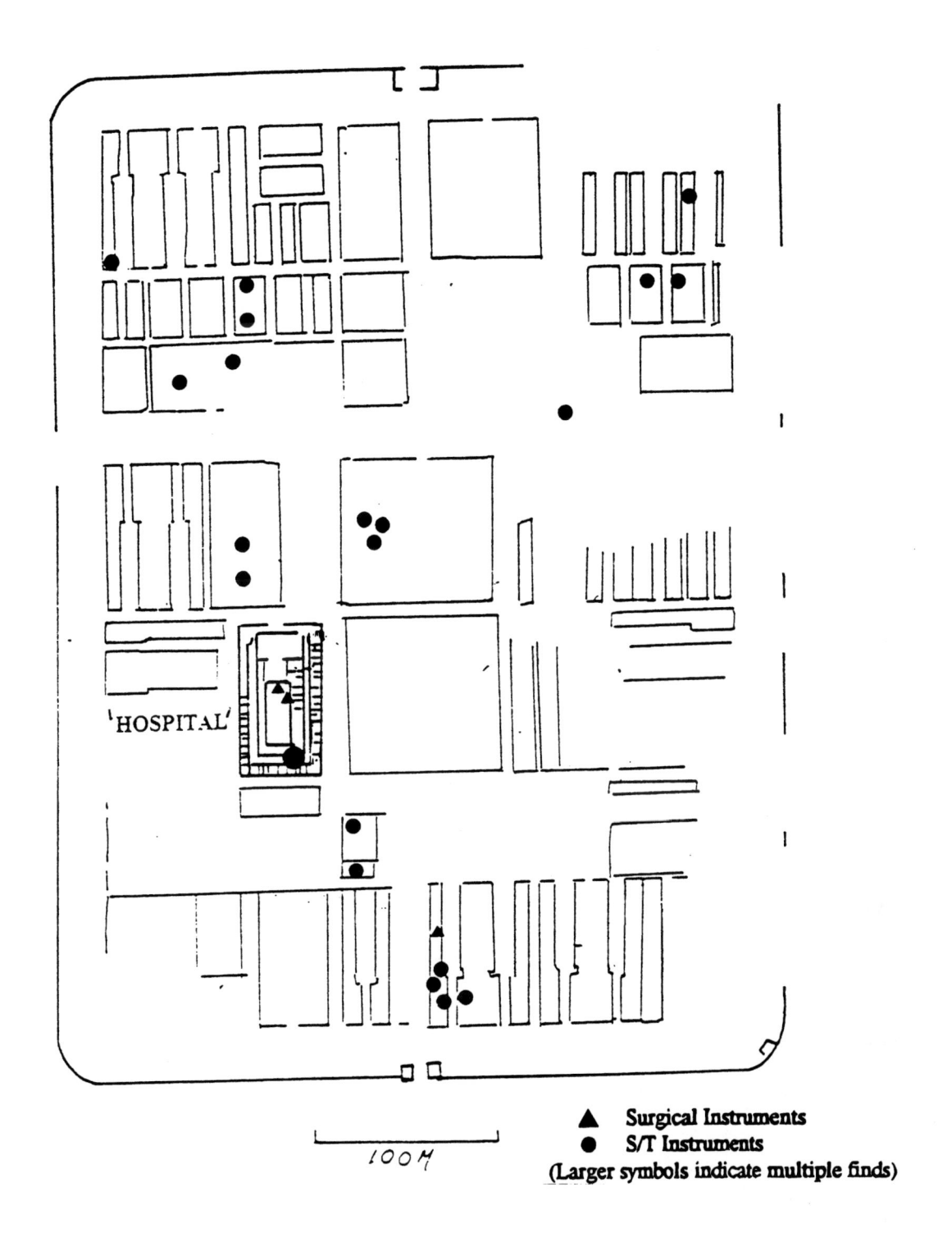

Fig. 5. Distribution of instruments at Neuss (modified from Johnson, 1983).

At Housesteads no instruments were found in the building claimed to be a hospital. The only surgical instrument found in the vicinity of the fort was a traction hook that was found outside the fort, possibly discarded there because it was broken. An ear probe was found outside the commandant's quarters. The minimal finds from the site do not necessarily indicate that the building identified as a hospital was one.

The distribution of instruments, therefore, shows that the sick and wounded soldiers might have been treated in a number of areas within the fortifications. Many of the so-called hospital buildings do not have surgical instruments, but other finds tend to suggest the structures might have been used for storage or for workshops, or later for depositing rubbish. The structure at Neuss had a number of instruments from one room that could suggest storage, yet the shell fragments and pottery sherds found with them tends to suggest dumping, so perhaps the room was not being used for storage, but as a place for refuse deposition. Novae had instruments found within the 'hospital', but a number of pottery and glass sherds, lamps and armour were also found

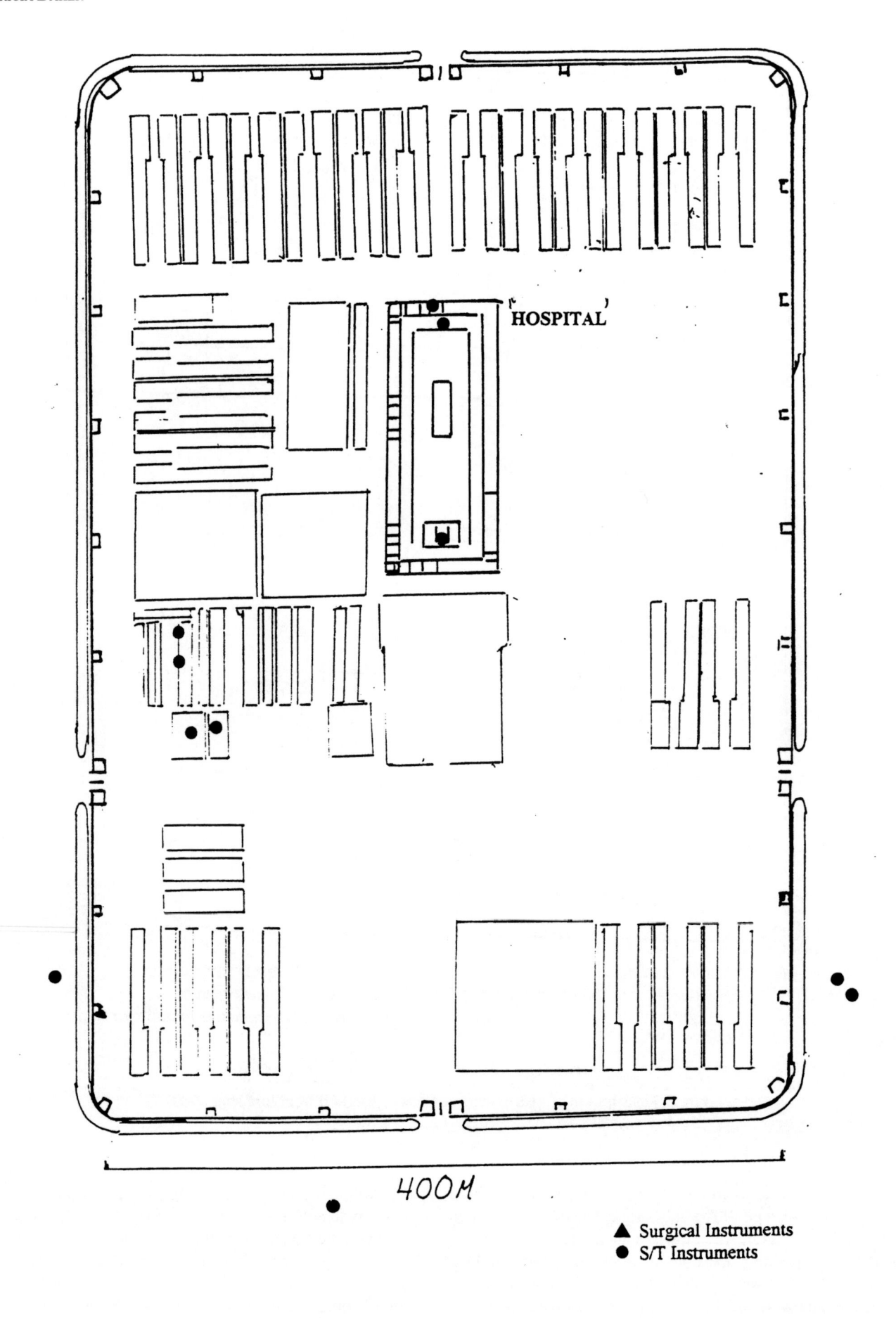

Fig. 6. Distribution of instruments at Chester (modified from Strickland in Frere, 1983).

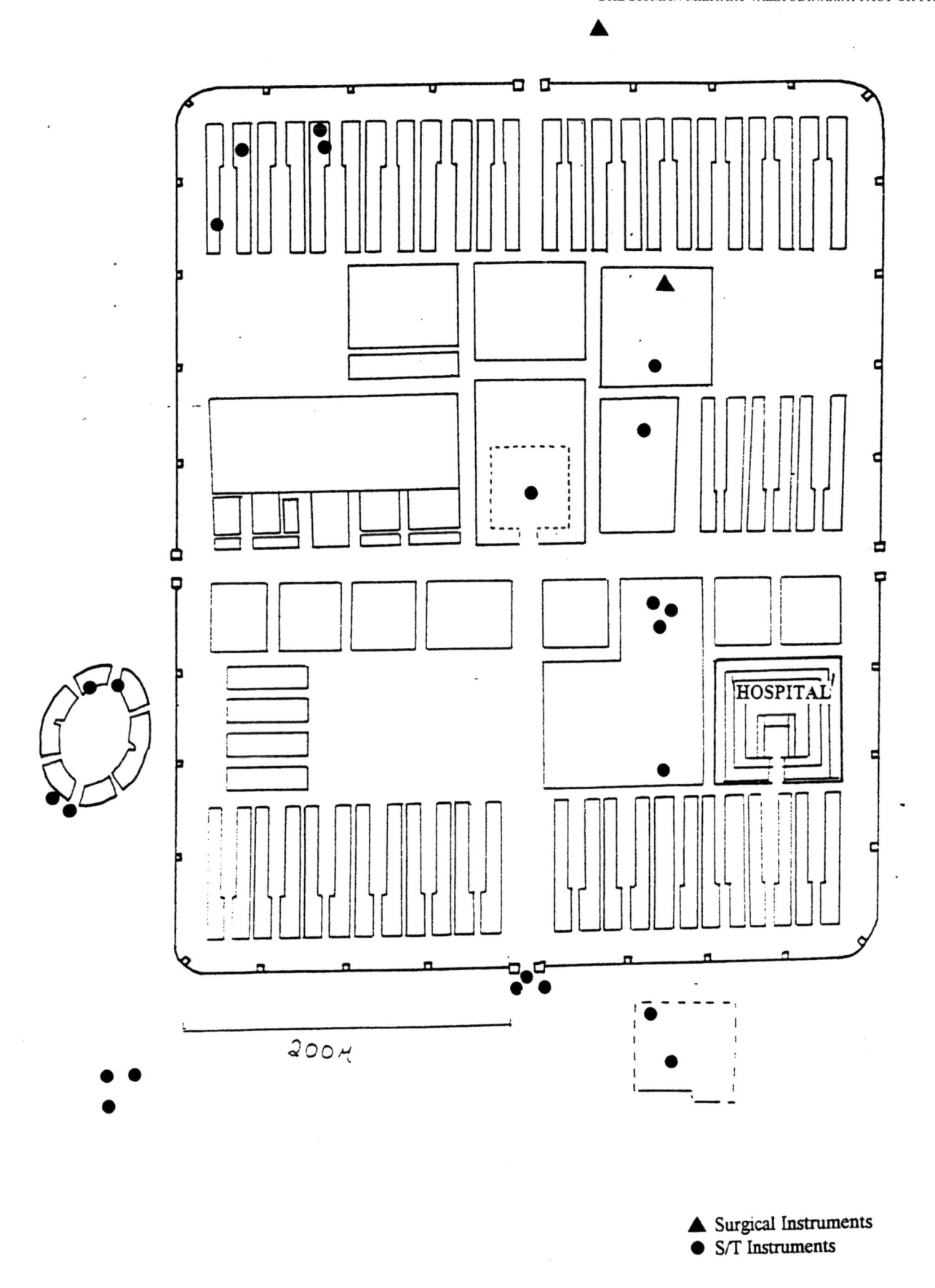

Fig. 7. Distribution of instruments at Caerleon (modified from Boon and Williams, 1967).

with them. Again, it seems as if the place was either used for storage or workshops, as one might ask why armour was present in the structure. It could be that the soldier was wounded and carried in wearing his armour; however, this is not a convincing explanation, as one would expect that his armour would have been removed from the structure. The 'hospital' building at Vindobona has a very high number of pottery and glass vessel fragments, suggesting that it might have been used for the storage of food. This also seems to be the case with the wine amphorae from Caerleon, and although the type of wine contained in the vessel may have been used for medicinal purposes, it might not have been stored in the hospital. Clearly from the evidence of finds, the structures identified as hospitals do not seem to have been very clean, at least in their final stages of use. It seems more likely that the buildings were used, or also used, for storage or as workshops, which is supported by the constant arguments from auxiliary structures that the buildings were either hospitals, *fabrica* or for storage. Thus, the artefactual evidence does not support the argument that the buildings were meant to be hospitals.

As a final note of caution, although it is important to look at the finds from each structure to attempt to determine its function, it must be remembered that artefacts can be moved from one place to another, and are not necessarily found in the locations where they were used or originally deposited (Schiffer, 1987). For example, certain buildings might have gone out of use, and the objects in them could have been moved to another structure. The obsolete building might then have been used to deposit trash. Roman archaeologists sometimes assume that artefacts occur in the same place that they were used, implying they were dropped as 'primary' refuse. Undoubtedly the situation is much more complex. Thus by looking at the find spots of the instruments it is rather difficult to give a precise idea about where they were intended to be used. This study does show that there are few assemblages of instruments, indicating that the doctors either cared for their instruments — making it difficult to say where they worked — or that they were recycled (many being made of bronze). The spread of instrument find spots across forts does indicate that the hospitals cannot be determined from finds alone, as the excavator of Neuss and archaeologists who followed have tended to accept uncritically.

CONCLUSION

The identification of the Roman military hospital merited re-examination because the hospital has been identified on very insubstantial evidence. When making comparisons of the archaeological remains in design and the structure, it seems that we are too eager to make the hospital fit a standard form, and this is based on the idea of the modern hospital as it has developed from the middle of the nineteenth century. This study was not made to state that the military *valetudinaria* were not hospitals, but to show that their identification is questionable, and to show how we can so easily place our views onto something and apply it as fact for the organisation of the Roman military medical practise.

ACKNOWLEDGEMENTS

I am most graetful to Dr J. Pollard and Professor P. J. van der Eijk for reading and commenting on the drafts. I would also like to thank Mr R. Arnott for accepting a late contribution to the TAG session.

BIBLIOGRAPHY

Abbreviations

AE   *L'Annee Epigraphique: Revue des Publications Epigraphiques Relatives a l'antique Romaine.* 1888–. Paris.

BGU   *Berliner Griechische Urkunden Ägyptische Urkunden aus den Königlichen Museen zu Berlin.* 1895–.

CIL   *Corpus Inscriptorum Latinorum Consilio et Ductoritate Academie Litterarum Regiae Borussical.* 1862–. Berlin: Academie der Wissenschaften.

P. Mich.   *Papyri in the University of Michigan Collection.* Ann Arbor: University of Michigan Press.

Primary Sources

Julius Caesar
   Commentariorum De Bello Gallico. R. du Pontet (ed.) 1900–1908. Oxford: Clarendon Press.

Celsus
   Corpus Medicorum Latinorum (vol. I). F. Marx (ed.) 1915. Stuttgart: B. G. Teubner.

Hyginus Gromaticus
   Liber de Munitionibus Castrorum. W. Gemoll (ed.) 1879. Leipzig: B. G. Teubner.

Livy
   Ab Urbe Condita. C. F. Walters and R. Conway (eds.) 1974. Oxford: Clarendon Press.

Scriptores Historia Augusta
   D. Magie (Trans.) 1921–1932 (Loeb Classical Library). London and New York: William Heinemann Ltd.

Tacitus
   Historiarum Libri. C. D. Fischer (ed.) 1967. Oxford: Clarendon Press.

Secondary Sources

Bidwell, P.
(1997) *Book of Roman Forts in Britain*, London: B. T. Batsford/ English Heritage.

Boon, G. C. and Williams, C.
(1966) *Plan of Caerleon Isca: Legio II Augusta, Discoveries to December 1967*, Cardiff: National Museum of Wales.

Bowman, A. K. and Thomas, J. D.
(1991) 'A military strength report from Vindolanda', *Journal of Roman Studies* **81**: 62–73.

Bowman, A. K. and Thomas, J. D.
(1994) *The Vindolanda Writing Tablets (Tabulae Vindolandenses II)*, London.

Campbell, J. B.
(1994) *The Roman Army 31 BC–AD 337: A Sourcebook*, London and New York: Routledge.

Carlin, M.
(1989) 'Medieval English hospitals', in L. Granshaw and R. Porter (eds.), *The Hospital in History*, New York and London: Routledge, pp. 21–40.

Conrad, L., M. Neve, V. Nutton, R. Porter and A. Wear.
(1995) *The Western Medical Tradition*, Cambridge: Cambridge University Press.

Crow, J.
(1995) *Housesteads*, Bath: B. T. Batsford/ English Heritage.

Davies, R.
(1989) 'The Roman military medical service', in D. Breeze and V. Maxfield (eds.), *Service in the Roman Army*, Edinburgh: Edinburgh University Press, pp. 209–36.

Doppler, H. W.
(1970–71) 'Baden in römischer Zeit', *Helvatia Archaeologica* **2**: 26–32.

Evans, C.
(1990) "'Power on Silt': towards an archaeology of the East India Company', *Antiquity* **64**: 643–61.

Frere, S. S.
(1983) 'Roman Britain in 1982', *Britannia* **14**: 279–356.

Henderson, J.
(1989) 'The hospitals of late-Medieval and Renaissance Florence: a preliminary survey', in L. Granshaw and R. Porter (eds.), *The Hospital in History*, New York and London: Routledge, pp. 63–92.

Horstamanshoff, H. F. J.
(1995) 'Galen and his patients', in Ph. J. van der Eijk, H. F. J. Horstmanshoff and P. Schrijvers (eds.), *Ancient Medicine in its Socio-Cultural Context*, Amsterdam and Atlanta: Rodopi Press, pp. 83–99.

Jackson, R.
(1988) *Doctors and Diseases in the Roman Empire*, Norman and London: University of Oklahoma Press.

Johnson, A.
(1983) *Roman Forts*, London: Adam and Charles Black.

Koenen, C.
(1904) 'Beschreibung von Novaesium', *Bonner Jahrbucher* **111/112**: 97–242.

Majno, G.
(1975) *The Healing Hand*, Cambridge, Mass. and London: Harvard University Press.

Miller, T.
(1985) *The Birth of the Hospital in the Byzantine Empire*, Baltimore and London: The Johns Hopkins University Press.

Neumann, A.
(1965) 'Spital und Bad des Legionslagers Vindobona', *Jahrbuch des Römisch-Germanischen Zentral Museums, Mainz* **12**: 99–117

Nutton, V.
(1969) 'Medicine and the Roman army: a further reconsideration', *Medical History* **13**: 260–70.

Pitts, L. and St. Joseph, J. K.
(1985) 'Inchtuthil, The Roman legionary fortress', *Britannia Monograph Series no.* 6, London: The Society for the Promotion of Roman Studies.

Póczy, K.
(1976) 'Investigation of the Aquincum legionary camp and the restoration of its ruins', *Budapest Régisegei,* **24** (**1**): 27–9.

Press, L.
(1988) 'Valetudinarium at Novae and other Roman Danubian hospitals', *Archeologia* **39**: 69–89.

RCHME
(1959) *City of Cambridge*, London: HMSO.

Scarborough. J.
(1976) *Roman Medicine*. Ithaca: Cornell University Press.

Schiffer, M. B.
(1987) *Formation and Processes of the Archaeological Record*, Alberquerque: University of New Mexico Press.

Schönberger, H.
(1979) 'Praetorium oder Fabrica', *Germania* **57**: 135–41.

Schultze, R.
(1934) 'Die römischen Legionslazarette in Vetera und anderen Legionslagern', *Bonner Jahrbücher* **139**: 54–63.

Thomas, J. C.
(1990) 'Some other analogie', in F. Baker and J. Thomas (eds.), *Writing in the Past*, Lampeter: St. David's University Press, pp. 18–24.

von Petrikovitz, H.
(1975) *Die Innenbauten römischer Legionslager während der Prinzipatzeit*, Berlin: Westdeutscher Verlag.

Wilamanns, J. C.
(1995) *Der Sanitätsdienst im Römischen Reich. Medizin der Antike (2)*, Hildesheim, Zurich and New York: Olms Weidmann.

THE INTERPRETATION OF MEDICINAL PLANTS IN THE ARCHAEOLOGICAL CONTEXT: SOME CASE-STUDIES FROM POMPEII

Marina Ciaraldi

INTRODUCTION

The history of humanity goes hand in hand with the continuous search for cures and remedies to relieve the body of pain. Even today, despite the sophistication of our technology, medical research is still engaged in a difficult battle against disease. The production of chemical drugs and the availability of complex medical equipment has, however, not completely replaced the use of natural remedies. Plants in particular still provide a variety of raw materials used in many pharmaceutical preparations (for instance Griggs, 1981).

The use of drugs derived from plants is well-attested in early documents (for instance the Eber Papyrus (Bryan, 1974)) and provides evidence of the high level of knowledge of the natural world that typifies ancient populations. The modern knowledge of the medicinal properties of plants is the result of many centuries of experiments, and it has its foundation in the work of the early herbalists (Nutton, 1995a; 1995b; Weatherall, 1996).

The study of the evolution of medicine and pharmacy represents one of the most fascinating branches of the history of science. Treaties of early medicine and pharmacy have been intensively investigated, producing a lively debate on aspects as diverse as the philosophical perception of the human body and the origin of diseases (Riddle, 1985; Nutton, 1996).

Archaeology has much to contribute to the discussion on ancient medicine. Its contribution not only supports the written evidence, but it can also highlight aspects of the past or of human populations otherwise not documented (see, for instance, Albarella, 1999). The occasional finding of medical tools (Bliquez, 1994), the analysis of residues from drug containers (Sjöqvist, 1960; Scatozza Horicht *et al.*, 1993) and the study of human pathologies, represent only a few of the many types of archaeological evidence that can shed light on ancient medicine. The interpretation of the archaeological evidence is, however, not always straightforward.

Archaeobotany, the study of plant remains from archaeological sites, has the potential to clarify many of the issues debated by historians on the use of medicinal plants. In reality, however, the use of medicinal plants in archaeological contexts is difficult to prove. The finding of plants with a medicinal potential does not necessarily imply their use for such purpose. Studies that successfully demonstrate the pharmaceutical use of plants are rare (Robinson, 1985; Buurman, 1988; Zias *et al.*, 1993; Prioreschi and Babin, 1993; Dickson, 1996).

The aim of this work is to show how an integrated approach that takes into account archaeological and historical evidence can help in the identification of the medicinal use of plants in the archaeological record.

IDENTIFICATION OF MEDICINAL PLANTS IN THE ARCHAEOLOGICAL CONTEXT: THE CASE OF VILLA VESUVIO

Plant remains recovered from archaeological sites are an invaluable source of data for understanding the relationship between plants and past populations. Their interpretation, however, is often complex. This is due to the existence of a large number of unknown variables that contribute to the formation of archaeological assemblages. An example of this complexity is represented by the interpretation of seeds of plants known for their medicinal use in charred plant assemblages. How do we know whether a plant is present in such assemblages as a consequence of its use as a medicinal plant? The answer to this question can sometimes be found in the understanding of the mechanism through which the plant was incorporated into the assemblage. The relation between the mechanisms of inclusion and the process of drug production also has to be analysed. We need to understand whether there may have been stages in the preparation of a medicine during which part of a plant might have been preserved and later found in archaeological deposits.

Attempts to reconstruct the formation processes of plant assemblages and their association with the specific use of a plant have proved to be successful in a number of cases. For instance, an extended literature on the interpretation of the archaeological evidence associated with cereal crop processing is now available (Hillman, 1984; Jones, 1984; etc.). Other cases refer to plants used as dyes (Hall, 1995; Tomlinson, 1985), or associated with stable manure (Kenward and Hall, 1997).

Comparative ethnographic studies have been fundamental in the determination of the formation process of plant products (Hall, 1995; Hillman, 1984; Jones, 1984). Ethnographic evidence has also provided information on the differential preservation of the various parts of the plant and the likelihood of their preservation in archaeological deposits. Ethnographic models, however, are not always available and cannot be applied to all situations. Their applicability can, for instance, be geographically limited. Historical sources can provide essential comparative data for the interpretation of archaeological assemblages (Albarella, 1999), especially in those cases in which the ethnographic evidence cannot provide suitable interpretative models.

Recent work on plant remains from excavations at Pompeii (Ciaraldi, 2000; Ciaraldi, forthcoming) has proved to be a useful case for the comparison of historical and archaeological data. The first case discussed is represented by the plant assemblage recovered from Villa Vesuvio, Scafati. During the excavation of a *villa rustica* (farmhouse), seven *dolia* (large vats partly embedded in the ground and generally used as food containers) were discovered in its cellar. One of the *dolia* contained a 30 cm thick deposit of peach stones and walnuts. These were preserved under waterlogged conditions. A rich organic deposit was recovered from the bottom of the *dolium*. This contained large quantities of seeds, other plant remains, mainly reptile and amphibian bones. On the basis of the species of plants and animals identified, the assemblage was tentatively interpreted as the residue of drug preparation (Ciaraldi, 2000). Other archaeological evidence, such as the presence of a particular kind of cooker, supported this interpretation. The representation of the same kind of cooker on a Roman stele depicting a soap factory or a pharmacy suggested that this structure may have been associated with workshops where drugs or soap were prepared (Rostovtzeff, 1957).

Many of the plants found in the *dolium* are mentioned for their medicinal use in ancient texts (Ciaraldi, 2000) and are still used today in pharmaceutical preparations (Newall *et al.,* 1996; Youngken, 1951; Stuart, 1979; Duke, 1985). In an attempt to further substantiate the interpretation of the plant assemblage from Villa Vesuvio, this has been re-examined in the light of historical data. The processes used for the preparation of medicines, as described in the historical record, were considered in detail. The re-examination of the plant assemblage from this new perspective was attempted in order to explain the processes involved in the formation of the deposit. Two aspects related to the use and preparation of medicinal plants were taken into account. First, the documentary evidence for the use of specific parts of the plant was considered. Secondly, the way the plants were processed during the production of drugs was noted. These two aspects were not always described in the ancient texts and often this probably depended on the level of familiarity that the ancient writers had with the plants described.

It seems that in the past, medicinal plants were processed using less destructive techniques than those used nowadays. Since medicinal plants were not necessarily pounded, ground or juiced, the survival of well preserved parts of plants, such as the seeds, is compatible with the interpretation of the plant assemblage from Villa Vesuvio as the remains of a drug preparation. Nowadays the location of the active compounds within a plant is well understood but this might not have been the case in ancient times. Consequently medicinal properties might have been assigned to the entire plant rather than to specific organs. This proves that the use of our modern knowledge of medicinal plants to interpret archaeological assemblages can lead to erroneous conclusions.

The comparison between the written evidence and that resulting from the analysis of the plant assemblage from Villa Vesuvio has produced some interesting results. The species identified at Villa Vesuvio were compared with the historical evidence, in particular as concerns the parts of the plants used and the process of preparation. The ancient books used as reference were the Greek herbal of Dioscorides (as translated by Gunther, 1959 and discussed by Riddle, 1985) and Pliny's Natural History (translated by Rackam and Jones, 1963–69). These two ancient texts are generally considered complete and reliable (Weatherall, 1996). Even more importantly, their works were written in the first century AD, which means that they are contemporary to the deposit under analysis, dated to AD 79. Pliny's book also has strong links with the Italian reality and with Campania, the region where Villa Vesuvio is located, in particular. Pliny owned a house in Miseno, a locality just to the north of the Bay of Naples. He died in AD 79 during the eruption of Mount Vesuvius.

A comparison between the anatomical parts found in the *dolium*, those used in modern medicine, and those mentioned in ancient sources was carried out for each medicinal plant found in the assemblage from Villa Vesuvio. The way medicinal plants were processed in ancient times was also considered whenever the information was available. The results of the comparison prove that the presence of certain anatomical parts of medicinal plants in the *dolium* is consistent with some of the processes described in ancient sources (Table 1).

In a few cases medicinal plants were generically mentioned as having medicinal properties but no further details were given. This was, for instance, the case of elder (*Sambucus nigra* L.), mentioned by both Pliny and Dioscorides. For other plants, a longer and more detailed account of their preparation is normally provided, sometimes accompanied by long lists of medicinal properties and anecdotes, for example in the case of the opium poppy (*Papaver somniferum* L.) (Pliny NH XX.109–204; Dioscorides *Mat.Med.* IV.65). This could be an indication of the fact that certain plants were better renowned for their medicinal properties than others.

The comparison (see Table 1) provides interesting indications. There is consistency between the anatomical parts used as a medicine according to Pliny and Dioscorides and those found in the *dolium*. On the contrary, in a few cases there is a substantial difference in the use of plants as described by ancient and modern texts. This is so, for instance, in the case of the mallow (*Malva sylvestris* L.).

The processing of plants for drug preparation seems to have been different in the past. Decoctions, infusions, and soaking in wine were common practices. Grinding, powdering and pounding are also mentioned, but perhaps they were not as common as we would expect on the basis of modern references.

Seeds were by far the most common finds in the plant assemblage at Villa Vesuvio. Written evidence shows that seeds, or indeed parts of the plants that might have contained seeds, were frequently used in the preparation of drugs. This seems to be in contrast with the recurrent argument that seeds of medicinal plants in archaeological contexts cannot be taken as evidence of the use of a plant as a medicine. Due to their toughness and durability, seeds tend to be commonly found in archaeological contexts. A few species found at Villa Vesuvio were not mentioned as medicinal plants in ancient sources. These included bud scales of beech (*Fagus sylvatica* L.), seeds of common chickweed (*Stellaria media* L.), and immature flowers of the strawberry tree (*Arbutus unedo* L.). These plants may have ended up in the assemblage accidentally. This seems to be so, for instance, in the case of the bud scales of beech. Beech nowadays grows in the Apennine, between 1000 and 1700 metres (Pignatti, 1982). Its presence in the plant assemblage of Villa Vesuvio might indicate that buds and bud scales of beech were introduced accidentally in the assemblage, perhaps through the use of mushrooms picked up in the woodlands and used as one of the ingredients of the mixture. The other two species might

Table 1. Species identified in the *dolium* at Villa Vesuvio

TAXON	PLINY	DIOSCORIDES	MODERN AUTHORS
Abies alba (sc/c)	unguent XII.134; resin XV.30		
Cupressus sempervirens (sc/s)	oil (perfumes); berries (for herb wine) XIV.112; pounded leaves, **globules** and **seeds**/roasted fruits/shreds of barks XX.12,XXIV.15–16		
Juglans regia (nut/bud sc)	oil (*caryinum*) X.V28, XXIII.88; shells (wool dye) XV 86–91; **nuts** XXIII.147–149; Mithridates: dried pounded walnuts XXIII.149	burnt 'putamen'; oil (hair dye) I.178	leaves, bark
Ficus carica s	juice; leaves, unripe fruits, young shoots, ripe fruits decoction XXIII.117–30	fruits soaked in water, decoction I.181–186	
Cannabis sativa s	**seeds**; juice from seeds; roots boiled XX.259	oil from **seeds**, III.165	flowering tips, **seeds** for oil; leaves
Urtica dioica s	**seeds**; seeds and pounded leaves (?); dried roots XXII 31–6		leaves for decoctions, roots, **seeds**, herb, juice
Portulaca oleracea s	juice and **seeds**; pounded **seeds** in honey XX.210–15	juice, II.151	
Ranunculus sardous s		leaves, stalks, dried roots pounded II.208	
Papaver somniferum s	calyx pounded and taken in wine; **seeds**; juice from the calyx; **seeds** pounded with juice; heads and leaves boiled (*meconium*) XX.198–204	leaves, heads in water; *meconium*: pounded heads and leaves; pounded **seeds** IV.65	juice from unripe capsule; plant boiled in oil, capsule decoction, **seeds** decoction, **seeds**
Chelidonium majus s	juice of flowering plant XXV.89–90; crushed roots in vinegar XXV.170	juice from heads, roots II.211	whole plant; powdered dried roots; leaves; flowers boiled in lard
Brassica cf. *rapa* s		**seeds** in antidotes and treacle II.134	
Rosa sp. s	oil; petals (juices extracted), flowers and fruits (taken in drinks), dried leaves XXI.121–5	leaves to make oil (*rosaceum*) I.53	ripe fruit
Prunus persica st	pounded leaves and kernel XXIII.132		bark, leaves; oil from seed
Vitis vinifera s/be/tendril	Various	leaves, **tendrils**, V.1	
Malva silvestris s	leaves; 'mallows rotten in urine and boiled', roots, **seeds** in wine XX.222.230	decoction of **seeds** and leaves, pounded green and dried **seeds** II.144/III.163	herb, flowers, juice from roots
Bryonia dioica s	boiled stalks, leaves, fruits (in preparation for leather), roots, ointment, pessary XXIII.21–8	tendrils, leaves, roots, fruits IV.184	resin; roots
Myrtus communis s/be	oil from **berries** XV.124, **berries** and berry juice, juice to darken hair, pounded dried leaves, pessary, young stalks XXIII.159–66	oil from leaves, I.48	leaves
Caucalis platycarpos s	juice, **seeds** XXII.83		
Daucus carota s	roots and **seeds** XXV.112 and XXVI.89	**seeds** in drink, roots, pounded, leaves III.59	herb, **seeds**, roots
Apium graveolens s	leaves boiled, juice from roots, **seeds** XX.112–15	**seeds**, roots, III.74	herb, oil from **seeds**, leaves, roots, seeds, decoction of seeds
Marrubium vulgare s	leaves, **seeds** pounded together, boiled stalks, juice		flowering plant
Anagallis sp. s		juice, II,209	whole plant
Galium cf. *aparine* s	**seeds** in wine, leaves and juice XXVII.32		flowering plant
Symphytum officinale s	roots XXVI.45/ 81; decoction of entire plant XXVI.137/161	roots, entire plant, IV.9–10	rhizome decoction, mucilage, leaves
Verbena officinalis s		leaves, IV.60	whole flowering plant, leaves
Lamium sp. s	leaves and roots XXII.37–8		
Solanum nigrum s		leaves, juice, IV.71	
Hyoscyamus sp. s	juice XXII.124, oil XXIII.94; **seeds** in wine, roots XXVI.152	oil (dried/green pounded **seeds** macerated in hot water) I.42	oil from leaves, leaves, powdered **seeds**, herb, **seeds** in wine and suppository
Sambucus nigra s			flowers, berries, bark
Valerianella dentata s		roots, stalks, I.7	
Eupatorium cannabinum s		pounded leaves, **seeds** and plant in wine, IV.41	
Sonchus asper s	juice and boiled roots XXII.89–90		
Sonchus oleraceus s	as above		

The part of the plants found in the deposit from the *dolium* at Villa Vesuvio, Scafati are compared to those mentioned in ancient texts and by modern authors. Part of plants mentioned in ancient and modern sources and which correspond exactly to those found at Villa Vesuvio are in bold. Part of plants whose use might explain the presence of the anatomical part found at Villa Vesuvio have been underlined.

have been present in the surrounding areas of the site and been accidentally included in the assemblage.

SEEDS FROM DRAINS

The importance of the general archaeological context in the interpretation of the plant assemblage has already been pointed out for Villa Vesuvio (Ciaraldi, 2000). This is also the case for seeds recovered from hospital drains. The presence of seeds of medicinal plants found in such contexts has convincingly been interpreted as evidence of their use as medicinal plants (Robinson, 1985; Dickson, 1996). But how about medicinal plants found in domestic drains? Can we also assume their medicinal use?

During excavations at the House of the Vestals (VI,1, 6–8, Pompeii) an elaborate drain system was uncovered (Bon et al., 1997). The drain fills contained a rich assemblage of mineralised plant remains (Ciaraldi, 1996). Most of the plant remains were from plants used as food, and included fruits, spices and legumes. The deposit also included some plants known for their medicinal properties. In some of the samples collected from the drain fill a good number of seeds of Queen Anne's lace or wild carrot (*Daucus carota* L.) were recovered. This plant is typical of disturbed ground, and it is often found along roads and paths but rarely in cultivated fields (Hanf, 1990). Unlike other species of the same family, Apiaceae, its seeds are not used as spices. Its presence in the plant assemblage of the Vestals raises some questions on its interpretation. The seeds of the wild carrot are known to have been used as a medicine and Riddle (1994; 1997: 51) states that they act as a 'strong contraceptive if taken orally immediately after the coitus'. Their efficacy has proven to be valid during laboratory experiments on rats (Sharma et al., 1976 and Kalival et al., 1987 cit. in Riddle, 1997), as it seems to impede the implantation of the ovule. The use of wild carrot seeds as a contraceptive was known in ancient times (Hippocrates, cf. in Riddle, 1994; 1997; Dioscorides *Mat.Med* 3.83) and is still adopted in Northern American and Indian folk medicine (Riddle, 1997: 51). Can the presence of wild carrot seeds at the House of the Vestals be taken as evidence of their use as a contraceptive? It is difficult to be certain but the possibility has to be considered. The medicinal use of plants has sometimes been neglected in the interpretation of plant assemblages from archaeological sites. The example from the House of the Vestals may act as a good reminder of the fact that plants may have been used for purposes other than food and these should not be discounted when interpreting the archaeobotanical evidence.

CONCLUSIONS

The presence of medicinal plants in archaeological deposits is not always proof of their use as medicine. The often-incomplete understanding of the processes of deposition can make the interpretation of an archaeobotanical assemblage difficult. The possible medicinal use, in particular, can be obscured by many taphonomic variables involved in the formation of the assemblage. Ethnographical studies, widely used as a source of evidence in the interpretation of plant assemblages (e.g. crop processing assemblages), are not always available and have been little explored as far as medicinal plants are concerned. Alternative sources of information can come from ancient texts. Historical sources have been used to support the interpretation of the plant assemblage from Villa Vesuvio as a residue of drug preparation. The analysis of Pliny's and Dioscorides' works on the use of medicinal plants suggests that in ancient times plants were used and processed differently. The plant remains identified from the deposit from Villa Vesuvio are consistent with some of the descriptions related to drug preparation provided by the two ancient writers. This consideration, together with the more general archaeological evidence, strongly supports the idea that the assemblage represents the residue of drug preparation. A similar approach, which takes into consideration historical sources, has also been used in the case of the interpretation of the seeds of wild carrot recovered from the drain at the House of the Vestals. In this case, however, the evidence is less conclusive and it highlights the need for more studies of plant assemblages from similar contexts, in the absence of suitable archaeological and ethnographic comparisons.

Historical sources generally represent a most useful tool for the understanding of archaeological assemblages. The analysis of the plant assemblages from Pompeii hopefully highlights the usefulness of an integrated approach in the interpretation of the archaeological evidence.

ACKNOWLEDGEMENTS

I would like to thank Robert Arnott for his encouragement in the submission of this paper, NERC for financial support of the research project of which this paper is part and Umberto Albarella for comments on an early draft.

BIBLIOGRAPHY

Albarella, U.
(1999) 'The mystery of husbandry: medieval animals and the problem of integrating historical and archaeological evidence', *Antiquity* **73**: 282, 867–75

Bliquez L. J.
(1994) *Roman Surgical Instruments and Other Minor Objects in the National Archaeological Museum of Naples*, Zeben, Mainz.

Bon, S. E., Jones, R., Kurchin, B. and Robinson, D. J.
(1997) 'The context of the House of the Surgeon: investigation in Insula V,1 at Pompeii', in S. E. Bon and R. Jones (eds.), *Sequence and Space at Pompeii*, Oxford, Oxbow Monograph **77**: 32–49.

Bryan, C. P.
(1974) *The Papyrus Ebers,* Chicago: Ares Publishing.

Buurman, J.
(1988) 'Roman medicine from Uitgeest', in H. Küster (ed.), *Der Prähistorische Mensch und Seine Umwelt*, Stuttgart: Verlag pp. 341–51.

Ciaraldi, M.
(1997) 'Plant remains', in S. Bon, R. Jones, B. Kurchin and D. Robinson (eds.), *Anglo-American Pompeii Project*

1996, Bradford Archaeological Sciences Research 3, University of Bradford, pp.17–23
(2000) 'Drug preparation in evidence? An unusual plant and bone assemblage from the Pompeian countryside, Italy', *Vegetation History and Archaeobotany*, 9: 91–8.

Dickson, C.
(1996) 'Food, medicinal and other plants from the 15th century drains of Paisley Abbey, Scotland', *Vegetation History and Archaeobotany*, 5: 25–31.

Gunther, R. T.
(1959) *The Greek Herbal of Dioscorides*, New York, Hafner Publishing.

Duke, J. A.
(1985) *CRC Handbook of Medicinal Herb*, Boca Raton, Fla: CRC Press.

Griggs, B.
(1981) *Green Pharmacy: A History of Herbal Medicine*, London: Norman and Hobhouse.

Hall, A.
(1995) 'Archaeological evidence for woad (*Isatis tinctoria* L.) from Medieval England and Ireland', in Kröll and R. Pasternak (eds.), *Res Archaeobotanicae*: Proceedings of the 9th Symposum, Kiel 1992, Kiel, pp. 33–8.

Hanf, M.
(1990) *Le Infestanti d'Europa*, Bologna: Edagricole.

Hillman, G.
(1984) 'Interpretation of archaeological plant remains: the application of ethnographical models from Turkey', in W. van Zeist and W. A. Casparie (eds.), *Plants and Ancient Man: Studies in Palaeoethnobotany*, Rotterdam: Balkema pp. 1–41.

Jones, G.
(1984) 'Interpretation of archaeological plant remains: ethnographical models from Greece', in W. van Zeist and W. A. Casparie (eds.), *Plants and Ancient Man: Studies in Palaeoethnobotany*, Rotterdam: Balkema, pp. 43–61.

Kaliwal, B. B., Nazeer Ahamed, R. and Appaswomy Rao, M.
(1984) 'Abortifacient effect of carrot seed (*Daucus carota*) extract and its reversal by progesterone in albino rats', *Comparative Physiology and Ecology*, 9: 70–4.

Kenward, H. and Hall, A.
(1997) 'Enhancing bioarchaeological interpretation using indicator groups: stable manure as a paradigm', *Journal of Archaeological Science*, 24: 663–73.

Nutton, V.
(1995a) 'Medicine in the Greek world, 800–50 BC', in C. I. Lawrence, M. Neve, V. Nutton, R. Porter and A. Wear (eds.), *The Western Medical Tradition*, Cambridge: Cambridge University Press, pp. 11–38.
(1995b) 'Roman medicine, 250 BC to AD 200', in C. I. Lawrence, M. Neve, V. Nutton, R. Porter and A. Wear (eds.), *The Western Medical Tradition*, Cambridge: Cambridge University Press, pp. 39–70.

Pignatti, S.
(1982) *Flora d'Italia*, Bologna: Edagricole.

Prioreschi, P. and Babin, D.
(1993) 'Ancient use of cannabis', *Nature* 364: 680.

Rackam, H. and Jones, W. H. S.
(1963–69) *Pliny the Elder, Natural History*, Loeb Classical Library, London, Heinemann.

Riddle, J.
(1985) *Dioscorides on Pharmacy and Medicine*, Austin: University of Texas.
(1994) 'Birth control in the Ancient World', *Archaeology* 47: 30–5.
(1997) *Eve's Herbs*, Cambridge Mass and London: Harvard University Press.

Robinson, M.
(1985) 'Plant and invertebrate remains from the priory drains', in G. Lambrick, 'Further excavations on the second site of the Dominican Priory', *Oxoniensia* 50: 196–201.

Rostovtzeff, M.
(1957) *The Social and Economic History of the Roman Empire*, Oxford: Clarendon Press.

Scattozza Horicht, Lucia A., Chianese, L., Piccioli, C. and Sacchi, R.
(1993) 'Prime osservazioni ed analisi sul contenuto di alcuni recipienti in vetro rinvenuti nell'area archeologica di Pompei', in L. Franchi-Dell'Orto (ed.), *Ercolano 1738–1988, Convegno Internazionale Ravello, Ercolano, Napoli e Pompei 30 Oct.–5 Nov. 1988*, Roma: L'Erma di Bretscheneider, pp. 551–64.

Sharma, M. M., Lal, G. and Jacob, D.
(1976) 'Estrogenic and pregnancy interceptory effects of carrot *Daucus carota* seeds', *Indian Journal of Experimental Biology* 14: 506–08

Sjöqvist, E.
(1960) 'Morgantina: Hellenistic medicine bottles', *American Journal of Archaeology* 64: 78–83.

Stuart, M. (ed.)
(1979) *The Encyclopaedia of Herbs and Herbalism*, London: Orbis Publishing.

Thomlinson, P.
(1985) 'Use of vegetative remains in the identification of dyeplants from waterlogged 9th–10th century AD deposits of York', *Journal of Archaeological Science* 12: 269–83.

Weatherall, M.
(1996) 'Drug treatment and the rise of pharmacology', in R. Porter (ed.), *The Cambridge Illustrated History of Medicine*, Cambridge: Cambridge University Press, pp. 246–77.

Youngken, H. W.
(1951) *Pharmaceutical Botany*, Philadelphia: Blakiston, 7th edition.

Zias, J. et al.
(1993) 'Early use of cannabis', *Nature* 363: 215.

ROMAN SURGERY: THE EVIDENCE OF THE INSTRUMENTS

Ralph Jackson

Medical implements and surgical instruments are the most tangible remains of Roman medical practice. They are fascinating and instructive in many ways, not least in their design and manufacture, yet they undoubtedly raise more questions than they answer. For that reason, I have framed this paper in the form of an introduction and a series of questions to which I have offered a few possible answers. Needless to say, they are neither exhaustive nor conclusive.

INTRODUCTION

With few exceptions, surgical instruments of clearly identifiable and recurrent form were not widespread until the beginning of the first century AD. From this time onwards, however, surgical instruments of diagnostic type were made and used throughout the Graeco-Roman world. Although there was some variation in the choice of materials and decor, the individual forms, once developed, remained surprisingly constant. As a result, perhaps, of their distinctive and recognisable form, there is a perception in some quarters that Roman surgical instruments are quite numerous. In fact, this is not the case. Rather, it is an illusion created by recent renewed interest in the archaeology of medicine, by a spate of publications on the subject, and by the fact that museum curators tend to put on display all the instruments they recognise, unlike other classes of material. As an example, and to put this into perspective, the Romano-British finds at present include little more than fifty scalpels, the commonest (and most readily identifiable) distinctive surgical instrument. Only the undiagnostic quasi-medical implements (Fig. 1), which have toilet and cosmetic uses as well as medical and surgical applications, are at all common. Unfortunately, published examples are often classed as 'medical'. The great majority are ligulae, spatula probes, scoop probes and the small tweezers, ear-scoops and nail-cleaners which have looped heads for suspension on a ring or cord. In fact, the presence of a looped terminal and suspension ring, which is characteristic of toilet implements, almost never occurs on surgical tools. Of the modest sample of distinctive surgical instruments, few are well-contexted or even well-provenanced, let alone precisely dated. Important here is the recognition of fragmentary instru-

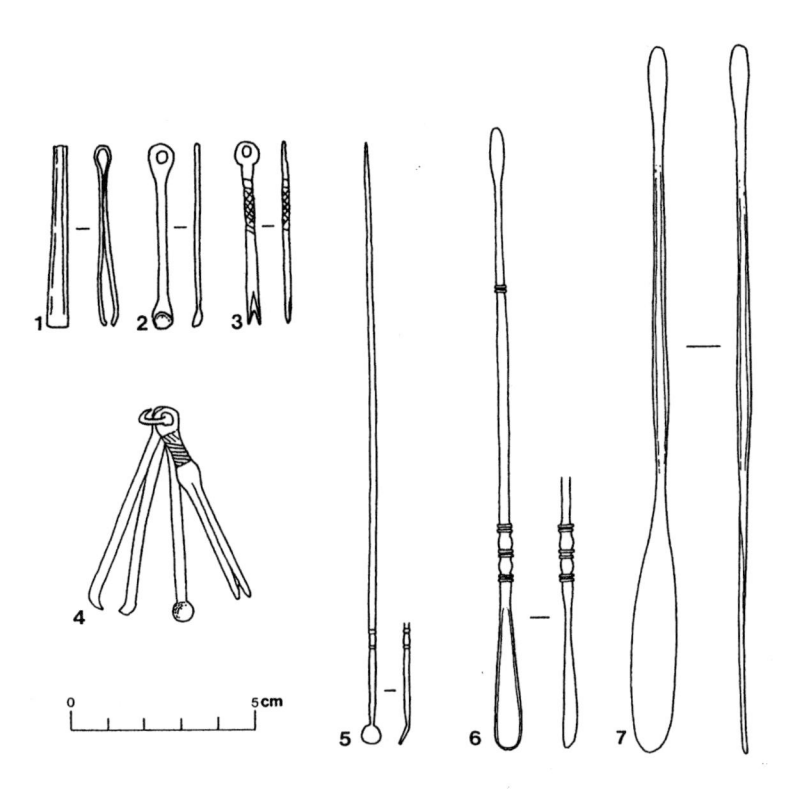

Fig. 1. Roman toilet and multi-purpose implements. 1–3: tweezers, ear-scoop, nail-cleaner, King Harry Lane, St Albans (after Stead and Rigby, 1989); 4: toilet set, Bucklersbury House, London (after Merrifield, 1965); 5–7: ligula, scoop probe, spatula probe, Italy (after Jackson, 1986).

ments which not only shed light on prevalence but also often provide dated contexts for complete but uncontexted instruments.

Research since the late 1970s has resulted in the establishment of an increasingly secure database of Roman instrument types and their chronology. Notable works include Künzl (1983; 1996); Krug (1985); Bliquez (1994) and Jackson (1986; 1990; 1994a). These, and others, have allowed a much clearer understanding of the instrumentation potentially available to those who undertook surgery in the Roman imperial period, but there are still areas of ignorance or uncertainty.

The single most striking feature of surviving instruments is their quality. Some are exquisitely decorated and some are plain, but almost without exception they are carefully-crafted tools developed for a specific task or range of tasks. A few are made of iron, but most are of copper and its alloys, principally bronze and brass, which could be cast, forged or cold-worked. For bonding purposes tin-lead solder was used. Iron, chosen especially for blades and where strength was required, was always forged. Roman blacksmiths knew the technique of carburisation and produced steel tools, but in certain regions the ore yielded a natural steel especially favoured for surgical tools (Galen II 682K).

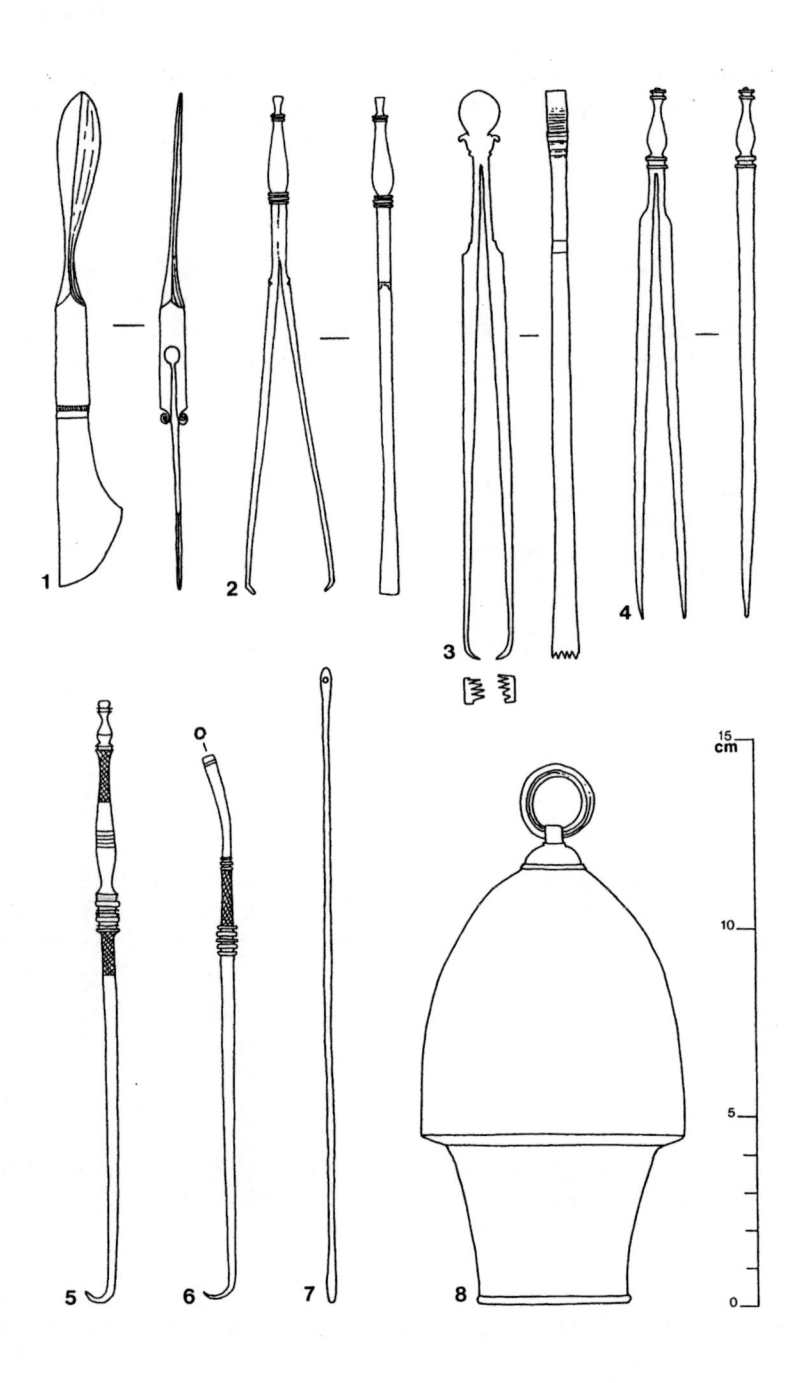

Fig. 2. The commonest distinctive types of Roman surgical instrument — core tools. 1: scalpel, London (after Jackson, 1990); 2: smooth-jawed fixation forceps, Cologne (after Jackson, 1990); 3: toothed fixation forceps, Pompeii (after Jackson, 1990); 4: pointed-jawed forceps, Italy (after Jackson, 1986); 5: sharp hook (retractor), Pompeii, Naples, Mus. Naz., Inv. 78042; 6: needle-holder combined with sharp hook, London (after Jackson, 1990); 7: slender probe (eyed *dipyrene*), Colchester (after Jackson, 1994a); 8: cupping vessel, Pompeii (after Jackson, 1990). All copper alloy, except iron blade of 1 and (missing) iron needle of 6.

The core of a surgeon's *instrumentarium* comprised scalpels, forceps, hooks, needles and probes, normally in some numbers. The scalpel (Fig. 2: 1) soon acquired a standard form with an iron blade and a bronze handle. Like many Roman surgical instruments, it was double-ended, and the handle usually terminated in a spatula used above all for blunt dissection. In addition to the common 'bellied' type of blade, a variety of other shapes is known, including straight–edged, concave, convex and hooked types in a variety of sizes. When the blade broke or wore out it was possible to remove it from the handle and fit a new one. In order to do this, the practitioner could have gone to a blacksmith, a specialist instrument-maker or a cutler.

Depictions on stone, together with archaeological remains, demonstrate that sets of scalpels were commonly kept in hinged wooden cases. Sometimes other instruments were contained in the same case, notably forceps and hooks. Forceps, essentially a mechanical extension of the fingers, were usually single-ended instruments made of bronze, although occasionally they were combined with a second forceps or another instrument. Several specialised types were used, but those most frequently found are pointed-jawed, plain fixation or toothed fixation forceps (Fig. 2: 2–4), all three of which enabled the surgeon to cover most eventualities. A ring-slide on the fixation forceps enabled the jaws to be locked for a firm and prolonged grip when fixing and raising skin or tissue, while the ridging on the inner face of the tips of some pointed-jawed forceps, like that on modern anatomical forceps, also permitted a secure grip, but without causing tissue damage.

Wound edges were held apart with retractors, small sharp hooks on slender handles (Fig. 2: 5–6), and a surgeon might possess several. They were also used to raise and excise small pieces of tissue, as in tonsillectomy. To ensure a firm grip the narrow handle was often decorated with elaborate mouldings or finely-cut facets. Blunt hooks were used for more sensitive work.

The other indispensable component of surgical kits was a set of probes. These were of especial importance in the preliminaries to any operation, particularly those on internal parts, which involved careful exploration. Very fine flexible bronze probes (Fig. 2: 7) were used for this sort of work, but in addition stouter probes, spatulae, scoops, spoons and needles were used both for preparing and applying medications and for many other medical and surgical applications.

Needles were widely used: those with an eye comprising a simple domestic type, for stitching the end of a bandage, and surgical needles for suturing, ligating and passing a thread. Fine-pointed needles, probably commonly made of iron or steel, and sometimes mounted in socketed copper-alloy handles (Fig. 2: 6), were required for dissection, cauterisation, perforating, puncturing, transfixing and raising tissue and structure, while a distinctive copper-alloy variety was developed for the operation to couch cataract.

One of the few instruments that was normally made of iron was the cautery. Very few have survived, but their use was evidently extensive, for Greek and Roman medical authors frequently recommended them. Their success must have been due in large part to the fact that through heat sterilisation the incidence of post-operative infection was minimised.

Scalpels, hooks, forceps and probes are the most commonly found types of Roman surgical instruments, and together with needles and cauteries they were the basic tools of surgery. More specialised instruments include dental tools, instruments of bone surgery, special toothed forceps, anal and vaginal dilators, clysters, syringes, drainage tubes and catheters, cataract needles and lithotomy instruments.

HOW CAN SURGICAL AND MEDICAL INSTRUMENTS BE DISTINGUISHED FROM OTHER IMPLEMENTS AND TOOLS?

Some Roman instruments are specific and distinctive, while others conform closely to their modern medical counterparts. Almost invariably they are precision tools made to the highest standards. Additionally, the frequent use of bronze, or the combination of bronze and iron, sets them apart from most other craft tools or domestic implements, which were generally of iron or bone, or a combination of the two. However, some pieces are more difficult to identify, especially individual unassociated site finds and, of course, corroded and broken examples. Naturally, therefore, association is of the greatest importance since it allows us to give a medical context to types of instrument which hitherto had no assured medical application. Conversely, it can remove spurious tools from the typology of Roman medical instruments. Both processes result in a more complete and precise understanding of Roman instrumentation.

Nevertheless, allowance still has to be made for multiple use or adapted usage of apparently medical tools, and, conversely, for the medical usage of seemingly non-medical implements. The find from Bingen, Germany (Como, 1925; Künzl, 1983: 80–5), is a case in point. This *instrumentarium*, from a cremation burial of the late first–early second century AD, comprises some forty instruments, several of which are distinctive tools of bone surgery. More problematic, however, are several iron tools in the set which, without a medical context, would have been characterised as carpenter's tools. Should they be regarded simply as tools for carpentry irrespective of the medical context? Are they carpentry tools that had been borrowed for or adapted to surgical use? Are they additional instruments that had been 'made-to-order' for use in bone surgery? Or are they carpentry tools that the Bingen healer required to make medical aids and apparatus of wood, e.g. splints, crutches, walking sticks, windlasses etc.? Perhaps the Bingen healer was both a carpenter and a surgeon. Our current state of knowledge does not permit an unequivocal answer.

Another example, the cataract-couching needle, illuminates further the problem of identification and also demonstrates how profoundly important surgery can be carried out with the simplest of equipment, in this case a solid pointed needle. In fact, the Classical accounts of the operation to couch cataract (to break up and move a cataractous lens), which include descriptive details of the instrument (Celsus *De medicina* VII. 7. 14; Paul of Aegina VI. 21), have enabled the recognition of a specific type of needle, found in some Roman surgical kits, as the cataract-couching needle (Scalinci, 1938; Künzl, 1983: 26–7; Feugère, Künzl and Weisser, 1985). It is a single-piece copper-alloy instrument with a slender stem, often embellished with decorative inlay or mouldings, and surmounted with an olivary terminal. The needle, which projects from the other end of the stem, is straight, smooth and circular-sectioned with a slightly blunt-pointed tip. This type corresponds closely to the descriptions of Celsus (early first century AD) and Paul of Aegina (seventh century AD), but good preservation of the complete instrument is necessary in order to make an unequivocal identification: if the needle component is broken or corroded it is usually impossible to differentiate the instrument from a broken example of the much more ubiquitous, multi-functional (and not necessarily medical) scoop probe (*cyathiscomele*). Furthermore, even where an identification is secure, it should neither be assumed that cataract-couching was done only with this one type of needle nor that the cataract needle was restricted solely to this one operation. The cataract needle would have served many other surgical roles described in the texts, while couching could be performed with other varieties of needle, including those not primarily intended for surgery, as long as it had a tip 'pointed enough to penetrate (the eye), yet not too fine' (Celsus *De medicina* VII. 7. 14D).

The use of such 'loan tools' is a critical factor to be borne in mind when attempting to assess the level of medical and surgical activity. Just as craft or household knives might substitute for the scalpel, and some domestic glass or pottery vessels might be pressed into service for cupping in the absence of a purpose-made cupping vessel (Celsus *De medicina* II. 11. 2), styli, quills, spoons, razors and strigils are among the 'cross-over' utensils mentioned in medical texts and sometimes found in sealed assemblages or sets of medical instruments (Jackson, 1994a: table 3; Künzl, 1983).

To summarise, many purpose-made surgical and medical instruments are clearly distinguishable in the archaeological record, but other tools capable of medical and surgical applications are not.

HOW REPRESENTATIVE A SAMPLE ARE THE SURVIVING INSTRUMENTS?

As is clear from the Classical medical literature (e.g. Celsus, *De medicina*; Soranus, *Gynaecia*; Galen; Pseudo-Galen; Paul of Aegina), healers in the Roman world could, potentially, draw upon a wide arsenal of medical equipment. Much would have been made from organic materials, and Celsus mentioned implements of wood, leather, cloth, papyrus, reed, feather etc. (Jackson, 1994a). Few examples have survived in the archaeological record, and rare, too, is the preservation of such vulnerable materials as bone and glass. Thus, the majority of surviving identifiable medical equipment comprises surgical instruments and implements made of metal. But differential preservation applies also to metals, and those objects made of thin sheet or slender rods — notably bronze vessels and containers, iron blades, probes and needles (especially suturing needles) — have often perished or have corroded beyond recognition. It is therefore of the utmost importance to bear in mind how partial a picture even the better surviving archaeological finds provide of Roman *instrumentaria*.

As with other classes of artefact finds we should be surprised not at the relative rarity of many types of Roman medical instrument, but that even as many as exist have survived. They had value — sometimes probably considerable value — and their loss or removal from circulation requires explanation. Different processes are at work in the differing contexts of finds and, as ever with artefact studies, these have to be taken into consideration when interpreting their meaning. Broadly, there are three categories of finds: individual site finds, grave finds and 'disaster' finds. Individual finds on sites are unlikely to represent 'accidental' or 'casual' loss, but the actual circumstances of deposition can seldom be reconstructed with confidence. Nevertheless, whether from general layers or more specific contexts they can help to consolidate or broaden distribution patterns and sharpen the chronology of instrument types. Even in the absence of a secure context they can provide valuable new intrinsic information (e.g. Jackson, 1997a), and they may, at least, attest medical activity, through not necessarily at the precise site of discovery.

Grave finds provide a clearer and often undisturbed context, an especially secure resting place for instruments. Their burial was a controlled action, a deliberate, conscious decision to remove them from circulation and place them in the grave. In order to maximise the evidence retrieved from burials, a particularly sensitive excavation technique is required, as exemplified recently by the discovery of the mid-1st century AD 'Doctor's Burial' at Stanway, Essex (Crummy, 1997; Jackson, 1997b). The securely-dated context of associated artefacts in graves has been the single most valuable source of evidence for Roman medical instrumentation. However, the ritual aspect of ancient burial practice is seldom uncontentious, and generally it cannot be discerned or reconstructed with any great degree of certainty. For example, as yet there is no convincing explanation as to why valuable, functional medical tools were consigned to graves in this way. It is a burial rite that does not extend to other Roman crafts or professions. Furthermore, it is seldom clear whether, or how much, selection took place, and therefore it is rarely possible to determine whether or not the interred instruments represent a complete set, a part-set or merely a token instrument or instruments. Certainly, bulky items are not found. Were they intentionally excluded? Critically, too, although the integrity and preservation of instruments are favoured in a burial context, those instruments had been removed from the setting in which they were used in life.

Thus, individual finds provide intrinsic, chronological and statistical data, and the sepulchral finds add to these information garnered from securely-associated medical and non-medical artefacts. To aim for the broader picture, however, to attempt to assess the reality of surgical instrumentation and to place medical practice in a social context, it is necessary to turn to the third category that may be termed 'disaster' or 'catastrophe' finds: shipwrecks, volcanic eruptions, conflagrations. These are unexpected, unpredictable or uncontrollable events that may isolate and preserve a whole assemblage of material remains in the place and form in which they were in use up to the moment of the disaster. Such finds are not numerous and, of course, seldom clear-cut. Furthermore, and ironically, their exceptional nature means that while they are of immense importance and provide invaluable information it is more than ever necessary to be cautious in attempting to generalise that information beyond the immediate provenance: they may give a vivid glimpse of a particular circumstance in a particular place at a particular time, but it is difficult to gauge how representative the set of circumstances may be. Like the other categories of find, there is variation from one context to another. Least secure are shipwrecks which seldom constitute a sealed context. The most notable examples are 'Plemmirio B' (Syracuse) (Gibbins, 1989), which yielded two scalpels and a handled needle, and a wreck site in the Gulf of Baratti (Populonia), as yet unpublished (but for interims see Spawforth, 1990; Gibbins, 1997), on which were preserved a variety of medical finds including many wooden drug boxes, a bronze cupping vessel and a *collyrium* stick (desiccated eye-salve).

The most celebrated disaster finds, and thus far the only example of preservation by volcanic eruption, are the instruments from sites around the Bay of Naples, principally Pompeii and Herculaneum, sealed by volcanic debris from the eruption of Vesuvius in AD 79 (Bliquez, 1994). Unlike Herculaneum, Pompeii was not totally sealed, and the upper parts of the highest buildings projected from the covering of lapilli and ash after the eruption had ended. Nevertheless, the subsequent scavenging is most unlikely to have had as its aim the retrieval of medical kits. More significant is likely to have been the effect of the longer period of evacuation that appears to have been possible at Pompeii. This would have enabled an unknown number of people to escape (at least beyond the town walls) taking with them an unknown quantity of possessions. That the fugitives included people with medical equipment is implied by a find from the 'Grande Palestra' (Maiuri, 1939: 218–21; Künzl, 1983: 12–15; Bliquez, 1994: 87–8, 207–8), where a man carrying a box of medical instruments was overcome as he vainly tried to flee the town. This circumstance (and others) necessarily tempers any attempt to gauge the overall medical provision for Pompeii based on surviving finds of instruments and equipment (see e.g., Künzl, 1998).

While circumspection is required as to the number and variety of healers identified at Pompeii, other useful information emerges, not least the survival of equipment seldom found in other contexts. For example, the Vesuvian towns have yielded a significant proportion of all the known examples of rectal and vaginal dilators, including the so far unique quadrivalve dilator (Bliquez, 1994: 62–6, 183–91). These large, undoubtedly expensive, metal instruments have seldom been found in burials or elsewhere on sites, and the Pompeii circumstance allows us the opportunity to set them in the context of the broader Roman instrumentation of that town in AD 79.

Conflagrations, that may simultaneously both destroy and preserve, are potentially the commonest of the disaster scenarios. The full publication of the two most important examples to date are still pending. The first, an extensive find of instruments on the floor of a house at the Roman town of Marcianopolis (Devnya), Bulgaria, burnt down in the mid-fifth century AD, was briefly reported (without illustrations) in 1983 (Minchev, 1983). It is said to include scalpels, shears, sharp hook, handled needle, uvula forceps, bone lever, lithotomy scoops, rectal and vaginal dilators, trepanning tool and embryo hook.

The second example is by far the largest single find of Roman surgical instruments yet known. Excavations by Dr Jacopo Ortalli at Piazza Ferrari, Rimini, between 1989 and 1997, brought to light the so-called '*domus* del Chirurgo', part of a maritime *insula* of the Roman town of Ariminium that was destroyed by fire in the mid-third century AD. Together with contemporary conflagrations elsewhere in Ariminium and at other nearby coastal sites this event has been linked to the Alamannic raids of AD 257/8. The subsequent walling of the town resulted in the desertion of the site (which was in the lee of the rampart and the intervallum road) and its destruction deposits were sealed and remained intact. They have disclosed a small wealthy residence, part of a larger complex, with several fine mosaics. Interim accounts of the site and a selection of the finds have already appeared (Ortalli, 1992; 2000), and work is under way on the final report. The medical equipment, found principally in one room, included over 100 instruments as well as drug boxes, melted glassware, and a graded set of stone mortars and pestles. As well as introducing instrument types never found before, the find is our best evidence yet of what the equipment of a practising healer may have looked like. Although all organic materials had been consumed by the fire, the intensity of which had also fused together many of the metal instruments, it sheds important light on the potential range of surgical and medical treatments available to the population of Ariminium in the mid-third century AD.

WHAT DID A 'NORMAL' KIT OF MEDICAL INSTRUMENTS LOOK LIKE?

In the Hippocratic writings a doctor was advised always to have ready to hand a portable kit of instruments for use away from the surgery (Hippocrates, *De decenti habitu* 8.10–13 (9.236–238L)). This is likely to have comprised one or more examples of each of the basic tools of surgery — scalpel, spring forceps, sharp hook, needle, probe, cautery and cupping vessel, which are the instruments most frequently referred to by Celsus in the surgical books (VII–VIII) of his *De medicina*.

Iconography tends to support this view, whether on votive reliefs or tombstones (see e.g., Tabanelli, 1958: pls. 10–15; Krug, 1985: Abb. 12, 18, 21, 26; Hillert, 1990: 187–97). However, caution is necessary here, because there is evidently a symbolic or emblematic role to the depictions. Instruments appear to have been seen as the healer's 'badge of office' or as representing the essence of healing, and they would thus be ready identifiers of 'doctoring' or 'medicine' (see e.g., Jackson, 1988: fig. 15). Therefore, the depictions should certainly not be regarded as unequivocal evidence of the true appearance of a healer's normal complete *instrumentarium*. Nevertheless, they are likely to show some of the key instruments, the commonest, most recognisable core tools; and that this is probably the case is suggested by archaeological finds of instrument kits, in virtually all of which core tools form an integral part or even the entire kit (Jackson, 1995: tables 1, 2).

Some of the best-contexted examples of small or moderate-sized core kits are those from Pompeii, Nijmegen, Wehringen and Luzzi. The Pompeii find, from the region of the so-called 'Grande Palestra', adjacent to the amphitheatre, was dropped in transit by a luckless fugitive from the Vesuvian eruption of AD 79. Beneath his skeleton was found the remains of a wooden box containing four scalpels, two hooks, two spring forceps, two needles, six probes and four medicine tubes (Maiuri, 1939: 218–21; Künzl, 1983: 12–15; Bliquez, 1994: 87–8, 207–8 (A21–A27), pl. XXIII). At Nijmegen, a sarcophagus burial of third century AD date included four scalpels, two hooks, a spring forceps, six needles, three probes, a bone lever, a chisel, a shears and at least eight assorted medicine pots and boxes (Leemans,

1842; Künzl, 1983: 93–6; Braadbaart, 1994). Also of third century date, an inhumation burial from Wehringen (Bavaria) was furnished with a kit of six instruments — three scalpels, a hook, a spring forceps and a bone lever — closely-packed, top-to-tail, in a leather case. In addition there was a spatula probe, stone palette and medicine box (Nuber and Radnoti, 1969: 34; Künzl, 1983: 120–1; Fasold, 1992). The slightly larger kit found with a late first century AD inhumation at Luzzi (Cosenza) comprised single examples of scalpel, hook and forceps, two probable cauteries, four probes, a dental forceps, a bone forceps and a bone lever, as well as four medicine containers (Guzzo, 1974: 469–75 (grave 17); Künzl, 1983: 106–7).

The broad similarity in the combination of instruments in these sets is a repeating pattern in other, and less well contexted kits, and it can also be identified as a component of more extensive *instrumentaria* (see e.g., Jackson, 1986; 1995: tables 1–2). We may cautiously accept that it reflects the composition of the metal tools in a typical set of basic medical instruments during the period of the Roman Empire.

HOW UNIFORM WAS SURGICAL EQUIPMENT AND SURGICAL PRACTICE THROUGHOUT THE EMPIRE?

Apart from certain categories of instrument, most notably the copper-alloy cupping vessel (Fig. 2: 8), which had already been developed in Greece by the late sixth century BC and was to continue virtually unchanged for the next thousand years (Berger, 1970: 63–87), it is not until the early first century AD that we begin to encounter instruments of distinctive and recurrent forms (Künzl, 1996: 2584–5). Then the first impression is of great uniformity throughout the Empire, a uniformity that may be attributed, at least in part, to the rapid spread of knowledge of medical theories, practises and equipment by the Roman army.

In fact, regional differences are beginning to emerge, though usually those differences relate to decor and manufacture rather than to the form of the functional part. In Britain and the North-western provinces, for example, there is a little evidence for the preferential use of iron over bronze. The medical kit in the Stanway 'Doctor's Burial' (Crummy, 1997) exemplifies the point. Of its thirteen instruments seven are of iron, two are composite iron and copper-alloy tools and only four are of copper alloy, a reversal of the normal ratio in Roman surgical kits. If this proves to be a widespread phenomenon then it has profound implications, not just for uniformity but also prevalence, in view of the fact that so little of a corroded iron assemblage is generally susceptible to unequivocal identification. Thus, of the seven iron instruments from the Stanway burial, probably only two would have been firmly identified as medical tools were they to have been discovered as unassociated finds. The difficulty with the Stanway *instrumentarium* is that its idiosyncracies are open to chronological as well as regional interpretation (Jackson, 1997b).

In some cases uniformity of surgical equipment was inevitable, in that the form of the instrument was dictated by human anatomy. If ancient healers, for example, wished to access the male or female urinary bladder via the urethra for the purpose of catheterisation, then the instrument was necessarily a slender curved tube, of particular gauge and length, with an opening near the tip and a smooth outer surface (Jackson, 1986: 126–7, 147–51; 1994a: 184–7) as, indeed, it remained up to recent times. Our challenge is to differentiate the corroded and often incomplete remains of Roman copper-alloy catheters from other Roman tubular artefacts of similar form.

While the appearance and composition of sets of core tools shed light on the degree of uniformity of basic surgical instrumentation, some instruments, like the catheter, were much more restricted in their surgical applications and their distribution can be taken as some kind of coarse guide as to the uniformity not only of surgical equipment but also of surgical practise. Thus, the presence of skull trephining instruments from Bingen in the West to Colophon in the East (Como, 1925; Caton, 1914) and of uvula forceps in most provinces of the Empire (Jackson, 1988: 124–5 pl. 32; 1994b) might be taken as evidence of continuity and conformity of practise, whether the drilling of skulls (for whatever precise reason) or the surgical removal of the uvula or haemorrhoids. Absences may be attributed either to gaps in the archaeological record or to a true reflection of differing practise: at present not a single confirmed find of a cupping vessel is known from Britain (Jackson, 1993: 94 and n. 125). Perhaps the clearest archaeological evidence for regional differences in the organisation of medical practise, if not in the practise itself, are the objects popularly known as oculists' stamps, but more correctly termed *collyrium* stamps. Their concentration in the North-western provinces of the Empire is indisputable, but the precise meaning of that distribution is still the subject of debate (for a digest of published works see Jackson, 1996a; 1996b. See also Voinot 1999).

In summary, the distribution of surgical instruments and equipment provides some evidence for a widespread uniformity of practise throughout the Roman Empire. It cannot, however, shed light on the consistency (or otherwise) of the theory (or theories) that lay behind the surgical interventions. In certain instances there is clear evidence for regional differences, and we should undoubtedly envisage a complex situation in which Graeco-Roman medicine interfaced with the varying healing traditions of culturally different regions of the ancient world.

WHO USED SURGICAL TOOLS, AND CAN THE INSTRUMENTS HELP US TO ESTIMATE THE LEVEL OF MEDICAL ACTIVITY?

Modern medicine has become very compartmentalised, but it is important to remember that this was not the case in antiquity. A healer might set himself up as a 'general practitioner' or as a specialist in one or more medical fields or, indeed, any combination of the two, without any legal impediment. Indeed, there were no exams, certification or courses of study required of those who called themselves *medici* (Jackson 1993). Similarly, although there were healers styled *chirurgus* or *chirurgicus*, surgery was evidently not their sole preserve. Thus, surgical instruments are to be seen depicted on the tombstone of the *medicus* Publius Aelius Pius Curtianus, from Palestrina (Tabanelli, 1958: pls. XIII–XIV). Furthermore, we should take seriously the critical comments of the early first century AD medical writer Scribonius Largus, who noted with sadness that there were skilled and experienced healers far removed from the 'medical profession', while many within the profession were ineffective or grossly negligent or knew only one aspect of the healing sciences (Hamilton, 1986). This is clearly a signal not to underestimate either the quantity or the quality of self-help, whether by the *pater familias* or others.

As to an estimate of relative levels of medical activity, ideally, yes, the numbers, types and distribution of instruments would supply some sound statistics. Practically, however, the answer is 'no'. Even at Pompeii a comprehensive study of instruments and their provenances could only supply pointers (Bliquez, 1994; Künzl, 1998). Similarly, as already discussed, the evidence from burials is equivocal, while both domestic implements and craft tools could always be pressed into service for medicine and surgery.

DO THE INSTRUMENTS ASSIST US IN GAUGING THE SUCCESS OF ROMAN PRACTITIONERS?

Here the answer has to be an unequivocal 'no'. With so many unknown factors to consider there is no way that they can do this. Instead, taken in conjunction with the contemporaneous medical texts they reveal what might be achieved under optimal conditions: if the texts provide evidence for the *potential* of medical theory then the instruments provide evidence for the *potential* of practise. Conversely, they can also be used to show what might occur in less than satisfactory circumstances, as in the introduction of bacteria or the cutting of an artery in mistake for a vein (Celsus, *De medicina* II, 10, 15).

On the positive side, it can be observed that just as the authors of medical texts often paid considerable and detailed attention to surgical technique and patient care, the surviving instruments usually attest a similar attentiveness on the part of their makers/designers to precision and quality of manufacture. In the end, however, despite the use of the very best instruments in the best of hands, chance would always have played a major role. The micro-organisms of disease could not even be seen or accurately characterised — let alone eliminated — and hence there was no appreciation of the need for sterile conditions. Under such circumstances probably the best that could be hoped for was that the healer would operate with confidence, instil trust, inspire hope, and avoid haemorrhage and infection. In short, not kill the patient, thus allowing nature to effect the healing process, an approach long since recognised by the Hippocratic writers: 'Practise two things in your dealings with disease: either help or do not harm the patient' (*Epidemics* I. 11).

CONCLUSION

Medical equipment and surgical instruments are the link between texts and patients. They can confirm the reality of the medical writings, but further than that, as part of the debris of daily life, they can shed light on the actuality of ancient medicine, on the practise of medicine at the level of the 'general public', in a way that other sources cannot. However, the insufficiency of their evidence precludes unequivocal answers to all but the most mundane questions. We should, therefore, be duly cautious, though not timid, in our attempts at interpreting that evidence.

BIBLIOGRAPHY

Bliquez, L. J.
(1994) *Roman Surgical Instruments and Other Minor Objects in the Archaeological Museum of Naples. With a Catalogue of the Surgical Instruments in the 'Antiquarium' at Pompeii by Ralph Jackson,* Mainz.

Braadbaart, S.
(1994) 'Medical and cosmetic instruments in the collection of the 'Rijksmuseum van oudheden' in Leiden, The Netherlands', *Oudheidkundige mededelingen uit het Rijksmuseum van oudheden te Leiden* **74**, 1994: 163–75.

Caton, R.
(1914) 'Notes on a group of medical and surgical instruments found near Kolophon', *Journal of Hellenic Studies* **34**: 114–18.

Como, J.
(1925) 'Das Grab eines römisches Arztes in Bingen', *Germania* **9**: 152–62.

Crummy, P.
(1997) 'Colchester: The Stanway burials', *Current Archaeology* **153**: 337–42.

Fasold, P.
(1992) *Römischer Grabbrauch in Süddeutschland.* Schriften des Limesmuseums Aalen 46, Stuttgart.

Feugère, M., Künzl, E., Weisser, U.
(1985) 'Les aiguilles à cataracte de Montbellet (Saône-et-Loire). Contribution à l'étude de l'ophtalmologie antique et islamique. Die Starnadeln von Montbellet (Saône-et-Loire). Ein Beitrag zur antiken und islamischen Augenheilkunde.' *Jahrbuch des Römisch-Germanischen Zentralmuseums Mainz* **32**: 436–508.

Gibbins, D.
(1989) 'The Roman wreck of *c*. AD 200 at Plemmirio, near Siracusa (Sicily): second interim report. The domestic assemblage 1: medical equipment and pottery lamps', *The International Journal of Nautical Archaeology* **18** (1): 1–25.
(1997) 'More underwater finds of Roman medical equipment', *Antiquity* **71**: 457–9.

Guzzo. P. G.
(1974) 'Luzzi. Località S. Vito (Cosenza). Necropoli di età romana', *Notizie degli Scavi* **28**: 449–84.

Hamilton, J. S.
(1986) 'Scribonius Largus on the medical profession', *Bulletin of the History of Medicine* **60**: 209–16.

Hillert, A.
(1990) *Antike Ärztedarstellungen.* Marburger Schriften zur Medizingeschichte 25, Frankfurt am Main.

Jackson, R.
(1986) 'A set of Roman medical instruments from Italy', *Britannia* **17**: 119–67.
(1988) *Doctors and Diseases in the Roman Empire,* London (repr. 1991, 1993, 1995, 2000).
(1990) 'Roman doctors and their instruments: recent research into ancient practice', *Journal of Roman Archaeology* **3**: 5–27.
(1993) 'Roman medicine: the practitioners and their practices', in W. Haase and H. Temporini (eds.), *Aufstieg und*

Niedergang der römischen Welt (ANRW) **II 37.1**, Berlin/New York, pp. 79–101.
(1994a) 'The surgical instruments, appliances and equipment in Celsus' *De medicina*', in G. Sabbah and P. Mudry (eds.), *La médecine de Celse. Aspects historiques, scientifiques et littéraires*, St Étienne, Centre Jean Palerne, Mémoires **XIII**: pp. 167–209.
(1994b) '*Staphylagra*, *staphylocaustes*, uvulectomy and haemorrhoidectomy: the Roman instruments and operations', in A. Krug (ed.), *From Epidauros to Salerno*, *PACT* **34**, 1992 (1994): 167–85.
(1995) 'The composition of Roman medical *instrumentaria* as an indicator of medical practice: a provisional assessment', in P. J. van der Eijk, H. F. J. Horstmanshoff and P. H. Schrijvers (eds.), *Ancient Medicine in its Socio-cultural Context*, Leiden, Clio Medica 27/28: 189–207.
(1996a) 'Eye medicine in the Roman Empire', in W. Haase and H. Temporini (eds.), *Aufstieg und Niedergang der römischen Welt (ANRW)* **II 37.3**, Berlin/New York, pp. 2228–51.
(1996b) 'A new collyrium-stamp from Staines and some thoughts on eye medicine in Roman London and Britannia', in J. Bird, M. Hassall and H. Sheldon (eds.), *Interpreting Roman London. Papers in memory of Hugh Chapman*, Oxbow Monographs **58**, Oxford, pp. 177–87.
(1997a) 'A novel Roman forceps', *The Ashmolean* **33**, Christmas 1997: 15–16.
(1997b) 'An ancient British medical kit from Stanway, Essex', *The Lancet* **350**: 1471–73.

Krug, A.
(1985) *Heilkunst und Heilkult. Medizin in der Antike*, München (reprinted 1993), pp. 70–103.

Künzl, E.
(1983) *Medizinische Instrumente aus Sepulkralfunden der römischen Kaiserzeit.* Unter Mitarbeit von Franz Josef Hassel und Susanna Künzl. Kunst und Altertum am Rhein 115. Köln/Bonn.
(1996) 'Forschungsbericht zu den antiken medizinischen Instrumenten', in W. Haase and H. Temporini (eds), *Aufstieg und Niedergang der römischen Welt (ANRW)* **II 37.3**. Berlin/New York, pp. 2433–639.

(1998) 'Instrumentenfunde und Arzthäuser in Pompeji: Die medizinische Versorgung einer römischen Stadt des I. Jahrhunderts n. Chr.', *Sartoniana* **11**: 71–152.

Leemans, C.
(1842) *Romeinse steenen Doodskisten*, Nijhoffs Bijdragen, Arnhem.

Maiuri, A.
(1939) 'Regione I (Latium et Campania). I. Pompei. Scavo della 'Grande Palestra' nel quartiere dell'Anfiteatro (a. 1935–1939)', *Notizie degli Scavi* **1939**: 165–238.

Merrifield, R.
(1965) *The Roman City of London*, London.

Minchev, A.
(1983) 'Roman Medicine in Marcianopolis', *Concilium Eirene XVI. Proceedings of the 16th International Eirene Conference, Prague 1982*, Prague, pp. 143–8.

Nuber, H. U. and Radnoti, A.
(1969) 'Römische Brand- und Körpergräber aus Wehringen. Ldkr. Schwabmünchen. Ein Vorbericht.', *Jahresbericht der Bayerischen Bodendenkmalpflege* **10**: 27–49.

Ortalli, J.
(1992) 'Edilizia residenziale e crisi urbana nella tarda antichità: fonti archeologiche per la Cispadana', in *Cultura sull'Arte Ravennate e Bizantina XXXIX*: 557–605.
(2000) 'Rimini: la *domus 'del Chirurgo'* ', in Mirella Marini Calvani (ed.), *Aemilia. La cultura romana in Emilia Romagna dal III secolo a. C. all'età costantiniana*, Bologna, pp. 513–26.

Scalinci, N.
(1938) 'Su alcuni antichi strumenti di chirurgia oculare nel Museo Nazionale di Napoli', *Atti e Memorie dell' Accademia di Storia dell'Arte Sanitaria* **37**, fasc. 5.

Spawforth, A. J. S.
(1990) 'Roman Medicine from the Sea', *Minerva* **1** (6): 9–10.

Stead, I. M. and Rigby, V.
(1989) *Verulamium. The King Harry Lane Site*, HBMCE Archaeological Report **12**, London.

Tabanelli, M.
(1958) *Lo strumento chirurgico e la sua storia*, Forlì.

Voinot, J.
(1999) *Les cachets à collyres dans le monde romain*, Monographies instrumentum **7**, Montagnac.

INVESTIGATING THE ANGLO-SAXON *MATERIA MEDICA*: ARCHAEOBOTANY, MANUSCRIPT ART, LATIN AND OLD ENGLISH

Debby Banham

Our knowledge of Anglo-Saxon medicine is based on four collections of recipes in Old English, all probably compiled or translated in the tenth or late ninth centuries: the Old English *Herbarium*, edited by de Vriend, 1984, the *Lacnunga*, edited by Grattan and Singer, 1952, and *Bald's Leechbook* and *Leechbook III*, both edited by Cockayne, 1864–6, vol. 2. To further our understanding of these texts, I am compiling an Anglo-Saxon *materia medica*, a directory of all the substances prescribed in them. Of these substances, the overwhelming majority are plant products, and so the greater part of the work is concerned with plant names, botanical remains, and other evidence for plants. This paper will explain some of the methodological problems that faced me when I started research on Anglo-Saxon plants in 1986, and still face me, essentially unchanged, today.

It would be perfectly possible, if not very exciting, to simply list all the plant names mentioned in the Anglo-Saxon medical texts, and the purposes they are prescribed for, but such an exercise would be of limited value. Specifically, it would not tell us what those plant names meant (a problem to which most of this paper will be devoted), nor, looking at the wider historical context, would it help us to establish the relationship of the texts to the actual practice of medicine in Anglo-Saxon England. This last is probably an ultimately insoluble problem, but one way of approaching it is from the point of view of the individual plants, and whether they can be shown to have existed in early medieval England. If not, we have to be pretty sceptical about their being used in Anglo-Saxon medicine, whatever the texts say.

Any study of Anglo-Saxon plants must start by establishing which of the plants concerned were known in Anglo-Saxon England. This may seem on the face of it straightforward, but in fact it is fairly complex, in that no single form of evidence is sufficient on its own to achieve it, and combining different kinds of evidence means combining the difficulties inherent in each.

Archaeological remains of a plant, from an Anglo-Saxon site for instance, show that the plant existed, at least in this particular location, in the period. Either it was growing here of its own accord, or someone was cultivating it, or it was imported in some form from where it did grow. In some cases, such as grape pips in an early Anglo-Saxon context, or the notorious fifteenth-century banana recently found in London, it is clear that we are dealing with an import. In other cases, such as cumin or coriander seeds, the plant could have been grown in this country, but in the early middle ages it is unlikely. In the case of native plants, it is most likely that they were growing wild, although in some cases, such as strawberry seeds from busy urban sites, we may suspect that they were either being cultivated, or else being gathered from the wild away from the site. But there is also a large number of plants which although not native to this country, are easy to grow here and capable of becoming naturalised. Many plants prescribed in Anglo-Saxon medicine, such as parsley, thyme, and others that have since become common culinary herbs, fall into this category; and thus, when they are found in archaeological deposits, it is difficult to tell whether they were imported, cultivated in this country (whether on the site or not), or collected from naturally occurring populations.

However they arrived on the site, we can at least be sure that plants represented in the archaeobotanical record for the period were available for Anglo-Saxons to use. We cannot be sure, however, that the Anglo-Saxons did in fact use them; to establish that we need more evidence. This could either be further archaeological evidence, for instance that the plant had been processed, or else some other kind of evidence to show that the Anglo-Saxons were actually aware of the plant's existence. Otherwise, it is highly likely that plants of little economic importance, especially, were born to bloom unseen, or confused with other similar plants. There's no evidence, for instance, that the Anglo-Saxons distinguished between different kinds of nettle.

The evidence of texts, on the other hand, providing a statement from an author mentioning a plant by name, whether or not it tells us anything substantive about that plant, shows that the author knew the name of the plant, and possibly a good deal more about it, but not necessarily that the plant itself was familiar to him or her, let alone to other Anglo-Saxons, in real life. Abbot Ælfric, for instance, explains in his homily for the tenth Sunday after Pentecost that (olive) oil grows on trees like wine, 'but olive trees grow larger, and the berries are bigger' (Pope, 1968: 552). This tells us that Ælfric expected his audience to be unfamiliar with olive trees, and also, I suspect that he himself had never seen one, either. (Interestingly, though, it does suggest that they had some idea of what a vine looked like, and by Ælfric's time there were probably a few vineyards in England — see Banham, 1990: 139–47.) If the homilist had not given himself away like this, we would have to turn to archaeology to see whether olives were known in Anglo-Saxon England. (In the present state of our knowledge, the answer is 'no'.) Irrespective of whether they had seen an olive (or an olive tree), however, Ælfric and his audience (at least after they'd heard or read his homily) did know that such things existed. There must be many less obvious cases like this, where a writer refers to a plant without ever having seen it, but does not happen to betray this ignorance to the modern reader. In particular, for the student of Anglo-Saxon medicine, there is the tantalising possibility that the compilers of the medical texts were simply copying over, or translating, texts of continental origin, without having any idea what the plants referred to were.

Another useful form of evidence comes from place-names, such as Peasenhall, Appleby, and so on (see Banham, 1990: *passim*, for more examples of names relating to food plants), which can tell us that a plant was recognisable in the landscape when the name was first used (usually at some point during the Anglo-Saxon period). However, place names rarely give us any indication of whether the plants mentioned were wild or cultivated, or why their presence was worth remarking upon in this way.

It might be thought that contemporary illustrations would help us establish which plants were known in Anglo-Saxon England, especially as Anglo-Saxon art is full of plants. But the vast majority of these are highly stylised, as for instance the vine-scroll of early Northumbrian sculpture (for examples of this, see Cramp, 1984). Even when plants are drawn in a more representational manner, it must be recognised that the purpose of portraying them was not usually identification. In most cases it was to glorify God. For instance, the tenth-century Benedictional of St Æthelwold shows St Æthelthryth, the founder of Ely, holding a lily to identify her as, despite her two marriages, a virgin saint (British Library, Additional MS 49598, folio 90b; for a colour reproduction, see Deshman, 1995, plate 28). The artist has been unable to resist the temptation to gild the lily, literally; and so anyone attempting to identify a real lily by reference to this illustration, let alone tell what kind of lily it is, would be totally at a loss. The same applies to the illustration in the *Old English Hexateuch*, also of the tenth century, of Noah tending his vines prior to becoming the first man to get drunk (British Library, Cotton MS Claudius B. iv, folio 17r; facsimile Dodwell and Clemoes, 1974). No-one would recognise a vine from it.

The only examples of Anglo-Saxon plant illustrations that may have been intended for identification are those in the eleventh-century illustrated manuscript of the Old English *Herbarium*, British Library, Cotton MS Vitellius C. iii (facsimile D'Aronco and Cameron, 1998). But even here, most of them would have been little use for that purpose. First of all, we can be quite sure that none of them was drawn from life. There is a long continental tradition of *Herbarium* illustration, with several branches, and connections with the pictures accompanying other texts, including Dioscorides. In the recent facsimile publication, Professor Maria Amalia D'Aronco has traced the relationships of the book's illustrations to that tradition, and demonstrated effectively that medieval respect for *auctoritas*, in illustrations as much as in text, was much stronger than trust in one's own observation of the real world. Mistakes and misunderstandings could be transmitted from one manuscript to another across the centuries, as well as being invented afresh at each copying, and in fact few of the illustrations in Vitellius C. iii resemble, to modern eyes, the plants they are supposed to portray.

The new facsimile also shows what many published reproductions do not: the sorry state of the manuscript. First of all, the green pigment used in the illustrations was a copper salt that in many places has eaten through the membrane, resulting in holes in practically every folio. Those that survive best are those with little green leaf or stem visible. Secondly, like other Cotton manuscripts, this one was damaged in the 1731 fire when the collection was at Ashburnham House. As a result, it is charred and shrunken, and in many places split along the edges of the folios, especially the top edges. Where this coincides with the corrosion caused by the green pigment, whole illustrations can be unintelligible. What should have been the most useful Anglo-Saxon manuscript for plant illustration is thus of only very limited value.

The ideal combination of evidence for any plant would therefore normally be archaeological, to show that the plant physically existed here, together with contemporary writings to tell us what the Anglo-Saxons knew or thought about it. But there is a crucial link that I have so far ignored: we must be sure that whatever forms of evidence we combine refer to the same plant. This depends on our ability to equate the plant names, both Latin and vernacular, used in Anglo-Saxon medical texts with the genera, species and varieties we recognise today, and to which archaeological specimens are identified. Needless to say, this is no easy task.

To take Old English names first (although many of the points I make are also relevant to Latin names), first of all, in strict epistemological terms, we can never be sure exactly which plant or plants an Old English name covers. Even where a name has a clear and continuous history throughout the Old, Middle and Modern English periods (and there are a few such cases), it can rarely be more than a logical supposition that it always applied to the same plant. To take a familiar example, the Old English *dæges ege*, literally 'day's eye', is obviously the etymon of Modern English 'daisy', and it is attested at frequent intervals throughout the history of the language. So it is fair to translate it 'daisy' (with all due caution). (For a systematic discussion of nearly all recorded Old English plant names, see Bierbaumer, 1975–9.) But which daisy? Is it the little lawn daisy, *Bellis perennis*, or the ox-eye daisy *Chrysanthemum leucanthemum*? Both are considered native to the British Isles, so both can be assumed to have existed in Anglo-Saxon England. It may perhaps be relevant that *Bellis perennis* was probably less common in the early middle ages than it is today, since its preferred habitat is short grass, an ecological niche that, in an age without lawns, would be confined largely to closely grazed, but not over-grazed, pasture. The ox-eye daisy, on the other hand, as a cornfield weed, would have been considerably more common. Whichever daisy was meant, and a third possibility is that no distinction was made between the two, it was a pretty important medical plant: its name translates the Latin *consolida minor*, and it was thus credited with the same properties as *consolida major*, comfrey. If we want to establish the contemporary reputation of medical plants, identification is more than academic.

Despite all the ramifications I enumerated, this was a fairly straightforward case. Another, even less problematic, would be *foxes glofa*, clearly the same name as fox-glove, again a native plant. And there are plenty of others. But there are also, as in any translation exercise, false friends. *Feferfuge*, for instance, is the same word as 'feverfew', and it does apply to *Chrysanthemum parthenium*, now famous as a migraine treatment. But it derives from the Latin *febrifugium*, 'that which puts fever to flight', and as such had a much wider meaning than does its Modern English descendant. It certainly applied to centaury, and we can rarely be sure in a particular case whether it means feverfew, centaury, or some other plant, or if a more general reference was intended.

Probably about two-thirds of Old English plant names resemble Modern English ones, and most of the rest are derived from Latin. One or two look like quite plausible Modern English plant names, but don't happen to have survived. Some of these can be etymologised, like *attorlothe*, meaning literally 'poison-hatred', but scholars have been unable to agree which particular plant inimical to poison it refers to. Another such is *brunwyrt*, which would give Modern English 'brownwort'. Old English *brun* has a slightly different semantic range from our 'brown': 'bright brown' is a possible combination in Old English, but makes little sense in Modern. The word seems to be especially associated with blood-stains, and *brunwyrt* is apparently the hart's tongue fern, which has rows of bright rusty-coloured spores underneath its fronds. In fact the study of colour vocabulary can shed a good deal of light on plant names, and Dr Carole Biggam, in the course of her work on Old English words for 'blue', has been able to establish that *hæwenhnydele*, previously thought to be the red dead-nettle, is in fact the cornflower (see Biggam, 1994; 1997).

Finally, there is a substantial minority of Old English plant names that remains quite indecipherable. One hopes they may eventually yield to scholars' efforts, but some are fairly intractable. One such is *tunsingwyrt*. The second element is clearly the common *wyrt*, 'herb' or 'plant', but the first appears nowhere else in Old English. It has been suggested that *tunsing* has something to do with brewing, which one does in a *tunne*, or tun, but the intrusive 's' would be hard to account for. Some variant spellings suggest that *tunsing* may actually be a garbled form of *tungils*, a star (which gives us Modern English 'tingle'). Where *tunsingwyrt* appears in glossaries, it usually translates some form of *helleborus*, but no hellebore resembles a star so clearly as to make an identification from these two pieces of information. At the moment, we can get no further with *tunsingwyrt*.

Many Old English plant names, as already mentioned, are derived from Latin. Others, like *tunsingwyrt*, are found in Latin–Old English glossaries. It might be thought that these names could be interpreted quite simply by reference to their Latin equivalents or etymons. But the glossaries themselves present problems, mostly connected with the fact that they are all related to each other to a greater or lesser extent (see Pheifer, 1974, for a discussion of the glossaries and their relationships). So the fact that the same translation appears in five or six glossaries may not mean that it is correct, or even that it was believed to be correct in the early middle ages. It could simply be that an ancestral mistake in one glossary was transmitted to the others by copyists and compilers. The same kind of caveat applies to the Old English *Herbarium*, translated from the Latin and therefore a potential source of Latin equivalents. However, it is not clear that the *Herbarium*'s interpretations of the Latin are independent of the glossaries, or indeed of the other Old English medical texts (see de Vriend, 1984, for an edition and discussion of this text, and D'Aronco and Cameron, 1998, for further discussion of its relationship to other texts).

But even if each occurrence of a Latin–Old English translation could be regarded as an independent witness, we still could not simply use them to read off the meaning of the Old English words involved. The Latin itself would have to be interpreted first. The meaning of Latin plant names has not remained static over the last thousand years, any more than that of English ones. Furthermore, much less work has been done on Latin than on Old English plant names, especially in recent years.

Sometimes it is clear from descriptions in Pliny's *Historia naturalis*, for instance, or the Latin version of Dioscorides' *Materia medica*, that a name did mean the same in classical Latin as it does in the botanical Latin of our own day. *Abies*, for instance, meant a fir-tree to Pliny, and it is the generic name for firs in modern taxonomy. Again, *artemisia* is used by Dioscorides (or rather, his translator) to describe various kinds of wormwood, as it still is by botanists today (see André, 1956, *sub verbis* for discussion of these terms in classical Latin). In these cases, therefore, it is reasonable to suppose that the meaning in the tenth century was the same as it was in the first and is in the twentieth. The process of taxonomical scholarship itself introduces change, however: taxonomists may decide that not all plants known by a single generic name in fact belong to the same genus, or conversely that plants previously known by a number of different names should be grouped together under a single generic name. The redundant names are then lost. This has been going on for a long time, of course, so historians may be better off looking at obsolete botanical terminology than that current today. But however far back we go, we have to recognise that change and revision was taking place. When Linnaeus invented the binomial system, he gave some plants new names, but for many he drew on names already current in scholarly Latin, which in his day was still a living, and therefore a changing, language (see Heller, 1964).

To take just one example, in this case of names that changed during the middle ages, it is odd that rape is botanically *Brassica napus*, while the turnip, from Old English *næp*, is *Brassica rapa*. One would expect them to be the other way round. It is not clear what exactly has happened to these names, but it does appear that, when Old English *næp* was taken over from Latin *napus*, the latter meant a turnip. *Rapa* on the other hand seems not to have been taken into Old English, but in the fourteenth century Middle English *rape* etc. means both a turnip and the seed-bearing plant we know as Modern English 'rape' (see *OED* for historical citations of both words in English). If both senses could be used in Middle English, the Latin word was probably in the course of changing its meaning. Whether *napus* was affected by this change, or changed independently, is not clear. The confusion was undoubtedly exacerbated by the fact that, like other *Brassicae*, both species are extremely variable, and both have produced forms exploited for their leaves and for their roots, although, as far as I know, turnip seed has never been a crop on a par with oil-seed rape.

Another phenomenon that has changed the interpretation of Latin plant names is the shift of focus from the Mediterranean to northern Europe (and more recently to other parts of the world). The genus *Abies*, for example, contains kinds of fir-tree that Pliny will never have seen growing in Italy. *Artemisia*, on the other hand, included, even in Dioscorides' day, plants that will not readily grow in England, and certainly do not do so without human intervention. So what an Anglo-Saxon understood by the word may have been rather different from the understanding of a classical Latin speaker, or indeed of a modern botanist. Nonetheless, here we are only dealing with a contraction or expansion of semantic range, not a complete break.

Sometimes, however, whether deliberately or unwittingly, writers may have applied Latin names to plants completely different from the ones they normally meant. The main reason for this will have been the need to find equivalents available in England for plants found in the Mediterranean region and therefore in classical and sub-classical medical texts, but not in northern Europe. That this was a problem we know from two sources. One is the eighth-century Bishop Cyneheard of Winchester's plea to a colleague in Germany to send medical books, because 'we have a certain number, but the foreign drugs in them are quite unfamiliar to us' (Tangl, 1916: 247). Presumably he was hoping for books compiled in Germany and therefore better adapted to northern European conditions. His comment is echoed two centuries later by the scribe or compiler of *Bald's Leechbook*, who, faced with a recipe calling for 'the bark that comes from Paradise', remarked that 'that would be hard to come by' (Cockayne, 1884–6, vol. 2: 114).

That substitutions did take place can be inferred from variant translations: the Old English *fel(d/t)wyrt*, for instance, sometimes translates *gentiana*, sometimes *verbascum*, a mullein. Who could possibly confuse a gentian and a mullein, we might ask; probably only someone pretty desperate. It may be, however, that, in the context of early medieval medicine, not having access to yellow gentian, a very important medicinal plant at that time, was a desperate situation. Desperate enough to make one seize on a plant that resembles it only in one particular, that of having a tall spike of yellow flowers. Here the use of the plant names suggests that one plant was being used instead of another, but how many other cases might there be of this, where no such clues remain? Substitution may have been widespread, and perhaps usually silent (there is no such text as a *Quid pro quo* in Anglo-Saxon medicine), leading to the transfer of names from one plant to another, more familiar, but possibly quite unrelated. That mistakes occurred, confusing unfamiliar plants with better known ones, is at least equally likely.

Thus every type of evidence, whether from place names, the visual arts, or texts in either Latin or Old English, has its difficulties or limitations. Archaeobotany too is not without its problems. Other authors in this volume are much better qualified than I to comment on these, but I could pick out two as being particularly relevant to this kind of synthesis. One is differential preservation, which means that some types of plant are over-represented in the archaeological record, while others are never found at all, despite there being no doubt that they did exist in the past. The second is the problem of identification. Some plants are instantly recognisable from their seeds or pollen, while in other cases the remains could belong to any one of several plants, not necessarily closely related.

In this paper I have concentrated on problems, but I would not like to give the impression that they are insurmountable. Because we have so many sources of information at our disposal, difficulties with one can often be circumvented by using alternative forms of evidence. Meanwhile, archaeobotanical techniques are constantly being improved, so that information that would have been irrecoverable a few decades ago is now becoming commonplace, and the results of archaeobotanical work are gathered together in the Archaeobotanical Computer Database (ABCD) from the University of York (see Tomlinson and Hall, 1995), saving enormous amounts of library legwork. An Anglo-Saxon Plant Name Survey (ASPNS) has now been set up at the University of Glasgow, under the direction of Dr C. P. Biggam, bringing under one umbrella people working on the plant names in different places and different disciplines, and potentially providing an invaluable repository of relevant information. The combination of technological progress with new opportunities for co-operation between interested scholars should mean a virtual explosion of new information on Anglo-Saxon plants, their uses and their names in the next few years.

BIBLIOGRAPHY

André, Jacques
(1956) *Lexique des termes de botanique en latin*, Paris: C. Klincksieck.

Banham, Deborah Anne Reyner
(1990) *The Knowledge and Uses of Food Plants in Anglo-Saxon England*, unpublished PhD thesis, University of Cambridge.

Bierbaumer, Peter
(1975–9) *Der botanische Wortschatz des Altenglischen*, 3 vols, Grazer Beiträge zur Englischen Philologie, Frankfurt am Main: Peter Lang.

Biggam, C. P.
(1994) '*Hæwenhnydele*: an Anglo-Saxon medicinal plant', *Botanical Journal of Scotland* **46.4**: 617–22.
(1997) *Blue in Old English: an Interdisciplinary Semantic Study*, Costerus new series 10, Amsterdam and Atlanta, Georgia: Rodopi.

Cockayne, T. O.
(1864–6) *Leechdoms, Wortcunning and Starcraft of Early England*, 3 vols., London: Rolls Series.

Cramp, Rosemary
(1984) *British Academy Corpus of Anglo-Saxon Stone Sculpture*, volume I, *County Durham and Northumberland*, Oxford: Oxford University Press.

D'Aronco, M. A., and Cameron, M. L.
(1998) *The Old English Illustrated Pharmacopeia: British Library Cotton Vitellius C III*, Early English Manuscripts in Facsimile 27, Copenhagen: Rosenkilde and Bagger.

Deshman, Robert
(1995) *The Benedictional of Æthelwold*, Princeton, NJ: Princeton University Press.

Dodwell, C. R., and Clemoes, P.
(1974) *The Old English Illustrated Hexateuch*, Early English Manuscripts in Facsimile 18, Copenhagen: Rosenkilde and Bagger.

Grattan, J. H. G., and Singer, Charles
(1965) *Anglo-Saxon Magic and Medicine: Illustrated Specially from the Semi-pagan Text 'Lacnunga'*, Oxford: Oxford University Press.

Heller, John Lewis
(1964) 'The early history of binomial nomenclature', *Huntia* **1**: 33–70.

OED
(1989) *The Oxford English Dictionary*, 2nd edition, Oxford: Oxford University Press.

Pheifer, J. D.
(1974) *Old English Glosses in the Épinal–Erfurt Glossary*, Oxford: Oxford University Press.

Pope, John C. (ed.)
(1968) *Homilies of Ælfric: A Supplementary Collection*, volume 2, Early English Text Society original series 260, London: Oxford University Press for Early English Text Society.

Tangl, M. (ed.)
(1916) *S. Bonifatii et Lullii Epistolae*, Monumenta Germaniae Historica, Epistolae Selectae 1, Berlin.

Tomlinson, Philippa, and Allan Hall
(1995) *The Archaeobotanical Computer Database (ABCD): A Guide for Users*, York: Environmental Archaeology Unit, University of York

de Vriend, Hubert Jan
(1984) *The Old English Herbarium and Medicina de quadrupedibus*, Early English Text Society original series 286, London: Oxford University Press for EETS.

BALD'S *LEECHBOOK* AND ARCHAEOLOGY: TWO APPROACHES TO ANGLO-SAXON HEALTH AND HEALTHCARE

Sally Crawford and Tony Randall

The Anglo-Saxon world offers relatively wealthy sources of both archaeological and documentary evidence for the study of Anglo-Saxon disease and medicine. Numerous excavated inhumation cemeteries from the fifth to the eleventh centuries provide skeletal material for study, and some of the grave-goods from the earlier furnished cemeteries include items such as animal teeth, rare stones, and small bronze boxes which might be interpreted as amulets to be used in ensuring good health (Meaney, 1981). Archaeological data also provide information about the environment, agriculture and climate of Anglo-Saxon England. The surviving documentary evidence comes from manuscripts dating almost exclusively to the tenth and eleventh centuries. Hagiography and other narrative documents provide some insight into disease and treatment within an ecclesiastical construct, but the most significant contribution to our knowledge of Anglo-Saxon medicine is provided by the Leechbooks, compilations of remedies apparently commissioned for practising doctors. A full publication and translation of the majority of these texts was provided by the Reverend Oswald Cockayne in his monumental three-volume work, *Leechdoms, Wortcunning and Starcraft of Early England* (Cockayne, 1864–6). These texts derive largely from the Greek and Roman schools of medicine, although some of the remedies seem to reflect an early, insular tradition of medicine based on charms and amulets; these quasi-magical remedies have received a disproportionate amount of attention from Anglo-Saxon scholars, to the detriment of more serious study of the bulk of Anglo-Saxon remedies, although the balance is being redressed (Storms, 1948; Grattan and Singer, 1952; Meaney, 1984; Cameron, 1993). The most important of the surviving medical texts is known as Bald's *Leechbook*. Written in the tenth century, a Latin colophon records that it was transcribed by a writer named Cild for Bald, who is assumed to be an Anglo-Saxon doctor or 'leech' (Cameron, 1993: 20). The surviving manuscript contains three volumes, the first two certainly part of Bald's commission, the last less certainly belonging to the whole. Bald's *Leechbook* is the earliest surviving book of medicine in the English language.

Given the existence of both archaeological and documentary evidence, it might seem obvious to combine the two in a study of Anglo-Saxon medicine, but in practice, this has not been the case. The study of medicine in the past is one where the problems of interfacing history and archaeology, in addition to the specialist knowledge required in a study of medicine, are particularly severe. Charlotte Roberts and Keith Manchester argued, in *The Archaeology of Disease*, for a 'biocultural' approach to disease, but they warn against the shortcomings of the documentary sources: 'imprecise and incomplete representation may transmit incorrect information' (Roberts and Manchester, 1995: 2). However, given the quantity of information offered by Bald's *Leechbook* and other medical texts from the period, archaeological sources have played an extremely minor role in the study of Anglo-Saxon medicine. A case in point is Professor Malcolm Cameron's excellent and highly informative book *Anglo-Saxon Medicine* (Cameron, 1993). It represents a thorough and reasonable attempt to evaluate and understand the corpus of medicinal knowledge to which the Anglo-Saxon doctor had access by studying the texts collected by Anglo-Saxon doctors such as Bald, testing the efficacy of the remedies and debating their origins. The one area of evidence Cameron omits from his study is archaeology. Professor Cameron limited the use of archaeological evidence in Anglo-Saxon medicine to two paragraphs. Cemeteries, he informed us, revealed that women were dying young, 'particularly in childbirth', but there are very few cases from the mortuary record where childbirth can be inferred as the cause of death (Crawford, 1999: 63). Whilst he correctly mentions that the skeletal evidence reveals signs of arthritis, he also claims skeletal evidence for a high incidence of 'rheumatism' and 'rickets' (Cameron, 1993: 13). While there is a high incidence of osteoarthritis or degenerative joint disease in the Anglo-Saxon skeletal record, the evidence for rheumatoid arthritis is sparse, and rickets is an extremely rare occurrence in the skeletal record, limited to a few cases from late urban cemeteries. The late Saxon and Medieval cemetery at Fishergate, York, for example, yielded not one single example of rickets in an analysis of over 400 skeletons (Stroud and Kemp, 1993: 189–241). Similarly, Cameron says that 'archaeological evidence shows that most persons lived in 'small, damp, dark hovels' ' (Cameron, 1993: 13). This is a view of Anglo-Saxon domestic arrangements popularised by E. T. Leed's vision of Anglo-Saxon living: 'In such cabins, with bare headroom, amid a filthy litter of broken bones, of food and shattered pottery, with logs or planks raised on stones for their seats or couches lived the Anglo-Saxons' (Leeds, 1936: 26). Such an interpretation of Anglo-Saxon settlement was refuted by Ralegh Radford's review of Anglo-Saxon housing in 1957, and recent archaeological discoveries in the last 50 years have only served to confirm that 'small, damp, dark hovels' are almost certainly a figment of the late nineteenth and early twentieth century historical imagination (Ralegh Radford, 1957; Hamerow, 1993: 8).

Just as the study of Anglo-Saxon medicine has tended to concentrate exclusively on documentary sources, so the archaeologist, usually writing up a cemetery site and giving a report on the skeletal evidence, has been entirely, and reasonably, concerned with what the skeletal record reveals about Anglo-Saxon health, specifically diseases that have caused bone change. So we have two distinct and methodologically separate approaches to Anglo-Saxon medicine. One investigates what Anglo-Saxon doctors thought they knew (or, following Greek and Roman authorities, what they thought they ought to know) about medicine at the millennium. These documents offer a literary construct that may or may not have had a bearing on actual disease suffered by the population and methods used to treat common illnesses. The second approach is limited to describing trauma and deformation of skeletal material using modern interpretation of disease, and reflecting a tradition of disease identification and diagnosis that would have been alien, or incomprehensible, to those who suffered from the illness.

As an illustration of this last point, it is instructive to consider whether the most commonly-identified disease in the archaeological record — osteoarthritis — has any place in the documentary record of Anglo-Saxon medicine. Osteoarthritic changes were present in the mortuary population in all the larger Anglo-Saxon cemeteries. At Raunds, Northamptonshire, a late Saxon church cemetery with a total of about 376 burials, osteoarthritis was present in 'virtually every one of the 197 adults over the age of 17' (Boddington, 1996: 117). The area most affected was the lower vertebral column, followed by the shoulder and hip, and at the cemeteries of St Andrew's, Fishergate, York, dating from the late Saxon to the Medieval period, degenerative joint disease was again commonplace, again with the spine as the most common site. Hip and knee joints were frequently affected. Where there were severe bony changes to the hip joint, one hip joint rather than another was more likely to be affected (Stroud and Kemp, 1993).

Today, a patient suffering from osteoarthritic changes in the hip might consult a General Practitioner with symptoms such as a constant dull background ache in the hip, and sharper pain on particular movements, and there is no reason to suppose that an Anglo-Saxon sufferer would give a different account to their leech. A modern doctor might recommend X-rays, and could offer a range of treatments including hip replacement, but would an Anglo-Saxon doctor such as Bald be able to identify the cause of the illness, and how could he treat a patient with such a complaint?

Bald's first problem would have been that the aches complained of by his patient are not visible to the eye, and even palpation of the patient would not make it clear what the problem was. With no knowledge of 'osteoarthritis' as a diagnosis, Bald's written authorities would offer him a range of remedies to cover non-specific internal pains. He might suggest one of his remedies 'for pain in the groin':

'take two pennies weight of betony, add to two bowls of sweet wine, mix with hot water, give to drink after a night fasting. Also take groundsel, beat and give the juice to drink after a night fasting' (*Leechbook* I: 22).

Or perhaps a remedy for 'pain in the thigh':

'smoke the thighs thoroughly with fern. Also, to drink, pepper, wine, dwarf elder, honey. In addition, apple tree, thorn, ash, quick-beam, carline thistle, vervain, elecampane 'bishopwort', ivy, betony, ribwort, radish, *Rhamnus Frangula*, pepper, mastic, costmary, ginger, nettle, blind nettle. Make this into a drink' (*Leechbook* I: 23).

Alternatively, he might hazard 'bone ache' as a diagnosis:

'for bone ache, white hellebore, henbane, dwarf elder, old oatmeal and vinegar, hart or goat or goose grease, mix together then lay on. Also for bone pain, for a drink, elecampane, butcher's broom, dwarf elder, horehound, crowfoot, pound, place in water that is over-running, bathe by a hot fire, clean the ache with the water, clean daily. Then make an ointment from white hellebore, from elecampane, from wolf's bane, from wormwood, equal quantities of all, boil thoroughly' (*Leechbook* I: 28).

Without the medical tools to see beyond the skin, and, given the medical knowledge base available to him, a doctor such as Bald could have no hope of identifying and diagnosing the disease that is so obvious to the modern observer in the archaeological record. Like so many doctors today, his ignorance must have left him with feelings of inadequacy. He might have wanted to protect himself from patients seeing his failure and thus recommended remedies that were difficult to follow; it is typical of such diseases that, in Bald's *Leechbook*, the greater the range of ingredients in the remedy, the less the disease was likely to be treatable. Of Bald's fifteen recorded remedies for ear-ache, for example, none contains more than four ingredients (including the lubricant), and four contain only one ingredient (*Leechbook* I: 3). The majority of the remedies involve dripping lukewarm oil, mixed with one or two other ingredients such as garlic juice, honey or breast milk, into the affected ear. While these remedies would not have been successful for all ear-aches, the warm oil would have softened any build-up of earwax, and the other additions may have successfully soothed inflammation in the ear. The ingredients for the remedies for ear-ache such as ivy juice, goat's urine, honey, ash sap, rose oil, chicken fat and goose fat were, on the whole, readily available. This selection of ingredients contrasts markedly with some of the exotic ingredients such as ginger and pepper in the remedy for 'pain in the thigh', and with the long list of requirements to make up the drink for 'pain in the bone'. The failure of treatment in these more difficult compounds would then be the responsibility of the patient, or their carer, rather than intrinsic either to Bald's diagnosis or remedy. On the positive side, Bald did the best he could, and at least the warm herbal massage might have brought some relief to our hypothetical sufferer from osteoarthritis. In practical terms, there was nothing Bald or his fellow Anglo-Saxon doctors could have done for patients with osteoarthritis, even had they been able to recognise the condition.

It is clear from the evidence of Bald's *Leechbook* that internal disorders gave the doctor most trouble: there is little evidence within the Anglo-Saxon medical world for internal surgery — small wonder when infection would have meant surgery would be fatal — and any treatment of internal ailments relied on a hopeful mix of herbs acting as poultices or drinks. The Anglo-Saxon method of treating parts of the body as separate entities (a model inherited from the Mediterranean world) meant that the documentary sources show only occasional recognition of syndromes, where problems affecting different parts of the body might have one root cause.

As an index of the wide gap between the Anglo-Saxon doctor's written perception of the medicinal needs of his patients and the archaeological evidence of identifiable diseases in the skeletal record, the analysis of the human material from the Raunds cemetery is instructive. The population of c. 376 identified burials from the church cemetery, dated to the late tenth century was carefully analysed, and diseases consisted of: osteoarthritis, injury to bone (fracture and dislocation), osteitis (including some infections associated with leprosy, some with tuberculosis and/or poliomyelitis), orbital osteoporosis, (probably, but not certainly, an indicator of anaemia), sacrilisation of the lumbar vertebrae, one case of cleft palate and dental disease (Boddington, 1996). Other examples of bone pathology, such as spina bifida occulta, would have had little or no impact on the individual and are interesting as genetic or congenital abnormalities, but are not within the bounds of this discussion (some of these archaeologically-identifiable diseases have already received detailed attention in other contexts today). Of these diseases, osteoarthritis, as we have seen, is missing from the Anglo-Saxon list of specific illnesses, as are orbital osteoporosis and spina bifida. Leprosy, if equated with the Anglo-Saxon disease 'hreofle', may have been identified by the Anglo-Saxon doctor, but 'hreofl' may have been used to describe a number of cutaneous conditions (Cameron, 1993: 96–7). Anaemia was not recognised as such. Only bone fractures and disclocation and toothache receive any specific commentary in the *Leechbook*, although an operation to repair hare-lip, often associated with cleft palate, is recorded by Bald.

This comparison poses a question. Given the absence of Anglo-Saxon recognition/diagnosis of some of the most common ailments visible in the archaeological record, can Bald's *Leechbook* and other late Old English medical texts be assumed to give us an accurate insight into the diseases and traumas suffered by a typical Anglo-Saxon population? Bald could only comment on diseases within his own limited frame of reference, working within the well-established genre of medical writing.

However, a study of Bald's *Leechbook* and other medical texts indicates that some of the written remedies, athough following a Mediterranean model, and while often copying or translating remedies from the Latin, had a practical application (Cameron, 1983). Using these collections and recipes, an Anglo-Saxon doctor could, and did, recognise the symptoms of, diagnose and successfully treat diseases he could observe. Take this discussion from Bald's first *Leechbook* of a swollen throat:

'There are two forms of the disease. One is in the jaws and when the patient opens his mouth it is swollen and is red about the uvula, and the person cannot breathe easily, but is suffocated, also he cannot swallow, or speak easily, nor has a voice, however the disease is not dangerous. Another is when the throat is swollen and pussy and he cannot speak, and the swelling is in the neck and the tongue. The patient cannot breathe easily, nor twist his neck, nor lean his head forward to see his navel, and unless he is speedily treated he will be dead in about three days. If the patient's temperature from the disease is high but there are no outward signs of it, it is dangerous' (*Leechbook* I: 4).

The diagnosis and prognostication is not far from a modern GP's immediate response. Equally impressive is Bald's diagnosis and treatment of gangrene:

'If the swelling skin eruptions or the red mould come externally from wounds or cuts or blows, treat the condition immediately with scarification and applications of barley, in the way that knowledgeable doctors well know how; you will make it better. If the blackened area is so deadened that there is no feeling in it, then you must immediately cut away all the dead and numb parts back to the living body so that none of the dead area is left of that which, when tested, could feel neither ice nor fire. After that, treat the wound as you would the part which still has some sensation and is not completely dead. You must pull and draw the blood from the deadened place with frequent scarifyings, sometimes severe, sometimes light. Treat the cuts like this: take bean meal or oat meal or barley meal, or such meal as you think will do to apply, add vinegar and honey, cook together and apply and bandage on to the sore places. If you want the ointment to be more powerful, add a little salt to it and bandage on occasionally and bathe with vinegar or with wine. If needs be, give a herbal drink occasionally, and always consider when you are giving potent medicines what the strength is, and the condition of the patient, whether he is strong or vigorous and may easily cope with strong medicine, or whether he is delicate and frail and weak and cannot stand the medicine. Apply the medicine according to the condition of the patient, because there is a great difference between the bodies of men, women and children, and in the strength of the daily labourer and the leisured, of the old and the young and of those used to hardships and those who are unused to such circumstances. It is a fact that a pale body is weaker and more tender than tanned and sunburnt ones. If you intend to chop or cut a limb from the body, then consider the condition of the area and the strength of the place, because some areas fester more readily if they are not carefully attended. Some react to the treatment later, some sooner. If you must chop or cut an unsound limb from a healthy body, then do not cut on the border of the healthy area, but cut much more or chop in the well and healthy area so that you will make it better and cure it more quickly' (*Leechbook* I: 35).

The remedy offers a clear description of the problem, offers an effective treatment, including an operation and advice on how much flesh to cut, and makes a telling observation that different patients will react differently to the same treatment, and therefore treatment needed to be adjusted accordingly. Such remedies also illustrate that, what an Anglo-Saxon doctor could see, he would try to treat. The Leechbooks or medical recipes demonstrate that the diseases the Anglo-Saxon doctor felt most competent to treat were those he could observe.

Furthermore, just as the documentary sources are silent on some of the diseases identifiable in the archaeological record, so the skeletal evidence can offer no commentary on the very diseases that the Anglo-Saxon doctor was most competent to cure or treat. Anglo-Saxon doctors appear to have given the most practical and relevant advice for diseases they could see and feel and for specific symptoms that their patients relayed to them. These diseases and pains almost always concern the flesh and muscle, and many were sudden, infectious diseases. Many, but not all, of these ailments — unspecified eye-ache, headaches, stomachaches, fevers and ulcers, jaundice and meningitis — were diseases that usually leave no trace at all in the archaeological record.

Occasionally in the field of Anglo-Saxon medicine, archaeology and documentary sources coincide to allow the subject to be studied within a 'biocultural' framework, where the exact nature of the trauma and the probable cause of the trauma were obvious to the Anglo-Saxon doctor and the archaeologist alike. Head wounds fall into this category. Archaeologically-attested examples of healed head wounds in Anglo-Saxon mortuary contexts indicates that these were not necessarily fatal (Roberts and Manchester, 1995: 82). The documentary evidence indicates that the Anglo-Saxon doctor was able to play a significant part in ensuring that such a wound would heal. Bald's first book recommends the following:

> 'and if the brain is visible, take egg yolk and mix a little with honey and fill the wound and bandage with tow and then leave it alone, and after about three days look at the wound, and if the healthy skin has a red ring around the wound then you will know that you cannot heal it' (*Leechbook* I: 1,14).

Bald prescribes a useful clever paste; something to physically seal the wound and something to act as an osmotic agent, much as one might use magnesium sulphate today. In practice, the *Leechbook* really does show a high degree of sophistication in the management of wounds in general.

The limitations of an understanding of Anglo-Saxon disease through a study of the archaeological record, where soft tissue does not survive, are clear. There can be no study of Anglo-Saxon medicine without further source material. However, Bald and the modern archaeologist look blankly at each other; their accounts of disease and medicinal treatment in the Anglo-Saxon period are based on widely different knowledge bases. The explanation for the divorce between archaeology and historical accounts of Anglo-Saxon medicine seems clear. More positively, medicine provides one area of social history where the documentary sources do not make the archaeology redundant and vice versa. An understanding of both the limitations and the sophistication of Bald's medical knowledge, combined with a detailed study of the evidence yielded by the archaeological resource, must provide the best way forward for an overall understanding of health and disease in Anglo-Saxon England.

BIBLIOGRAPHY

Boddington, A.
(1996) *Raunds Furnells: The Anglo-Saxon Church and Churchyard*, English Heritage Archaeological Report 7

Cameron, M. L.
(1983) 'Bald's 'Leechbook': its sources and their use in its compilation', *Anglo-Saxon England* **12**:153–82.
(1993) *Anglo-Saxon Medicine*, Cambridge Studies in Anglo-Saxon England 7, Cambridge: Cambridge University Press.

Cockayne, O.
(1864–6)*Leechdoms, Wortcunning and Starcraft of Early England,* 3 volumes, London: Rolls Series.

Crawford, S.
(1999) *Childhood in Anglo-Saxon England,* Stroud: Sutton Publishing.

Grattan, J. and Singer, C.
(1952) *Anglo-Saxon Magic and Medicine Illustrated Specially from the Semi-Pagan Text 'Lacnunga'*, Oxford: Oxford University Press.

Hamerow, J.
(1993) *Excavations at Mucking Volume 2: The Anglo-Saxon Settlement*, English Heritage in association with the British Museum Press.

Leeds, E. T.
(1936) *Early Anglo-Saxon Art and Archaeology: Being the Rhind Lectures Delivered in Edinburgh 1935*, Oxford: Oxford University Press.

Meaney, A. L.
(1981) *Anglo-Saxon Amulets and Curing Stones*, British Archaeological Reports, British Series 96.
(1984) 'Variant versions of Old English Medical Remedies and the Compilation of Bald's *Leechbook*', *Anglo Saxon England* **13**: 235–68.

Roberts, C. and Manchester, K.
(1995) *The Archaeology of Disease*, 2nd Edition, Stroud: Sutton Publishing.

Storms, G.
(1948) *Anglo-Saxon Magic,* The Hague.

Stroud, G. and Kemp, R. L.
(1993) *Cemeteries of the Church and Priory of St Andrew, Fishergate*, published for the York Archaeological Trust by the Council for British Archaeology.

Wright, C. E., and Quirk, R. (eds.)
(1955) *Bald's Leechbook: British Museum Royal Manuscript, 12.D.XVII,* Early English Manuscripts in Facsimile 5, Copenhagen: Rosenkilde and Bagger.

THE *MARY ROSE* MEDICAL CHEST

Brendan Derham

INTRODUCTION

By 1545, the English-occupied areas of France had been reduced to the ports of Boulogne and Calais. For the French to mount a successful capture of these towns, their communication with England had to be disrupted. To this end, in the summer of 1545, the French fleet launched an assault on the English maritime forces gathered at Portsmouth, the homeport of the English fleet. Henry VIII had gathered 60 ships here, including the second largest ship in the fleet, the recently rebuilt *Mary Rose*. In the opening skirmishes of the battle the *Mary Rose* attempted a very abrupt turn about. This manoeuvre resulted in the sea rushing in through the open gun-ports, which led to the rapid sinking of the ship. As the ship sank, it impacted into the seabed and keeled over onto its starboard side. She settled with decks facing into the tidal currents, and so the exposed port side of the ship was rapidly swept away. This allowed the more protected starboard side to be buried in fine silt. Further layers of coarser, more resilient sediments were deposited over a longer time-span.

The wreck remained undisturbed until its excavation in the 1970s and the eventual lift of the hull in the summer of 1982. The excavation yielded a wide range of artefacts: 'Gold Angels', bronze artillery pieces, personal artefacts such as combs, tankards and crockery. The rapid covering of the structurally sound hull with cold, anaerobic silt had also resulted in the preservation of the half section of the ship's hull. Three cabins were revealed on the right hand side of the main gun deck. Excavation produced artefacts of both a personal and a professional nature. The cabins appear to have been occupied by some of the skilled artisans necessary to crew a sophisticated ship. The front cabin contained navigational equipment possibly belonging to the Pilot. The rear cabin contained several chests full of woodworking equipment. Inside the middle cabin was a collection of equipment and supplies belonging to a barber-surgeon (Rule, 1982).

The presence of barber-surgeons on board major ships became fairly standard practice during the Late Medieval and Renaissance Periods. A considerable amount has been written about the medical practices of Medieval and Renaissance Physicians (McCray Beier, 1987). In contrast, little consideration has been given to barber-surgeons, who, having served a full 7–9 year apprenticeship, were highly experienced in the more pragmatic skills necessary to provide primary health care and surgery. During the sixteenth and seventeenth centuries, textbooks began to be printed in the vernacular by experienced surgeons for the edification of the Guild's more junior members. John Woodall's book *The Surgeon's Mate*, originally published in 1617, contains much information regarding the surgical equipment and practices employed at the time (Kirkup, 1978). Woodall's textbook demonstrates how to deal with a wide variety of wounds and traumas, giving details of what were considered to be beneficial therapeutic practices. The texts covered the removal of arrows and shot, the setting of broken or dislocated limbs and when necessary their amputation. The texts provided not only details of therapeutic practices, but also recommended kit for surgeons. The equipment included a robust wooden chest for the secure storage of medicines and a wide range of surgical apparatus.

A wide range of equipment was recovered from the *Mary Rose*. Some of the items were found scattered around the barber-surgeon's cabin, whilst most were from inside a large wooden chest (about 4ft × 2ft × 2ft). Several of the artefacts are personal possessions such as coins, pewter ware and items of clothing such as shoes and a hat. Others are the artefacts of a barber, such as combs, brushes, razors and a shaving bowl. The collection also included artefacts of a more therapeutic nature, such as surgical equipment, drug jars and bandages. As most of the surgical instruments at the time were made of iron or steel only a few survived, but as degraded metal-wood complexes. In contrast a wide range of artefacts made from non-ferrous materials such as ceramic and wood have survived. Artefacts recovered included two syringes, which appear to have survived due to being constructed from pewter. Woodall's books recommend 2 syringes or clysters, one large, one small, used for the treatment of chronic constipation and gonorrhoea. A large number of containers also survived, including eight large earthenware jugs and 21 lathe-turned wooden canisters (Pl. 1).

The 44 samples analysed were associated with a wide range of the artefacts that came from inside the medical chest, as well as from those scattered around the barber-surgeon's cabin. Samples were taken from the wooden containers, ceramic jars, syringes, bandages and a few that were possibly a spillage lying loose within the chest. The question therefore was whether the samples represent the original contents of the containers or

Plate 1.

merely background detritus. The actual samples consist of a wide variety of materials, with the only obviously botanical material being a canister of peppercorns. The samples include inorganic powders and concretions, mixtures of organic and inorganic material and also various organic resins and lipids. The problem, therefore, was how to analyse the samples systematically to obtain a coherent set of results for the whole collection, whilst allowing for their great variation in physical and chemical composition. The results discussed here represent a small fraction of the samples analysed.

The first phase was an elemental analysis of the crude material (Table 1). The figures represent the total percentage of carbon, hydrogen and nitrogen (CHN) and the atomic ratio of carbon to the hydrogen present. The %CHN figures indicate the percentage of the sample that is organic (as opposed to inorganic metals and silicates), whilst the C:H ratio reflects whether they are present as part of a complex organic molecule or not. Complex organic molecules produced by bacteria, plants and animals give a C:H ratio of between 1–1 and 1–2. In contrast, simple carbon based minerals and organic compounds that have been geologically modified give much more extreme values.

The CHN data divides the samples present in the collection into 3 main groups. The first group had a CHN content of less than 10% and an extreme C:H ratio, i.e. outside 1–2. These are the kind of figures one would expect from samples that are essentially inorganic in nature. The second group had a CHN of less than 50% and a C:H ratio of between 1–2. This indicated an essentially inorganic sample with some organic material present, this being the product of either contamination of an organic sample with marine silt, or the deliberate blending of inorganic material with natural plant or animal products.

The third group had a very high CHN content, greater than 50% and again a C:H ratio of between 1–2. This group represents samples that were predominantly organic with some inorganic material present.

The second phase of the analysis consisted of sample preparation, separating each sample into three fractions. This was achieved by sequential solvent extraction of the sample in an ultra-sonic bath followed by centrifuging to separate out the insoluble portion. The two solvents used were dichloromethane/methanol (3:1), and then methanol/water (4:1).

Fraction A contains the non-polar compounds such as resins, fats and oils.

Fraction B contains any more polar constituents such as alkaloids. The detection of any alkaloids present is particularly important. As a group, alkaloids contain many pharmacologically-active chemicals such as the nicotine in tobacco and the morphine in opium.

Fraction C contains insoluble material, such as any botanical remains or any inorganic material present.

The third phase was the actual analysis of the three fractions from each sample.

A wide range of analytical techniques was used in the project. The organic fractions (A and B) were analysed by gas chromatography-mass spectrometry (GC-MS). Small quantities of material were treated with N,O-bis(trimethylsilyl)trifluoroacetamide (BSTFA) to convert any viscous compounds into their more volatile TMS derivatives. The gas chromatography (GC) serves to separate the samples into their individual components, highly volatile compounds coming off very quickly and less volatile ones later. The individual compounds are then immediately inserted into a mass spectrometer. This breaks each of the components into a series of fragment ions with characteristic m/z ratios from which the actual chemical structure can be interpreted. The inorganic material (fraction C) was analysed by X-ray Fluorescence (XRF) and X-ray Diffraction (XRD). The technique of XRF causes the sample atoms to emit X-rays at a wavelength characteristic of the atom itself. It is therefore possible to identify the elements that are present. The emission or fluorescence intensity is measured in counts per second (cps). In contrast the technique of XRD is based on the characteristic scattering pattern that results when X-rays impinge on crystalline material. This made it possible to identify the chemical and physical relationships of the elements present. Selective staining and optical microscopy were used on the occasional botanical remains recovered.

Table 1. Sample details and CHN analysis.

Sample no.	Sample description	Artefact No.	C:H Ratio	%CHN	CHN group
Samples from inside the chest					
2	Amorphous contents of chest	80 A 1217	1:1	84	Group 3
4	Amorphous contents of chest	80 A 1530	1:0	10	Group 1
12	Contents of wooden canister	80 A 1538/1-2	1:2	34	Group 2
17	Contents of wooden canister	80 A 1561/1-2	–	–	botanical
Samples from inside the cabin					
28	Contents of wooden canister	80 A 1690/1-2	1:1	84	Group 3

In the case of organic compounds for which the mass spectrum could not be identified by comparison with that of a known standard, further work was necessary. Several milligrams of the unidentified compound had first to be isolated by non-destructive techniques. The crude sample was first fractionated by sequential elution on a short chromatography column. The individual compounds are then isolated and purified by Thin Layer Chromatography (TLC). The structure of the purified constituent could then be determined by Nuclear Magnetic Spectroscopy (NMR), Infra-red Spectroscopy (IR) and Mass Spectrometry (MS).

RESULTS

Example 1

GC-MS analysis of the organic extracts from the first group of samples confirms an absence of any significant organic material, as one would expect from the CHN results mentioned earlier. The XRF results of the inorganic material from sample 4 show significant peaks at values that are characteristic of 3 elements: silica (1.74 KeV), calcium (3.69 KeV) and iron (6.40KeV) (Fig. 1). These are elements that constitute the vast bulk of most marine silts. This sub-group of samples would appear to consist of marine silt and concretions formed by corroding iron artefacts becoming associated with marine silt.

Example 2

Sample 2 is representative of the third group in that it contains only very low quantities of inorganic material. If one examines the XRF plot, one again sees the peaks for a mixture of silica, iron and calcium (Fig. 2). The plot also contains fluorescence peaks for copper (8.04 KeV) and lead (10.55 and 12.61 KeV). By comparing the fluorescence intensities with standards of marine silt spiked with known quantities of copper and lead salts, it becomes clear that these elements are present only at trace levels. The main constituents of this sample are in fact organic and are detected on the GC-MS, eluting around 16–17 minutes (Fig. 3). The constituents consist of a group of chemicals based around a tricyclic diterpene molecule. Whilst many *Coniferae* produce diterpenes, the ones in question — pimaric and abietic acids — are produced predominantly by members

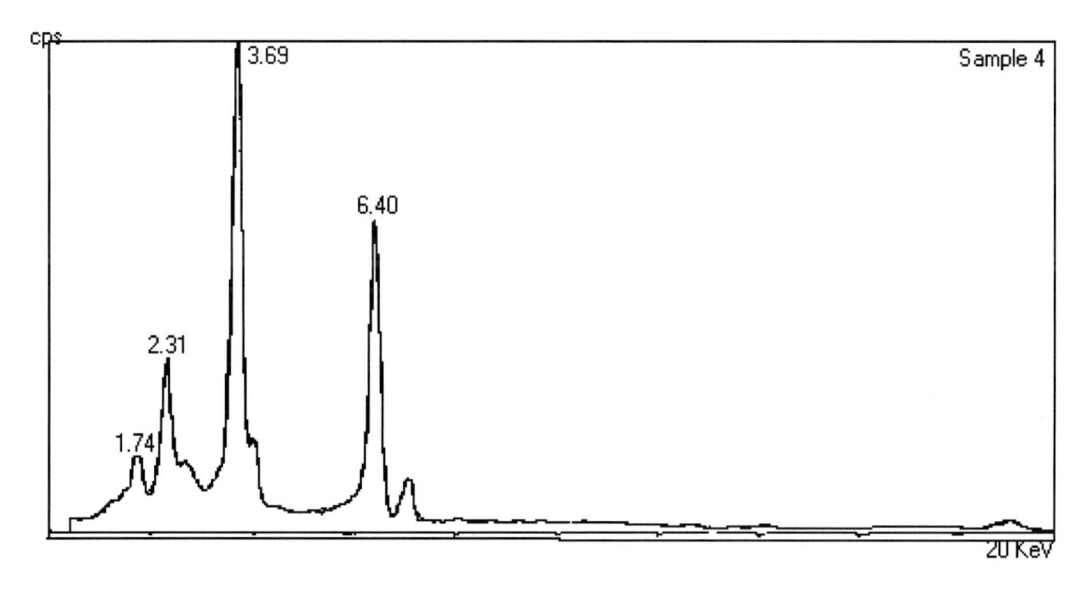

Fig. 1.

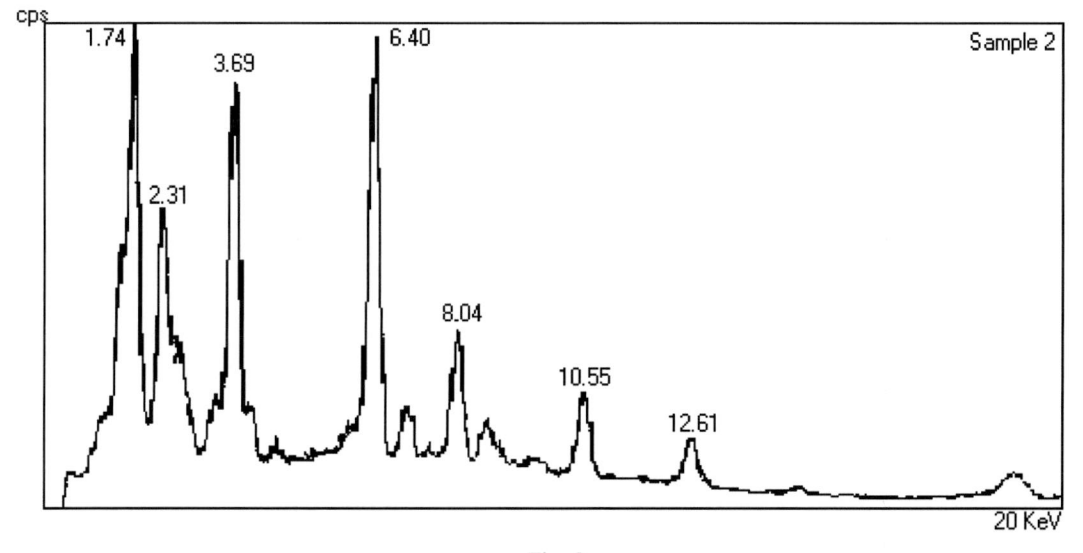

Fig. 2.

of the *Pinaceae*. This family includes pine, fir and larch trees. The main compound in the sample is in fact dehydroabietic acid, a compound readily formed by aerobic oxidation of abietic acid. The compound itself is readily identified by its mass spectrum (Fig. 4).

Beck *et al.* (1997) have demonstrated that when a pine resin is extracted by the heating of wood, various derivatives of the resin's constituents will be produced. These chemical alterations are caused both by esterification with the methanol present in the wood and by degradation due to the heat. Analyses by Evershed *et al.* (1985: 181–92) of tar barrels from the hold of the *Mary Rose* demonstrated the preponderance of these methyl esters of the diterpenes and their degradation products, the inference being that the samples represented crude pitches produced by the high-temperature cooking of conifer wood. In relation to the sample from the medical chest, however, there is a complete absence of any methyl esters and only low levels of retene (a decarboxylated and oxidised derivative). This infers that the resin had been collected by tapping from a live tree and not by heating wood scraps.

Example 3

Sample 28, the contents of a wooden ointment canister found within the chest, contains very little inorganic material. Results of the GC analysis of the organic fraction demonstrate that the constituents are diterpene based (Fig. 5). However, most compounds present had been heavily degraded. Retene, identified by its distinctive mass spectrum, constituted a major compound in this sample (Fig. 6). The degraded diterpenes are formed by heating a pine resin in an oxidising atmosphere to such an extent that the functional groups attached to the structure are broken off. The surviving intact diterpenes are present, like the previous sample, as the free acid and not the methyl ester. Therefore, this resin also must have been tapped from a living tree. In contrast, this resin must then have been heavily degraded so as to convert much of the resin acids into retene, the resin deliberately degraded to produce what is termed a rosin oil.

Example 4

Sample 12, representative of the second group in that it consists of both organic and inorganic material, originated in one

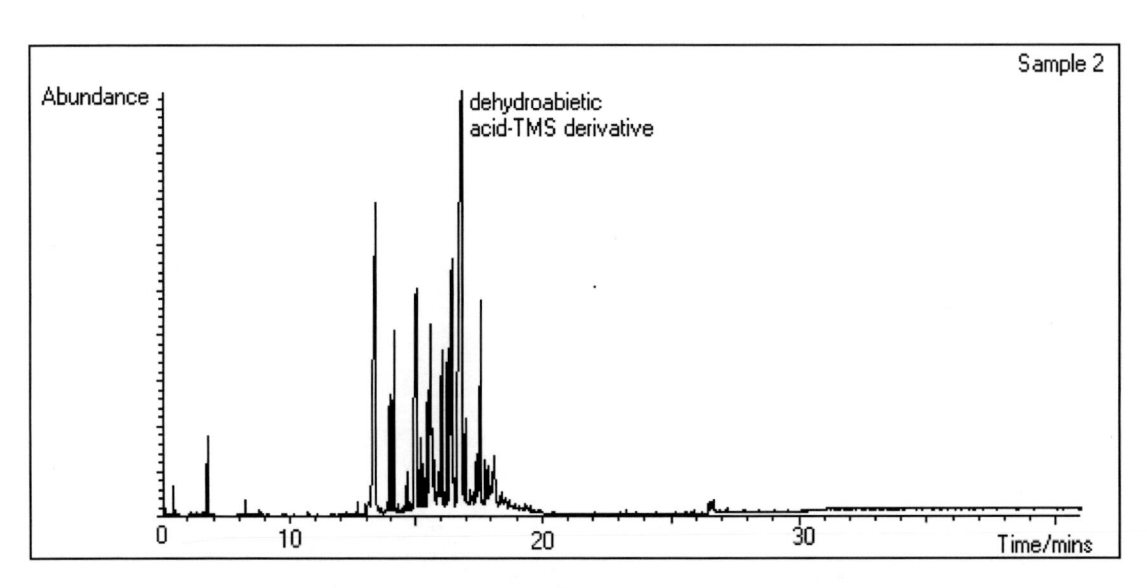

Fig. 3

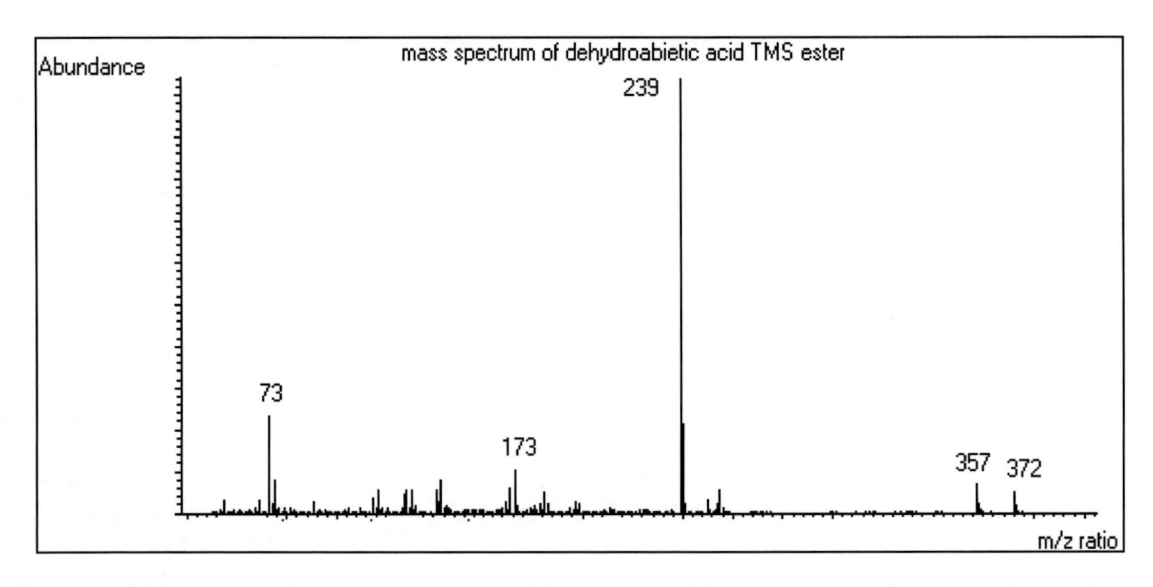

Fig. 4.

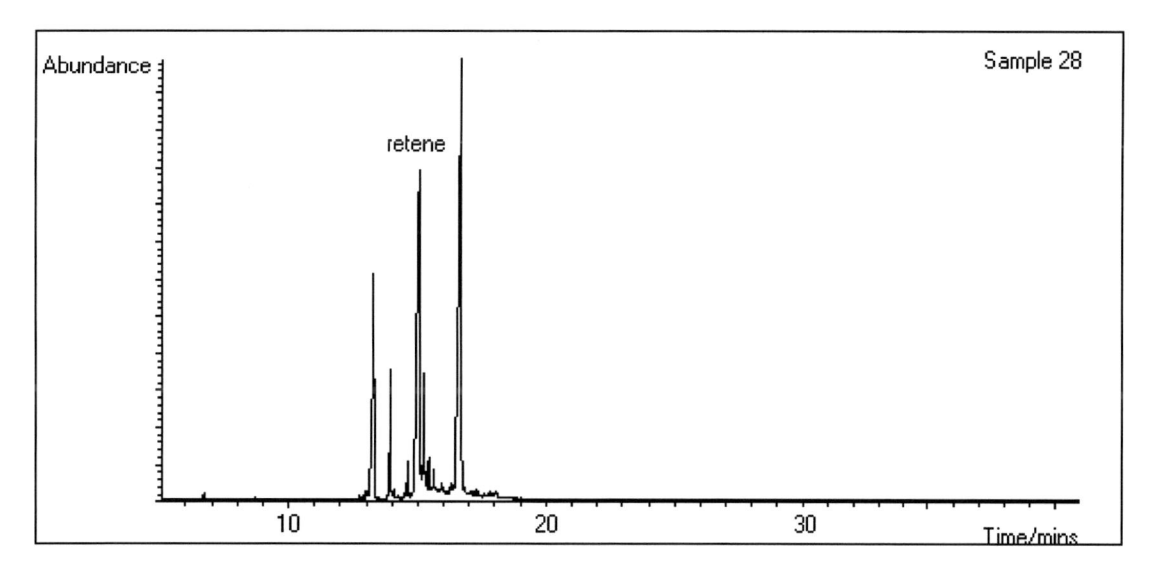

Fig. 5.

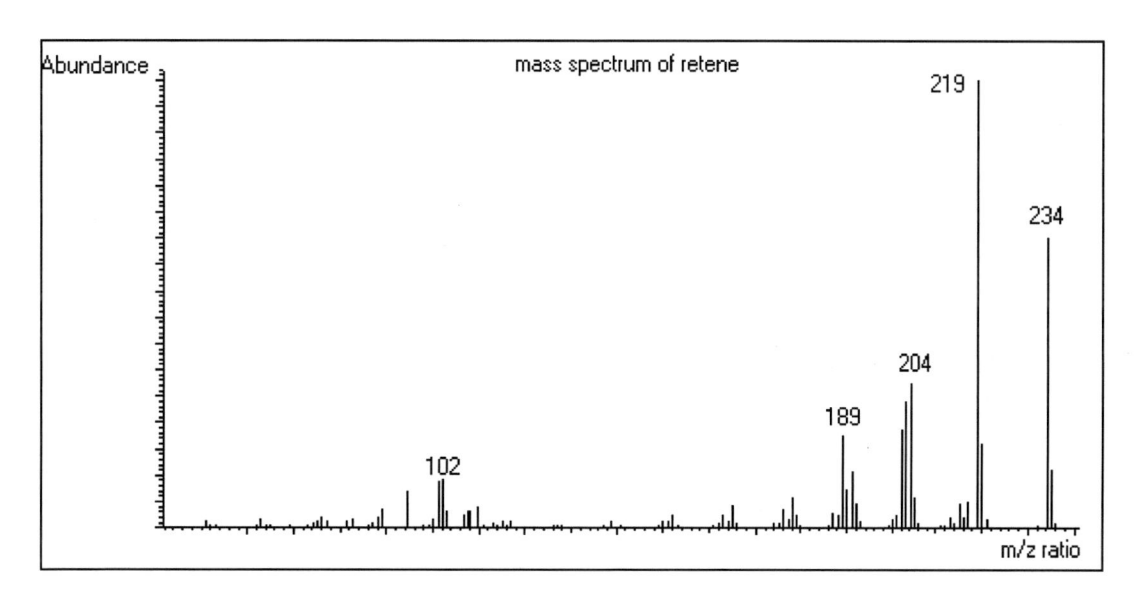

Fig. 6.

of the poplar canisters found inside the chest. Analysis of the inorganic residue by XRF again shows the presence of low levels of silica, iron and calcium (Fig. 7). The main peaks, however, are all due to the presence of significant quantities of lead (10.55, 12.61 and 14.76 KeV). Analysis of the organic material shows the presence of a homologous series of wax esters of hexadecanoic acid (Fig. 8). In this case, the (peak 17) tetra-, (peak 18) hexa-, (peak 19) octacosanoic, (peak 20) triacontanoic and (peak 21) dotriacontanoic acid esters are present. The presence of these compounds, the TMS derivatives of their hydrolysed degradation products (peaks 13, 14, 16) and a homologous series of even carbon number alkanes (peaks 9, 10, 11, 12) have been shown to reflect an aged beeswax (Heron et al., 1994). The presence of TMS derivatives of a range of saturated fatty acids (peaks 1, 2, 3, 6), as well as unsaturated oleic acid (peaks 4 and 5) and its degradation product 10-hydroxystearic acid (peak 8) would indicate that some form of lipid is also present. This is confirmed by the TMS ether of what is probably cyclolaudenol (peak 15) a plant sterol (Fig. 9). The only reported common oil in which cyclolaudenol is the predominant sterol is poppy oil (Goad and Goodwin, 1972: 113–98). This would seem to infer that the plant oil is possibly poppy seed oil. The sample would therefore appear to consist of a lead compound that had been dispersed in a base of beeswax and a plant oil, possibly poppy seed oil.

CONCLUSION

The results of analysis of several other samples consisting of a mixture of organic and inorganic compounds give a similar picture. The results demonstrated the use of a wide range of metallic compounds; mercury, tin, zinc and copper dispersed in organic matrices. In general, botanical remains were significant by their absence apart from the peppercorns and the occasional flax fibre. The fragments of plant macrostructures one would

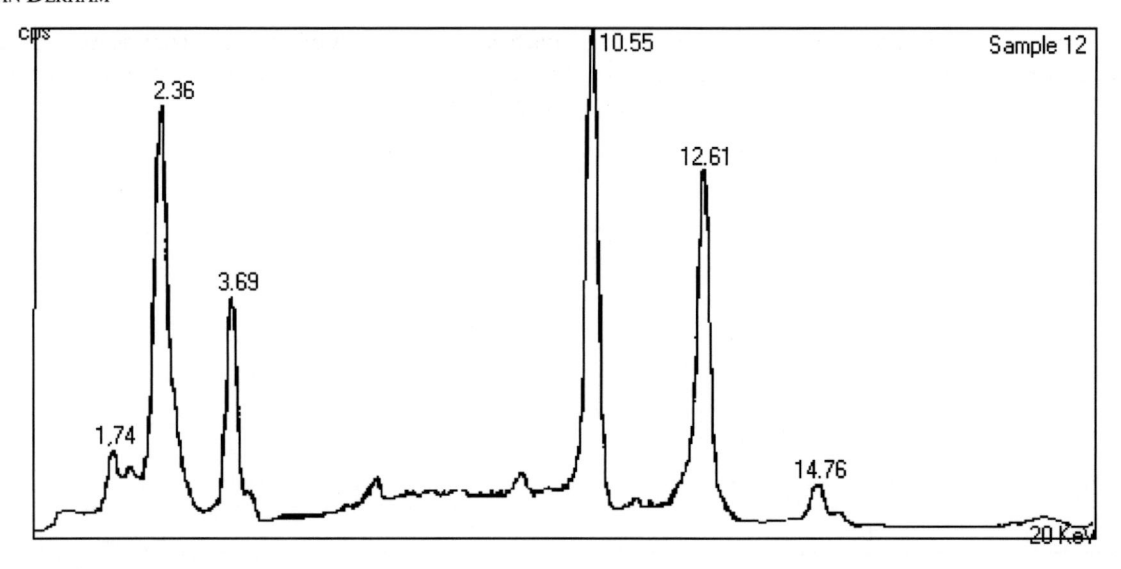

Fig. 7.

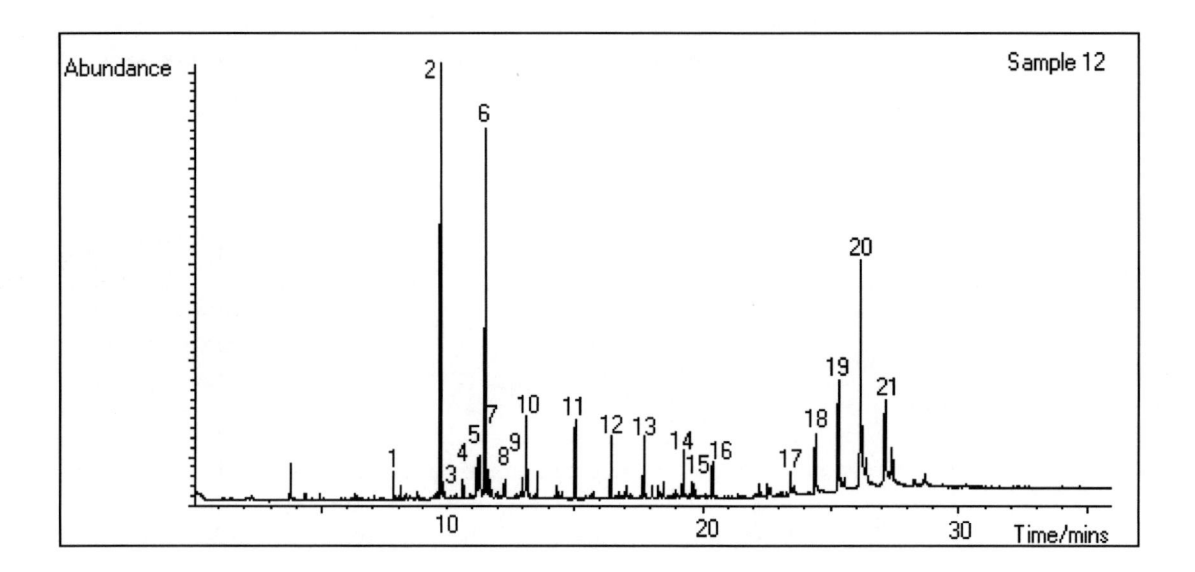

Fig. 8.

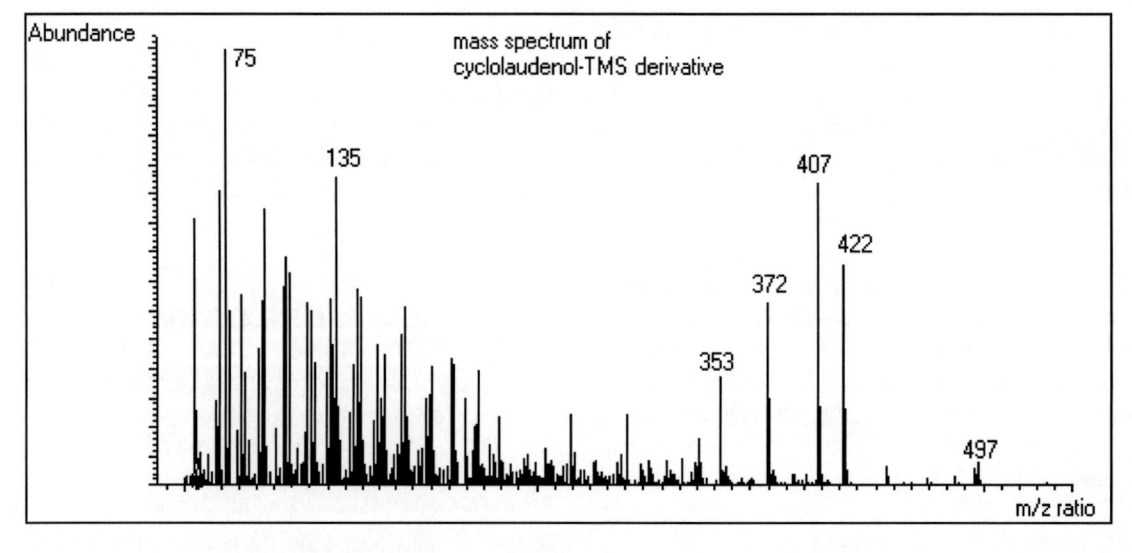

Fig. 9.

expect from the herbal medicine normally associated with the Middle Ages were absent. That botanical material survived intact in a few of the containers implies that their absence from most was due not to poor preservation but to their absence from the original pharmaceutical preparations.

The therapeutic use of natural products has a long history. The examples presented above serve to reflect the range of pharmaceutical formulation available in the sixteenth century. These included simple botanical material such as peppercorns imported from the East, conifer resins, widely available across most of Europe and also galenicals. Galenicals were complex mixtures of several natural products, produced by blending a wide range of natural materials. In the archaeological sense the project has established that archaeo-pharmacological residues containing a wide variety of materials may be analysed. The sample handling procedure developed serves to demonstrate that it is possible to effectively separate complex and amorphous archaeological residues into meaningful fractions. Each of these fractions can then be analysed by an appropriate technique or techniques. The extent to which the analyses can be interpreted is another matter entirely, being hampered by a lack of analytical standards for degraded natural products.

The results have demonstrated the use of a wide range of natural products, the therapeutic use of which continued down into the 21st century. The 1941 *Martindale Pharmacopoeia* published by the Pharmaceutical Society of Great Britain give potentially effective therapeutic roles for many of the substances detected:

- Pepper for treating intestinal spasms.
- Lead ointments for treating burns and severe bruising.
- Mercury ointments for treating syphilis.
- Copper salts for the treatment of skin ulcers.
- Zinc oxide or calamine lotion for skin diseases and burns.
- Pine resins as a haemostat, used to stop haemorrhaging from tooth sockets and in treating sepsis.

Whilst most of these preparations have been superseded by developments in modern pharmaceutical chemistry, the potential therapeutic efficacy of traditional empirical expertise should not be overlooked, giving reasons for the continuation of research into archaeo-pharmacology.

ACKNOWLEDGEMENTS

I would like to thank the Thackray Medical Museum Research Trust for providing funding for this research.

BIBLIOGRAPHY

Beck, C. W., Stout, E. C., and Janne, P. A.
(1997) 'The pyrotechnology of pine tar and pitch inferred from quantitative analyses by gas chromatography-mass spectrometry and carbon-13 nuclear magnetic resonance spectrometry', in Brzezinski and Piotrowski, W. (eds.), *Proceedings of the First International Symposium on Wood, Tar, and Pitch,* State Archaeological Museum, Warsaw: pp. 181–92.

Evershed, R. P., Jerman, K., and Eglinton, G.
(1985) 'Pine wood origin for pitch from the Mary Rose', *Nature* **314**: 528–30.

Goad, L. J., and Goodwin, T. W.
(1972) 'The biosynthesis of plant sterols', in Reinhold, L. (ed.), *Progress in Phytochemistry, Volume 3*, Interscience Publishing, London: pp. 113–98.

Heron, C. P., Nemcek, N. and Bonfield, K. M.
(1994) 'The chemistry of Neolithic beeswax', *Naturwissen Schaften* **81**: 266–9.

Kirkup, J.
(1978) *The Surgeon's Mate by John Woodall*, Bath: Kingsmead Press.

McCray Beier, L.
(1987) *Sufferers and Healers*, London: Routledge and Kegan Paul.

Rule, M.
(1982) *The Mary Rose*, London: Conway Maritime Press.

MORBID OSTEOLOGY

Mouli Start

INTRODUCTION

This paper has arisen from work undertaken on the skeletal remains recovered from excavations at the site of Newcastle Infirmary at the Forth, Newcastle upon Tyne (hereafter referred to as Newcastle Infirmary) during 1997 and 1998. The project was funded by The International Centre for Life, Newcastle upon Tyne. The author's role in the commercial project was as one of a team of three osteologists, working for ARCUS (Archaeological Research and Consultancy at the University of Sheffield), responsible for post excavation analysis. This paper has two main foci, firstly the unique skeletal evidence recovered for autopsy and dissection, and secondly the use of this, and other evidence, to try and understand the experience of being a patient in an institution like Newcastle Infirmary.

THEORETICAL BACKGROUND

A primary concern within osteology as a sub-section of archaeology, perhaps to an even greater extent than archaeology itself, is to employ a 'scientific' and 'standardised' approach to the analysis and discussion of human remains (Buikstra and Ubelaker, 1994: 1). There are valid reasons for adopting a standardised scientific approach in terms of recording procedure and osteological methodology, particularly where reburial is an issue as was the case with Newcastle Infirmary (all of the human remains from the Infirmary site are now reburied). Without a standardised understanding of the information that we seek to record, our investigation of the evidence is useless to any other researchers. We need a common language in order to communicate. For example, without a common set of standards for assessing the age and sex of individuals, we cannot compare the demographic structure of one population with another, and without these comparisons we cannot understand how human populations have changed over time.

This scientific approach to the evidence is often extended into its discussion, and traditionally published osteological discussions of human remains focus on the remains as sets of empirical data. Yet we cannot get closer to people in the past than their skeletons; after all, these are the actual physical remains of people and not simply sub-sets of skeletal elements. A recent volume, *The Loved Bodies Corruption,* has explored the possibility of writing subjectively about work in the fields of funerary archaeology and palaeopathology (Downes and Pollard, 1999: x). As a contributor to this volume, I recognised that I engage emotionally and personally with the people whose remains I study, and that this enhances my understanding of their lives (Kirk and Start, 1999: 200–8). I make my engagement with people in the past through my 'subjective' attempt to understand what their lives were like by reference to my own world-view. I found that my connection to the people who were patients at Newcastle Infirmary came through trying to understand what the experience of being a patient felt like. I am now a medical student, and so my interest in patient's experiences is not surprising. The evidence for post-mortems and dissection also fascinated me, scientifically and emotionally. Through the acknowledgement of my own subjectivity, I hope to enhance both the reader's involvement in my discussion (because they understand why I focus where I do), and the reader's own engagement with the people whose remains form the basis of this paper.

THE EVIDENCE

Having established my approach to writing this paper, this section presents the reader with the evidence on which my discussion and ideas are based. This includes an introduction to the Infirmary as an institution, a presentation of the skeletal evidence for autopsy and post-mortem, and a discussion of the demographic composition of the burial population.

The Infirmary

One of the great advantages of working in the post-medieval period is the support offered by historical writing and contemporary documents. For example, admission and burial registers from Newcastle Infirmary are extant, and they can be used in combination with osteological and archaeological evidence in order to create a fuller picture of life at the Infirmary. John Nolan, who directed the excavations, has drawn on historical sources, contemporary documents, and his archaeological findings to give a detailed picture of the Infirmary (Nolan, 1998). A very brief summary of Nolan's work on the Infirmary is outlined here in order to provide some context for the discussion of the patients and their experiences.

Newcastle Infirmary was a product of 'the age of philanthropy' (Nolan, 1998: 23). During the early–mid eighteenth century charitable hospitals were founded ostensibly to provide medical treatment for people who were too poor to pay for private medical attention. Its founders were a group made up of prominent Newcastle citizens, including five surgeons, who publicly advertised their proposal to found a pauper hospital (Nolan, 1999: 23). The proposal attracted subscribers, usually wealthy local businessmen and industrialists, who donated money to the proposal, and, after the donation of a suitable piece of land, building began in 1751, with the first patients admitted to the Infirmary on 8 October 1753.

The Infirmary would have been an imposing sight to patients entering through a large classically pedimented and columned doorway. The building took an L-shaped plan consisting of a basemented, three-storied south-facing wing and a two-storied east-facing wing that also contained an attic ward. The Infirmary contained a chapel to St. Luke, a boardroom, the physicians' consulting room, a surgery, a matron's parlour, seven male wards and three female wards (offering beds for 90 in-patients in total), an operating theatre, and a medical library (Nolan, 1998). Plates 1 and 2 show the operating theatre and library.

The Infirmary had a formally stated admissions policy that excluded children under the age of seven, pregnant women, the insane, and sufferers from measles, smallpox, incurable cancer, consumption and infectious fevers. These exclusions must be understood in their historical context in terms of the kind of medical knowledge they were based on. Diagnosis was based purely on observation and the examining physician's experience. For example, the term consumption implies pulmonary tuberculosis or primary lung infection. However, diagnostic accuracy during the eighteenth and nineteenth centuries was an expanding science, and many diagnoses of consumption may not have been strictly tubercular. People diagnosed as consumptive may have been suffering from bronchitis or non-tuberculous pneumonia rather than tuberculosis (Roberts and Manchester, 1995: 135). Osteological analysis provided secure diagnosis of two cases of tuberculosis, and *Mycobacterium tuberculosis* has been recovered from rib samples from the articulated burials from the Infirmary (Gernaey *et. al.* 2000; Boulter, Robertson and Start, 1998: 91). Clearly these patients were not successfully excluded from the Infirmary, although their admission may well have been made on the basis of other conditions. Indeed, consumption is one of the most common causes of death listed on the Infirmary burial registers (29 cases), so exclusion of those with this condition cannot have been strictly adhered to. Children were also admitted to the Infirmary despite the stated exclusions. Among the disarticulated remains three children under the age of 7 are represented (Table 1).

The Infirmary had an instructive as well as curative function. One of the published statutes of Newcastle Infirmary, dated to 1801, states 'an account of every case, operation, or dissection, which is rare and curious, and instructive, shall be drawn up by the physician or surgeon, under whose care it has been; and be entered in a register to be preserved as the property of the infirmary' (Nolan, 1998: 30). These accounts were held in the Infirmary library shown in Plate 2. Surgeons and physicians at Newcastle Infirmary were also allowed to take on fee-paying students and apprentices who provided them with an important source of income. Students were allowed to be present at surgical operations and on ward rounds, but they were not allowed to prescribe drugs or perform operations.

Burial at the Infirmary

Burial at the Infirmary started in the same year that the first patients were admitted, 1753, and continued for 92 years until 1845. Burial was continuous throughout this period except for a three-year break between 1835 and 1838 that may have arisen through overcrowding. Burial ceased in 1845, and hereafter all patients who died at the Infirmary were buried elsewhere. Burial registers survive for the years 1803–1815 and 1822–1845. Only those patients whose bodies went unclaimed were interred in the Infirmary burial ground. Unfortunately, since burial and admissions registers do not survive for the entire period of use of the burial ground, exact figures for the numbers of dead patients who went unclaimed cannot be known. As a guide to probable numbers, during the period 1838–1842 burial registers and House Committee Minutes, which contained discharge details, both survive and these attest that 75% of those patients who died at the Infirmary were buried elsewhere (Nolan, 1998: 41).

The burial ground suffered significant disturbance during two phases of building works on the Infirmary. Between 1801 and 1803 the south wing of the Infirmary was extended to the west and in 1852–1855 a new wing, the Dobson Wing, was built over the western end of the burial ground. Nolan suggests that it is reasonable to assume that cessation of burial in 1845 and the construction of the Dobson Wing were connected, although there are no surviving records to prove this link (Nolan, 1998: 41). This is despite the archaeological and osteological evidence that clearly demonstrate that the remains of at least 407 people were disinterred and reburied in a rather unceremonious way in large charnel pits in other parts of the Infirmary grounds (Nolan 1998: 41; Boulter, Robertson and Start, 1998: 21–8). These disturbance events created interesting osteological problems in terms of analysis of the burial population. Some burials were undisturbed and recovered as discrete individuals in neat ordered rows in the burial ground (in total 210 people). But by far the larger portion of the skeletal sample came from large charnel pits, and these disarticulated remains represented a minimum of 407 people. The apparent casualness with which these people were treated, some of whom would have been very recently dead, is at odds with accepted ideas of mid-nineteenth century reverence for the deceased.

Post-mortem Medical Intervention

The instructive and explorative roles that Newcastle Infirmary filled were not limited to surgical and medical treatment of live patients. The skeletal collection from Newcastle Infirmary was unique in terms of the sheer number of bones that presented evidence of post-mortem medical intervention. The term 'post-mortem medical intervention' in this context refers to cuts made to bones after death, either as part of autopsy or dissection, anatomical teaching and learning, or as training and experimentation in surgical techniques.

In total 130 skeletal elements, from both the articulated and disarticulated samples presented evidence of cuts made to the body after the death of the patient. Of these 86% originated from the disarticulated charnel pit contexts. When these figures are translated into numbers of people, 14% of all the patients who were buried at Newcastle Infirmary had been subjected to post-mortem medical intervention (Boulter, Robertson and Start, 1998: 144). As to why the disarticulated contexts contained larger numbers of bones that presented evidence of post-mortem medical intervention, several possible explanations exist. It could simply be a question of numbers. The articulated burials total 210 individuals, yet the disarticulated sample is made up of the remains of a minimum of 407 people. There also exists the possibility that the disarticulated material contains 'dumps' of dissected human remains that were not given proper burial. Unfortunately this theory cannot be either proved or disproved by the archaeological evidence. Nolan proposed that there is a possibility that at least some of the material that makes up the disarticulated sample originated from the exten-

Table 1. Demographic data from burial registers, articulated burials and disarticulated remains, Newcastle Infirmary at the Forth, Newcastle upon Tyne.

Demographic Data from Burial Registers, Articulated Burials and Disarticulated Remains, Newcastle Infirmary at the Forth, Newcastle upon Tyne

Demographic Data from the Burial Registers: Newcastle Infirmary

	Infant 1 (1–6 years)	Infant 2 (7–12 years)	Juvenile (13–17 years)	Young Adult (18–25 years)	Prime Adult (26–45 years)	Older Adult (46+ years)	Total
Male	–	3	15	57	137	77	289
Female	1	1	2	34	49	30	117
Total	1	4	13	84	167	107	406

Demographic Data from the Articulated Burials: Newcastle Infirmary

	Infant 1 (1–6 years)	Infant 2 (7–12 years)	Juvenile (13–17 years)	Young Adult (18–25 years)	Prime Adult (26–45 years)	Older Adult (46+ years)	Total
Male				19	85	25	129
Female				20	36	6	62
?	3	8	8				19
Total	3	8	8	19	38	76	210

Demographic Data from the Disarticulated Remains: Newcastle Infirmary

	Infant 1 (1–6 years)	Infant 2 (7–12 years)	Juvenile (13–17 years)	Young Adult (18–25 years)	Prime Adult (26–45 years)	Older Adult (46+ years)	Total
Male				25	94	43	162
Female				66	67	22	155
?	–	2	4				6
Total	–	2	4	91	161	65	323

(after Boulter, Robertson and Start, 1998: 39–48)

Plate 1. Pre-1906 print of the operating theatre at Newcastle Infirmary at the Forth (reproduced with permission of Newcastle City Library).

Plate 2. Pre-1906 print of the medical library at Newcastle Infirmary at the Forth (reproduced with permission of Newcastle City Library).

sion of the south wing in the early nineteenth century. This would imply that the disarticulated sample could contain a significant portion of earlier burials, so maybe dissection occurred more frequently during the earlier life of the Infirmary. It is not possible to make a clear correlation between the disarticulated material as early and the articulated material as late because significant clearance of the burial ground also occurred with the building of the Dobson Wing in the early 1850s.

Several different kinds of cut were represented in the skeletal material. The most common form of post-mortem cuts were craniotomies (64 skulls and 39 isolated cranial elements from the collection as a whole), reflecting a known medical interest in the functions and structure of the brain at this time (Porter, 1997: 528). A craniotomy removes the top portion of a cranial vault in order to allow access to the brain — a procedure that remains a standard part of autopsy and anatomical dissection today. Present day craniotomies are performed using a circular electric saw, and the author's observations of modern post-mortems can attest that this is a difficult procedure. During conversation with a mortuary technician at Sheffield's Medico-Legal centre it transpired that among the staff at the mortuary, it was possible to tell which technician had made a particular craniotomy cut from its pattern and position. It was hoped that it might be possible to identify similar patterns in the skeletal material from Newcastle Infirmary to give us information about how many post-mortem medical intervention cuts were made by different individuals. As yet this hope is unrealised, and since this line of enquiry concerns the people performing these procedures, they are not the focus of this paper.

During the eighteenth and nineteenth centuries craniotomy cuts would have been made with a hand-held surgeon's saw, an instrument that resembles a butcher's saw. A metal head brace was placed on the top of the skull and four screws — one on either side of the head above the ears, one in the centre of the forehead and one matching this at the back of the head — held the brace in place. The brace acted as a cutting guide and it had a handle on top which allowed easy removal of the 'lid' of the cranial vault once the entire circumference of bone had been cut through. Given the practical difficulties of making a craniotomy cut with these tools, the neatness of some of the craniotomy cuts recovered is remarkable and a testament to the care and skill of the person undertaking this procedure. However, not all craniotomy cuts were neat and careful. Among the collection several examples of false starts, bone steps and lips were recovered along the line of the craniotomy cut. The position of the cut also varied. In every case the frontal and parietal bones were also cut through, but it was variable as to whether the temporal and occipital bones were included in the main craniotomy cut. In some cases the cuts were also somewhat lopsided with the temporal bone included on one side, with the cut then rising considerably to miss the temporal bone completely on the other side of the skull. Another variation involved complete cuts through the frontal and parietal bones, but rather than cutting through the occipital at the back of the skull, an instrument was inserted into one of the lambiod sutures literally 'popping' the lid of the vault off. One such example is shown in Plate 3.

Post-mortem medical intervention cuts were also recovered from other areas of the body, though not in the same numbers as craniotomies. Some of these cuts, like craniotomies, are very similar to cuts made now as part of autopsy or teaching dissections. Ribs and clavicles presented cuts consistent with an investigation of the organs of the thorax. Other kinds of cuts attest directly that anatomy was being taught at Newcastle Infirmary. When teaching anatomy, it is usual to prepare prosections. These are parts of the body, for example a limb, which has been removed from a whole corpse and cut in cross section to display how soft tissues relate to each other and the underlying bone. Among the skeletal material from the Infirmary, thoracic, lumbar and sacral vertebrae and tibiae had been cut to produce prosections.

Thus far there has been little distinction made between autopsies that would have been made in order in determine cause of death or investigate pathology, and teaching dissections either made to teach students or to increase physicians' or surgeons' understanding of the human body. Only in the case of the prosections can we say categorically that anatomy was taught at the Infirmary.

Among the articulated burials that provide evidence of post-mortem medical intervention, Skeleton 86 is worthy of particular mention (see Plate 3). This patient's body had been subjected to a craniotomy, four ribs were cut and four separate amputations had been performed on the right humerus, femur, tibia and fibula (Witkin, 1997). It is highly unlikely that these amputations were performed on a live patient — if the upper leg (femur) were being amputated, why bother to also amputate the lower leg (tibia and fibula)? This patient's body was clearly used for surgical practise or teaching, as well as being dissected.

A significant question raised by the abundance of post-mortem medical intervention evidence in the burial population from the Infirmary is who among the patients that went unclaimed were chosen for these procedures? If dissections were performed in order to investigate disease, it might be expected that bones presenting evidence of post-mortem medical intervention would also present evidence of pathology. However, the attempt to correlate osteologically identifiable pathology with post-mortem medical intervention cuts yielded insignificant results. Of the nine people from the articulated burials who presented post-mortem medical intervention cuts, five had no pathological change at all. Three presented with minor spinal joint disease and one of these three also presented evidence of iron deficiency anaemia. The final individual had suffered a broken nose and fractures to clavicles and ribs, but all of these injuries were well healed and could hardly be considered to warrant post-mortem investigation.

Among the disarticulated material with evidence for post-mortem medical intervention, only ten bones presented evidence of pathology. Nine of these were minor cases of joint disease, non-specific infection and iron deficiency anaemia. The tenth example was the external lid surface of a cranitomied skull that presented lesions characteristic of venereal syphilis, shown in Plate 4. In this single example it would be safe to assume that the pathology witnessed osteologically was the basis for post-mortem investigations. It would seem that pathology did not always provide the motivation for post-mortem procedures to be undertaken. Of course, it is wise to point out that only chronic conditions affecting bone can be recovered osteologically. Any condition that was acute enough to kill a patient quickly, or that

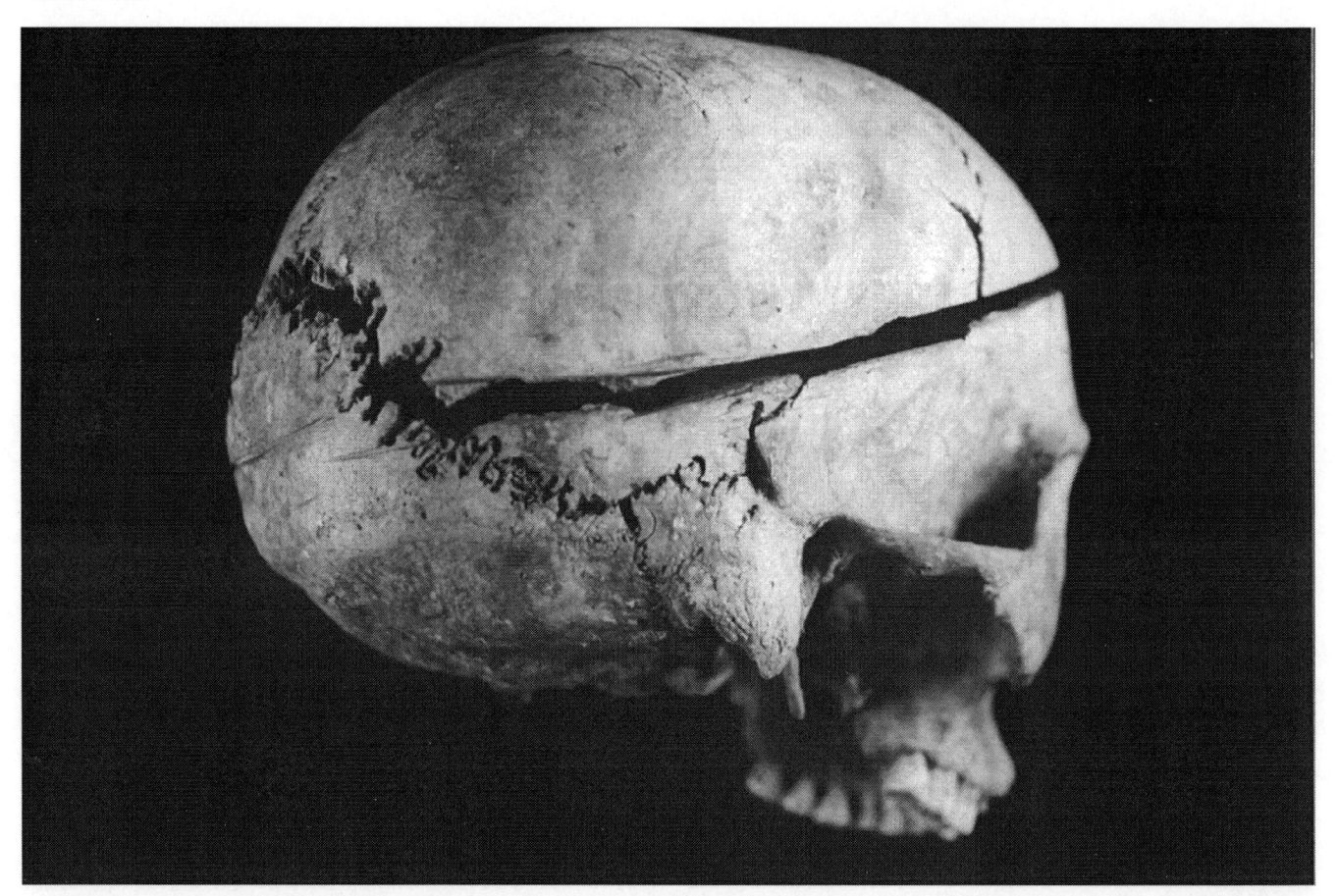

Plate 3. Craniotomy cut through skull of skeleton 86 from the articulated burials recovered from excavations at Newcastle Infirmary at the Forth (reproduced with permission of the International Centre for Life).

Plate 4. Craniotomied skull from the disarticulated material recovered from excavations at Newcastle Infirmary at the Forth. Note the characteristic 'caries sicca' lesions of venereal syphilis (reproduced with permission of the International Centre for Life).

did not involve the bone, would go undetected. Also, the majority of the bones that show evidence of post-mortem medical intervention originate from the disarticulated contexts, and any investigation of pathology is severely hampered when only an isolated skeletal element is available for study. This is because secure diagnoses in osteology are reliant on the observation of the whole skeleton of an individual. So, since pathology does not seem to provide an answer to the question of who was subjected to these procedures, I will now examine who these patients were, and through this investigation try to understand why they were chosen for post-mortem medical intervention.

The Patients

In order to find out who the patients at Newcastle Infirmary were, a combination of evidence is drawn upon. The Infirmary was set up, and referred to, as a pauper hospital established for 'The Sick and Lame Poor' of the counties of Durham and Northumberland. However, the term pauper in this context only implies the inability to pay for private medical treatment. Those who were admitted to the Infirmary normally had to have a letter of recommendation from one of the hospital subscribers. Subscribers were allocated a certain number of letters per year based on the size of their contribution to the Infirmary's coffers (Boulter, Robertson and Start, 1998: 1). Those with letters attended for a consultation on Thursdays when they were classed as in- or out-patients by the physicians (Nolan, 1998: 36). In cases of acute injury or accident, admission could be made at other times suggesting that the Infirmary filled a role somewhat similar to a modern Accident and Emergency department. The burial registers sometimes list the occupations of patients, and these included among the male patients pitmen, labourers, soldiers and various artisans. Much is made of the charitable nature of institutions like Newcastle Infirmary in modern medical history writing (Porter, 1997). Yet the nature of these occupations suggest that admission was aimed at least in part at treating and curing workers so that they could resume their duties (Nolan, 1998: pers. comm.; Boulter, Robertson and Start, 1998: 1).

The burial registers were less informative about the occupations of the female patients, and many were listed simply as married or spinster, although sometimes details of a patient's husband's occupation were given. In 1830 the Infirmary took over the functions of the Lock Hospital, a charitable institution which catered largely for prostitutes, and an 1851 census of female patients listed 41% of them as having the profession of prostitute (Nolan, 1998: 37). How many female patients before 1830 were also prostitutes is not known. If a link can be drawn between patients who were prostitutes and sexually transmitted diseases, then four cases of *Lues Venera* among female patients were recorded in the burial registers. Mary Wilson who died at the age of *c.* 25 was from Newcastle and no occupation is recorded for her. Margaret Wilson, who was 22 when she died, came from Rothbury and again no occupation is given. Mary Davidson came from Newcastle and she is listed as single and her age is not given, and finally Mary Brown has very little information recorded for her — only that she was 28 (Nolan 1998; Appendix 4). Among male patients, James Corby aged 25 also has *Lues Venera* listed as his cause of death. No occupation is given for James, but his origin is stated as Italian.

Among the articulated burials, 1.8% of patients presented skeletal evidence of venereal syphilis. In the disarticulated remains, the prevalence rate was 2.6% — and the real rate may well have been higher since this figure can only be based on isolated bones that present the classic *caries sicca* lesions (Boulter, Robertson and Start, 1998: 92).

The Infirmary, when it opened, contained seven male and only three female wards. As mentioned above, while working on this project we started to suspect that one of the motivations of subscribers, and functions of the Infirmary, was to treat workers in order to cure them and get them back to work. The majority of subscribers to the Infirmary were local industrialists and businessmen. Since a letter of recommendation was required from a subscriber in order to gain admission to the Infirmary in normal cases, it is not surprising that it was anticipated in the planning of the Infirmary that more male patients with artisanal occupations would be admitted to the Infirmary than women.

In terms of the group of people who were buried at Newcastle Infirmary, the demographic structure of the burial population was examined using both contemporary and osteological sources. Osteologists borrow demographer's methods in order to investigate population structure (Chamberlain, 1994: 18). The surviving burial registers provided the opportunity of comparing the demographics of those listed in the registers with that of the burial population. Despite the gaps in the burial registers, it was expected that the demographic patterns predicted by the burial registers would be reflected in the osteological demographic patterns for both the articulated and disarticulated human remains. After all, these three sets of information refer to the same burial population who were all patients who died and subsequently were buried at Newcastle Infirmary. In total, 289 male and 117 female patients were listed on the surviving burial registers (covering the periods 1803–1815 and 1822–1845). More than twice as many men as women appear on these registers reflecting the bias mentioned above in regard to numbers of wards available for treatment of male and female patients.

Osteological assessments of age-at-death and sex from the skeletal evidence were also used to examine the demographic structure of the burial population at Newcastle Infirmary. This was one area where the disarticulated nature of a large portion of the skeletal material caused problems. Where a whole skeleton is available for study, it is possible in the majority of cases to assign age-at-death and sex estimates to an individual, and this was fairly straightforward in the case of the 210 articulated burials. However, when analysing disarticulated material it was not possible to pick out all 206 bones that belong to one person from the thousands that made up our sample, and therefore it is not possible to examine complete skeletons in order to assess the age-at-death or sex of individuals. It was also not possible to use the 407 minimum number of individuals estimate to construct a demographic profile for the disarticulated sample. This is because it was based on bones that only give information about whether the person they originated from was an adult or a child; specific age-at-death information and reliable sexing information can not be retrieved from most isolated skeletal elements. The only elements that are useful in isolation for assessing age-at-death and sex are bones from the pelvis and whole crania. Minimum number estimates that included the demographic data these elements provided were 324 people for the crania and 236 people for the os coxa (pelvis). Since the crania provided demographic information about the largest portion of the disarticulated sample, demographic investigations used the data from these totals.

The burial registers gave specific age-at-death for the patients who appear on them, but osteological assessments are not specific to exact chronological age-at-death. Rather, osteological ageing techniques give information about the biological stage of life that a person died at (Chamberlain, 1994: 20; Buikstra and Ubelaker, 1994: 36; Start and Kirk, 1998: 167). Instead of age in years, individuals are assigned to an age-at-death category that corresponds to a broad chronological age range. For the skeletal remains of the patients at Newcastle the following categories were employed: Infant 1 (1–6 years); Infant 2 (7–12 years); Juvenile (13–17 years); Young Adult (18–25 years); Prime Adult (26–45 years) and Older Adult (46+ years). No children under 1 year of age were recovered from the human remains. A further limitation in analysing osteological remains is that in some cases age-at-death and sex assessment are not possible, even when a whole skeleton is available. To overcome this, unaged or unsexed remains are proportionally redistributed among the securely known age-at-death and sex categories. Table 1 presents the redistributed final demographic data from all three sets of evidence (burial registers, articulated burials and disarticulated material).

The final demographic totals for each of the three forms of evidence were expressed as percentages and presented graphically below in Fig. 1. In each case sub-adult individuals have been excluded because they form such a small part of the sample, and in the case of osteological information, sub-adults cannot be sexed and therefore a direct comparison between the burial registers and skeletal evidence cannot be made.

When the demographic profiles generated for the burial registers and the articulated burials are compared, the two patterns match fairly well in terms of a smaller overall percentage of female patients compared to male. This pattern also holds more specifically within the prime and older adult age categories — again the percentage of male patients is at least double that of female patients in both profiles. However, when the percentage of young adult females in the articulated burials is compared to that predicted by the burial registers, the two patterns do not match. There are too many young adult females among the articulated burials from the Infirmary.

This discrepancy in percentages of male and female deaths in the young adult category is even more pronounced when the burial register profile is compared to that for the disarticulated material. Once again there are far too many young women among the people who make up the disarticulated skeletal sample. In fact, there are almost equal numbers of men and women in the totals for the disarticulated material (162 men: 155 women), whereas in the burial registers (289 men: 117 women) and articulated burials (129 men: 62 women) men outnumber women more than 2:1.

Why are there so many young women in the skeletal remains that are invisible in the burial registers? And why are there so many more women in the disarticulated remains as compared to the articulated burials, or the burial registers? With regard to the excess of young women in both portions of the burial population, a usual osteological explanation for large proportions of young dead females in burial populations is the danger associated with childbirth. We know from the admissions policy that pregnant women were specifically excluded from admission to the Infirmary. Even if they had been admitted, no new-born children were recovered from the burial ground. It remains possible that women who were dangerously ill following childbirth might be admitted on an Accident and Emergency basis.

While giving a paper discussing this sample at the Museums North Conference in Newcastle entitled 'Close to the Bone', a member of the audience suggested that possibly this excess of young women had suffered abortions that had caused infection or internal bleeding. It is the author's understanding that it is unlikely abortions would have been performed at the Infirmary but, as with childbirth complications, patients could have been admitted on an Accident and Emergency basis. The author knows very little about the history of abortion and so cannot comment further on this idea, but it seems an entirely plausible one.

If our inference, from the 1851 census, that prostitutes formed a significant part of the female patient population is correct, might they be more likely to remain unclaimed, either through lack of family or sufficient funeral funds? Perhaps these patients were more likely to contribute to the burial population but remain unrecorded in the registers.

Nolan has suggested the possibility that the disarticulated portion of the sample is earlier in date than the articulated burials (Nolan, 1998: pers. comm.), and the burial registers cover later periods of the burial ground's use. If this is the case it is possible that equal numbers of men and women went unclaimed during the earlier phase of the Infirmary's life, while in later phases of use more men went unclaimed than women did.

The surviving admission and burial registers reveal that during the eighteenth and very early nineteenth centuries patients at the Infirmary were almost exclusively locals from Newcastle and surrounding areas. After 1803 some patients appear whose origins are given as Irish, Scots, foreigner, Italian, Prussian, and Norwegian amongst other places. These patients with more exotic origins are almost exclusively men, perhaps seamen. This increased internationalisation of the patient population is attested by the survival of ward notices from 1863 forbidding the smoking and chewing of tobacco, printed in English, French and German (Nolan, 1998: 38). It would seem less likely that the body of a patient who came from further afield would be claimed by his family for burial. So perhaps the higher proportion of unclaimed male patients in the burial registers and possibly later articulated burials is accounted for at least in part by the increased numbers of foreign male patients in the living patient population.

DISCUSSION

In addition to the osteological uniqueness of the abundance of skeletal evidence for post-mortem medical intervention evi-

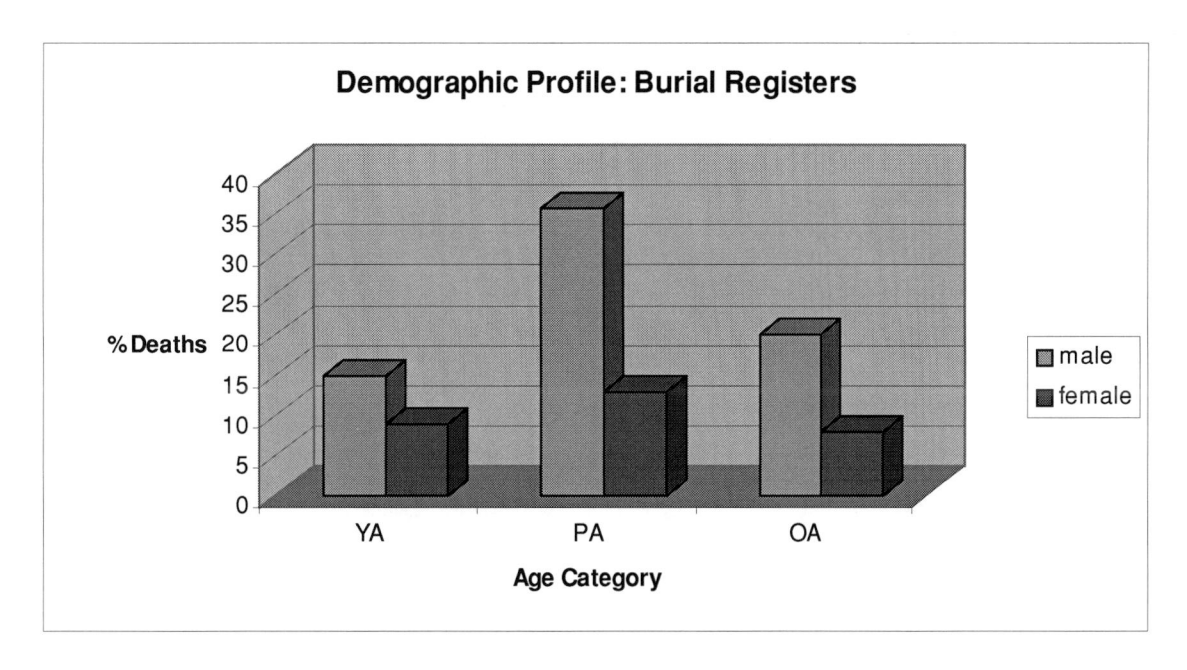

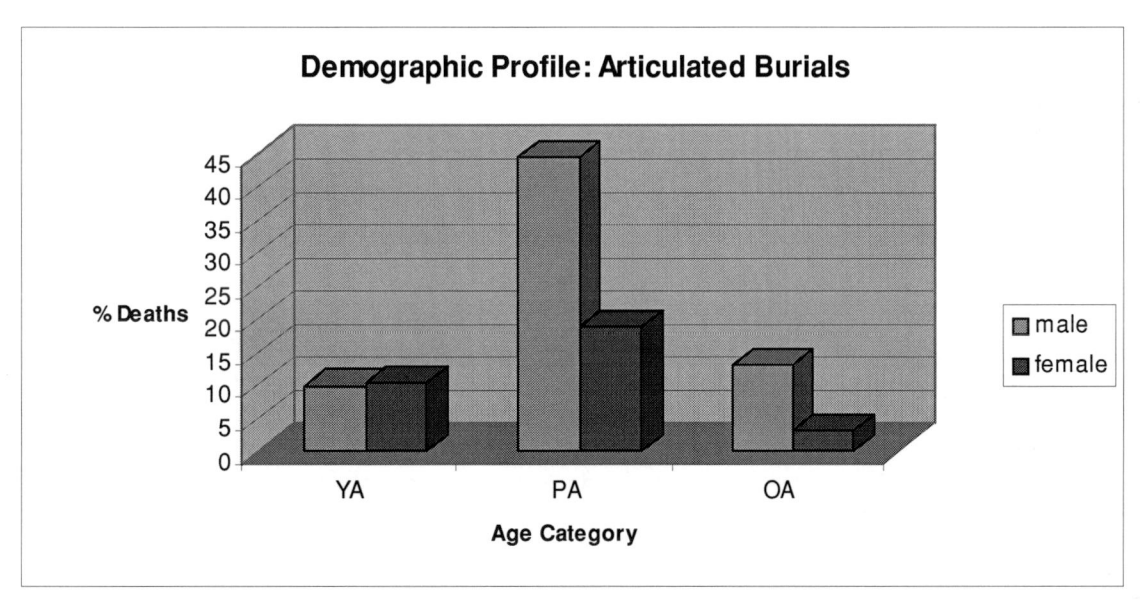

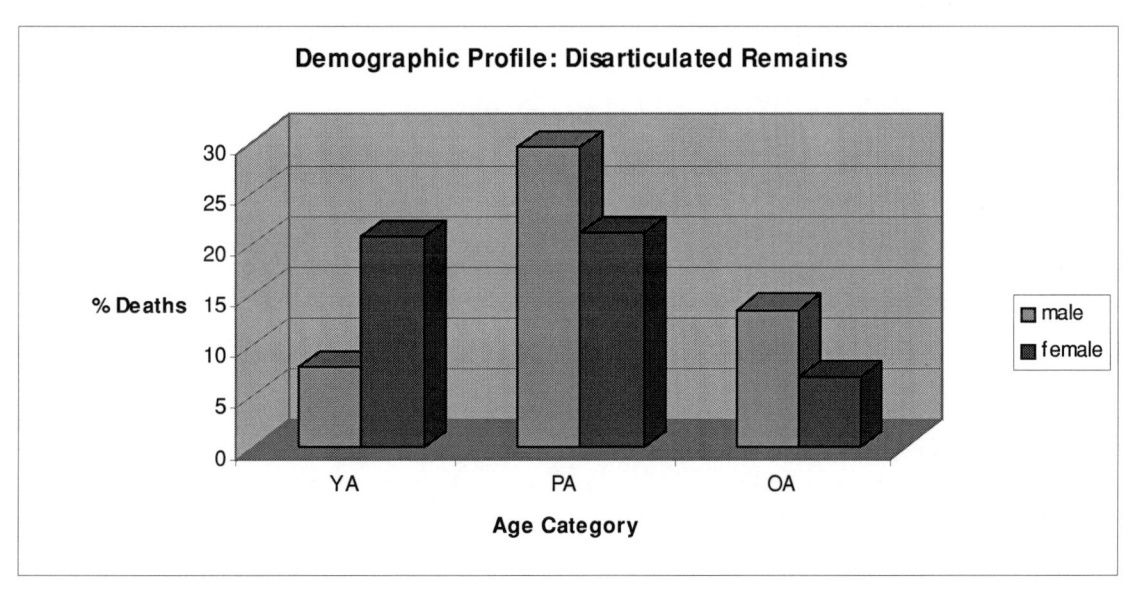

Fig. 1. Demographic profiles from the burial registers, articulated burials and disarticulated remains, Newcastle Infirmary at the Forth, Newcastle upon Tyne.

denced in the bones of the people buried at Newcastle Infirmary, there are important social and historical questions that arise from the analysis of this burial population. Before the passing of the Anatomy Act in 1832, dissection was illegal unless the body was that of a hanged murderer, and yet 14% of the patients buried at Newcastle, the majority of whom would have been interred prior to this date, had been subjected to post-mortem medical intervention. The published 1801 statute mentioning dissection evidences the Infirmary's attitude towards dissection that would remain technically illegal for another thirty-one years.

It is worth presenting a brief history of dissection in order to give context to this discussion of the patients at Newcastle Infirmary. This section relies heavily on the work of Ruth Richardson (1988), and I would recommend her work to anyone interested in the social history of dissection as an antidote to medical histories of the period. During the seventeenth and eighteenth centuries, there was a growing acceptance that a good knowledge of anatomy allowed physicians and surgeons to better understand the human body and therefore how to treat it. Unfortunately for the medical and artistic people who wanted to gain a better knowledge of anatomy, dissection was illegal and completely socially unacceptable.

In 1752 an Act of Parliament was passed with the aim of 'better preventing murder' (Richardson, 1988: 35). This gave judges the power to substitute dissection for gibbeting in chains as a further post-mortem punishment in addition to being sentenced to death in the first place. After the passing of this Act, surgeons became legal agents of the crown with the right to remove bodies from the gallows specifically to dissect them. Popular reaction to dissection was in many cases riotous. In Carlisle in the 1820s the friends of a hanged and dissected man attacked the medical men involved and killed one of them, and the Tyburn riots in London in 1749 are well documented (Richardson, 1988: 53). These riots and attacks on medical men demonstrate the strength of public revulsion towards dissection, and public distrust of medical professionals. This often publicly contested supply of bodies proved too scarce for the needs of teaching hospitals, anatomy schools and private individuals. Hence the profession of grave-robbing arose in order to supply this demand and the human body became a commodity. Again, public response condemned 'body snatchers' and local groups were set up to guard cemeteries against their activities (Richardson, 1988: 59–63). Teaching hospitals were widely believed to use the bodies of their dead unclaimed patients for dissection and surgical practise, and the osteological evidence from Newcastle Infirmary supports this. The bodies of the patients who died at Newcastle Infirmary and who went unclaimed were regarded as hospital property, teaching aids and as material to aid the advancement of the science of medicine.

This attitude to patients can also be found in their treatment during life. Patients had no other access to medical treatment, and they had to go to one of the hospital subscribers for a letter granting them admission to the Infirmary. Surgeons and physicians at the Infirmary used their charitable service there in order to build reputations on which their private practises were based, and were allowed to take on fee-paying students and apprentices. Surgeons and physicians were expected 'to unite tenderness with steadiness, and condescension with authority, as to inspire the minds of their patients with gratitude, respect and confidence' (Rules, 1801). We are left in little doubt about how patients were expected to view their time at the Infirmary.

From a modern perspective the people at Newcastle Infirmary would have had a harrowing patient experience. Imagine becoming ill enough to need medical or surgical treatment and having to go cap in hand to a wealthy Infirmary subscriber for your letter of recommendation admitting you to a charitable hospital. Once in the hospital you were expected to be filled with gratitude and respect, and to play your part in the furthering of medical knowledge through your treatment. You would have been in considerable pain, and if you needed surgery this would have been done without anaesthetic. Great advances in medical knowledge were made during this period, and experimental surgery was known to be carried out on poor charity patients rather than on fee-paying private clients (Richardson, 1988: 44). If you didn't survive and your body was not claimed, either because you had no one to claim you, not enough money to pay for a funeral or you were a long way from home, you might become a dissection subject. Dissection during this period was a legal punishment for heinous murder, and after the passing of the Anatomy Act in 1832, dissection was sanctioned on the bodies of the unclaimed poor. These uncomfortable connotations of dissection were more likely to be uppermost in the minds of patients who might become subject to it, than the supposed benefit it might bring to medical science.

The skeletal evidence that unclaimed bodies of patients were regularly being dissected at Newcastle Infirmary well before the passing of the Anatomy Act in 1832 will come as no surprise to medical historians. What is unique about this evidence is that for the first time we were able to investigate the actual physical remains of the people who were the subjects of dissection. Their permission, and their families' permission, was not sought, although they would have been well aware of their possible fate. Working with the remains of these people inspired an interest in their lives and compassion for their experiences. As a modern beneficiary of the medical advances that these patients were essential to, I believe it is important that we attempt to understand what their experiences and lives would have been like.

ACKNOWLEDGEMENTS

I would like to thank the International Centre for Life, and in particular Dr Cliff Jessett, for their support of the project throughout and permission to publish this article. The warmest thanks to my colleagues and friends Sue Boulter and Duncan Robertson, we were an osteological team of three and more than the sum of our parts. John Nolan, Andrew Chamberlain and Annsofie Witkin were central to the project and all were instrumental in the development of this paper. The staff at ARCUS, particularly Jim Symonds, are also thanked. Finally, conversations with Cathy Pink, Rupert Till and Bill Bevan helped give me the confidence to develop the ideas that resulted in this paper.

BIBLIOGRAPHY

Boulter, S., Robertson, D. and Start. H.
(1998) *The Newcastle Infirmary at the Forth, Newcastle upon Tyne. Volume 2: The Osteology: People, Disease and Surgery*, Sheffield: ARCUS.

Buikstra, J. E. and Ubelaker, D. H. (eds.)
(1994) *Standards for Data Collection from Human Skeletal Remains*, Fayetteville: Arkansas Archaeological Survey Research Series No. 44.

Chamberlain, A.
(1994) *Human Remains*, London: British Museum Press.

Downes, J. and Pollard, T. (eds.)
(1999) *The Loved Bodies Corruption: Archaeological Contributions to the Study of Human Mortality*, Glasgow: Cruithne Press.

Gernaey, A. M., Minnikin, D. E., Copley, M. S., Power, J. J., Ahmed, A. M. S., Dixon, R. A., Roberts, C. A., Robertson, D. J., Nolan, J. and Chamberlain, A. T.
(2000) 'Detecting ancient tuberculosis', *Internet Archaeology* 5 available on http://intarch.ac.uk/journal/issue5/gernaey_toc.html.

Kirk, L. and Start, H.
(1999) 'Death at the undertakers', in Downes, J. and Pollard, T. (eds.), *The Loved Bodies Corruption: Archaeological Contributions to the Study of Human Mortality*, Glasgow: Cruithne Press, pp. 200–8.

Nolan, J.
(1998) *The Newcastle Infirmary at the Forth, Newcastle upon Tyne. Volume 1: The Archaeology and History*, Newcastle: Northern Counties Archaeological Services.

Porter, R.
(1997) *The Greatest Benefit to Mankind: A Medical History of Humanity from Antiquity to the Present*, London: Harper Collins.

Richardson, R.
(1988) *Death, Dissection and the Destitute*, London: Penguin Books.

Roberts, C. and Manchester, K.
(1995) *The Archaeology of Disease: Second Edition*, Ithaca, New York: Cornell University Press.

Start, H. and Kirk, L.
(1998) 'The Bodies of Friends — the osteological analysis of a Quaker burial ground', in M. Cox (ed.), *Grave Concerns: Death and Burial in England 1700–1850*, York: Council for British Archaeology, pp. 167–77.

Witkin, A.
(1997) The Cutting Edge: aspects of amputations in the late 18th and early 19th century. MSc Dissertation, Department of Archaeology and Prehistory, University of Sheffield.

RECOGNITION AND UNDERSTANDING OF AGE-RELATED BONE LOSS AND OSTEOPOROSIS-RELATED FRACTURES IN THE EIGHTEENTH AND NINETEENTH CENTURIES

Megan Brickley

Over the last decade age-related bone loss and osteoporosis in post-menopausal females has generated considerable interest in the medical literature and wider media. Growing awareness of the condition in the present population has led to a number of studies of age-related bone loss in archaeological material (Brickley, 1998; Mays, 2000; Lees et al., 1993). Analysis of archaeological bone from nineteenth century London collections demonstrated that the pattern of bone loss recorded was broadly the same as that recorded from modern samples of bone (Brickley and Howell, 1999). Given the relatively recent date of this material, this finding is not surprising. However, in view of the significant morbidity and mortality associated with osteoporosis-related fractures and the enormous social concern that the condition raises today, examining the understanding and response of past peoples to this condition is of importance. A comprehensive review of historical literature relating to age-related bone loss and fractures has never previously been undertaken.

The term osteoporosis has been in use for 150 years, but in the past it was applied to a wide variety of conditions. Linguistically the term is derived from the Greek *osteon* meaning bone and *poros* meaning little hole, literally meaning 'porous bone' (Schapira and Schapira, 1992). It is only recently that the term has been applied specifically to age-related bone loss.

A widely accepted definition of the condition states that 'osteoporosis is a disease characterised by abnormalities in the amount and architectural arrangement of bone tissue that leads to impaired skeletal strength and an undue susceptibility to fracture risk' (Melton et al., 1992). Fractures are a common feature of osteoporosis in modern clinical literature (Dempster and Lindsay, 1993: 797–80) with common sites being the proximal femur (hip), distal radius (wrist) and vertebral bodies (spine). Fractures of the proximal femur are regarded as being the most serious (Barlow, 1994), and it is this type of fracture that will be examined in this paper.

Clearly it is not possible to be completely certain that cases from the early medical literature are definitely related to osteoporosis. However, information regarding the fracture and the circumstances of its occurrence will give an indication of whether it was related to osteoporosis. Important features in determining if a fracture was due to osteoporosis include:

1. age of the individual;
2. sex of the individual;
3. circumstances of the fracture;
4. descriptions of bone given in autopsy notes.

Osteoporotic fractures commonly occur in older individuals, with women more often affected than men, and are often characterised by minimal trauma. The simple act of a person stepping down from a pavement may be sufficient to induce a fracture. Descriptions of the physical qualities of bone that include characteristics such as cortical thinning and loss of trabecular bone would also be indicative of osteoporosis. If cases reported contain a number of these criteria, there is a strong possibility that what is being described is a fracture due to osteoporosis.

HISTORICAL TEXTS

In the presentation of information gathered from the various sources it has not been possible to separate out information relating to each of the features of osteoporosis-related fractures as done above. This is due to the nature of the texts used and levels of understanding of the fractures. The nature of texts documenting medical matters is undoubtedly influenced by the ways in which health care provision was made during the period. Hospitals in London, established by voluntary contributions from wealthy individuals, or money provided by the church, were intended for the good and worthy poor who could not afford to pay for medical treatment. In many reports of fracture treated in hospital, details of moral character appear to have been considered more important than clinical features of the fracture. In a number of case notes examined, where an individual died, the doctor commented that the patient was not a very upstanding citizen or had immoderate habits, as if these were almost the cause of demise.

Those who could afford to do so would have employed the services of a doctor privately. A doctor with a good reputation would make a better living, so many doctors were reluctant to admit any sort of failure. This can clearly be seen in the debate surrounding fractured femora. Personal rivalry is also shown in the writings of Mr Pott criticising Mrs Mapp, a well known bone setter of the period. He wrote of the 'absurdity and impracticability of her promises,' referring to her as an 'ignorant, illiberal, drunken female savage' (Pott, 1767).

Age-related changes in bone structure were clearly observed and commented upon, even if the reasons for the occurrence of the changes were not well understood. A number of features associated with osteoporosis-related fractures were clearly identified relatively early on.

John Aitken was the earliest author discovered in the present research who wrote specifically about changes in bone structure with age. He noticed that the bones of the older individuals appeared to be far more 'fragile' (Aitken, 1771) than those of younger individuals. Another observation made was that the bones of younger individuals and animals seemed to heal far more successfully than those of older individuals. Describing the differences between the bones of these two age groups he wrote: 'This difference is so remarkable between these two conditions of the bones, is perhaps to be entirely ascribed to some degree of *pliancy* or *tenacity* which the bones of young animals possess, and of which they are afterwards deprived by age' (Aitken, 1771: 23).

Aitken observed that there were changes in all parts of the body with age, both in hard and soft tissues, and put forward a possible reason for the increasing brittleness of bones of older individuals:

> 'This great accumulation of the earthy principle in bones, would seem to be the cause producing that extreme rigidity and fragility, which those of very old people are observed to possess' (Aitken, 1771: 26).

The suppleness of the bones of younger individuals was put down to their greater lubrication with fluids, which he referred to as glutens. This quotation also demonstrates that another feature of osteoporosis related fractures had been recognised; the difficulty of getting fractures to heal successfully (Sneed and Van Bree, 1990). Aitken also observed another very important feature of osteoporosis related fractures, the limited trauma required to break a bone: 'In some cases, the texture of the bones has been so much perverted, as from the smallest violence, and even muscular effort, to suffer fracture' (Aitken, 1771: 38).

Joseph Amesbury, writing a little later (Amesbury, 1831), also noticed changes in bones and bone structure with age and stated the link between age, changes in bone and fractures in a clearer manner than any previous author. He observed: 'The bones become brittle in proportion as persons advance in years, and in old age they are sometimes fractured by very slight causes' (Amesbury, 1831: 2). Sir Astley Cooper (Cooper, 1824) elaborated on the changes associated with age in bones, and described the typical alterations in bone structure seen with osteoporosis very clearly:

> 'That regular decay of nature which is called old age, is attended with changes which are easily detectable in the dead body; and one of the principal of these is found in the bones, for they become thin in their shell, and spongy in texture. The process of absorption and deposition varies at different periods of life; in youth the arteries, which are the builders of the body, deposit more than the absorbents remove, and hence is derived the great source of growth. In the middle period of life the arteries and absorbents preserve an equilibrium of action, so that with a due portion of exercise the body remains stationary; whilst in old age the balance is destroyed by the arteries doing less than the absorbents, and hence the person becomes diminished in weight; but more from the diminution of the arterial than from an increase of the absorbent action. This is well seen in the natural changes of the bones, their increase in youth, their bulk, weight, and little comparative change during the adult period, and the lightness and softness in the more advanced stages of life' (Cooper, 1824: 107).

Another writer who discussed in some detail changes occurring with age throughout the human body (including bones) was R. W. Smith, who also noticed that such changes were more pronounced in females:

> 'Among all the striking and varied changes which the human system suffers under the influence of that inevitable decline of organisation, which is attendant upon advanced age, there are few more remarkable than those which affect the osseous system. These strange modifications of structure are supposed to affect the skeleton of the aged female much more frequently than that of the male' (Smith, 1847: 66).

> 'Changes which predispose the neck of the thigh bone to fracture from the most trivial causes; under such circumstances, as has been jointly observed by Mr Adams, the fracture should in many instances, be looked upon as more a stage of morbid alteration, from which no amendment is to be expected' (Smith, 1847: 68).

This extract appears to point to fracture through minimal trauma, one of the features noted as being typical of modern fractures related to osteoporosis (Barlow, 1994: 27).

Early death registers give very little information about the individual or cause of death. It is only towards the end of the period of study that more information such as cause of death is routinely provided. In the registers examined for this study, cause of death was given as 'Fracture of the thigh' in a number of cases (Table 1). This term was used to describe intra-capsular fractures of the femur, fractures that would today commonly be referred to as hip fractures. Such fractures were a clearly recognised and distinguished type and Cooper when writing about them referred to them as a 'different species' (Cooper, 1824: 101). Many of these individuals were elderly, often in their seventies or even older, and where date of admittance to hospital is given, it can be seen that they frequently lived only a matter of months. It is suggested that the examples provided and those like them may be due to osteoporosis. When information such as the age of patient are given, all are consistent with osteoporosis.

Case notes made by doctors of the period are also a valuable source of information often containing details that allow the possibility that fractures were related to osteoporosis to be evaluated. A good example of these types of case notes is given below.

> 'Mary Clement, aged eighty-three and a half years, when walking across her room, October 1st 1820, supported by her stick, which from the debility consequent upon her age she was obliged to employ, unperceived by herself, placed her stick in a hole of the floor, by which loosing her balance, and tottering to recover herself from falling, which she would have done but for those near her, she found she had, as she supposed dislocated her thigh-bone. When called to her she was lying upon her bed in much pain, with the thigh shortened and the foot everted. 'Examination' which fully confirmed me in the opinion that some part of the neck of the femur was broken' (Cooper, 1824: 139).

In this case sufficient information is given that all the criteria set out at the start of this paper can be evaluated and it is possible to suggest the above case was almost certainly related to osteoporosis.

Table 1. Examples of cases of femoral neck fracture which may be due to osteoporosis, taken from the death registers at St. Bartholomew's Hospital.

Age	Sex	Injury	D.O.A	D.O.D
77	Female	Fracture thigh	09.01.1840	02.03.1840
72	Female	Fractured thigh	11.11.1840	30.11.1840
82	Male	Fractured thigh	01.07.1841	17.07.1841
82	Male	Fractured thigh	01.03.1841	20.07.1841
72	Female	Broken thigh	30.07.1843	18.06.1843
69	Male	Fractured thigh	28.10.1843	04.11.1843
94	Male	Fractured thigh	15.11.1844	20.11.1844
90	Female	Fractured thigh and collarbone	16.10.1845	15.01.1845

D.O.A. is the date of admittance to hospital, D.O.D is date of death.

Fracture of the femoral neck is still regarded by many in the medical profession in the same terms as those described by Cuming: 'This is the most difficult fracture to manage in the whole body, and what surgeon is there who in the course of his practice has not witnessed the most unpleasant consequences resulting from it?' (Cuming, 1806: 243).

One of the features that has focused so much attention onto osteoporosis recently is the very high mortality that fractures can produce. Although many people survive the actual fracture, they often die within a relatively short space of time. Today, one in four women who sustain an osteoporosis-related fracture dies prematurely (Spector, 1991: 7). The shock of a serious accident such as a fractured hip in an elderly individual seriously weakens them, leading to greater susceptibility to many other conditions such as pneumonia, which are the ultimate cause of death. Cases where death closely followed a hip fracture were observed in the death registers from St. Bartholomew's Hospital as well as hospital reports, as the following extract from the writings of Smith demonstrates: 'Of five compound fractures of the femur, only one recovered' (Smith, 1847: 65).

Smith described the problems such fractures caused in more detail: 'Sometimes the patient dies in a few days from the effects of the shock upon a system already enfeebled by age; very frequently bronchitis sets in, and terminates fatally before ten days have elapsed' (Smith, 1847: 106).

As mentioned previously, a common feature of osteoporotic fractures today is the low level of force (trauma) that is required to produce them. Sir Astley Cooper noted the comparatively normal circumstances surrounding many of the hip fractures that he encountered.

'That this state of bone in old age favours much the production of fractures, is shewn by the slightest causes often producing them. In London the most frequent source of this accident is from a person, when walking on the edge of an elevated footpath, slipping upon the carriage pavement; and though it be a descent of only a few inches, yet, from its occurring so sudden and unexpectedly, and from the force acting perpendicularly, with the advantage of a lever in the cervix, it produces a fracture of the neck of the thigh bone; and as the fall is the consequence of this fracture it is imputed, by ignorant persons, to the fall, and not to its true cause' (Cooper, 1824: 109).

Cooper made a number of observations about fractures that came to his attention which indicate that the propensity of older individuals, particularly females, to sustain certain types of fracture was widely accepted.

'Women are much more liable to this species of fracture than men; we rarely in hospitals observe it in the latter, but our wards are seldom without an example of it in the aged female... the fracture of the neck of the thigh bone within the capsular ligament, seldom happens but at an advanced period of life, whilst the other fractures I have described happen at all periods of life. Old age, however is a very indefinite term; for it is as strongly marked at sixty, as in others at eighty years' (Cooper, 1824: 107).

Sir Astley went on to define in unambiguous terms the exact ages at which these fractures arose, and the ages he gave clearly match those encountered in modern cases of osteoporotic fracture: 'Between fifty and eighty years is the most common period at which the fracture occurs' (Cooper, 1824: 106–7).

It has been noted that fractures occur more frequently in the winter (Barlow, 1994: 73) and this may also have been the case in the period under study.

'An intensely cold or frosty state of the atmosphere has been thought, in like manner, to render the bones more than ordinarily fragile. The frequency of fractures during frosty weather, seems to have given rise to this opinion; — the greater slipperiness and hardness of the earth in this than in soft weather, the one occasioning more falls, and the other fractures account for this fact independent of the notion of increased frostility' (Aitken, 1771: 40).

DISCUSSION AND CONCLUSIONS

Overall, although it is not possible to be certain that the cases discussed in the literature are definitely related to osteoporosis, it appears likely that osteoporosis-related fractures did present a problem to the population and medical practitioners of the period.

In spite of the limitations of the historical sources, the pattern that emerges from the early medical literature mirrors that reported for osteoporosis today. It was predominantly older people who were affected, with women more frequently affected than men, fractures were sustained after a low energy impact, and there were clearly observed changes to both cortical and trabecular bone.

The great debate surrounding the treatment of femoral neck fractures, and the concern about the problems encountered in trying to get such fractures to unite, suggests that fractures that occurred constituted a serious problem. It is also clear from the writings of the period that there was a great deal of pain and disability associated with such a fracture, and many individuals never recovered. As in the present population, such fractures were related to significant morbidity and mortality. Quantification is impossible, but such fractures must have been reasonably common for so much time and energy to have been devoted to them.

It is also clear that the aetiology of these fractures was poorly understood. Inclusion of all material collected is not possible in a short article, but some material examined suggests that such fractures were viewed with a certain amount of inevitability and fitted with views of the feebleness of women current at the time. Today, there is fear and concern amongst the general population, particularly women, regarding sustaining a fracture in old age. During the period under study this was not the case; any fear and concern that did exist was felt by the medical profession and related to their inability to treat such fractures.

BIBLIOGRAPHY

Aitken, J.
(1771) *Essays on Several Important Subjects in Surgery: Chiefly on the Nature of the Fractures of the Long Bones of the Extremities*, London: E&C Dilly.

Amesbury, J.
(1831) *Practical Remarks on the Nature and Treatment of Fractures of the Trunk and Extremities*, London: Longman.

Barlow, D. H. (ed.)
(1994) *Report by the Advisory Group on Osteoporosis*, Whitehall London, Department of Health.

Brickley, M.
(1998) *Age Related Bone Loss and Osteoporosis in Archaeological Bone: A Study of Two London Collections, Redcross Way and Farringdon Street*. PhD thesis, University of London.

Brickley, M. and Howell, P. G. T.
(1999) 'Measurement of Changes in Trabecular Bone Structure with Age in an Archaeological Population', *Journal of Archaeological Science* **26**: 151–7.

Cooper, A.
(1824) *A Treatise on Dislocations and on Fractures of the Joints* (3rd edn.), London: Longman.

Cuming, R.
(1806) *The naval, military and private practitioners amanuesis, medicus et chirurgicus: Or a practical treatise on femurs and on amputation, gunshot wounds, trismus, scalds etc. and with new successful methods of treating mortification, of amputating at the shoulder joint, and of curing femoral fractures.* London: Mathews & Leigh.

Dempster, D. W. and Lindsay, R.
(1993) 'Pathogenesis of osteoporosis', *Lancet* **341**: 797–801.

Lees B., Molleson T., Arnett T., and Mays S.
(1993) 'Differences in proximal femur bone density over two centuries', *Lancet* **341**: 673–5.

Mays, S.
(2000) 'Age-dependent cortical bone loss in women from 18th and early 19th century London', *Amer.J.Phys.Anthrop.* **112**: 349–62.

Melton, J. L. III, Chrischilles, E. A., Cooper, C., Lane, A. W., and Riggs, L. B.
(1992) 'Perspective, how many women have osteoporosis', *Journal of Bone & Mineral Research* **7**: 1005–10.

Pott, P.
(1767) *Some Few Remarks on Fractures and Dislocations*. Printed for L. Hawes, W. Clarke and R. Collins.

Schapira, D. and Schapira, C.
(1992) 'Osteoporosis: The evolution of a scientific term', *Osteoporosis International* **2**: 164–7.

Smith, R. W.
(1824) *A Treatise on Fractures in the Vicinity of Joints and on Certain Forms of Accidental and Congenital Dislocations*. Dublin: Hodges & Smith.

Sneed, N. V. and Van Bree, K. M.
(1990) 'Treating ununited fractures with electricity: nursing implications', *Journal of Gerentological Nursing*, **16**: 26–31

Spector, T. D.
(1991) 'The epidemiology of osteoporosis', in J. C. Stevenson (ed.), *Osteoporosis*. Guilford: Reed Healthcare: pp. 7–9.

CONTRIBUTORS

Robert Arnott
Centre for the History of Medicine
The Medical School
University of Birmingham
Birmingham
B15 2TT

Dr Patricia Baker
School of European Culture and Languages
Cornwallis Building
University of Kent at Canterbury
Canterbury
Kent
CT2 7NF

Dr Debby Banham
Department of History and Philosophy of Science
University of Cambridge
Free School Lane
Cambridge
CB2 3RH

Dr Megan Brickley
Department of Ancient History and Archaeology
University of Birmingham
Birmingham
B15 2TT

Dr Marina Ciaraldi
Birmingham University Field Archaeology Unit (BUFAU)
University of Birmingham
Birmingham
B15 2TT

Dr Sally Crawford
Department of Ancient History and Archaeology
University of Birmingham
Birmingham
B15 2TT

Dr Brendan Derham
29 Kings Barton Street
Gloucester
GL1 1QX

Joyce M Filer
Department of Egyptian Antiquities
The British Museum
Great Russell Street
London
WC1B 3DG

Dr Chrissie Freeth
Department of Archaeological Sciences
University of Bradford
Bradford
BD7 1DP

Professor John Hunter
Department of Ancient History and Archaeology
University of Birmingham
Birmingham
B15 2TT

Ralph Jackson
Department of Prehistory and Early Europe
The British Museum
Great Russell Street
London
WC1B 3DG

Dr Niall McKeown
Department of Ancient History and Archaeology
University of Birmingham
Birmingham
B15 2TT

Dr Charlotte Roberts
Department of Archaeology
University of Durham
South Road
Durham
DH 3LE

Mouli Start
16 Carr Road
Waklkley
Sheffield
S2 2WZ